almost grown

OWL

Also by James Miller

The Passion of Michel Foucault

*"Democracy Is in the Streets": From Port Huron
to the Siege of Chicago*

Rousseau: Dreamer of Democracy

History and Human Existence—From Marx to Merleau-Ponty

almost grown

the rise of rock

James Miller

WILLIAM HEINEMANN: LONDON

First published in the United Kingdom in 1999 by William Heinemann

1 3 5 7 9 10 8 6 4 2

William Heinemann
Random House UK Limited
20 Vauxhall Bridge Road, London SW1V 2SA

Random House Australia (Pty) Limited
20 Alfred Street, Milsons Point, Sydney,
New South Wales 2061, Australia

Random House New Zealand Limited
18 Poland Road, Glenfield
Auckland 10, New Zealand

Random House South Africa (Pty) Limited
Endulini, 5a Jubilee Road, Parktown 2193, South Africa

Random House UK Limited Reg. No 954009

A CIP catalogue record for this book is available from the British Library

Papers used by Random House UK Limited are natural, recyclable products made from wood grown in sustainable forests. The manufacturing processes conform to the environmental regulations of the country of origin

Printed and bound in Great Britain by Creative Print and Design (Wales) Ebbw Vale

ISBN 0 434 00791 9

Contents

6: Stairway to Heaven

when there's no future

how can there be sin

we're the flowers in the dustbin

we're the poison in your machine

we're the future

your future

JONES/ROTTEN/MATLOCK/COOK
"GOD SAVE THE QUEEN"
THE SEX PISTOLS, 1977

Preface

A Rock and Roll Chronicle

The history of rock and roll now spans half a century—a chastening thought for anyone ever excited by the novelty of this once freshest of popular forms. As innovative artists have continued to come and go, from Little Richard to the Sex Pistols, from Frank Zappa and the Mothers of Invention in 1966 to Radiohead some thirty years later, my own interest in rock has waxed and waned, but never quite disappeared. Still, if I'm honest, the most thrilling moments all came early, in the Fifties and Sixties, when the music was a primary focus of my energy, shaping my desires, coloring my memory, and producing the wild fantasy, widely shared, that my generation was, in some inchoate way, through the simple pleasure we all took in rock and roll, part of a new world dawning.

It was a world that I had first discovered in 1956. I was sleeping over at the house of an older cousin—he was eighteen, I was nine. It was Christmastime. Every night he fell asleep with his radio on. And every night, as I lay in the upper deck of his bunk bed, I would hear the beat and blare of a late-night disc jockey's theme song, "Night Train," a honking saxophone playing a lazy blues to a striptease beat. As the music faded, the disc jockey started up his patter, a manic rush, words tumbling, pure jive, mainly nonsense to me. Then came the records. I had grown up on the decorum and consonance of symphonies and Broadway musicals, so I was unprepared for the off-hand directness of a song like "Green Door" with its chintzy ragtime feel, or "Don't Be Cruel," with its sultry vocal, bounding electric guitar line, and a slap-happy drum sound unlike anything I'd ever heard.

These records touched me in ways that I'd never been touched before. Enthralled by this noise, I began to seek it out, to the consternation of my parents. I became a fan—short for "fanatic." I began to collect records. I looked forward to seeing my favorite artists when they made a television appearance—a relatively rare event in the beginning. I bought an electric guitar and learned enough licks to form my own band, write a few songs, and make some money by playing at dances in high school and college. When I wasn't listening to records or practicing the guitar, I was reading *Dig, 16,* or *Hit Parader,* all full of stories about the latest teen hairdos and dance steps and up-and-coming rock idols.

And so it went for much of the next thirty years of my life: I could not hear enough, or know enough, about the sounds that had first moved me during that winter of 1956.

Time passed. What had once seemed exotic grew familiar. Inspired by the Beatles, a new generation of performers, from Bob Dylan to Jim Morrison and the Doors, helped choreograph a cultural revolution that turned rock and roll from a disparaged music for kids into a widely watched, frequently praised mode of serious cultural expression. By the end of the Sixties, rock had turned into a multibillion-dollar global industry. And my passion had turned into a job.

I became a professional critic, publishing my first record review in *Rolling Stone* in 1967—it appeared in the third issue. For the next quarter century, I covered the pop music scene for a variety of publications, from *The New Republic* to *Newsweek,* giving my readers tangible evidence of rock's mainstream respectability.

As a young fan in the Sixties, I had seen the Beach Boys in Hawaii, the Zombies and Searchers and Rolling Stones in a Chicago amphitheater, the Byrds on Sunset Strip, Janis Joplin in Berkeley, the Grateful Dead at a Love-In, and Eric Clapton's band Cream at the Savile Theatre in London. I had also made frequent pilgrimages to the old Regal Theater on the South Side of Chicago to see James Brown and Jackie Wilson and the Four Tops and Bobby "Blue" Bland in their prime.

As a professional journalist in the Seventies and Eighties, I got the chance to see a great many more artists in even more intimate settings: Bob Marley and the Wailers in their first North American appearance (with only thirty other people in the club); Bruce Springsteen and the E Street Band on the brink of fame; the artist formerly known as Prince on his first important American tour. I also got the chance to meet and talk with a great many of my musical heroes, old and new, from Sam Phillips and Paul McCartney to David Bowie and Elvis Costello and Bono of U2.

In many ways, it was an exhilarating time to be listening to popular music, and to be writing about rock and roll. Yet despite a steady stream of new artists and a relentless flood of publicity for every passing fad—and despite the fact that for many years I made my living by contributing to the flood of publicity—the rock world as I came to know it professionally seemed to me ever more stale, ever more predictable, ever more boring.

What had seemed mysterious to a nine-year-old boy, and what augured a revolutionary youth culture in the mind of an impressionable nineteen-year-old, became, to the adult critic, a routinized package of theatrical gestures, generally expressed in a blaze of musical clichés.

Not that rock and roll was diminishing in popularity; on the contrary, more people than ever bought records and flocked to hear the latest bands. The best-selling album of the twentieth century, Michael Jackson's *Thriller*, was released in 1982. And the scale of rock's biggest theatrical events has grown ever more gargantuan. Once upon a time, the music had been performed live in clubs and small halls, the kind of venues where I first saw Jimi Hendrix and the Who in the 1960s. Thirty years later, to see a major rock act like U2 or Pearl Jam, one usually had to journey to an arena or stadium where the artists were dwarfed by their surroundings, never mind the size of the crowd assembled to witness the event.

Disenchanted yet still intrigued, not least by my own disenchantment, I sensed that it was time to step back, take stock, and try to untangle and think through a series of events, a great many of which I had either undergone with impassioned abandon or been asked to write about with factitious enthusiasm (a constant temptation for cultural critics who are expected to celebrate the new).

Since leaving *Newsweek* in 1991, in part because I no longer felt able to feign enthusiasm, I have worked primarily as a teacher, currently at the New School. By academic training, I am an intellectual and cultural historian: and like a good historian, I resolved to understand, to my own satisfaction, where rock and roll had come from—and what it had come to.

Hence this book: a reflective look back at selected episodes in the history of the world's most popular form of music.

My narrative combines research into contemporary sources with an analysis of what I take to be the essential issues, informed by a quarter century of experience working inside the music business. I have eschewed any effort to be comprehensive, or to indulge my own continuing affection for the music of various artists, such as Bo Diddley, Sam Cooke, the "5" Royales, the Moonglows, Jerry Lee Lewis, Buddy Holly, the Everly Brothers, the Flamingos, James Brown, Phil Spector, the Beach Boys, the Searchers, Bobby Bland, Curtis Mayfield and the Impressions, the Kinks, Otis Redding, the Byrds, Led Zeppelin, Kenny Gamble and Leon Huff, Captain Beefheart, Al Green, Donna Summer, Elvis Costello, and the Pretenders—to name only a few of the musical figures scanted in the survey that follows. I have also resisted the temptation to cover up the sometimes embarrassing centrality of "bad" white boys in the cultural history of rock and roll after the advent of Elvis. Among artists popular in the Sixties, for example, it seems to me obvious that Aretha Franklin and Dionne Warwick and Dusty Springfield all are greater *musical* artists than, say, Mick Jagger of the Rolling Stones, or Jim Morrison of the Doors. But it has been Jagger and Morrison, for better or worse, who symbolize various aspects of the *cultural* essence of rock and roll in a way that the others have not, however glorious the music they made.

In order to clarify this elusive cultural essence, I have focused on a sequence of events, some well known, others not, that led to the invention, and subsequent refinement, of the musical genre and set of emblematic values that we, today, associate with the word "rock." In addition to describing, briefly, what really happened, I have also tried to explore its broader implications, using anecdotes to elaborate a tacit critique.

The story I tell is, superficially, one of triumph. As an integral part of the entertainment industry, rock today is glamorous, profitable, vibrant. For teenagers from Tokyo to Topeka, the music remains a large part of growing up, offering a focus for shared fantasies of romance and rebellion.

As a mode of social interaction, on the other hand, rock has many of the features of a finished cultural form—a more or less fixed repertoire of sounds and styles and patterns of behavior. The music I once found fraught with strange, even subversive meanings now often seems to mean nothing at all. Its essential possibilities have been thoroughly explored, its limits more or less clearly established. Though new variants of rock have continued to appear, from rap in 1979 to grunge, trance, house, and trip-hop in more recent years—and though new acts, from Queen Latifah and En Vogue to My Bloody Valentine and the Cardigans still sometimes catch my ear—I believe that the genre's era of explosive growth has been over for nearly a quarter century. Like such other mature pop music forms as the Broadway musical and the main currents of the jazz tradition, from swing to bop, rock now belongs to the past as much as to the future.

My narrative thus ends with the death of Elvis Presley in 1977, because by that time, in my view, the essence of rock and roll—as a musical style, as a cluster of values, as an ingredient in a variety of youthful subcultures around the world—had been firmly established. ✳ Rock, when it is entertaining, offers the sound of surprise: not the surprise of virtuosos improvising new ways to play (the thrill of jazz), but rather the surprise of untrained amateurs, working within their limits, finding a voice of their own—and sometimes even elaborating new song forms unthinkable to more highly skilled musicians. Without an air of ingenuous freshness and earnest effort, rock as a musical form is generally coarse, even puerile—full of sound and fury, perhaps, but characteristically spurning the subtle creativity and seasoned craftsmanship that is the glory of such other mature vernacular pop music genres as jazz and the blues, country and gospel.

The apparent reason for this difference is both simple and, in a sense, self-evident: unlike every other great genre of American pop, rock is all about being young, or (if you are poor Mick Jagger) pretending to be young.

I was nine when I bought my first rock record—it was "Don't Be Cruel" by Elvis Presley. At the time, my interest in such music was regarded as relatively precocious. A generation later, when my oldest son turned nine, he was already a veteran rock fan who had long shared his interest with his peers, collecting songs, swapping tapes, offering proof—if proof were needed—that rock can still produce a shared sense of exhilaration, not least among preteens and young adolescents just discovering the world.

Meanwhile, most of *my* friends (discounting those who have continued to make their living by writing about, or recording, popular music) long ago stopped listening to rock. As they settle into middle age, their old albums gathering dust, their current musical tastes are now attuned to quite different styles of music, from country-western to classical, from show tunes to patriotic women's choruses from Bulgaria—almost anything, in fact, but the once beloved soundtrack of their adolescence and early adulthood.

How did such a distinctively youthful form of music come to play a defining role in the global culture of the postwar period? Why should rock have become the musical lingua franca of the last half of our century? And what can its evident power—and equally striking limits—tell us about the broader cultural character of our time?

As I quickly discovered when I began to address these questions, my knowledge of rock history, even after all the years I had written about it, was surprisingly incomplete. In the last decade, there has been an outpouring of celebrity memoirs, often painful to read, but also often full of new information. At the same time, a handful of revelatory new works has appeared, for example John A. Jackson's carefully researched studies of Alan Freed and Dick Clark, Fredric Dannen and Fred Goodman's insider accounts of the seamier sides of the rock music business, Peter Guralnick's eye-opening biography of Elvis Presley, Mark Lewisohn's painstaking day-by-day chronicle of the Beatles, and Jon Savage's richly detailed recounting of the rise of punk rock in England in the 1970s. Record companies have meanwhile thrown open their vaults in search of previously unreleased scraps of music. It is now possible to hear Elvis Presley auditioning for Sam Phillips, Little Richard rehearsing "Tutti Frutti," the Beatles playing live in Hamburg, Germany, and the Sex Pistols working through multiple versions of "Anarchy in the U.K." It is also possible to read solemn academic treatises on how the heavy metal played by rock bands like Iron Maiden and Megadeth "articulates the anxieties and discontinuities of the postmodern world." (No, I'm not making this up.)

A generation ago, without the benefit of all this new material, I took a different approach to the topic as the original editor of *The Rolling Stone Illustrated History of Rock & Roll.* I structured that volume by inviting prominent critics to write essays on a pantheon of distinguished musicians: within this framework, Sam Cooke and Jackie Wilson and Otis Redding and Buddy Holly and the Beach Boys got equal billing with the Rolling Stones and the Doors. Like the subsequent institution of The Rock and Roll Hall of Fame, *The Rolling Stone Illustrated History* made it seem as if the music revolved around an admirable group of natural geniuses. To some extent, of course, it has: without Elvis Presley and the Beatles, there might not be a Rock and Roll Hall of Fame.

Still, a survey only of heroic musicians cannot help but leave a misleading impression of what rock and roll is, and of how it has evolved. By breaking apart a familiar and essentially romantic narrative, and exploiting the latest memoirs and research to look again more closely at a handful of events, one can see the story of rock's global triumph more clearly for what it is: an enduring puzzle that has yet to be properly appreciated, much less explained.

Here, then, is a look back, a chronicle of some critical moments in the advent of rock and roll when, for better or worse, the course of events changed—and a new form of popular culture appeared.

1

Life **C**ould **Be a Dream**

"Good Rockin' Tonight"

As epochal events go, it was modest, unimpressive—
and, at the time, all but ignored. The site was a nondescript recording studio in Cincinnati, Ohio. The occasion was a recording session
for a company unknown to most Americans, King. The agent of
change was a singer named Wynonie Harris, thirty-two years old,
also practically unknown. In most respects, there was nothing noteworthy about the setting, the singer, or his songs. But one of the
songs Harris sang on December 28, 1947, "Good Rockin' Tonight,"
would become a best-selling hit, played on jukeboxes and aired on
radio stations across black America. And by popularizing the word
"rock," Harris' recording would herald a new era in American popular culture.

Nobody noticed. In December of 1947, the music we now call
"rock and roll" hadn't yet been named, much less invented. When
Harris sang his pathbreaking song, he was simply doing what he had
done for years, practicing a time-honored craft he had mastered in an
old-fashioned way, through trial and error, learning how to make
music that would lift listeners up, put people into motion, and let
them dance the night away.

"Hence the dance hall as temple," the novelist and critic Albert
Murray has written: "Hence all the ceremonially deliberate drag
steps and shaking and grinding movements during, say, the old
downhome Saturday Night Function, and all the sacramental strutting and swinging along with all the elegant stomping. . . . And hence
in consequence the fundamental function of the blues musician (also
known as the jazz musician), the most obvious as well as the most
pragmatic mission of whose performance is not only to drive the
blues away and hold them at bay at least for the time being, but also
to evoke an ambiance of Dionysian revelry."

In the way that Wynonie Harris had lived his life, and made his
music, his objective was plain and simple: it was revelry, the more
"Dionysian" the better. At the time he recorded "Good Rockin'

Tonight," he was already a minor legend. Renowned for his fast living and hard drinking, he'd been playing Saturday Night Functions
from coast to coast since the mid-Forties, building up a reputation as
one of the wildest black showmen of his day. Photographs show a
coffee-colored Clark Gable, debonair, cocky, a gleam in his eyes, the
promise of pleasure on his lips.

A generation later, Harris would have become a pinup for kids, a
pop culture icon, just like Michael Jackson or Prince, two of his spiritual heirs. But in 1947, he was, by comparison, a nobody—an
anonymous journeyman. In those days, there were few magazines devoted to pop music, no TV shows about it (television was still in its
infancy), and little mainstream media coverage of Negro stars like
Wynonie Harris.* Despite the widespread popularity in America of
black dance music and of certain black entertainers, such as Louis
Armstrong, the Mills Brothers, and the Ink Spots, patterns of social
segregation cut deep. Inhabiting a common culture, whites and
blacks still lived largely in worlds apart.

Harris had first achieved fame in the world of black music with
Lucky Millinder, who led one of Harlem's hottest dance bands. After
scoring a vocal hit with the Millinder band in 1945—it was a good-
natured blues novelty, "Who Threw the Whiskey in the Well?"—
Harris went solo, recording for several different small labels, and
selling just enough copies to sustain his career.

His session for King after Christmas in 1947 hardly promised anything out of the ordinary. As was customary in those days, the session was scheduled to last three hours and produce three or four
usable takes of three or four new songs. The band consisted of seasoned musicians, most of them jazzmen like Oran "Hot Lips" Page,
an alumnus of Count Basie's renowned Kansas City band. As usual,
the label's A&R man (for "artists and repertoire") had selected the
songs for the band to play. The tunes ran the gamut. One was a
risqué novelty, long since forgotten, called "Lollipop Mama." Another tune, "I Believe I'll Fall in Love," was even less distinguished.
Songs like this—and the fare was typical—did not give a singer much
to work with. Still, if luck was with him—if Harris caught the right

*I should explain the racial terms used in the book. "Colored" and "Negro" were
terms in common usage in America well into the Sixties, when "black" became preferred in many contexts, just as "African-American" is often preferred today. All of
these terms appear at various points in this text, as the historical context dictates.

feeling, if his band hit a relaxed rhythmic groove—even the most hackneyed of songs might let a blues musician fulfill his fundamental function, making music of sufficient energy and earthiness to provoke an outburst of emotion that carried listeners away.

The composer of "Good Rockin' Tonight" was a young singer named Roy Brown, a native of New Orleans and a fan of Wynonie Harris. Legend has it that Brown, inspired by hearing Harris in person, wrote the song on a paper bag and offered it to "Mister Blues" (his nickname) backstage. When Harris refused the gift, Brown sang the song himself at his first recording session. Brown's version was selling well in the South, and so came to the attention of Harris' new A&R man at King, Henry Glover, a big band veteran charged with finding fresh "repertoire" for his "artists."

The song's rhythmic style was apt. This was the heyday, in black popular music, of a relaxed kind of boogie-woogie—the musical backbone of "Good Rockin' Tonight." Almost offhandedly, Harris and his combo transformed the song into a celebration of everything dance music can be: an incantation, an escape, an irrepressibly joyous expression of sheer physical existence.

They took Brown's song at an easy lope. The band was loose, Harris in rare form. A sax riffed, a piano pumped, and Harris shouted: "Have you heard the news? There's good rockin' tonight!"

Five months later, the news was out. By June of 1948, Harris' record was spinning on jukeboxes from coast to coast. The era of "good rockin' " had arrived.

Or so it would later seem. To chronicle the past is to search for some place to start, some more or less arbitrary moment to begin: and more than one historian of rock has thought to open his story with "Good Rockin' Tonight." Not that experts can agree. In 1992, an account of fifty pioneering rock and roll recordings demonstrated the intractability of the question posed by the book's title, *What Was the First Rock 'n Roll Record?*

Questions of historical priority scarcely preoccupied Wynonie Harris. Born in 1915 in Omaha, Nebraska, he had honed his talents in the Midwest, performing as a buck dancer, a drummer, a singer, touring with carnivals, doing vaudeville, entertaining at minstrel shows, covering a territory that ran from the Dakotas in the north to Oklahoma in the south.

The undisputed cultural capital of this territory was Kansas City. And it was in Kansas City that Wynonie Harris first heard Joe

Turner—and first found his true calling. "He went crazy over the big blues shouter," Preston Love, one of Harris' lifelong friends later recalled. "He thought the blues was a way of life—an only life, and he patterned himself as a singer after Joe Turner."

In the 1930s, when Harris first visited Kansas City, Joe Turner was tending bar, bouncing bums, and singing the blues at a club called the Sunset—the kind of place that later rock and roll stars could only dream about. Located at Twelfth and Woodlawn, the club was surrounded by dozens of other saloons, promising an endless supply of whiskey, women, and song. Tricks were two dollars an orgasm, marijuana three sticks for a quarter. In these days, Kansas City was a mecca for white revelers and black musicians, attracting one of the greatest concentrations of jazz talent in history: Count Basie, Lester Young, Ben Webster, Buck Clayton, Andy Kirk, Mary Lou Williams, Jay McShann, Charlie Parker—the list goes on. Every night after hours, musicians like this converged on the Sunset to blow the blues away, in the process refining the jazz form called swing—dance music with a sleek pulse, bursting with energy and brimming with riffs: short fusillades of melodic ostinato, repeated, developed, elaborated, repeated again, reinforcing the music's rhythmic thrust, cutting through the air like the night train to Memphis.

The Sunset was a tiny place, roughly twelve feet wide and sixty feet deep, a "black and tan" with a bandstand at one end and a rope down the middle to separate the black patrons from the whites (or "tans"), who in the Thirties were numerous—this, after all, was the heyday of swing, the style of popular music preferred by most Americans, white and black. The Sunset's house pianist in these years was Pete Johnson, the best in the city, a boogie-woogie virtuoso with a rock-steady sense of time that sent patrons flocking to the dance floor. A primitive amplification system piped the music into the darkened streets, allowing Johnson's partner, Big Joe, to "call his children home," summoning customers inside. Turner served drinks and sang at the same time. He handed down the bleakest of lyrics—"you may be beautiful, but you gonna die some day"—with unswerving authority and infectious good humor. Sometimes, as Turner later recalled, "we'd start playing around three in the morning. The bossman would set up pitchers of corn-likker, and we'd rock"—which gives an idea of one thing that Wynonie Harris may have had in mind when he sang about "good rockin' " ten years later.

The world had changed in the interim. Kansas City's wonder years were over. But the city's riffing style of swing lived on, not least in the music of Wynonie Harris.

A tall, handsome man from a racially mixed background (one of his wives would later claim that his father had been an American Indian by the name of Blue Jay), Harris was dapper and slim, with striking eyes of bluish green and a pencil-thin mustache—a far cry from Joe Turner, who was a blues version of Paul Bunyan. During World War II, Harris, like Turner, had joined the great black migration of these years to the West Coast, where work could be found in wartime factories running round the clock. Both men ended up in Los Angeles, where they regularly performed together, sometimes staging a friendly "cutting" session, as if to summon the memory of times past at the Sunset.

In 1947, Harris and Turner recorded a series of duets, including a boisterous "Battle of the Blues" that nicely illustrates the difference in their styles. Swapping boasts about their sexual prowess, Turner as usual sounds earthy, offhand, almost absentmindedly lustful—a force of nature, untamed and sublime. Harris by contrast is dogged, strident, strenuously energetic.

He made a career out of bellowing off-color novelties, drinking songs, and raucous blues. "I Want My Fanny Brown" was one jukebox favorite, "I Like My Baby's Pudding" another. Dumb double entendres didn't faze him. A prototypical "rock" singer, he attacked the most inane of lyrics with melodramatic gusto.

The 1940s was a time of change in the music that most Americans listened to. In mainstream pop, the big bands were being replaced by crooners like Vaughn Monroe and Perry Como. In the world of jazz, dance music was out, bebop was in, turning the art of improvisation into a form as demanding as anything heard in European concert halls. As jazz ceased to be a truly popular music, even among blacks, the so-called race charts published by the music trade magazine *Billboard*—charts meant to document the recorded music black Americans preferred to hear—registered a historic shift: the hot new style was jump, a simplified and superheated version of old-fashioned swing, often boogie-woogie based, usually played by a small combo of piano, bass, and drums, with saxophone and trumpet.

From its streamlined riffs to the genre's very name, jump owed a large debt to the Kansas City scene of the 1930s. Count Basie had shown the way with "One O'Clock Jump." But the genre's greatest postwar exponent was the singer and saxophonist Louis Jordan, a native of Arkansas later based in New York City and Los Angeles. In a string of popular recordings that began in 1942, and included four million-sellers ("G.I. Jive," "Caldonia," "Choo Choo Ch'Boogie," and "Saturday Night Fish Fry"), Jordan perfected a propulsive, boogie-woogie-based style of swing, animated by a clownish stage manner he had inherited from Louis Armstrong, Fats Waller, and Cab Calloway. At the height of Jordan's career, between 1944 and 1946, his recordings were as popular with whites as with blacks. One of his biggest hits, "G.I. Jive," actually topped the normally lily-white "folk" (or country-western) chart in 1944, becoming the first recording in history to top simultaneously all three *Billboard* charts (pop, race, and folk). Despite his huge white following, Jordan was unapologetically black. Before him, the black stars most popular with white listeners, such as Louis Armstrong, the Mills Brothers, and the Ink Spots, had hurdled America's racial divide by singing Tin Pan Alley material. Jordan took a different tack, singing songs filled with images from ghetto life ("Saturday Night Fish Fry," for example, recounts a police raid on a block party). And though his flair for comedy took the sting out of his lyrics, and sometimes brought Jordan to the brink of self-parody, he was a committed entertainer, a peerless bandleader—and for any up-and-coming jump blues star, the man to beat.

For one striking moment—in the studio that December day in 1947—Wynonie Harris did just that. Like Jordan's classic hits, Harris' "Good Rockin' Tonight" swings effortlessly. An epitome of the jump genre, the record opens with a growling trumpet fanfare. The bass player doubles the pianist's pumping left hand, and hand-clapping reinforces the drummer's backbeat. Knocking out a perfect boogie beat, the group hews to a formula, but the formula is tried and true: ten years later, it would be all but impossible to locate five musicians able to animate the same simple riffs with such style and élan. Harris himself was in rare form. Uncommonly subdued, he sings with blithe artistry. Apart from a feverish sax solo, the song glides by.

Harris' recording turned into one of the biggest race hits of 1948: in June, it topped *Billboard* magazine's weekly lists of both Most-Played Juke Box Race Records and Best Selling Retail Race Records. Its popularity triggered a small boom in race records that highlighted ford "rock." In the months that followed, there was Joe er's "Rockin' Boogie," the tenor saxophonist Wild Bill Moore's

"We're Gonna Rock, We're Gonna Roll," vocalist Roy Brown's "Rockin' at Midnight," Jimmy Preston's "Rock the Joint," and yet another Wild Bill Moore disc, this one with the pithy and prophetic title "Rock and Roll."

Prophetic or not, these records at first changed little in the music most Americans listened to, or in the culture that most Americans inhabited. Distributed primarily on jukeboxes located in Negro clubs and bars, none of these pioneering "rock" records reached the larger white audience—not even Wynonie Harris' exuberant version of "Good Rockin' Tonight."

The primary problem was not the color of the musicians' skins—Louis Jordan after all played a virtually identical brand of music. The problem was the word "rock." As the record's A&R man, Henry Glover, later explained, "we were restricted with our possibilities of promoting this song because it was considered filth"—and though "filth" was acceptable on a ghetto jukebox, it was not acceptable on most radio shows: "They had a definition in those days of the word 'rock,' meaning the sex act, rather than having it known as 'a good time,' as they did later."

In the late 1940s, Glover was a talent and song scout for King. A label founded in 1943, King was owned and operated by Syd Nathan, a Cincinnati record retailer. Priding himself on his prowess as a salesman, Nathan had made a small fortune by "selling records in a location that nobody could sell a record in," as he told his sales staff in 1951—"it was like trying to sell a grand piano out in the desert. But we done business because we knew how to do business."

Nathan had started up King by recording hillbilly artists, and quickly made his mark in the folk field. Branching into race music, Nathan in 1946 hired Glover, a former trumpeter and arranger in Lucky Millinder's big band, and one of the first black men in the postwar record business to be given any creative clout. It was Glover's job to help his label's artists by finding songs, booking studios, hiring musicians, and supervising the recording sessions. Like Nathan, Glover "knew how to do business." One of the first artists he signed and supervised for Nathan was Bullmoose Jackson, a popular baritone who would produce naughty novelties and lugubrious ballads for King starting in 1946.

The commercial success of labels like King in these years was symptomatic of a number of concurrent changes in the American music industry. As cheap and improved record players came on the market after World War II, retail sales of recordings grew rapidly, particularly in the areas of country music and rhythm and blues. Registering the change, *Billboard* in May 1948 augmented its old charts listing jukebox favorites with two new charts listing the week's best-selling retail recordings of race and folk music. The new popular interest in both black and country music grew out of the wartime experience of a large number of Americans: thanks to the regional and racial mixing that had occurred in the armed forces, and also thanks to the heterogeneous musical fare piped round the world on armed forces radio programs and V-Discs, a generation had been exposed to a range of musical styles far wider than anything heard on the live variety shows broadcast by America's national radio networks in the 1930s. At the same time, the country's established labels, faced with a shortage of shellac during the war, had sharply cut back their involvement in musical genres they deemed marginal. The reluctance of the major labels to meet a growing demand left the field wide open for independent entrepreneurs like Syd Nathan.

The postwar independent record business was risky and brawling—but Syd Nathan was a pugnacious entrepreneur. As an associate later recalled, he was a "short, round, rough, gruff man with a nose like Porky Pig and two Coca-Cola bottles for eyeglasses." He smoked cigars, growled hoarsely, and governed his record label like a modern-day fiefdom, barking out orders to underlings. He turned King into one of the few vertically integrated operations in the music business. He owned his own studio, he owned the plant that stamped his records, and he owned the press that printed King's record jackets. He also drove hard bargains, offering his race and folk artists a flat fee to record, and taking care to purchase the copyright on virtually every song that his label issued. The most lucrative aspect of the music business is song publishing: whoever owns the publishing rights to a piece of music is in a position to make money every time the sheet music or a recording of the song is sold, and virtually every time the music is performed live, or a recording of it is broadcast. Trying to maximize his profits, Nathan became a virtuoso at imaginatively exploiting his catalogue of songs, having his folk acts record race songs that he owned, and vice versa: one of Wynonie Harris' biggest hits was a remake of an earlier country hit for King, Hank Penny's "Bloodshot Eyes." Cheerfully philistine by temperament, Nathan took special pride in making money from smutty songs no other label would touch, churning out off-color records with titles like "I Want a Bowlegged Woman," the notorious "Work With Me Annie," and its equally notorious sequel, "Annie Had a Baby."

"The first thing you learn is that everyone is a liar," Syd Nathan once snapped to an inquiring reporter: "The only thing that matters is the song. Buy the song, own the song, but remember, no matter what anyone tells you, they are liars until they have convinced you they are telling the truth."

Nathan's vulgarity was legendary—but in Wynonie Harris, he met his match. In 1947, Nathan and an associate journeyed to New York City to talk Harris into signing with King. As Nathan told the story a few years later, they found Mister Blues "in a backstreet dingy hotel in Harlem. . . . And when we knocked on the door, he says 'come in,' and there were three gals in the room with him. All naked. So one of them opened her mouth, and he threw her out in the hall without any clothes on. . . . So we sat there talking to this drunk, stupid individual—and if he were here I'd tell it to him (he's got a little more sense since then)—till six o'clock in the morning." As the sun rose in the east, Harris signed with King.

"Good Rockin' Tonight" was the first in a series of best-sellers that Harris recorded for Nathan's label. The consistent popularity of his recordings for King over the next five years made him wealthy and famous.

"As a statement of fact, clean of any attempt to brag about it, I'm the highest-paid blues singer in the business," Harris boasted in 1954 (just as his star was starting to fade). "I'm a $1,500 a week man. Most of the other fellows sing for $50 to $75 a night. I don't. That is why I'm no Broadway star. The crooners star on the Great White Way and get swamped with Coca-Cola-drinking bobby-soxers and other 'jail bait.' I star in Georgia, Texas, Alabama, Tennessee and Missouri and get those who have money to buy stronger stuff and my records to play while they drink it. I like to sing to women with meat on their bones and that long, green stuff in their pockets. You find them mostly down south. As a matter of fact, I like all kinds of women, regardless of what color they are or what size and shape they may have. Just so long as they're breathing, that's me!"

Such vainglory was a sign of "good rockin' " to come. For Wynonie Harris and those who would follow in his footsteps, from Chuck Berry to Mick Jagger to Prince, the new music would, in time, become what Big Joe Turner's blues had been at the Sunset in Kansas

City—"a way of life," a free life, an "only life." Organized, like jump, around the single-minded pursuit of simple musical pleasures, rock, too, would hold out the promise of wealth, of fame, of physical gratification without measure or limit. And all for a song!

October 29, 1949:

Red Hot and Blue

The sun had set and the radio was rocking. The deejay's patter was manic, his voice a blur, his words a jumble. "Get your bald-headed nanny goat runnin' through the front door," the man said breathlessly, jamming together syllables and words and sentences without pause, as if without punctuation, "tell 'em Phillips sencha down there from *Red Hot 'n' Blue* the next fifteen minutes of *Red Hot 'n' Blue* is comin' to ya through the courtesy of that good Old Amigo Flour we're gonna play the next record for LeAnn Sandwich for Erma King Annie L. Sandwich for Cathy for W.J. Johnson also for Yumma Black for Ernie Black for Porter for Ruby Young I believe it is a call for Monroe Williams and the title is 'Say you ever get booted' here's a record that's gettin' hot man 'Booted' by Roscoe Gordon!"

A drum rolled. A raspy voice shouted out, "Jack, man! Have you ever been booted?"

A chorus shouted back. "Did you say booted?"

"Yeah, man. Booted!"

A piano shuffled into a boogie beat—and another hour of the Dewey Phillips show began on radio station WHBQ in Memphis, Tennessee.

Phillips first aired his show on October 29, 1949, filling a forty-five-minute slot from 10:15 until 11:00 at night. But within weeks, Phillips was on the air from 9:00 till midnight, hawking flour, spinning records—and changing, forever, the way white people would hear black music.

Memphis in 1949 was a boomtown. It was also a bastion of segregation, with separate (and unequal) parks, schools, and restaurants set aside for the city's rapidly growing black population (nearly 40 percent of the city's total of 300,000). Most of the black newcomers had come straight from small towns and farms in adjacent Mississippi. The mechanization of cotton harvesting in the 1930s had destroyed the sharecropper system, triggering a mass migration from the Delta, a wedge of fertile farmland that stretched south from Memphis toward Vicksburg, Mississippi. Some of the migrants moved farther north, to St. Louis or Chicago. But others, unwilling to stray far from home, looked for work in Memphis. The newcomers brought with them country habits and a taste for old-fashioned country blues, an elemental and harshly rhythmic style of music that Dewey Phillips would make a mainstay of his radio program.

A music of relative simplicity and raw power, the form of blues commonly heard on the Delta differed from the styles popular in other areas. As the music historian Robert Palmer has observed, "the Mississippi Delta's blues musicians sang with unmatched intensity in a gritty, melodically circumscribed, highly ornamented style that was closer to field hollers than it was to other blues." Where the jazz-based jump bands that came out of Kansas City were sleek and swinging, the Delta blues bands were jagged and rough; where a singer like Joe Turner projected a feeling of easy mastery, a classic Delta bluesman like Charley Patton howled and growled, mangling diction, swallowing words, in some recordings from the 1930s carrying on what sounds like a febrile conversation with himself, using different voices, from a piercing falsetto to a sandpaper baritone.

It was rough-and-ready music for a Saturday Night Function, and Dewey Phillips hawked it like snake oil. A freckle-faced redhead raised in rural Tennessee, he had become a fixture on the Memphis scene after the war. Before joining the staff of WHBQ, he had worked the public address system at Grant's Dime Store downtown, blaring records and jabbering advertisements, developing the wild delivery he would perfect on *Red Hot and Blue*. Broadcasting from the mezzanine of the Old Chisca Hotel on Main Street, he brought the savage sound of the Delta blues to Memphians of all races, filling the air with barrelhouse boogie. To hear the latest in black music, there was now no need to sneak into a juke joint, or steal across the tracks to visit a record store. After the evening of October 29, 1949, one simply had to keep the radio set on Memphis' all-purpose (and most powerful) radio station, WHBQ—and wait till nightfall for *Red Hot and Blue*.

Dewey Phillips epitomized a new phenomenon: the celebrity disc jockey. A strictly regional radio star who talked with a strictly regional accent, Phillips made a virtue out of being different, spurning the conventions of radio broadcasting from the down-home drawl in his delivery to the down-home music he aired. Throughout the 1930s, local radio programming had been largely supplied by *national* networks. The network announcers, as the official voice of a self-consciously *national* medium, invariably sounded urbane, educated, colorless, using clear diction and a soothing tone to summon Americans together to hear melodramas, news, fireside chats by the President, live broadcasts of everything from dance concerts to the Metropolitan Opera—almost anything, in fact, but recordings; and least of all, recordings of identifiably regional styles of music. For better or worse, the national networks in these years functioned as great cultural equalizers, transmitting more or less the same variety of live entertainment and news to every listener, whether white or black, rich or poor.

All this changed with the introduction of commercial television after World War II, though it took some time for the new medium to reach the hinterlands (Memphis, for example, got its first TV station only in 1948). As national broadcast networks like NBC and CBS shifted their resources from radio to television, local radio affiliates were forced to devote more and more time to local programming, much of it, by necessity, featuring prerecorded music. Disc jockeys—the men who chatted with the audience and played the recordings—assumed a new importance. In order to be competitive, announcers had to have an edge, an image, a distinctive on-air personality; and it didn't hurt if they played a distinctive style of music, too. As never before, stations were willing to experiment with new formats. And by the end of the 1940s, it was clear that shows featuring race records were attracting a large and growing audience, particularly in the South.

These shows would, in time, help break down old barriers between white and black, quickening America's movement toward black civil rights. But the race format was itself a by-product of segregation. For years, advertisers interested in pitching certain products at Negro consumers had sponsored separate radio segments that featured black-themed programming. The national radio networks had routinely featured the big bands of Duke Ellington and Count Basie, while in Memphis WHBQ had long made a practice of airing the *Midnight Ramble,* a show featuring black musicians staged for an all-white audience every Thursday night at the Palace Theater. The trick, particularly in the segregated South, was to pitch products at black listeners without surrendering control to black personalities. In the early years, the vast majority of disc jockeys airing black music were white, from Dewey Phillips in Memphis and "John R." Richbourg in Nashville to Zenas "Daddy" Sears in Atlanta and Hunter Hancock in Los Angeles.

These disc jockeys prospered by exploiting a lucrative new market. After the war, the income of African-Americans, historically depressed, grew even more quickly than that of whites. In a city like Memphis, certain commodities were disproportionately bought by blacks. A pioneering survey of Negro consumers in Memphis, conducted in 1952, revealed that black Memphians consumed 80 percent of the city's packaged rice, 70 percent of its canned milk, and 65 percent of its all-purpose flour. The same survey showed that radios, once beyond the means of the average black family, had become a standard appliance—in Memphis alone, 93 percent of black households owned a radio, and 30 percent owned two. Advertisers eager to reach this newly affluent audience naturally turned to radio shows that featured race music.

Memphis became a national leader in black radio programming. In addition to *Red Hot and Blue,* the catalyst was WDIA, the nation's first radio station to feature all-black music played by an all-black staff of disc jockeys, a policy instituted in 1948. Though it broadcast only from dawn to dusk, WDIA by the fall of 1949 was one of the most popular radio stations in Memphis. It was, in fact, the size of WDIA's daytime audience that convinced WHBQ to experiment with the race format at night.

Red Hot and Blue was an instant hit. As WHBQ's program director later recalled, Phillips "got something like seven requests his first night. Well, the next night, I don't know the exact amount, but it was more like seventy requests. Then, even more incredible, the next night, it was closer to seven hundred."

For nearly a decade, Dewey Phillips was the most popular radio personality in Memphis. At the peak of his popularity in the mid-Fifties, he reached an estimated 100,000 listeners on an average night. A big part of the appeal was Phillips himself. His on-air patter blazed with bizarre asides and absurd non sequiturs, delivered in a primeval piney-woods drawl, evoking the sharecropper's son as unbuttoned hipster.

The earliest known aircheck of the show, recorded on December 3, 1951, captures the mood and texture of a typical night—and demonstrates that Phillips routinely programmed the roughest and most down-home kind of Delta-style blues. After starting with Roscoe Gordon's "Booted," a stomping boogie, Phillips continued with Muddy Waters' "She Moves Me," a now classic piece of Chicago blues, featuring Little Walter on harmonica. Briefly he changed the pace with a seasonal tune, Lowell Fulson's "Lonesome Christmas," before closing the fifteen-minute slot (during which he kept constantly plugging Old Amigo Flour) with Elmore James and his slashing original version of "Dust My Broom," featuring Sonny Boy Williamson on harmonica.

This set of songs was a reflection of regional taste. In 1951, Roscoe Gordon lived in Memphis, while Elmore James and Sonny Boy Williamson worked out of West Memphis, Arkansas. Though Muddy Waters had moved to Chicago in 1943, he had grown up in Clarksdale, Mississippi, in the heart of the Delta, some sixty miles south of Memphis. Even Lowell Fulson, who by 1951 was based in California, had gotten his start in the Southwest, working a territory that included Memphis.

The music all of these men played was evidently what the listeners to *Red Hot and Blue* wanted to hear—and a far cry, ironically, from the more urbane and jazz-oriented fare broadcast during the day on WDIA. Because it was earthy and often musically crude, the brand of music that Phillips routinely played was regarded as demeaning by many educated Negroes—the core of the audience that WDIA initially wished to attract. In these years, it was, paradoxically, easier for a white deejay like Phillips to air unrefined Delta blues on a predominantly white-oriented station like WHBQ than it was for a pioneering black deejay like Nat D. Williams to play the same music on an all-black station like WDIA. And that was not the end of the paradoxes. For the fact that this music was aired on a predominantly white station gave it a new kind of cultural cachet among blacks, even as it permitted white listeners to tune in without guilt.

In effect, Dewey Phillips turned every night in Memphis into a kind of make-believe "Midnight Ramble." Working in the most ephemeral of mediums—it is all but impossible today to hear even a sample of what Phillips in his prime sounded like—he presided over a new kind of community, one that was largely invisible (since most of his listeners were sitting at home) and at first inconsequential (since as radio surveys showed in the early Fifties, a surprising number of his listeners turned out to be teenagers). But soon enough, the signs of this new community would be everywhere in Memphis, from the blues records on the jukeboxes in soda fountains to the black bands hired to play at white country clubs.

It wasn't the end of segregation—but it was the beginning of the end. And in time, every city in America would experience its own version of this musical great awakening, often through the magic of a show like *Red Hot and Blue*. The sun would go down. The radio would light up. And for a small but rapidly growing number of young white listeners, many still largely unknown to one another, the very strangeness of the music—its dreamlike distance from any world they had personally experienced—made it a powerful antidote to boredom, an invitation to fantasy, an image of freedom.

April 1950:

Fender Guitars

The bands heard on the race hits of the late 1940s were small combos, usually featuring a boogie-woogie pianist, a honking saxophonist, and sometimes a lead guitarist. They played loose and loud. Music with a big beat, it still wasn't loose enough, or loud enough, to be rock and roll. For that, something else was needed—instruments able to make a bigger noise.

In 1950, such an instrument appeared. It was the Fender Esquire, the first mass-produced, solid-body electric guitar. The instrument's fret board was bolted to a flat plank of wood equipped with a pickup—a magnet wound with a steel coil that converted the vibrations of the metal strings into an electronic signal, which was in turn converted into sound by means of an amplifier and loudspeaker.

Over the next decade, this solid-body design was refined and perfected by Leo Fender—the Thomas Edison of the rock era. Fender wasn't the first person to build an electric guitar, nor were his electric guitars the best—only the most memorable. It seems fitting that the tombstone of rock's first martyr, Buddy Holly, should depict the silhouette of a Fender Stratocaster, the futuristic solid-body guitar he had played. By 1959, the year of Holly's plane crash, the outline of Fender's uniquely formed guitar perfectly symbolized the dead man, and his musical gift to the world.

Acoustic guitars use a hollow wooden cavity to project the sound of the vibrating strings out toward listeners. At first, inventors tried simply to amplify this sound. Too often, the result was distortion and unwanted feedback, a piercing howl produced when an amplified signal is inadvertently amplified again. A radio repairman by vocation, Leo Fender had watched in the 1930s as early electric guitarists struggled to tame their unruly instruments. Near the end of his life, Fender explained how his electric guitar differed from all those that had come before. "On an acoustic electric guitar you have a string fastened to a diaphragm top, and that top does not have one specific frequency. If you play a note the top will respond to it and also to a lot of adjoining notes," producing distortion, particularly at higher levels of amplification; "a solid-body doesn't have that, you're dealing with just a single note at a time." In effect, Fender's solid body design, by eliminating the diaphragm top, allowed each string to be amplified cleanly, without unwanted feedback—thus enabling electric guitarists to play louder than ever before.

The Esquire was only one of Leo Fender's inventions. Born on a farm near Anaheim, California, in 1909, just eight years after Marconi succeeded in using wireless radio waves to transmit the letter S across the Atlantic Ocean, he had come of age in a world where phonographs and radios were still awe-inspiring innovations, machines with a conjurer's power to reproduce sounds. Fascinated by the prospect of harnessing that power, Fender developed a passion for electrical engineering. A lifelong country music fan, he began to tinker with guitars in his teens, and by the 1930s he was experimenting with the pick ups used to amplify guitars. In 1931, Fender opened a radio, music, and record store in Southern California. In the years that followed, he experimented with new electric guitar designs, and also built his own public address amplification systems, which he rented out for sporting and entertainment events. At the same time, he was working on other devices, among them a reliable record changer. After the war, Fender decided to sell his design for the record changer, using the profits to build a new plant in Fullerton, California, for manufacturing electric guitar equipment.

In 1948, when Fender's first guitar rolled off his plant's assembly line, amplified instruments were still something of a novelty. The sound of swirling violins marked the mainstream pop of the era, while the timbres of the big band—trumpets, saxes, piano—still dominated jazz and jump blues. Even in country music, where the guitar had long been ubiquitous as a rhythm instrument, it was still generally strummed in the background, leaving the melody and improvisation to a banjo, or mandolin, or a keening fiddle.

Fender's electric guitars would help change all that—but change was already in the air. Earlier in the decade, a Texas musician named T-Bone Walker had introduced the electric guitar as a lead voice in jump blues, while Oscar Moore, inspired by Charlie Christian, Benny Goodman's pioneering electric guitarist, had kept the instrument popular in jazz circles with his impeccably swinging solos in the King Cole Trio. In country music, Merle Travis was similarly in the midst of rewriting the rules, transforming the amplified guitar into a stringed equivalent of the pianoforte—an instrument capable of producing melodies as well as harmonies, with more or less percussive force, at a volume that could compete with brass, woodwinds, and drums. Grasping all of these possibilities and elaborating them still further by building his own solid-body electric guitar was Les Paul, who released his first recordings several years before Leo Fender brought the Esquire to market.

Unlike Les Paul, who was an able musician in his own right, Leo Fender was fascinated, above all, by the sheer romance of electronics. He represents a recurrent type in postwar culture: the technological tinkerer as Promethean innovator.

Just as the introduction of the microphone in the 1920s had revolutionized the practice of popular singing, so did the amplification of the guitar transform the craft of popular musicianship. In both cases technological innovations facilitated the cross-fertilization of new vernacular approaches to music. With the aid of a microphone, singers could address listeners with unprecedented intimacy, just as the jazz style popular in the Twenties encouraged them to phrase with rhythmic flexibility. A similar metamorphosis occurred with the electric guitar: amplification allowed guitarists to play fluid and hornlike solos, while the country and jump blues genres popular in the late Forties encouraged them to elaborate a more percussive and riffing style.

In 1948, there was an outpouring of guitar boogie records. John Lee Hooker offered "Boogie Chillen," playing a primal style—one blaring chord, banged out at a boogie tempo. Arthur Smith sounded jaunty and crisp on his influential "Guitar Boogie," a hit with country fans later that year. And then there was Les Paul, whose tongue-in-cheek "Hip-Billy Boogie" was characteristically clever, setting bright riffs in cheerful counterpoint to a bluesy solo, thanks to Paul's pioneering use of sound-on-sound tape recording, or overdubbing.

The guitars that Leo Fender introduced in 1950 proved to be the right product at the right time. The instrument's construction was sturdy, yet elegant. A neck of solid maple was bolted to a gently curved body of flat, solid ash. Two pickups were mounted in the body, one of them angled next to the bridge, to produce the crispest possible treble tones. The headstock, gently curved like the instrument's body, announced in spaghetti lettering that this was a guitar made by Fender.

The new instrument—first dubbed the Esquire, then the Broadcaster, and finally the Telecaster—caught on quickly. By 1951, business was booming—and Fender was putting into production his next major invention, the electric bass.

Musicians were drawn to the Telecaster by its rugged construction and the unusual palette of sounds it could produce. Mute the strings and the notes popped percussively; raise the volume and the notes hung in the air, as if by magic defying the quick decay of the naturally plucked string. Using the pickup nearest to the bridge produced a sound that was preternaturally bright and twangy, while using the pickup nearest the neck created a mellower tone, reminiscent of that produced by previous electric guitars.

But Fender was more than a skilled instrument maker. He has also rightly been hailed as the electric guitar's Harley Earl—an engineer with a flair for futuristic design. Like Earl's famous tailfin designs for General Motors cars in the 1950s, Fender's guitars flaunted the artificiality of their shape, using swept-back contours to evoke a fantasy of power and speed. Fender's Stratocaster model, introduced in 1954, was offered in a host of shocking colors, from Fiesta Red to Shoreline Gold. Unlike the saxophones and trumpets played by a big band musician, or even the synthesizers and electronic keyboards fashionable today, these were instruments that made a fashion statement. Musicians sported them like necklaces, waved them like scarves, collected them like rare pearls.

Fender's instruments did more than change the sound and look of postwar pop music; above all, they changed the range and variety of people who would be able to make music. The guitar has long been an inviting instrument for amateurs: easily portable, it is also relatively easy to play. But Fender's innovations made it even easier. By doing away with the hollow, resonating cavity of wood that was the musical heart of the old-fashioned Spanish guitar, Fender's solid-body design sharply reduced the importance of controlling each string's resonance precisely, enabling players to mask fingering mistakes. Suddenly even a clumsy novice could sound almost musical: plug in a Telecaster, tap a string, and sound poured effortlessly out, at a volume that was previously unimaginable.

Fender's guitar inaugurated a new era for the design and manufacture of electronic instruments. Fender himself worked on the first electric pianos, which his company produced in the mid-Sixties. A generation later, with the use of computers in synthesizers, drum machines, and sequencers—devices able to store and program patterns of sound electronically—a variety of sophisticated electronic instruments had all but obviated the need for a musician to acquire, through practice, a certain level of manual dexterity. On a modern electronic synthesizer, one need only touch a button or a key, and samples of every conceivable sort of timbre and sound pour forth effortlessly. Whether this superficial ease of access to the means of producing sound has brought the world more music of beauty is, of course, another question entirely.

"Let's be realistic about this," Frank Zappa remarked in 1979, usefully summing up Leo Fender's contribution to global culture. "The guitar can be the single most blasphemous device on the face of the earth." Powerful, flashy, unspeakably loud, a handy tool for those with little in the way of previous musical experience, the electric guitar became the archetypal weapon in rock's attack on the decorum and orderliness of previous forms of fine music, profaning its empire of well-tempered tones and refined artistry, and allowing a new spirit—of deliberate musical brutishness—to ring in listeners' ears.

Winter 1950–1951:

"The Tennessee Waltz"

In 1949, the editors at *Billboard,* then as now the American music industry's most important trade magazine, announced a change in the nomenclature they would use to label different genres. Henceforth, what had previously been classified as "race" music would be known simply as "rhythm and blues"; at the same time, what had previously been described as "folk" music would henceforth be called "country and western." One of the *Billboard* staff writers behind the name changes, a young jazz buff named Jerry Wexler, explained that "rhythm and blues" seemed "a label more appropriate to an enlightened time": to his ears, "race" sounded too much like "racist."

So the names changed. But the use of racially coded labels remained intact. These labels reflected real musical—and racial—divisions. But they also artificially reinforced the divisions by making certain genres of music, by definition, marginal to a mainstream that could scarcely have existed without all the tributaries feeding into it. In these years, it often happened that a country or rhythm and blues recording would sell hundreds of thousands of copies, and yet barely register in *Billboard*'s weekly pop chart, which was labeled simply "Best-Sellers in Stores." At the same time, a handful of race and folk recordings, even in the mid-1940s, were simply too popular to ignore. Country singer Al Dexter went to number one on the *Billboard* chart of (mainstream) best-sellers with "Pistol Packing Mama" in 1943, while jump blues star Louis Jordan topped the same chart a few months later with "G.I. Jive." It was all American music, after all; and with growing frequency, it was all on the air, free for anyone to hear, available for anyone to buy, accessible for anyone to copy—as is shown by the story behind the biggest pop hit of the postwar, prerock era, "The Tennessee Waltz."

The song was composed in 1946 by bandleader Pee Wee King and Redd Stewart, the vocalist in King's Golden West Cowboys. Born Julius Frank Kuczynski, and raised in Milwaukee, Wisconsin, King had learned how to play the fiddle from his father, a professional polka musician, and how to act from Gene Autry, with whom he toured and made cowboy movies in the 1930s. During his time with Autry, King became adept at playing Western swing, a genre of dance music influenced equally by old German fiddle tunes, the vogue for Hollywood Westerns—and the jumping brand of jazz fashionable in Kansas City. A regular on the Grand Ole Opry in the decade after 1936, King made waves when his band's guitarist was permitted to play an electric instrument on the ultraconservative show. But King by temperament was neither an innovator nor a rebel. Like most people in any field, he made a career out of imitating others, be it Bob Wills, the father of Western swing, or Bill Monroe, the inventor of modern bluegrass and the composer of "The Kentucky Waltz"— the song that inspired King and Stewart to knock off "The Tennessee Waltz."

As the two men later recalled, they were sitting in the band's equipment truck and listening to Bill Monroe's version of "The Kentucky Waltz" on the radio when Stewart commented that no one had yet written a "Tennessee Waltz." King suggested writing new lyrics for the melody of a "No Name Waltz" that the Golden West Cowboys had been using as an instrumental theme. Stewart jotted the words down on a matchbook cover. In a matter of minutes, the men had composed a piece of music so simple that it sounded ageless.

King and Stewart first recorded "The Tennessee Waltz" in 1948, two years after it was written. King's original version is plodding but plangent. The melody is first stated by a fiddle, then an electric pedal steel guitar, to an oom-pah oom-pah accordion accompaniment. Redd Stewart declaims the lyrics in an earnest light baritone that suggests Bing Crosby fronting a polka band; his diction is colorless. Apart from the keening timbres of the fiddle, the recording scarcely sounds a note that is overtly "country," or "western." (On stage, on the other hand, the Stetson hats worn by the band made the genre of their music easier to identify.)

Shortly after its release in 1948, King's recording of "The Tennessee Waltz" appeared on *Billboard*'s folk chart, where it stayed for over half a year, inspiring several competing folk versions, including one by Cowboy Copas, and another by Roy Acuff. The song became a country music standard. And there the story might have ended, had it not been for trumpeter Erskine Hawkins, a veteran jazzman, the composer of "Tuxedo Junction," and the leader for the past decade of a big band popular with dancers in Harlem. The self-styled "Twentieth Century Gabriel" had a flashy style and a flair for ostentatious display. In 1950, he rearranged "The Tennessee Waltz" as a dirge for jazz band. Sung by Jimmy Mitchell with unctuous sentimentality, Hawkins' version is notable mainly for the lead trumpet part, which makes the song sound weirdly like "Taps."

Enter Patti Page. Twenty-two years old, she was a native of Oklahoma and a veteran radio star with sweet pipes, good looks, and a perky style. After a short stint singing with Benny Goodman, she had first caused a stir in 1948 by releasing a record that featured her singing four-part harmony with herself, a feat she had accomplished by recording four separate vocals on four separate acetates and then having her engineer play the four acetates together, to record on a fifth, and final, acetate. (The new technique of recording on magnetic tape, which allowed for much greater flexibility in shaping and editing a performance, was just being introduced in these years.)

In the fall of 1950, Page's manager, Jack Rael, chanced to meet Jerry Wexler in the offices of *Billboard* magazine, where Wexler was working at the time. Page was then preparing to record a Christmas novelty, "Boogie Woogie Santa Claus," and Rael needed a song for the flip side. Wexler suggested that Page listen to Erskine Hawkins' new recording of "The Tennessee Waltz." A few days later, she produced her own famous version of the song.

In a bow to the Erskine Hawkins arrangement that inspired it, Page's recording opens with a mournful trumpet obbligato played by Buck Clayton, the Kansas City jazzman famed for his playing with the Count Basie big band of the 1930s. Page sings with chaste restraint, letting the nostalgia in the lyrics speak for itself. But what grabs a listener's attention is not the song, not the singer, and certainly not the musicianship of a legendary trumpeter: what fascinates is, rather, the recording as such. In a pathbreaking piece of sonic legerdemain that sounds almost quaint a half century later, Page sings four-piece harmony with herself, creating a delicate latticework of sound. The music is simultaneously direct and ethereal, plain yet highly ornamented, with an aura of childlike magic, not unlike that once associated with music boxes.

The popularity of Page's recording prompted still more cover versions of "The Tennessee Waltz." Singer Anita O'Day rushed out one, as did Jo Stafford, Guy Lombardo, and the Fontane Sisters. But the only version that proved able to compete with Page's recording on its own terms was that produced by Les Paul—a man who knew even more about electronic gimmicks than Patti Page.

Besides being a virtuoso electric guitarist, Les Paul throughout the 1940s had experimented extensively with recording techniques. At roughly the same time that Page was making her first voice-on-voice recordings, Les Paul was using studio technology to speed up and slow down his guitar lines, in addition to using, as Page had, sound-on-sound techniques to create layer upon layer of music. Shortly afterward, Paul began to work with singer Mary Ford, orchestrating miniature concertos for voice and electric guitar.

Despite the competition from Les Paul and Mary Ford, Patti Page's version of "The Tennessee Waltz" prevailed over all rivals, selling more than six million copies—a staggering sum at the time. For months her recording seemed to be everywhere—on jukeboxes, on radio stations, and on the turntables of the rapidly growing number of Americans who owned record players. One of the biggest hits in the history of the recording industry, it effected a revolution in the way that popular music was produced.

"The Tennessee Waltz" was, after all, a synthetic new kind of music, the hybrid product of several different vernacular genres. The song's lyrics were shockingly simple, a far cry from the clever wordplay favored by Tin Pan Alley's resident tunesmiths.

And the sheer *sound* of Page's recording was unprecedented. A tricked-up, technologically evolved sort of pseudo-folk song, Patti Page's hit was hard to categorize, impossible to reproduce on stage, and instantly unforgettable. Above all, it created a new standard for the manipulation of artificially produced sounds—a standard that would prove central to the aesthetics of rock and roll.

Winter 1950–1951:

"Teardrops From My Eyes"

The growing sophistication of techniques for reproducing sound had by 1950 dramatically transformed the uses to which music could be put, creating a new public of private listeners—and a new breed of cognoscenti. Symphonies that a person living in the nineteenth century would have been lucky to hear once were available for repeated listening on home phonographs, as were previously esoteric types of dance music from remote corners of America. Unable to read music, never trained to play an instrument, often detached from the living social context of the music, a new kind of aficionado—the record collector—was nevertheless equipped to make a host of more or less discriminating judgments about the grain of a voice, the pulse of a beat, the inimitable sound of a recording like Patti Page's "Tennessee Waltz."

It took time for the intuitions typical of the record collector to affect how recordings were made and marketed. In its early years, the industry had been dominated by men who had grown up plugging sheet music—before the invention of the phonograph and radio, the only medium for the mass marketing of music. After World War II, however, a new breed began to leave its mark on the music business, following the lead of John Hammond, Milt Gabler, and Alfred Lion, men who had collected jazz records before beginning to produce them. And of these younger record producers, none would prove more influential than Ahmet Ertegun—the founder and creative force behind Atlantic Records, the most successful independent label of the rock and roll era.

Ertegun was an exotic character. Born in Turkey, he grew up in Washington, D.C., where his father served as Turkey's ambassador. A paragon of studied cool who (in the words of Jerry Wexler) "affected a small continental stutter" that hinted at his upper-class pedigree, Ertegun was an elegant dresser, a cultivated dandy with tortoiseshell glasses, a patrician manner, and a prodigious knowledge of classic jazz. At the age of fifteen, he and his older brother, Neshui, were profiled in a piece on jazz record collectors that *Esquire* magazine published in 1938. As one acquaintance later remarked, the Erteguns "knew every record and who played on it, like other kids knew about football and baseball teams." The two boys were constantly plotting ways to commandeer the family limousine in order to trek into black Washington neighborhoods, in search of the latest discs by Lester Young or Lucky Millinder.

While studying at Georgetown University, Ertegun went to work at the local race record outlet, "Waxie Maxie" Silverman's Quality Music Shop at Seventh and T Streets. There he learned about the retail side of the record business—and discovered the commercial potential of jump blues. "Black people were clamoring for blues records," he recalled years later, "blues with a sock dance beat. Around 1949, that was their main means of entertainment. Harlem folks couldn't go downtown to the Broadway theaters and movie houses. Downtown clubs had their ropes up when they came to the door. They weren't even welcome on Fifty-second Street where all the big performers were black. Black people had to find entertainment in their homes—and the record was it." *weren't welcome anywhere*

Convinced that the success of labels like King was no fluke, Ertegun persuaded a family friend to loan him the money to start a record company of his own. For his first partner he chose a veteran race record man and jazz collector, Herb Abramson, who had helped produce best-selling recordings for Billy Eckstine and the black comic Dusty Fletcher, whose novelty song "Open the Door, Richard" became one of the biggest pop hits of 1947.

Later that year, Ertegun and Abramson launched their new label, Atlantic Records. Both men were connoisseurs of recorded jazz, unlike King's owner, Syd Nathan. They worked hard to produce "a strong and clean rhythm sound," as Ertegun later recalled: "To get that clean rhythmic punch, we found it necessary to use written arrangements." Trying at first to balance their love of jazz with their wish to make money, Ertegun and Abramson began by recording hopelessly compromised instrumentals—"pseudojazz," as Ertegun later called them. It was only in 1949, with the success of a blues novelty, "Drinking Wine, Spo-Dee-O-Dee, Drinking Wine," that the label found its stride. The breakthrough came one year later, with a series of jump blues hits that began with the label's first number one best-seller, "Teardrops From My Eyes," featuring Ruth Brown.

Born in 1928, Ruth Brown had grown up in Portsmouth, Virginia, where her father worked as a dockhand and also served as choir director of the local African Methodist Episcopal Church. As a teenager she had begun to sing in nightclubs, coming to the attention of Lucky Millinder, the same band leader who had launched Wynonie Harris' career. A contralto who tried to model herself after Billie Holiday and Ella Fitzgerald, she specialized in ballads and smoky blues, delivering songs in "a sandy voice with squeaky little curls," as the writer Arnold Shaw described it.

Brown was no virtuoso. But Ertegun and Abramson, desperate for talent, snapped the singer up in 1949. At first, they worked the pop side of the fence, trying to marry Brown's faintly gospel-tinged delivery with classy pop tunes. They tried recording her with the white Chicago jazz revivalist Eddie Condon, and also with the Delta Rhythm Boys, a smooth black vocal quintet with a best-selling record to its credit, a harmony version of Duke Ellington's "Just A-Sittin' and A-Rockin'."

None of these early recording sessions really clicked; but Brown's recordings sold moderately well in the rhythm and blues market, so Ertegun kept trying. The most important thing that he should have learned from Waxie Maxie was the value of a simple song. Ruth Brown's first records were a bit too fussy. So Ertegun modified his formula, and devised a new recipe: hire seasoned musicians willing to knock out simple riffs with relaxed aplomb; record songs that were rougher than mainstream pop, with lyrics that conjured up the raw, volatile emotions of an adolescent; and then ask the featured singer, no matter how worldly or sophisticated, to communicate these emotions with feigned feeling.

Years later, reminiscing off the cuff, Ertegun put it this way: "When I first met Ruth Brown, her main number, the song she liked best," as he recalled, was by a white songbird, Doris Day, "or Jo Stafford, or one of those. . . . And there's nothing wrong with those songs, and there's nothing wrong with the urban black man getting into the general taste of the world, you know, except that that taste is never as good as what he had to begin with."

Ertegun, in short, instructed Ruth Brown to sing more like a "real" Negro.

Putting this recipe to the test on a session held in the fall of 1950, Ertegun asked the veteran saxophonist Budd Johnson to create a honking jump blues arrangement of a new song of heartbreak and erotic yearning called "Teardrops From My Eyes." Since she was a singer of pop ballads by inclination, Brown sounded faintly uncomfortable with the song's chugging tempo, a discomfort that imbued her performance with a paradoxically piquant sense of drama. It was an awkward, almost clumsy rendition of a clever though generic race lyric—but the band rocked from start to finish, delivering a "sock dance beat."

Ertegun soon knew he had a winning formula. Ruth Brown's recording of "Teardrops From My Eyes" first appeared on the *Billboard* chart of Best Selling Retail Rhythm and Blues Records in October 1950, and remained there for a long, long time—half a year. For eleven weeks (during roughly the same period that white America was riveted by Patti Page's version of "The Tennessee Waltz"), *Billboard* ranked "Teardrops From My Eyes" as the number one rhythm and blues recording in America.

The recipe, though simple, was hard to execute properly. In order to transform himself into a successful producer of "urbanized, watered-down versions of real blues"—Ertegun's honest description of his pioneering hit recordings with Ruth Brown—he had to suspend old standards of judgment, setting aside the discriminating intuitions he had refined as a jazz record collector. The abilities of his favorite musicians were in chronic tension with the modest music he asked them to play. It was difficult to find the right kinds of songs and the right kind of singer. The artfulness of the formula was at odds with the air of abandon it was meant to simulate. Despite its impromptu flavor, after all, "Teardrops From My Eyes" was the result of hard work, a thoughtfully arranged and carefully rehearsed piece of music (unlike, for example, Wynonie Harris' version of "Good Rockin' Tonight").

It was worth the effort. Brown would go on to become the most successful of Atlantic's early artists, setting a pattern copied by many of the label's other successful acts, from the Clovers to Clyde McPhatter. Atlantic, for its part, would become one of the most prosperous and influential record labels of the 1950s, releasing a long series of recordings that cleverly juggled the artistic finesse of jazz, the elemental backbeat of jump blues, and the slick arrangements of postwar pop.

In effect, Ertegun and his partners were elaborating a new kind of pop music for a new kind of listener—call it "white Negro" music.

The notion of the "white Negro" comes from Norman Mailer. In an incisive (and notorious) essay published in 1957, Mailer described a new breed of youthful hipster, modeled after those found in urban locales like Greenwich Village where (in Mailer's words) "the bohemian and the juvenile delinquent came face-to-face with the Negro." As Mailer described the youthful hipster's salient traits, he was a self-made "psychopath," rejecting conventional inhibitions and struggling "to live the infantile fantasy" of a life of impulsive freedom, in the process elaborating an ethic of "immoderation, childlike in its adoration of the present," all in the hope of regaining a lost power—the "chance to act as he has never acted before."

Race played a special role in the psychic economy of this self-made psychopath. As an object of endless fantasy in the mind of the youthful white hipster, the Negro came to symbolize a universe of forbidden pleasures: a creature of "Saturday night kicks," the hipster's Negro had relinquished "the pleasures of the mind for the more obligatory pleasures of the body," pleasures he conveyed to others through the mode of music, which "gave voice to the character and quality of his existence, to his rage and the infinite variations of joy, lust, languor, growl, cramp, pinch, scream and despair of his orgasm."

For the youthful white hipster, it was orgasm—achieved in the teeth of repression—that represented the Hidden God. "To be with it," as Mailer explained the hipster's real goal, "is to have grace, is to be closer to the secrets of that inner unconscious life which will nourish you if you can hear it, for you are then nearer to that God which every hipster believes is located in the senses of his body, that trapped, mutilated and nonetheless megalomaniacal God who is It, who is energy, life, sex, force, the Yoga's *prana,* the Reichian's orgone, Lawrence's 'blood,' Hemingway's 'good,' the Shavian lifeforce; 'It'; God; not the God of the churches but the unachievable mystery within the sex, the paradise of limitless energy and perception just beyond the next wave of the next orgasm."

With the promise of paradise regained in the air, it was no wonder that the white hipster, according to Mailer, craved nothing so much as the liberating sound of Negro music. No matter how "watered, perverted, corrupted, and almost killed," the "music of orgasm," even when conveyed in a "laundered popular way," still evoked "instantaneous existential states to which some whites could respond," as if awakening with a start from a deep narcotic sleep, stirred by a song that "was indeed a communication by art because it said, 'I feel this, and now you do too.' "

"Joy, lust, languor"—the mass marketing of such emotions in a "laundered popular way" became the stock-in-trade of Atlantic Records, paving the way for other enterprising companies to pull off the same feat. On the label's tenth anniversary, in 1957, Ahmet Ertegun accurately summed up his company's achievement. "We discovered that white kids started buying these records because the real blues were too hard for them to swallow," he explained. "What we did manage to achieve was something like the authentic blues, but cleaner, less rough, and perforce more sophisticated."

This is accurate enough—and said with an irony characteristic of a true hipster. But in the winter of 1950, even as "Teardrops From My Eyes" was in the midst of establishing Atlantic as a profitable record company, there was still little tangible evidence that a critical mass of white kids had any serious interest in blues, whether real or fake. Atlantic was pioneering a new style of music. But a new breed of record collectors—and a new generation of self-styled hipsters— had yet to discover it.

Top 40

Their epiphany happened in an empty bar, as Todd Storz and Bill Stewart later told the story. At the time—it likely happened in 1951, though nobody later could recall just when—Storz and Stewart were young media executives in a tertiary radio market, starting at the bottom. They had been hired to turn around KOWH, a radio station that was currently ranked dead last in Omaha, Nebraska, commanding less than 5 percent of the available audience.

It was a tough place to sell entertainment. A cow town smack in the bleak middle of the Great Plains of America's upper Midwest, Omaha, like Council Bluffs, Iowa, just across the Missouri River, was a place of prim houses, clean lawns, weekly church dinners, and the most wholesome population of white folk imaginable, hardworking descendants of sturdy European stock. Winter was long, the land was featureless, and for most people life was pretty dull.

Storz and Stewart were stumped about what to do next. The market was dominated by network-affiliated stations, running a typical variety of programs, from crop reports in the morning to news and drama shows at night. Storz was searching for some formula, some recipe for success—some new mix of music and news that might excite listeners and attract advertisers.

One night, Storz suggested to Stewart that they repair to a local watering hole to conduct some informal market research. As they drank, they listened to what the clientele wanted to hear on the jukebox. And as they listened, Storz was struck, again, by a paradox.

While in the army during the war, he had noticed that soldiers took pleasure in hearing exactly the same songs played over and over again. In the bar, he noticed the same thing: "The customers would throw their nickels into the jukebox and come up repeatedly with the same tune. Let's say it was 'The Music Goes Round and Round.'" Even more striking was the reaction of the bar's waitress. After almost all the patrons had left, with her pick of songs to play, "what number would she select? Something she hadn't heard all day? No—invariably she'd pick 'The Music Goes Round and Round.'"

Storz (or perhaps it was Stewart) had a bright idea (their memories later differed). Why not play records on their radio station in the same way that patrons were playing them on the jukebox—over and over again?

It was a crazy idea. Ever since the invention of radio, most commercial stations had tried to air a wide variety of programs, featuring different kinds of music: opera, polkas, jazz, hillbilly—name it, and a local station likely aired it at some time during the day. The national networks were more cautious but equally catholic in their programming. They called it *broad*casting for a reason.

But perhaps people didn't want variety at all. Perhaps they wanted *repetition*. Given the chance, they would choose to hear "The Music Goes Round and Round" not once, not twice, but over and over again. If people preferred to hear the same song repeatedly, why not give people what they wanted?

The idea was simple. Putting it into practice proved a little more difficult. Despite the publication of charts like those in *Billboard* listing the most popular records in the country as a whole, it was not easy in 1951 to know what people in any given city really wanted to hear. Nor was it easy to foresee how the public would respond to a radio station that played a handful of recordings repeatedly. At the time, the vast majority of radio programs that featured prerecorded music were hosted by disc jockeys who decided what to play, and when; like Dewey Phillips, they took pride in the idiosyncrasy of their programming, carefully sequencing instrumentals and vocals, new songs and old, patter and music.

Repeatedly playing a few records nevertheless had certain advantages. By having KOWH adhere to a standardized blueprint for programming, Storz could hire virtually anyone to spin records and pitch products. And by accelerating the velocity of the programming, Storz could minimize the danger of boredom. Announcers would sprint through the news, prerecorded commercials would brighten the sound mix, and disc jockeys, unable to program their own music, would project a sense of personality through jokes, gimmicks, and a cacophony of noise—gongs, bells, whistles, horns—all geared to reinforce a carefully contrived atmosphere of frenzy.

Storz was of course not the first person to perceive the importance of repetition to music listeners. The idea of airing a small number of popular songs was at least as old as *Your Hit Parade,* an American broadcasting institution for over a decade. Starting on radio in 1935 and moving to television in 1950, the weekly show rehearsed the nation's favorite tunes, working from number ten up to number one. Just how these numbers were computed remained something of a mystery: the announcer on *Your Hit Parade* vaguely indicated that the show's list reflected a survey of sheet music sales, jukebox plays, record sales, and live performances on radio (and, later, TV). Still, by the late 1940s, the music business was driven by the *idea* of rank-ordered hit songs, never mind how the rank ordering was done. In a sense, the Storz Top 40 format simply turned a radio station into *Your Hit Parade* writ large.

By the end of 1951, it was clear that the Storz format was a smash hit, at least in Omaha. In the course of the year, KOWH had shot to the top of the local market, moving from a meager 4.4 percent share of the radio audience to a commanding 45.2 percent. Over the next few months, similarly styled stations began to sprout up, mainly in the American heartland. In the towns of the high prairie, where Top 40 first took root, the high-voltage format warmed up housebound families huddled against the winter winds. Refining the formula, the Top 40 stations began to target teenagers after sunset. Forget about good taste; if kids wanted to hear a song, a Storz station would play it, over and over again.

A great many veteran music men in New York City were frankly appalled by Storz and his mindless new format. They argued that the repetitive playing of only a few recordings amounted to a form of brainwashing. They deplored the stridency of the disc jockeys, the gimmickry of the station promotions, the limits of the play list. Above all, they complained about the music: most of the time, they feared, people, if left to choose for themselves, would choose junk—a betrayal of the industry's avowed commitment to good taste and high musical standards.

Storz was a businessman. He was more interested in his own profit margin than in someone else's idea of cultural uplift. "I do not believe there is any such thing as better or inferior music," he remarked at the height of the controversy over Top 40 in the mid-Fifties: "If the public suddenly showed a preference for Chinese music, we would play it."

In order to ascertain the public's preference, Storz kept track of local jukebox plays, sheet music sales, and retail record sales. The personal taste of the station's own personnel was rigorously discounted, on the grounds that it was both irrelevant and unrepresentative. "About the time you don't like a record," one Storz station manager explained to his station's disc jockeys, "mama's just beginning to hum it. About the time you can't stand it, mama's beginning to learn the words. About the time you're ready to shoot yourself if you hear it one more time, it's hitting the top ten."

In theory, this all added up to a recipe for cowardice, bringing to popular music one of the most insidious trends in postwar American society, the deployment of market research to create a placid emporium in which consumers are given the dubious satisfaction of never finding, or fulfilling, a fresh or disturbing desire.

In practice, the results, at first, were rather different. In the same months that KOWH was introducing its Top 40 format, it had become clear that what much of the public wanted to hear was neither Chinese music nor so-called good music, but rather bluesy riffs, country reels, tricked-up pseudo-folk songs like "The Tennessee Waltz," pop with a backbeat like "Teardrops From My Eyes," histrionic ballads like Johnnie Ray's sobbing rendition of "Cry"—one of the most popular records of 1951. For roughly a decade, during its era of greatest influence, between 1956 and 1965, Top 40 became a crucial conduit for giving people what they wanted to hear—particularly when what they wanted to hear was not what the guardians of cultural taste supposed that they should hear.

At the same time, Top 40 radio would change the way music was made. The systematic repetition of popular recordings on radio stations reinforced the popular taste, marked in any era, for essentially repetitive musical forms. As Top 40 spread, melodies gave way to riffs, riffs became jingles, jingles became "hooks"—instantly recognizable sound patterns, either melodic or rhythmic, designed to snare a listener's attention. Looking for the musical equivalent of a fishing lure, record producers began to fiddle with the arrangement of new songs, searching for gimmicks, trying to create strikingly new combinations of sounds—the voice-on-voice recordings of Patti Page and Les Paul were just a beginning.

Through sheer repetition of the finished recordings, Top 40 changed as well the way that this highly styled and often utterly artificial new kind of pop music was perceived. Speeding up the circulation of songs generated a kind of "dynamic obsolescence" that bred a certain restless quest for sheer novelty, while restricting the number of records that were aired during any given week ensured that a handful of really big hits were drummed into every listener. As never before, music could be passively absorbed. The collective unconscious acquired a new sonic dimension. And access to this dimension was easier than ever, thanks to the infinite repeatability of the sounds stored on recordings.

It has been said that rock and roll, like popular music generally, was never meant to last. On one level, that is doubtless true: people like Wynonie Harris, Patti Page, and Ruth Brown were not trying to make music for the ages. But through sheer repetition, the recordings of people like Harris, Page, and Brown became a permanent factor in the psychology of countless listeners. Specific recordings functioned like cue cards, reminding people of where they had been and what they had felt when they first heard a song. And a genre of music that was more repetitive than jump blues, simpler than "The Tennessee Waltz" and aired on standardized Top 40 formats, would soon enough facilitate an unprecedented outpouring of almost instant nostalgia, fueling a wistful longing for the past—the most profound sentimental basis of rock and roll, and one reason for the surprising durability of its most popular recordings.

for the end

March 21, 1952:

The Moondog Coronation Ball

On the evening of Friday, March 21, 1952, thousands of black youngsters in Cleveland anticipated a night of "sacramental strutting and swinging" (in Albert Murray's phrase). A new local radio personality, Alan Freed, was hosting a rhythm and blues concert and "Coronation Ball" at the area's largest hall, the Cleveland Arena. Freed's late-night show, *The Moondog House*, had been on radio station WJW for less than a year, but already his rhythm and blues format had fired up Cleveland's previously inert population of black teenagers. Billing himself as "The King of the Moondoggers," Freed addressed his listeners as if they were denizens of a make-believe kingdom of hipsters and nighthawks, united in their love for Negro music. The idea of coming together to witness the mock coronation of this kingdom's make-believe king was irresistible—and so was the slate of performers scheduled to perform at Freed's "ball."

Within a week of Freed's announcing the Moondog Coronation Ball, 7,000 tickets had been sold. Capitalizing on the unexpected demand, Freed and his partners printed and sold several thousand more tickets, how many nobody knew—they had stopped counting.

At dusk on a rainswept night, the kids converged on the Cleveland Arena. Freed had taken a calculated risk in booking his ball into an old hockey rink that could accommodate 10,000 people. By nightfall, it was obvious that the rink would sell out, but the crowd was still growing. At 8:30, with the hall jammed beyond capacity, the doors were locked shut and the show began.

Still more fans kept coming, tickets in their hands. There was no place for them to go. They pressed forward anyway, trying to force their way into the old arena, jostling, shoving, pushing, waving useless tickets in frustration.

Inside, the jump blues saxophonist Paul Williams and his band were rocking, evoking an ambiance of Dionysian revelry.

Outside, the crowd grew larger and pushed harder. Suddenly, one of the doors burst open. The angry mob flooded onto the arena floor. The police, unprepared, retreated in bewilderment. The lights were low, the saxes were honking, and the joint was jumping.

As the band played on, and the crowd was jammed ever more tightly against the stage, tempers flared. Fists flew, knives flashed.

Some tried to move toward the exits, while others joined in the melee. One gang of kids stormed the stage, tearing down the sequined "Moondoggers" sign that was hanging on the curtain behind the bandstand. Stunned, the band stopped playing. The fighting grew worse.

Caught off guard, the police were slow to react. They called for reinforcements, and phoned city hall for advice. When city officials finally arrived, they canceled the concert and ordered the crowd to disperse.

As quickly as it had begun, the riot was over. But Cleveland was stunned. The city had never seen anything quite like it.

"Moondog Ball Is Halted as 6,000 Crash Arena Gate," screamed the headline in Saturday's *Cleveland Plain Dealer.* That afternoon, the city's other major daily, the *Cleveland Press,* reported that the mob had numbered 25,000 "hepcats"—in this context, "hepcat" functioned as a racial code word, communicating the fact that the crowd consisted largely of black teenagers. The city's black establishment weighed in with its own expressions of outrage. Writing in the city's black newspaper, *The Cleveland Call and Post,* a columnist declared that "the shame of the situation lies not in the frustrated crowd that rushed to the Arena, but in a community which allows a program like this to continue and to exploit the Negro teensters!"

The target of this racially pointed barb was white. And because he was white, Alan Freed, like Dewey Phillips in Memphis, in fact felt no compunction about playing whatever his audience wanted to hear, even if it propagated "bum taste, low morality, and downright gutbucket subversions," as the columnist for the *Call and Post* complained.

City hall meanwhile accused Freed of reckless disregard for the public safety. Charging that the promoters had printed and sold too many tickets, city officials threatened legal action.

Under attack on all sides, Freed took the first opportunity to defend himself. The Saturday night after his abortive Coronation Ball, the Moondog addressed his radio audience directly.

"I promise you that everything will be righted," Freed said solemnly—and then announced an impromptu plebiscite. "I'd like to have you do this for me tonight when you call in your requests to our Moondog show on this Saturday night. I would like you to tell . . . when you call in, that you are with the Moondog. And if you're not with the Moondog, you can tell them that, too, because if enough of you can show your faith tonight through your telephone calls, through your telegrams, through your cards and letters over the weekend, we will continue the show. If not"—Freed paused melodramatically, the hitch in his delivery expressing a martyr's conviction of total innocence—"the Moondog program will leave the air!"

Freed was a genius at this sort of spiel. It is hard to believe he meant a single word. After all, the riot was a publicity windfall, turning Freed into a local celebrity overnight. The notoriety was priceless—and so was the aura of danger that now surrounded him. Chaos! Disorder! A fount of moral turpitude! And all right here in River City!

The managers of his radio station, WJW, immediately increased the airtime allotted to Freed's nightly program. In the weeks that followed, his popularity soared.

Quite apart from his real moral defects—and they were many—Freed was an unlikely pied piper for Cleveland's black teenagers. The son of Lithuanian Jewish immigrants, he had a passion for classical music, calling one of his daughters Sieglinde, after the character in

Wagner's *Ring of the Nibelungen*. A veteran disc jockey and television announcer, he had an abrasive personality that repeatedly landed him in trouble. In 1951, with his broadcast career on the skids and his liquor consumption on the rise, Freed, then twenty-eight, struck up a conversation that changed his life. He was drinking at a bar with Leo Mintz, the owner of the Record Rendezvous, one of Cleveland's largest record stores. Mintz had already helped Freed get a job playing classical recordings on Cleveland radio station WJW—as a longtime sponsor on the station, Mintz had clout. Now the businessman offered Freed the prospect of a quite different kind of job, playing a completely different kind of music. Mintz explained to Freed that he had noticed an upsurge in rhythm and blues sales at his store in the past few months. Hoping to broaden the market for such recordings, Mintz proposed that he buy several hours of late-night airtime on WJW—and that Freed serve as the host of a new show devoted exclusively to rhythm and blues recordings.

Freed was reluctant. Negro music wasn't his cup of tea. But he needed work and had no choice. And so on July 11, 1951, Freed started playing rhythm and blues records on WJW.

The few airchecks of the program that have survived suggest that Freed played an eclectic variety of music popular with black listeners: everything from up-tempo swing and jump blues to sloe-eyed ballads. Freed's on-air manner was energetic and faintly smarmy. Inspired by an offbeat instrumental called "Moondog Symphony" that had been recorded by a colorful New York City street musician who called himself Moondog, Freed decided to use the record as his show's theme music—and to borrow the musician's moniker. Every show began with the sound of bones rattling, drums beating, and dogs howling, while Freed jabbered genially: "All right, Moondog, get in there, kid! Howl it out, buddy!" Using a cowbell and telephone book as props, he rang the bell and pounded the book, sometimes shouting into an open microphone when the music got really hot, all in a homey effort to convey excitement. But compared to a wildman like Dewey Phillips, Freed was positively low-key. He took his time announcing the dedications to each song, and he took care to enunciate clearly not only the title of each record he played, but also the record company that had released it.

Freed was neither the first nor the best of the white rhythm and blues radio stars. But his location gave him an edge. In these years, the music industry closely watched Cleveland, regarding it as a "breakout" city—a regional market where national trends started. Bill Randle, the city's top-rated disc jockey, was widely credited with launching the career of more than one recording artist, including Johnnie Ray, whose sobbing rendition of "Cry" had set a new standard for the histrionic display of emotion on a popular recording. A scholarly music buff who had started his radio career by broadcasting jazz, Randle had long ago given up any effort to impose his own musical tastes on his programming: "I don't care what it is," he famously remarked in the early Fifties. "I want to make hits." When Freed's popularity began to soar, Randle took notice—and so did the pop music business in New York City.

Within a year, Bill Randle had begun to play a smattering of rhythm and blues records on *his* radio show. Tapes of Alan Freed's program began to air in the New York City area. And the show business tabloid *Variety*, sensing a new national trend in the making, remarked on the "strong upsurge" of popular interest in rhythm and blues.

On July 20, 1953, Alan Freed returned in triumph to the Cleveland Arena. That night, he hosted "The Biggest Rhythm and Blues Show," a package tour that would become the largest-grossing R&B revue up to that time. The headliners were Ruth Brown and Wynonie Harris. And though the audience that night, like the audience for Freed's ill-fated Coronation Ball, was overwhelmingly black, the racial equation was about to shift. After the near riot the year before, the music doubtless struck many as more unsavory than ever. But now that it was spreading over the airwaves, Wynonie Harris' brand of "good rockin' "—its promise of pleasure subtly transformed by the new aura of menace—was poised as never before to break out.

August 1952:

"Kansas City"

It was an old story, really, a saga of erotic fantasies and racial conflict, of cultural stereotypes and collective self-expression, with black music as the pretext and sexual freedom as the prize, all the more exciting for seeming taboo, at least to the God-fearing white farmers who joined in the dances of their slaves. "Toward the close of an evening," a visitor to Virginia remarked in 1776, "when the company are pretty well tired, it is usual to dance jigs; a practice originally borrowed, I am informed, from the Negroes."

Jigs were just the beginning. By the last half of the eighteenth century, a new kind of music had taken shape in the New World, combining elements from Africa and Europe. The ways in which this hybrid music originally evolved remain obscure: the half million slaves brought to America came from peoples scattered across a continent, and once in the New World, skilled musicians were often able to eke out a living as free men, working as itinerant entertainers. Their travels brought black performers into frequent contact with white audiences, promoting a sustained interchange of musical ideas between the two races that often makes it hard to distinguish African and European elements in any given piece of music, from "Zip Coon," which uses the melody of "Turkey in the Straw," to "Tutti Frutti," which uses a number of lines ("I got a gal her name's Sue," "I've been to the east, I've been to the west," etc.) that musicologists can trace back to sources in England and Ireland.

The first widely popular form of American entertainment associated with this hybrid musical idiom was minstrelsy. For roughly a hundred years after 1820, audiences enjoyed the jigs and skits of minstrels who appeared in blackface, using burnt cork to "black up" and portray characters like Zip Coon, a city dandy, and Jim Crow, a plantation slave. Minstrelsy produced the first pieces of American music to be popular internationally, and also launched the career of countless American musicians, from the composer Stephen Foster to the singer Al Jolson. The majority of minstrel artists were white, like Foster and Jolson; but countless black performers also worked the minstrel circuit (though blacks as well as whites were required to "black up").

The institution of minstrelsy provoked an understandably ambivalent response from African-American observers. As James Weldon Johnson, writing in *Black Manhattan* (1931), summed up his feelings, "Minstrelsy was, on the whole, a caricature of Negro life, and it fixed a stage tradition which has not yet been broken. It fixed the tradition of the Negro as only an irresponsible, happy-go-lucky, wide-grinning, loud-laughing, shuffling, banjo-playing, singing, dancing sort of being."

Still, as Johnson conceded, the minstrelsy tradition "did provide stage training and theatrical experience for a large number of coloured men," and it did provide a public and genuinely popular outlet for the expression of facets of the black American experience that would otherwise have been all but invisible. The pioneering black blues stars Ma Rainey and Bessie Smith both got their start by singing with Fat Chappelle's Rabbit Foot Minstrels; the jazz saxophonist Lester Young got his start with a black minstrel show; so did Louis Jordan and Wynonie Harris a few years later. Out of minstrelsy grew ragtime, jazz, and rhythm and blues—genres that turned African-American music into an independent cultural force and lucrative commercial property.

Joined in admiration for black musicians, and brought together, too, by the organizations and institutions that produced their shows and distributed their music, blacks and whites nevertheless tended to respond somewhat differently to the same cultural form. A Saturday Night Function that occasioned Dionysian revelry and sentiments of solidarity among blacks, for whites also functioned as a spectacle of sensual abandon—and a pretext for feats of cultural phantasmagoria. George Gershwin's *Porgy and Bess* is a fine musical example of the creative power of highly elaborated white fantasies about the soul of black folk. And so, too, is Jerry Leiber and Mike Stoller's 1952 composition, "Kansas City"—a hipster's reverie.

At the time, Leiber and Stoller were both still teenagers. Serious jazz record collectors and ardent fans of Negro dance music, they had begun collaborating on rhythm and blues songs in 1950, shortly after meeting—both were students at Los Angeles City College. Though their temperaments were antithetical—Leiber was outgoing, Stoller quiet and reserved—their backgrounds and interests, as they quickly came to realize, were surprisingly similar.

Leiber had grown up in Baltimore, the son of Jewish émigrés from Poland; his mother owned a small grocery store on the edge of Baltimore's black ghetto, which is where he first fell in love with jazz and the blues. Stoller had grown up in New York City, the son of a middle-class Jewish family with left-wing politics and cosmopolitan cultural tastes; as a young woman, Stoller's mother had danced in the chorus line of Gershwin's *Funny Face*.

Leiber was the team's lyricist, Stoller the musician. As a boy, Stoller had fallen in love with boogie-woogie. His parents sent him for piano lessons with James P. Johnson, the great jazz pianist (and one of George Gershwin's musical idols). By the time he was four-teen, Stoller was a trained connoisseur of Negro musical idioms, equally at home with the complex harmonies of bebop and the buoy-ant dance rhythms of boogie-woogie.

In 1949, Stoller's family moved to Los Angeles. This was an era when the jazz scene on Central Avenue in L.A. rivaled that of Fifty-second Street in New York City—and the rhythm and blues scene was, if anything, livelier. New records were easy to find at places like Norty's Record Shop, while on the radio Gene Norman broadcast the latest in jazz and Hunter Hancock aired the hippest in rhythm and blues.

Leiber, whose family had moved to L.A. four years earlier, was also an avid fan of black music. His lyrics, he later recalled, "came out of the blues I was listening to on the black stations." Working at a Fairfax Avenue record store, he jotted down couplets in his spare time. Unable to write music, he began to look for a possible collabo-rator—and so came to meet Mike Stoller, who was then studying classical composition. (In the late 1950s, at the height of his popular-ity as a rock and roll songwriter, Stoller would resume his studies, working with the serial composer Stefan Wolpe, and eventually com-pleting several major works, including a symphony and string quar-tet.)

It did not take long for Leiber and Stoller to discover their shared passion for black culture. "Actually, I think we wanted to be black," Leiber remarked years later. "Black people had a better time. As far as we were concerned, the worlds we came from were drab by com-parison. . . . I was alienated from my own culture and searching for something else"—not unlike the archetypal hipster analyzed by Nor-man Mailer.

Precocious rebels, the two boys expressed their shared sense of alienation by dating black girlfriends, by hanging out in Negro neighborhoods—and by listening almost exclusively to black music. Children of left-leaning families, they expressed themselves politi-cally, too, by joining a commune organized around egalitarian and interracial principles. While their young comrades found work in the aerospace industry—Stoller once described their political tendency as "Marxist-Lockheed"—Leiber and Stoller struggled to make money from their music. They kept writing rhythm and blues songs, care-fully crafting each one to sound "authentic"—that is, as "black" as possible.

Their ambition was nothing new. In the middle of the nineteenth century, Stephen Foster had acquired an international reputation based, in part, on composing "Ethiopian songs" in a gimcrack Negro dialect, for example, "Camptown Races" and "Old Black Joe." A century later, white songwriters like Hoagy Carmichael and Johnny Mercer were still writing music in the same minstrel vein: the lyrics of Louis Jordan's biggest pop hit, "G.I. Jive," came from the pen of Mercer, who deployed a hipster argot that, in Jordan's mouth, almost sounded genuine.

Black entertainers had long before learned that by singing material with a comic flavor they could play to two audiences simultaneously—blacks on the one hand, and whites on the other. And white aficionados of Negro music realized that they could service black performers with songs and theatrical productions that helped them to play this two-faced cultural game with irony, even brio. It was just a matter of time before the latest styles in rhythm and blues prompted a new generation of songwriters to produce a rocking variant on Gershwin, Carmichael, and Mercer—a new hybrid of black and white idioms.

At the time that Leiber and Stoller were composing their first songs, the most popular black musical style was jump blues. Wishing to write songs that sounded as "black" as possible, they worked hard to produce earthy lyrics and artless melodies. Since a number of independent rhythm and blues labels were located in Los Angeles, it was easy to find customers for their songs, especially after one of their first compositions, "Hard Times," became a hit in 1951 for the blues pianist Charles Brown. At the time, Leiber and Stoller were eighteen years old.

Other composers might have been content with skilled mimicry—but not Leiber and Stoller. As serious about their songwriting as they were about their left-wing politics, they refused to settle for clichés and musical formulas. Their first creative breakthrough came a year after "Hard Times," in the summer of 1952. The occasion was a recording date for Little Willie Littlefield, a second-string Texas singer and piano player, perhaps best remembered as the man who gave Fats Domino the idea of using piano triplets—one of the most salient musical characteristics of rock and roll by the mid-Fifties.

As was customary in those days, three hours of studio time had been set aside to record four songs. The A&R man from Littlefield's label had commissioned Leiber and Stoller to write four new songs for the date. To fulfill the commission, the two young men did what they always did: Stoller fooled around at the piano and Leiber improvised lyrics. Most tunes they completed in under ten minutes.

But one of songs they wrote for Littlefield involved, by design, a little more work. Originally called "K.C. Lovin' " (though better known under the title "Kansas City"), the song was an experiment. Instead of knocking out yet another variation on a generic twelve-bar blues, Stoller composed a mellifluous, flowing melody. Leiber responded in kind, taking pains to craft a plain-spoken lyric full of picaresque detail, evoking Kansas City as a timeless utopia of wine, women, and song. As Stoller later explained, the song "*is* a twelve-bar blues, but it's a *melodic* one, as opposed to a traditional blues melody, which is basically a series of inflections. I wanted to write something that, if it was played on a trumpet or a trombone, people could say it was a particular song, instead of that's a blues in E Flat or F. I wanted something you could listen to instrumentally, and say, 'I know that song.' " By applying their knowledge of conventional songcraft, Leiber and Stoller produced a new kind of song, combining the artfulness of classic pop with the timeless feel of a folk song—a kind of "Tennessee Waltz" in blackface.

Littlefield's recording "K.C. Lovin' " was not a success. It was only seven years later, in a 1959 version by Wilbert Harrison, that the song became widely popular. And it was still another version, recorded by Little Richard in 1955, that inspired the Beatles to record the song in 1964—turning "Kansas City" into one of the first "standards" of the rock and roll era.

By then, Leiber and Stoller had firmly established themselves as the foremost composers working in the rock and roll field. In the same month that they wrote "K.C. Lovin' " they also composed "Hound Dog," a runaway bestseller in 1953 for Willie Mae "Big Mama" Thornton. Prolific and consistently successful, they were hired by Ahmet Ertegun in 1956 as staff producers for Atlantic Records, where they worked with Ruth Brown and the Drifters, and created a classic series of recordings for the Coasters, joining a theatrical sense of humor with sturdy blues melodies.

In later years, Leiber and Stoller were disarmingly modest about their youthful achievements. "We were writing songs that we loved and that we were *compelled* to write," Stoller once remarked: "But we didn't think they had any lasting value." In the mid-Sixties, feeling cramped by the limits of a musical genre that they, as much as anyone, had helped to invent, the team stopped producing rock and roll altogether, instead writing art songs (including one minor masterpiece in this genre, "Is That All There Is?," composed for Peggy Lee in 1969).

In 1952, though, any ambivalence that Leiber and Stoller felt was purely political. It was one thing to craft songs about "Hard Times," and so honor the wretched of the earth; it was quite another thing to express some part of one's all-too-white cultural patrimony—and then make money, lots of it, in the bargain.

"One day in 1953" (as Greil Marcus has memorably retold the story), "Jerry Leiber and Mike Stoller rushed back to their Marxist-Lockheed commune with big news. Willie Mae Thornton's 'Hound Dog' had topped the charts. They had their first number one R&B hit. Their comrades replied with a lecture. Pop music had no social value; commercial success only proved the masses were victims of a commodity fetish and that Leiber and Stoller were its unwitting purveyors." The teenage tunesmiths were duly purged.

And that is just as well. Free to follow their muse without political self-censorship, Leiber and Stoller blazed a path that would lead from Willie Mae Thornton to Elvis Aron Presley, transforming the character of American popular song—and injecting a new taste for blues-inflected "authenticity" into white America's ongoing love affair with black musical idioms.

Summer 1953:

Elvis Hears Voices

Sometime in the summer of 1953, an aspiring young singer with a guitar walked through the doors of the Memphis Recording Service at 706 Union Street. The incident has since been dramatized countless times, though no one knows just when it occurred, or even precisely what happened. Still, a few bits of solid evidence do exist; and one eyewitness would later recall the scene in some detail.

The young man with the guitar told the woman at the front desk that his name was Elvis Presley. He said (as the woman later recalled) that he wanted to record two songs, to give his mother as a present.

Just eighteen and fresh out of high school, young Presley was nothing to look at. The photo in his high school yearbook shows a pimply adolescent with greasy hair and scruffy sideburns. Born in 1935 and raised an only child in Tupelo, Mississippi, he had moved with his mother and father to Memphis in 1948. His dad worked in a paint factory, his mom was a homemaker. At Humes High (still a segregated school, for whites only) Presley was regarded as an odd duck. In an era of crew cuts, his greasy sideburns stuck out.

It was a Saturday afternoon in late July or early August (memories differ), the air thick with heat. The waiting room was jammed with people waiting to make a personal recording, to cut a disc of themselves singing a song or reciting a poem for some loved one.

Something in Presley's carriage struck Marion Keisker, the woman behind the desk. The boy, she would later recall, was visibly nervous. To calm him down while he waited his turn, Keisker struck up a conversation, "a conversation I had reason to remember for many years afterwards, because later I had to tell the story so often."

Why was he there? "He said he was a singer.

"I said, 'What kind of singer are you?'

"He said, 'I sing all kinds.'

"I said, 'Who do you sound like?'

"He said, 'I don't sound like nobody.' "

He was boasting, of course. No one who is only eighteen has an entirely original style. And the young Presley had doubtless heard, and been influenced by, a variety of other singers.

He loved, above all, to listen to sacred singers, gospel divas, spiritual quartets, heavenly choirs. A faithful son of godly parents, he became an active member of the Assembly of God Church at 1084 McLemore in South Memphis, raising his voice in song every Sunday. The church sometimes presented programs of spirituals by the church's own Blackwood Brothers, a professional quartet with a national reputation. During services, members of the congregation could watch (at least) as the most enthusiastic, filled with song, trembled in rapture and spoke in tongues. To lift the soul in song was a great gift: as the young Presley confided to his girlfriend in these months, he dreamed of joining a spiritual quartet. He even auditioned for one, the Songfellows (he was rejected). He also sought out the even more ecstatic atmosphere at Negro Sunday services. He sometimes took his girlfriend to the East Trigg Baptist Church, a Negro congregation under the direction of W.H. Brewster, who preached, composed songs, and also led the church choir. (Mahalia Jackson had launched her career in 1947 with a million-selling version of one of Brewster's songs, "Move on Up a Little Higher.")

Still other aspects of Presley's musical influences are a matter of speculation and sketchy evidence. At the age of ten, while his family was still living in Tupelo, Mississippi, he had appeared in front of several hundred listeners at the annual Mississippi-Alabama Fair and Dairy Show and sung "Old Shep," a lachrymose ballad about a boy and his dog popularized by the country singer Red Foley. After the family moved to Memphis in 1948, Presley had also presumably heard Dewey Phillips spinning gospel and blues discs on WHBQ, as well as the mainstream pop fare the station broadcast during the day.

Still, apart from singing in church and his wish to join a spiritual quartet, there is little hard evidence that young Presley ever sang much of anything in public.

We should picture, instead, a loner, someone who practiced by singing songs to himself in his bedroom. He was a shy and nervous boy (as Marion Keisker had noticed), yet he had a quiet ambition (to judge by what he sang at the Memphis Recording Service) to sing, not just spirituals, but ballads and sweet love songs, just like those favored by the most famous and popular singers of the day, from Italian bel canto stylists like Dean Martin and Perry Como and Mario Lanza to black harmony groups like the Mills Brothers and Ink Spots.

During a Pentecostal church service, lifting one's voice in song is a liturgical exercise, a way of summoning the Holy Spirit. In his bedroom singing alone, perhaps pretending to be Mario Lanza or Bill Kenny (the lead tenor in the Ink Spots), young Presley summoned a more secular spirit, of romantic yearning and dreamy reverie.

When Presley's turn finally came that sultry summer afternoon in 1953, he recorded two ballads, both of them associated with the Ink Spots: "My Happiness," and "That's When Your Heartaches Begin." Since these recordings have survived, it is possible to hear at first hand the young Presley's commitment to mastering a musical language of decorous ardor. He accompanies himself on guitar, strumming softly. He has obviously studied the original recordings by the Ink Spots, taking care to copy the florid vocal ornamentation of Bill Kenny's tenor lead, and also the solemn recitative performed by Orville "Hoppy" Jones on "That's When Your Heartaches Begin."

Still, when Presley told Marion Keisker, "I don't sound like nobody," he wasn't just bragging: he was also being honest. Try as he might, he couldn't reproduce the polished sound of the Ink Spots. He sang with too much feeling. Where they were smooth, he was agitated; where they sounded calm, he seemed unsure; where they radiated self-confidence, he evoked an insatiable longing, for what, heaven only knows. Gifted with a supple voice able to execute vaulting shifts in timbre and pitch, Presley in 1953 approached the romantic clichés of "My Happiness" and "That's When Your Heartaches Begin" with scarcely veiled fear and trembling, like a sinner starving for absolution. He worried over words and mangled his enunciation, struggling to project an air of mature grace—and failing.

It would be several years before the originality of Presley's style sank in, but one of the key ingredients is already evident in these crude early recordings. Most great popular singers—from Louis Armstrong and Bing Crosby to Big Joe Turner and Frank Sinatra—develop one distinct voice. Not Presley. At the age of eighteen, he was already a man of many voices, blessed with an uncanny ability to mimic a variety of different singing styles. Within the span of one ballad, "That's When Your Heartaches Begin," he lurches intuitively from one voice to another, sounding now like a poised baritone, now like a keening tenor. (A classic later example of Presley's protean style is his 1956 recording of "I Want You, I Need You, I Love You.")

Marion Keisker listened as Presley sang. She liked what she heard. Quietly she switched on a backup recorder, to tape an extra copy. After the session was finished, Keisker handed Elvis an acetate disc of the songs—and filed away her tape recording. "Good ballad singer," she scrawled on the box—and that is apparently how her boss, Sam Phillips, first heard about Elvis Presley.

The owner of the Memphis Recording Service, Sam Phillips also operated his own small label, Sun Records. Born in 1923, Phillips had grown up on a farm in Alabama listening to spirituals and hillbilly music, and also to country blues, a music that touched him as deeply as black gospel music had touched Presley. Forced to drop out of high school in order to help support his family during the Depression, Phillips had taken a correspondence course in engineering. After graduation, he entered the radio business, moving to Memphis to work at radio station WREC, where he engineered the remote broadcasts of big bands and visiting pop singers from the Peabody, the city's classiest hotel, and also hosted a variety of shows playing a variety of different kinds of prerecorded music. Like Leo Fender, he loved to twist dials and turn knobs. And like his friend and colleague Dewey Phillips (no relation), he was a white man who kept his eye on the local black music scene, looking for his main chance. In 1950, the two men were briefly partners in the Phillips label, an abortive venture premised on recording "nothing but the best race and spiritual artists," as Sam put it in an early promotional letter. "I wanted to record the local talent," he recalled years later. "And I knew what I wanted. I wanted something *ugly*. Ugly and honest."

The Memphis Recording Service had opened for business in January 1950. The only studio in town, its facilities were available to anyone with money. Phillips traveled to weddings and funerals, and invited amateurs to cut songs for three dollars a shot. He kept his ears open, and made a point of recording the best local talent he could find. In the first months of the studio's operation, he had the luck—and good judgment—to produce some of the earliest commercial recordings by B.B. King and Howlin' Wolf. From the start, he left his mark on these recordings, coaxing the musicians into expressing themselves without inhibition, and using his own experimental studio techniques (what came to be known as "slapback" echo was his favorite gimmick) to imbue the performances with an artificial resonance and an air of mysterious depth.

At first, Phillips sold his recordings to other labels. Howlin' Wolf's sessions were released by RPM in Los Angeles and Chess in Chicago, while B.B. King signed a contract with Modern in Los Angeles—three of the independent companies that were competing with King and Atlantic for a share of the black music market. But after seeing the success that Chess and Modern had with Wolf and B.B. King, Phillips decided to launch a label of his own.

In its first months of operation, Sun released a variety of material: ersatz jazz, mediocre ballads by singers trying to mimic Dinah Washington or Billy Eckstine, some decent down-home Delta blues. Hoping to exploit the popularity of Leiber and Stoller's "Hound Dog," Phillips cut a flagrant imitation called "Bear Cat" with Rufus "Hound Dog" Thomas, a local black disc jockey.

The label got its first break when the national media took notice of one of its acts, the Prisonaires, a group of Negro convicts who recorded pop and gospel material for Phillips. But it was not until the summer of 1953 that Sun had its first solid hit. The featured artist was a singer named Little Junior Parker. A relatively sophisticated musician, Parker and his combo, the Blue Flames, specialized in jump blues. But what Phillips chose to release was a raucous one-chord boogie that the musicians had intended as a joke: "Feeling Good," a crude parody of John Lee Hooker.

Although Sun's early roster consisted primarily of black musicians, Phillips kept his ears open for hillbilly acts, for pop crooners, and also for white country boys who wanted to sing with blues feeling (a crossover style almost as old as the phonograph record, first popularized in the 1920s by Jimmie Rodgers, the "Singing Brakeman"). That is why Marion Keisker paid attention when she heard Elvis Presley sing that summer day in 1953. "The reason I taped Elvis was this," she later recalled: "Over and over I remember Sam saying, 'If I could find a white man who had the Negro sound and the Negro feel, I could make a billion dollars,' this is what I heard in Elvis."

But *what*, really, had she heard? It cannot have been any trace of Delta blues, because Presley did not sound at all like Howlin' Wolf or Charley Patton, nor was it any trace of white country blues, since Presley didn't sound remotely like Jimmie Rodgers either. What Keisker, like Phillips, probably had in mind was Presley's passing resemblance to Frankie Laine and Johnnie Ray—two white singers of the era who had launched their pop careers with emotive recordings that sounded so authentically "black" that both men were briefly bona fide black music stars. ("That's My Desire," Frankie Laine's 1947 recording debut, reached number three on the *Billboard* chart of Most-Played Juke Box Race Records, while "Cry," Johnnie Ray's debut in 1951, had reached number one on both the pop and rhythm and blues charts.)

Keisker herself, struggling years later to pinpoint what it was about Presley that made her take notice, boiled it down to a word. *"Soul,"* she called it, "this Negro sound. So I taped it. I wanted Sam to know."

Soul. The word itself is a term of theology, a word for the divine principle in man, his spiritual essence, the immortal core of his being. As a piece of American slang that gained currency in the 1960s, on the other hand, the word has a somewhat different resonance: as the black writer Claude Brown once defined it, "soul is bein' true to yourself" and—even more—it is "that uninhibited self-expression that goes into practically every Negro endeavor." A code word for something characteristic of African-American culture (as in the phrase "soul food"), it also came to stand for a certain spiritual vitality, a spark of spontaneous feeling.

Despite the evident anachronism involved in applying the word to Presley in 1953, *soul* sounds right. In 1953, he was no self-conscious student of black folk idioms like Mike Stoller, no cosmopolitan hipster like Ahmet Ertegun. But already, at eighteen, he *was* a singer of naked feeling, "unbelievably insecure," as Sam Phillips would later recall, "yet convinced, in his own mind, that he was destined to produce something great."

In 1953, however, there was scant evidence that Elvis Presley was destined to produce anything at all. He was one of countless kids in the mid-South strumming a guitar and daydreaming about a career in pop music. He had demonstrated a knack for singing a certain style of sweet ballad. Period. And when Elvis had finished his recording of "My Happiness" and "That's When Your Heartaches Begin," he went back to a job driving a truck, and also doubtless back to his bedroom, perhaps absorbing more of the wild sounds broadcast nightly on *Red Hot and Blue*, still singing to himself—and secretly hoping, one imagines, that Sam Phillips would call.

March 15, 1954:

"Sh-Boom"

The song opens a cappella, five voices raised in harmony. "Life could be a dream," they sing, "life could be a dream . . ." A small band—saxophone, guitar, piano, bass, drums—kicks into a bright bounce. Words sail by in a blur, half sung, half scatted, "sh-boom, sh-boom, yeah-da-da-da-da-da-da-da-da, sh-boom, sh-boom . . ." It's a lyric about love at first sight, and the words are dizzy: "Hello, hello again," the voices chant, "hey-na-nee-na-na."

In the summer of 1954, the Chords' recording of "Sh-Boom" helped launch an American fad for amateur black harmony groups. "Doo-wop," the genre would be called—although, as one expert has quipped, it could just as well be called "sh-boom." A dreamy style, it invited listeners to identify with the young singers; no other type of postwar popular music has inspired more affection. And though the singers, if compared with gospel groups or established harmony acts like the Ink Spots, were often barely melodic, there were moments when a doo-wop recording could seem to float over the airwaves, stopping time, and stopping hearts, with an unrehearsed vocal blend of sublime serendipity.

The typical doo-wop group consisted of four young men singing in four-part harmony. The lead singer was usually a tenor, with a blending baritone and bass offset by a wispy high falsetto. A sweet and gentle style, it first flowered on the mean streets of Harlem and the Bronx, where neighborhood kids gathered nightly to test their vocal mettle, vying for supremacy by crushing rival groups also struggling to imitate smooth pop singers and cool jazz harmonies. The competing groups developed different strengths: some emulated balladeers like the Ink Spots and Orioles, while others modeled themselves after up-tempo specialists like the Dominoes and "5" Royales, groups that joined the emotional directness of gospel music with the boogie-woogie backbeat of jump blues. Most of the kids could barely sing, but everyone had fun trying, and soon enough, record company scouts, looking for new songs and new acts, descended on high school playgrounds, looking for hot new groups and hoping to cash in on their spirit of can-do adventure and open-hearted optimism.

The Chords, like the majority of the groups, came from New York City. The lead tenor, Carl Feaster, was joined by tenors Jimmy Keyes and Floyd "Buddy" McRae, baritone Claude Feaster, and bass singer William "Ricky" Edwards, augmented by Rupert Branker, a pianist who doubled as the group's informal leader. (A childhood prodigy and the only trained musician in the group, Branker would go on to become pianist and music director for the most successful doo-wop group of all, the Platters.)

Feaster and the other Chords had grown up and gone to school together in the Bronx, attending P.S. 99 and Morris High. Every day after school was out, they joined each other to jam with other amateur singers, hoping to hit a sweet note, win a kiss, and keep out of trouble: those recognized as singers were excused from taking sides in the neighborhood's chronic gang warfare. In the Bronx alone, there were dozens of groups: besides the Chords, there were the

Crickets, the Fi-Tones, the Five Chimes, the Gayhearts, th
the Heartbreakers, the Jupiters, the Limelighters, the M
Wrens. Schools sponsored talent shows, churches hosted
dances. During the summer, parks became the arena for impromptu musical jousts, while on Wednesday nights, Harlem's Apollo Theater welcomed all comers, throwing its doors open to amateurs. As the doo-wop historian Philip Groia has written, the possibility of "signing a recording contract, becoming a star, hearing your own records on the radio, having your girlfriend telephone a local disc jockey to request your record, and making some money, created dreams that staggered the imagination." On the streets outside Morris High, the latest rhythm and blues hits blared from the loudspeakers of storefront shops. Fame beckoned—but as Groia writes, "the true test of how well a man could feel a note was how well he performed on the street for his buddies."

It was out of this milieu that the Chords rose to stardom. Originally calling themselves the Tunetoppers, they quickly claimed a position of preeminence within the neighborhood. More harmonically sophisticated than their competition, they prided themselves on their taste for "top-drawer" music. Besides learning the songbooks of the Ink Spots and Orioles, they worked hard to master the modern jazz voicings favored by such white groups as the Four Freshmen and Modernaires. Inspired by the jive gymnastics of Slim Gaillard and the vocal pirouettes of Ella Fitzgerald, they also taught themselves how to scat, using nonsense words and onomatopoeic sounds to improvise in the manner of a jazz horn soloist.

While woodshedding, the group began to toy with bits and pieces of melody, in time elaborating a nonsense song they called "Sh-Boom." "We tossed it around for months and months," Jimmy Keyes recalled years later. "We'd get happy for one part, and get a kick out of what we did a certain way. Then we might want to do it another way months later."

One day in 1953, on the way to catch a subway train, a talent agent overheard the Chords, who were characteristically singing as they walked into the same station. Impressed by the group's sound, the agent introduced himself, collected the boys' names—and later mentioned the group to Ahmet Ertegun and his new partner, Jerry Wexler, who had given up reviewing records at *Billboard* in order to make records at Atlantic. After auditioning the Chords, Ertegun and Wexler signed the group and booked them into a studio on March 14, 1954.

The two men were hoping to use the group to launch a new label, Cat Records. In the months before, Ertegun and Wexler had noticed that a number of their rhythm and blues records were selling well in stores located in predominantly white neighborhoods, particularly in the South. "The Southern bobbysoxers began to call the R&B records that move them 'cat' music," Ertegun and Wexler explained in an article they wrote, addressed to their industry peers. "Not all R&B qualifies as cat music. It has to kick, it has to move, and it has to have a message for the sharp youngsters who dig." By signing the Chords to the Cat label, Ertegun and Wexler hoped to pitch this type of R&B at white teens.

The song they chose to spotlight is revealing. It was not "Sh-Boom" (which they recorded only as an afterthought), but "Cross Over the Bridge"—a pseudo-gospel song that had recently been made into a huge hit by Patti Page, whose recording sold more than one million copies in the United States in 1954.

In those days, if a song promised to become widely popular, different record companies rushed to have different acts cover it. The practice was universal. Nobody thought twice about black groups knocking off R&B versions of pop hits, just as nobody thought twice about white acts knocking off pop versions of R&B recordings—as Patti Page (with the help of Jerry Wexler) had done in 1950 by covering Erskine Hawkins' version of "The Tennessee Waltz." As long as it seemed possible to sell another recording of the same song, the cover versions kept coming, much to the delight of the song's owners, who stood to profit from every single version, no matter the performer. In 1954 alone, the schmaltzy "Oh My Papa" was recorded not just by Eddie Fisher, but also by bandleader Ray Anthony; "Secret Love" was covered by black balladeer Tommy Edwards as well as Doris Day; and "Three Coins in the Fountain" was a hit for both the Four Aces, a white vocal quartet, and for Frank Sinatra. The trick was to pull a "switch," as record men called it, aiming a new version of an established song at a fresh segment of the pop music market, for example by having a country artist do a pop hit, or a pop singer do a country song, or a vocal group do a ballad made popular by a crooner.

That the Chords should venture to compete with Patti Page thus came as no surprise. The shock—for that is what Tin Pan Alley felt—came when disc jockeys flipped over the Cat recording of "Cross Over the Bridge" and started to play the flip side, "Sh-Boom."

It sounded like gibberish, but the song had a crazy bounce and it felt *great*. Within weeks, "Sh-Boom" was getting airplay nationwide on rhythm and blues radio stations. And that was just the beginning. In Los Angeles, the record quickly crossed over to pop radio formats and jukeboxes in white neighborhoods. By early summer, sales of the Chords' "Sh-Boom" in Southern California had eclipsed such competition as Perry Como's "Wanted" and Kitty Kallen's "Little Things Mean a Lot." Sensing that the song was a potentially lucrative property, Hill & Range, one of Tin Pan Alley's biggest song publishers, bought half of it from the current owners, an Atlantic song-publishing subsidiary (Atlantic needed the cash, and stood to profit if Hill & Range could pitch the song to some of the pop artists it routinely supplied with material).

Meanwhile, in Chicago, arrangements had already hastily been made to pay the Chords the highest possible compliment—by copying the group's homemade hit. The chore of doing a pop cover fell to a vocal quartet from Toronto called the Crew-cuts. They sounded the way they looked: very bland. Just a few years older than the singers in the Chords, the Crew-cuts had first met as choirboys singing in the 1940s in the Toronto Cathedral School Choir. Skilled at singing intricate harmonies precisely, the group projected a peppy, can-do exuberance that still conjures up a world of shy glances and shared milk shakes. Their first commercial recording, released in the spring of 1954, was a fluffy rhythm number called "Crazy 'Bout Ya Baby"—never mind that the Crew-cuts had no sense of rhythm.

With "Crazy 'Bout Ya Baby" at number eight on *Billboard*'s chart of best-selling pop records, an executive at their label, Mercury, asked the group to listen to "Sh-Boom." The idea was to have the Crew-cuts do a switch, working out a new version aimed at "cats" so square they'd never heard of the Chords.

With the help of orchestra leader David Carroll, the Crew-cuts came up with an entirely new arrangement. Gone were the a cappella opening and reedy jazz overtones of the original. Added was a brassy big band and a funny twist to the song's chorus: after the Crew-cuts finish chanting "sh-boom" in their inimitable glee-club style, the music suddenly stops—until the silence is broken by a tympani, sounding like a giant trampoline making an elephant airborne. Combined with the group's glee-club harmonies, the arrangement took the offhand whimsy of the original and turned it into a piece of surreal kitsch.

Throughout the summer of 1954, radio stations across America played both versions of "Sh-Boom," kitsch competing with whimsy. Both versions sold briskly. Buoyed by their wide exposure on pop radio stations, the Chords became the first black harmony group since the Ink Spots to crack the top ten on *Billboard*'s weekly chart of best-sellers in stores, reaching as high as number five. The Crew-cuts took "Sh-Boom" all the way to number one, selling more than a million copies in the process.

Suddenly, rhythm and blues harmony groups were the hottest new commodity on the pop futures market. Scouts from Tin Pan Alley began to poke around New York City's playgrounds and street corners, looking for the next pot of gold buried in Harlem or the Bronx.

The Crew-cuts went on to enjoy a brief run of hits, most of them pseudo-rhythm and blues, successfully applying the formula they had used with "Sh-Boom." The Chords, unable to summon at will the magic that had produced their masterpiece, were asked instead to imitate the Crew-cuts—yes, the Crew-cuts!—by adding a brassy big band to their next recording, a contrived piece of junk called "Zippity Zum." The song flopped, and most of the Chords (with the exception of Jimmy Keyes and Rupert Branker) melted back into obscurity.

Still, their moment of fame, though fleeting, left a mark. Inspired by the success of the Chords, the record industry found what it was looking for: more hit songs. After "Earth Angel" by the Penguins cracked the *Billboard* top ten in December 1954, there was no turning back: for nearly a decade, doo-wop brought homemade songs and wobbly singing into the mainstream of the music business, which eagerly cashed in on the naïveté—and raw emotion—of the amateur harmony groups. For the singers, it was the chance of a lifetime; and for kids watching, it was one vision of bliss. They didn't soon forget the day when the blue limo with the Chords' logo rolled through the streets of the old neighborhood, inspiring another generation of curbside Carusos—and offering proof that life could be a dream.

Fantasies like this are heady stuff. The harmonies the groups sang sometimes soared with desire. And even in the years after doo-wop had all but disappeared from the national best-seller lists, popular interest in the genre never entirely waned. Record collectors pored over obscure recordings, and collated information about the members of the old groups. Organizations appeared, wholly dedicated to preserving the genre. And throughout the Eighties and well into the

Nineties, Jimmy Keyes could still be seen performing with a group he called the Chords, still singing "Sh-Boom" to the mostly white and mostly middle-aged crowds at endless reunions of nostalgic doo-wop fans, captives of a common past, unable to get over the song that, forty years before, had stopped time, and stopped hearts, with its sublime serendipity.

July 30, 1954:

Elvis Discovers His Body

On July 30, 1954, Elvis Presley, age nineteen, appeared on stage at an outdoor concert in Memphis. Just days before, his music had caused a minor sensation in Memphis when disc jockey Dewey Phillips had aired his first Sun recording, "That's All Right" and "Blue Moon of Kentucky," playing both songs, so he later boasted, fifteen times in one night. Rushing to capitalize on the publicity, Sam Phillips had booked Presley at the last minute on a touring revue featuring Slim Whitman, a mustachioed country singer with slicked-back hair renowned for yodeling, in an ear-splitting falsetto, nostalgic treacle like "Indian Love Call" (originally popularized in 1936 by Jeanette MacDonald and Nelson Eddy).

The show was scheduled for Overton Park on Saturday, July 30. Ads ran the week before, one promising a newcomer named "Ellis Presley." The day of the show, Marion Keisker drove Presley to do his first interview, with a reporter for the *Memphis Press-Scimitar*. Years later, the reporter recalled how Presley looked: "Like the wrath of God. Pimples all over his face. Ducktail hair. Had a funny-looking thin bow tie on. . . . He was very hard to interview. About all I could get out of him was yes and no." Marion Keisker did most of the talking, plugging Presley's new songs: "Both sides seem to be equally popular on popular, folk and race record programs. This boy has something that seems to appeal to everybody."

At the time, the breadth of Presley's appeal was more pious wish than hard reality. His Sun debut was selling locally, but doing the Whitman concert—a big show before a large live audience—required a leap of faith. Despite playing a couple of songs at a hillbilly night-club a few days earlier, Presley was essentially untried and untested as a live performer. When Sam Phillips arrived backstage shortly before Presley was to appear, he was not surprised to find his latest musical protégé "looking kind of *pitiful*—well, maybe *pitiful* is the wrong word. I knew it was the way he was going to look: *unsure.*"

Presley would be performing with the same pair of musicians that Phillips had used on Presley's first Sun recording, bassist Bill Black and electric guitarist Scotty Moore, both relatively seasoned players, both older than Presley. Phillips and the two veteran performers tried to steady the singer before his stage call.

It was a typical midsummer day in the mid-South, hot and sticky. The stage itself was the size of the clubs that Black and Moore were used to playing; and thousands of people in picnic good spirits were waiting to see Slim Whitman. "We were all scared to death," Moore recalled years later. "Here we come with two little funky instruments and a whole park full of people," not to mention the fact that the lead singer was twitching with anxiety.

"My very first appearance was on a show in Memphis as an extra added single," Presley told a reporter two years later. "I was scared stiff. I came out, and I was doing a fast-type tune"—probably "That's All Right"—"and everybody was hollering, and I didn't know what they were hollering at."

"Elvis, instead of just standing flat-footed and tapping his foot, well, he was kind of jiggling," Scotty Moore says in *Last Train to Memphis,* the most trustworthy account, by Presley's best biographer, Peter Guralnick. "That was just his way of tapping his foot. Plus I think with those old loose britches that he wore—they weren't pegged, they had lots of material and pleated fronts—you shook your leg, and it made it look like all hell was going on under there."

The band next played "Blue Moon of Kentucky"—there weren't many tunes in their repertoire. "During the instrumental parts," Moore recalls, "he would back off from the mike and be playing and shaking, and the crowd would just go wild, but he thought they were actually making fun of him."

As they ran off stage, Presley turned to Moore. "What's makin' 'em holler so much?" he asked.

"It was your leg, man," Scotty Moore later recalled telling him. "It was the way you were shakin' your left leg. That's what got 'em screamin'."

The screams kept coming. Accounts differ about what happened next. In his biography, Guralnick has Presley doing "Blue Moon of Kentucky" one more time for his encore. But Dewey Phillips later insisted that the final song was his idea: a rollicking version of "Good Rockin' Tonight." And one can well imagine the scene: "Have you heard the news . . . ?" Elvis shouts, relaxed, letting himself go, his leg a jubilant blur, his unsteadiness melted by the applause. "There's good rockin' tonight!"

Two years later, all Presley could remember was the crowd's response. "I went back out for an encore," he said, "and I did a little more. And the more I did, the wilder they went."

For the novice showman, the crowd's reaction was exhilarating—and out of the blue. Letting go did not come naturally to Elvis Presley. Polite and pious to a fault, he addressed everyone either as "ma'am" or "sir." At first, his diffidence made realizing his equally obvious ambitions perversely difficult. He had spent a great deal of time studying Hollywood movies, and, as the sequel of his story would show, aspired to live a life like that of the matinee idols he had grown up admiring. He greased his hair back and wore shirts with the collar turned up, trying to look like Robert Mitchum or Tony Curtis or James Dean, deliberately projecting an air of rebelliousness and wounded vulnerability. Scotty Moore, who doubled in these months as Presley's manager, would later recall the sheer oddity of his manner, from the shocking color of his shirts to his unapologetic love of gospel music. Even before he was famous, he aimed to make an impression. But his humbleness was genuine, and his habits of deference died hard. The tension between his ingrained humility and his streak of defiant nonconformism colors all of Presley's pathbreaking work in these years.

Shortly after Presley's visit to the Memphis Recording Service the previous year, Sam Phillips had played the tapes of "My Happiness" and "That's When Your Heartaches Begin," and filed a mental note to keep the kid in mind. When a tape of a new song arrived in the mail a few months later, Phillips tracked down Presley, and asked him to drop by the studio at 706 Union. Presley listened to the song on the tape, a simple ballad called "Without You," sung with haunting soulfulness by an unknown singer. Phillips wanted Presley to go for a similar feeling. Presley tried—but he just couldn't do it. Undaunted, and also impressed by the boy's perseverance, Phillips put him in touch with guitarist Scotty Moore, twenty-two years old and just out of the navy. They began to rehearse with twenty-eight-year-old Bill Black, who played stand-up bass.

On July 5, 1954, Presley returned to the Memphis Recording Service with Moore and Black, armed with a new song, "I Love You Because," a country ballad popularized in 1949 by Ernest Tubb, a singer whose vinegary style made the lyrics sound plainspoken and dignified. Again, things went badly. Try as he might—and no fewer than six different takes of the song have survived—Presley could not sell the lyrics. In his hands, they sounded cloying, corny, lifeless.

What happened next has been recounted many times. The band took a break. And then, without a word, Elvis picked up his guitar and began to joke around. He laughed and strummed through a jaunty blues made popular by Arthur Crudup in the 1940s, "That's All Right," delivering the lyrics with a wink and a smile. Bill Black joined in, slapping his bass to create an exaggerated pop; Scotty Moore picked up his electric guitar and added a bouncy blues riff.

As Scotty Moore later recalled, Sam Phillips suddenly stuck his head out of the control booth "and said, 'What are you doing?' And we said, 'We don't know.' 'Well, back up,' he said, 'try to find a place to start, and do it again.' " A firm believer in making his own luck, Phillips was prepared to try and do with Presley's version of the blues what he had already done with Junior Parker's "Feeling Good": turn a tongue-in-cheek musical lark into a best-selling record.

Presley and the band ran through the song again. Phillips asked Moore to keep the guitar licks simple. And then Sam Phillips let the tape roll, capturing a fresh sound—a white boy's goofy blues, born of frustration and release.

Three weeks later, when Presley took the stage in Overton Park and, once again, got scared—and let go—the feeling of unexpected freedom captured by his recording of "That's All Right" found its visual emblem: the "Hillbilly Cat" with the shaking limbs.

No film or recording of the event survives; no one can be sure what Presley looked like or sounded like that particular night. That he sang both sides of his Sun single seems certain. And if he didn't do "Good Rockin' Tonight," he should have. The song suits the occasion perfectly.

Whatever happened at Overton Park, Presley did record "Good Rockin' Tonight" one month later, as the follow-up to "That's All Right." To hear the studio version of "Good Rockin' Tonight" is to begin to understand how a sun-baked crowd, waiting for a yodeler of hillbilly schmaltz, might go wild instead for the twitching kid with the funny-looking bow tie. Unlike "That's All Right," Presley's recording of "Good Rockin' Tonight" is the work of someone singing with self-conscious determination. Still, Presley is a bundle of nerves. Where Wynonie Harris took the tune at a relaxed lope, Presley is high-strung, histrionic, edgy. He attacks the words with manic intensity, his voice veering wildly between a smooth baritone and a hoarse, high tenor. His singing is relentless, as if the song's lyrics had to be strenuously evoked, dramatized, driven home—he's obviously working very hard to recapture the excitement generated spontaneously by "That's All Right." Instead of the sleek swinging tempo used by Wynonie Harris and his combo, Presley, Moore, and Black chop up the rhythm and improvise a frantic new vocal chorus, driven home by a lurching boogie riff on the electric guitar. "Well, we're gonna rock," Elvis shouts, "we're gonna rock! Let's rock! C'mon and rock!"

The recorded performance is a shock. Hearing it, one can easily imagine people reeling with pleasure; that certainly is how many Americans reacted to Presley on television two years later. Like a Pentecostal enthusiast bursting with the spirit, the young man is trembling in ecstasy and speaking in tongues.

"It's like your whole body gets goose bumps," Presley told a close friend two years later, describing how he felt when he performed. "It's like a surge of electricity going through you. It's almost like making love, but it's even stronger than that."

Uncanny forces—of frustration and release, of inhibitions dissolved, of a rapturous joy affirmed—had been set in motion. And in Memphis on July 30, 1954, Elvis Presley for the first time became their cynosure.

November 24, 1954:

Copyrighting "Rock and Roll"

It had been a bad day for Alan Freed. In the morning, he had been stripped of his right to use the on-air moniker Moondog after a judge ruled against him in a suit brought by Louis "Moondog" Hardin, the blind New York street musician whose "Moondog Symphony" had originally inspired the disc jockey to yap and howl. Now, scarcely two months after Freed had moved his Moondog radio show from WJW in Cleveland to WINS in the lucrative New York City market, he was going to have to come up with a new name, a new trademark.

That night, Freed and his cronies retired to P.J. Moriarty's, a restaurant on Broadway. "Alan was having a few drinks and bemoaning the fact that he had to come up with a new name," one witness later recalled. "To be honest with you, I couldn't say if Alan said it or somebody else said it. But somebody said 'rock and roll.' Everybody just went, Yeah. *Rock and roll.*"

Since Freed for months had been billing his show as the "Moondog Rock and Roll Party," it made sense simply to shorten the old name. Freed himself brushed aside the one obvious objection: whatever its broader musical connotations, "rock and roll" was still in 1954 black slang for sexual intercourse. "I don't give a shit," Freed erupted. "That's what I'm going to call the show!" Thus was born Alan Freed's *Rock and Roll Party.*

The phrase "rock and roll" was not, of course, a new one. In 1922, blues singer Trixie Smith had recorded "My Man Rocks Me (With One Steady Roll)" for a company called Black Swan—the first recording company owned and operated solely by African-Americans. Twelve years later, the Boswell Sisters, the best of the era's white jazz vocal groups, had a modest popular hit with their recording of a song called, simply, "Rock and Roll." In 1938, band leader Erskine Hawkins—whose recordings would later inspire Glenn Miller ("Tuxedo Junction") and Patti Page ("Tennessee Waltz")—released "Rockin' Rollers' Jubilee." And ten years later, Wynonie Harris' "Good Rockin' Tonight" had provoked a flood of songs with the word "rock" in the title. Freed himself had been using the phrase since 1952, promising radio listeners in Cleveland "a rock and roll *session* with *blues and rhythm* records."

Having decided to call his show a *Rock and Roll Party,* Freed went one step farther. Stung by the outcome of the court case that day, he and his friends hatched a scheme to copyright the phrase. The most famous of his partners in this ill-fated venture was Morris Levy, the self-styled godfather of New York's black music world, and a man widely feared for his ruthless business practices and rumored ties to organized crime. (In 1988, Levy finally went to jail, after being convicted on two counts of conspiracy to commit extortion.) Levy had made his fortune in the music business by running one of the most famous midtown jazz clubs, Birdland, which had first opened its doors in 1949. Levy next moved into song publishing. Until 1953, he trafficked almost exclusively in jazz and Latin music. But that changed after an associate, George Goldner, convinced Levy to help him promote the Crows, a pioneering doo-wop group. Using his influence with disc jockeys who played black music—and also offering cash bribes, or "payola"—Levy helped Goldner turn the Crows' recording of "Gee," released four months before "Sh-Boom," into the first doo-wop song to cross over from the rhythm and blues charts and sell as a mainstream pop hit (on *Billboard*'s pop chart, it reached number fourteen).

By the fall of 1954, when Freed moved his radio show from Cleveland to New York, Morris Levy had become a key figure in the city's rhythm and blues scene. With his long experience in booking and music publishing, Levy was an invaluable contact. Shortly after arriving in New York, Freed asked him to help book his local rhythm and blues concerts. The two men became partners. The copyright claim for the phrase "rock and roll" was eventually filed on behalf of Seig Music, a corporation consisting of Freed, Morris Levy, veteran promoter Lew Platt, and WINS, Freed's new radio outlet.

After his move to New York in September, Freed had quickly become one of the city's top-rated disc jockeys. Rhythm and blues fans, long accustomed to the relaxed patter of black disc jockeys like Tommy "Dr. Jive" Smalls, were at first stunned by the frenzy of Freed's style. Willie Bryant, a veteran soft-shoe dancer, singer, big band leader, and radio announcer, tried to rally Harlem residents to protest the use of a white man to air black music. But the protests fizzled out, and new listeners simply assumed that Freed's maniacal shouting during his shows was part of the atmosphere at any "rock and roll party."

The character of the music that Freed played did not, at first, change at all. An aircheck of a show broadcast early in 1955 captures Freed on a typical evening. The references to "rock and roll" are endless: "Hello, everybody, yours truly, Alan Freed, the old king of the rock and rollers, all ready for another big night of rockin' and rollin', let 'er go! Welcome to *Rock and Roll Party* number one!" But the range of the records that Freed plays scarcely differs from what he had been playing in Cleveland: ballads by singers like Dinah Washington; harmony records by doo-wop groups like the Cadillacs; and one unusually intense jump blues by Ray Charles, "I Got a Woman." In these months, "rock and roll" was simply Alan Freed's trademark name for rhythm and blues. It was just another euphemism for black music.

Still, the fact that Freed now called the music that he played "rock and roll" was not without significance. Working in New York City, the entire music industry could see what he was up to. And the change in his show's name by chance coincided with a dramatic—and widely remarked—shift in the racial composition of Freed's audience.

On January 14 and 15, 1955, Freed presented his first dance concert in New York City, at St. Nicholas Arena. A fit successor to the Moondog Coronation Ball, this concert was billed as a "Rock 'n' Roll Ball." (When Freed's trademarked phrase acquired its apostrophes is something of a mystery: the first *Billboard* story reporting the Freed show's new name spelled it "Rock and Roll.")

As Morris Levy, who promoted the concerts, would later recall, the demand for tickets caught everyone by surprise: "He made four announcements, six weeks before the dance, and $38,000 came in the mail. I says, Oh my God. This is crazy."

And that was only the first shock. The second shock came from seeing the crowd in person. Freed's ball featured a by-now predictable lineup of rhythm and blues talent: Ruth Brown, Joe Turner, the Drifters, Fats Domino, and two doo-wop groups, the Moonglows and Harptones. The musicians were all black. But the audience was nearly half white.

Both nights, the old arena was jammed with people. Inside, as Morris Levy later recalled, "the ceiling was actually dripping from the moisture. It was *raining* inside the St. Nicholas Arena."

Freed's "Rock 'n' Roll Ball" went off without a hitch. And music industry insiders, noting the size and composition of Freed's audience, laid plans to pay Freed for the privilege of billing selected new releases as bona fide "rock 'n' roll."

A new label had appeared. It only remained to make a new kind of music that fit the label.

Blackboard Jungle

The scene was repeated round the world. The lights in the theater dimmed. The film began to roll. Nervous drum fills accompanied a written prologue:

"Today we are concerned with juvenile delinquency—its causes—and its effects. We are especially concerned when this delinquency boils over into our schools. The scenes and incidents depicted here are fictional. However, we believe that public awareness is a first step toward a remedy for any problem. It is in this spirit and with this faith that BLACKBOARD JUNGLE was produced."

A snare drum cracked. Out of the theater's speakers boomed a voice: "One, two, three o'clock, four o'clock ROCK!" Against the backdrop of a blank blackboard, the film's credits flashed by. The drama in the voice intensified: "Nine, ten, 'leven o'clock, twelve o'clock ROCK! We're going to ROCK around the clock TONIGHT!" The band on the soundtrack jumped into a medium-tempo boogie, with the singer barely hugging the rhythm and the drummer nailing double rim-shots at the end of each line. On screen, after the credits had finished, with the song still blaring, a new image appeared: an elevated train hurtling into a jungle of tall buildings, an urban heart of darkness.

Stepping off the train, a man soberly dressed in suit and tie approached a somber brick building, NORTH MANUAL HIGH SCHOOL. In the asphalt schoolyard ahead of him, just visible through the school's wrought iron fence, a bunch of kids were dancing. As the stranger approached the front door, a few toughs hooted at him. In the background, a saxophone and electric guitar played a blaring riff in unison. The singer sounded jubilant: "When the band slows down we'll yell for more . . ." As the song finally faded into the background, the boys in the schoolyard surged forward, pressing against the fence to leer at a passing woman, their arms waving through the cast iron bars—like convicts in a prison, or apes in a zoo.

In the two minutes and ten seconds it lasted on screen, this combination of image and song—teenagers under detention, Bill Haley singing "(We're Gonna) Rock Around the Clock"—defined the cultural essence of the music that Alan Freed had just named. It would be all about disorder, aggression, and sex: a fantasy of human nature, running wild to a savage beat.

The director of *Blackboard Jungle*, Richard Brooks, was an earnest liberal. Genuinely concerned about chaos and violence in the nation's high schools, he had no personal interest in glorifying juvenile delinquency. But his style was melodramatic, and so was the movie's ad campaign: "A drama of teenage terror! They turned a school into a jungle!"

Released on March 25, 1955, the film hit a nerve. As one film critic, Andrew Dowdy, has remarked, "more important than the violence in *Blackboard Jungle* was the implication of irreversible cultural tensions." These tensions were dramatized in the film's most memorable sequence. In an effort to communicate with students, one of the teachers at North Manual High brings in to class his personal collection of old jazz recordings. But the punks don't dig Bix Beiderbecke. In a carnival of defiance, the kids trash the teacher's "vision of American popular culture, sailing the fragile 78's across the classroom, while the sound track blares their own competing music."

From Los Angeles to London, self-styled hoods reacted with glee. They danced, they sang, they slashed seats. The booming riffs of Bill Haley's opening song were a reveille. At Princeton University one night in May, a student broadcast Haley's recording of "Rock Around the Clock" out of a dormitory window, provoking others to join in, using their phonograph players to produce a thrum of chaotic noise. In the streets, a crowd gathered; a party began; parading through campus, the students set fire to trash cans.

Alarmed educators warned that the senseless violence was a preview of worse to come. *Time* deplored the aid and comfort the film was giving to Communist critics of America and its way of life. That fall, when *Blackboard Jungle* was announced as the U.S. entry in the Venice Film Festival, America's ambassador to Italy, Clare Boothe Luce, threatened to "cause the greatest scandal in motion picture history" unless the film was withdrawn.

Spurred, in part, by the controversy over *Blackboard Jungle* and its rock and roll anthem, educators, commentators, and politicians struck up an edgy debate over the state of America's youth. The U.S. Senate Subcommittee on Juvenile Delinquency held a hearing, asking experts to testify about the effects on teenagers of film violence. The very existence of this Subcommittee reflected America's preoccupation in these years with teen disorder. The problem had first been identified during World War II, when a small but influential group of criminologists reported that roving bands of unsupervised youth were running wild when they weren't quietly wreaking havoc— moral termites, gnawing at the foundations of civil society. "The psychopath, like the child, cannot delay the pleasure of gratification," the psychiatrist Robert M. Lindner warned in 1944 in his influential study, *Rebel Without a Cause—The Hypnoanalysis of a Criminal Psychopath.* The juvenile delinquent, as Lindner analyzed him, "cannot wait upon erotic gratification," so he rapes; he cannot wait for approval from adult society, so he grabs attention by becoming an outlaw, a menace to society, a rogue male, "a rebel without a cause, an agitator without a slogan, a revolutionary without a program."

As the popular reaction to *Blackboard Jungle* suggested, the spectacle of youthful anarchy had its charms—and not only in the eyes of the young and the restless. In his essay "The White Negro," Norman Mailer, citing Lindner, wrote about the psychopathic components of the hipster's personality with warm sympathy, going so far as to say that the psychopath "could become the central expression of human nature before the twentieth century is over." A few months later, the director Nicholas Ray and the actor James Dean gave a definitive (and truly glamorous) form to the figure of the psychopathic hipster in *Rebel Without a Cause*—a film with a script based on the work of Lindner as adapted by Irving Shulman, the author of the first important piece of pulp fiction about juvenile delinquents (*The Amboy Dukes,* published in 1947).

The ongoing public fascination with teen hooliganism, film violence, and its impact on the moral future of the United States of America helped turn *Blackboard Jungle* (like *Rebel Without a Cause* a half year later) into one of the benchmark films of 1955—and also one of the most profitable. The uproar also sold records. "(We're Gonna) Rock Around the Clock" entered *Billboard*'s chart of best-sellers on May 14, 1955. Two months later, it was number one in the United States; by the end of the year, it was number one in England as well; in the months that followed, as the film made its way into theaters around the world, "(We're Gonna) Rock Around the Clock" followed it, introducing a new genre of music to a large audience and turning Bill Haley into the world's first—and to this day, least likely—rock and roll star.

Thirty years old in 1955, Haley was no Greek god. A paunchy man with thinning hair, he had chipmunk cheeks, a spit curl lacquered to his forehead, and a dead eye that left him painfully self-conscious. A veteran of country-western radio and the Jersey shore nightclub scene, he was ill-suited to the global scale of his sudden fame, which had come about largely by chance, as an artifact of the wider controversy over *Blackboard Jungle*.

The basis for Haley's accidental apotheosis had been laid four years earlier. In 1951, the owner of a small Philadelphia record label had convinced Haley, until then strictly a country singer, to record a new version of a rhythm and blues hit recently produced by Sam Phillips in Memphis, a stomping barrelhouse blues called "Rocket 88." Haley's recording of the song was a flop; but his version proved popular in local nightclubs. He added other rhythm and blues songs to his repertoire. Though Haley had broken into show business by dubbing himself the "Ramblin' Yodeler," he couldn't ignore the popular response to his new material. So in 1952, Haley hired a new band of players schooled in jazz, and recorded a hot new version of a 1948 jump blues hit, "Rock the Joint," which sold well in the Philadelphia and New Jersey area. Doffing his cowboy duds, Haley donned a Scotch plaid jacket, and began trying in earnest to copy the classic jump blues shouters, men like Wynonie Harris and Joe Turner. A few months later, his makeover was complete when his version of a jive novelty, "Crazy Man Crazy," finally became his first, modest nationwide hit.

Haley's voice was solid as a plank—and as wooden. But his musicians knew how to swing. And Haley knew how to lead a band. Emulating the stage act of the Treniers, a tightly choreographed black rhythm and blues act popular in the Northeast, and instructing his band to emulate as well the musicianship of Count Basie, among other masters of the jump idiom, Haley and the Comets painstakingly refined their new style, creating a showy stage act to go with their blues riffs, which they delivered with a lumbering, distinctively heavy backbeat.

After "Crazy Man Crazy" had climbed to number twelve on the *Billboard* charts, a Philadelphia impresario named James Myers commissioned Max Freedman, a sixty-three-year-old Tin Pan Alley veteran, to write something with Haley in mind. Freedman's claim to fame was "Sioux City Sue," a cute song that Bing Crosby had popularized in 1946. His main talents were a knack for wordplay and a feel for the musical marketplace. Taking as his model "Rock the Joint," and drawing as well from "Around the Clock Blues," a song recorded in 1945 by Wynonie Harris, Freedman produced "(We're Gonna) Rock Around the Clock"—a generic jump blues, jointly credited to "Jimmy DeKnight," a pseudonym for Myers, who owned the song.

In the summer of 1953, Haley began to work the new song into his nightclub act. And on April 12, 1954, shortly after signing his first contract with a major national label, Decca, he recorded "(We're Gonna) Rock Around the Clock" in New York City.

The session was under the supervision of Milt Gabler, a producer who had previously worked with such jazz stars as Billie Holiday and Lester Young, and also with the great jump blues artist Louis Jordan. Gabler recorded Haley in the same Manhattan ballroom he had used to record Jordan, exploiting the hall's acoustic depth to juice up the beat. A veteran of the swing era, Gabler focused his energy on getting just the right drum sound; for the session, he hired a New York studio musician named Billy Guesack, placed three microphones around his drum kit, and asked him to hit rim-shots on the snare drum, in order to produce a heavy backbeat (a technique that jazz drummer Gene Krupa had perfected with Benny Goodman's band in the 1930s). The band played every stereotyped riff with panache and precision; Gabler's recording was alive, full of energy and excitement; the electric guitar solo, by the Comets' Danny Cedrone (a note-for-note reproduction of Cedrone's solo on Haley's version of "Rock the Joint"), was a model of real grace (and a fitting if modest homage to Cedrone's musical idol, jazz guitarist Charlie Christian).

Released on May 10, 1954, Haley's Decca recording of "(We're Gonna) Rock Around the Clock" reached the *Billboard* pop charts, but barely: it spent just one week at number twenty-three.

James Myers was undaunted. Convinced that Haley's version of "(We're Gonna) Rock Around the Clock" would make him a wealthy man yet, he set his sights on Hollywood. In the fall of 1954, shortly after Haley's second Decca record, a bowdlerized version of Joe Turner's "Shake, Rattle and Roll," had become a huge national hit, selling more than one million copies, Myers mailed dozens of copies of "(We're Gonna) Rock Around the Clock" to Hollywood producers, suggesting they consider using the song.

This was how Haley's song came, belatedly, to the attention of

Richard Brooks and the producers of *Blackboard Jungle*. Wishing to use the song as a symbol of youthful mayhem and menace, Brooks decided to add a crucial new dimension to the music—sheer volume. In those years, it was customary for Hollywood producers to lower the levels of the bass and treble on the music used on soundtracks, lest the audience in theaters be deafened by the giant loudspeakers behind the screen. For *Blackboard Jungle,* however, the producers ran Milt Gabler's recording of "Rock Around the Clock" wide open, letting the music hit listeners in the gut.

In a large theater, "(We're Gonna) Rock Around the Clock" was *loud*—for most people, it was the loudest music they had ever heard. The volume of the beat added to the menace of the scene on screen. A crude but effective symbolic association was put into play: the louder the sound, the more strongly it would connote power, aggression, violence. Haley's band may sound quaint when compared to Led Zeppelin or the Sex Pistols: but heavy metal and punk both have their origins in the shock waves produced by the soundtrack of *Blackboard Jungle.*

Freed's phrase for this loud new music seemed more apt than ever. If "(We're Gonna) Rock Around the Clock" wasn't rock and roll, what was? Oddly enough, Freed himself was less than thrilled. The sudden, overwhelming popularity of the term "rock and roll" made his copyright of the term all but unenforceable. And the defining association of the genre with images of disorder posed a potential public relations problem of a sort that Freed knew all too well, having weathered the outcry after the riot at his Moondog Coronation Ball two years earlier. "Hollywood is to blame," Freed complained, singling out *Blackboard Jungle*. "It was unfortunate," he said, that the song had been used in "that hoodlum-infested movie . . . [which] seemed to associate rock 'n' rollers with delinquents."

The charge that certain styles of music bred violence was an old one. Similar accusations had been leveled at swing. Not by coincidence, both rock and swing were styles broadly associated with African-Americans. The panic over the "violence" of such music was racially tinged, an indirect way of expressing the fear of miscegenation, a fear provoked by the fact that rock, like swing before it, was a music designed to put bodies in motion. But in contrast with swing, rock and roll to this day has never completely shaken its formative association with violence—one need only recall the riots that have greeted rap movies like *Boyz N the Hood* to realize how little has changed, despite the passage of nearly a half century. And an association that a businessman like Alan Freed viewed with understandable ambivalence, since recurrent episodes of real violence threatened the orderly exploitation of rock and roll, many of the young fans viewed with excitement, as offering a real and rare promise—of untrammeled freedom, of daring the unknown (no matter the brutality of some free acts) by doing "what one feels whenever and wherever possible" (as Mailer described the hipster ethos).

Haley's Decca recording of "(We're Gonna) Rock Around the Clock" sold at a hectic clip. By the end of 1955, it had become the most influential recording in the United States since "The Tennessee Waltz," selling an estimated six million copies (it remains, along with Bing Crosby's "White Christmas," one of the best-selling single records in history). Hoping to make more money still from Haley's current popularity, Hollywood producer Sam Katzman rushed out a short feature film starring Haley and featuring Alan Freed. Designed to rebut critics who linked rock and roll with juvenile delinquency, the plot was simple: Haley plays the new music at a dance, and proves to relieved parents that it needn't breed rioting. Freed, playing the role of a suave rock and roll disc jockey who is beyond moral reproach, stands up for the new music with a stream of smarmy speeches about the power of rock and roll to keep kids off the streets, and out of trouble. Fortunately (or unfortunately, depending on one's point of view), half of the seventy-minute film featured the new music, which spoke for itself. There were nine songs by Haley alone, including a reprise of the film's title hit, "Rock Around the Clock."

Shot in two weeks in January 1956, *Rock Around the Clock* was in theaters around the world three months later. Despite Freed's on-screen reassurances that rock and roll was innocuous—no more threatening, really, than the swing that mom and dad once danced to—more than one young audience around the world, inspired by the music, reacted with a display of more or less pointless violence, just like the jazz-hating hoodlums depicted in *Blackboard Jungle*.

In Minneapolis, a group of youngsters charged out of a theater showing *Rock Around the Clock* and briefly ran wild, committing acts of petty vandalism. In Hartford, Connecticut, a similar outburst prompted a local psychiatrist to call rock and roll violence a "communicable disease," spread by a "cannibalistic and tribalistic sort of music." Confirming the doctor's worst fears, teens in Dublin, Ireland, went on a rampage after watching the film, leaving exhibitors elsewhere in Europe understandably nervous. In Copenhagen, Denmark, a motorcycle gang roared through the streets after seeing the film, terrifying citizens. In Egypt, authorities denounced the movie as an American ploy, designed to sap the nation's morale by disturbing the peace. In England, things were calm until one crowd left a South London theater chanting Bill Haley songs—and proceeded to stall traffic on the city's Tower Bridge. The British tabloids couldn't resist blowing the incident up—and British teens couldn't resist imitating it. There was a national outbreak of dancing in the aisles, chanting in the streets, and deliberate rudeness toward assorted figures of authority: when the manager of a Croydon cinema reprimanded one mob, he was squirted in the face by a youth armed with a fire extinguisher. In a Manchester theater, the crowd lobbed lightbulbs from the balcony. In a show of official concern, the Queen screened a print of the controversial film. And in a gesture of self-defense, Bill Haley told London's *Daily Mirror*, "We don't make boys bad!"

It was too late. Nihilism had become a pop fad. In civilized old England, even more dramatically than in the United States, a lot of Haley's new fans took pride in being bad: that, to them, was what the new music was all about. Affecting an air of foppish brutality, they made rock and roll their own.

And in Liverpool, one of those boys, a fifteen-year-old fan named John Lennon, felt the sting of disappointment. At the theater where he had gone to see *Rock Around the Clock*, there hadn't been a riot.

2

Rock and Roll Music

"Ain't It a Shame"

In the weeks that followed the release of *Blackboard Jungle,*
a recognizably new form of music appeared, its shape defined by a
handful of recordings. Independently produced, each one made a different noise, told a different story, offered a different pattern to copy.
Some of these recordings renewed older traditions, some fused formerly divergent traditions, and some seemed to be products of pure
whim. As a whole, they nevertheless showed what the new style
would be, giving a fresh meaning to its name. By the beginning of
1956, "rock and roll" was not just another euphemism for black music. It was a genre in its own right, associated with a new matrix of
musical sounds, and a new cluster of emblematic cultural values.

Overshadowing this metamorphosis was one song, "(We're
Gonna) Rock Around the Clock," and one Mephistophelean figure,
Alan Freed. But the substance of the metamorphosis came from other
figures singing other songs, none more appealing than Antoine
"Fats" Domino and his breakthrough pop hit, "Ain't It a Shame."

A native of New Orleans, born in 1928 in the city's rural ninth
ward, Domino (his real name) sang with a warm Creole accent, and
hammered out piano triplets—his trademark—with hypnotic precision, producing a flowing, mellifluous brand of sweetly swinging
jump blues. He was a squat and baby-faced man, five foot five, two
hundred twenty-four pounds, nicknamed "Fats" because he looked
cuddly, but also in homage to one of his idols, the great jazz pianist
Fats Waller. The product of a musical family, Domino's father was a
violinist, and his brother-in-law, Harrison Verrett, was a guitarist
who had played with the Kid Ory and Papa Celestin bands. Drawn
to the piano, Domino emulated the boogie-woogie style of virtuosos
like Pete Johnson and Albert Ammons, and also the rougher, more
percussive barrelhouse blues of "Champion" Jack Dupree. (They
called it "barrelhouse" because the style had first flourished in the
gin mills, or "barrelhouses," that dotted the lumber camps and piney
woods of Mississippi, Louisiana, and East Texas.)

In 1946, Domino got his first steady gig, working with a band at the Hideaway Club. It was the heyday of jump blues, and Fats Domino made the style his own. He emulated the relaxed delivery of Big Joe Turner, and the good-natured showmanship of Louis Jordan. Starting with his first recording session for the Imperial label, in December 1949, Domino stood out as one of Jordan's most accomplished heirs, becoming one of the best-selling rhythm and blues recording artists of the early Fifties.

In these years, Domino's recording dates followed a typical pattern. The day before the session, Domino's arranger, producer, and A&R man, Dave Bartholomew, met with the pianist and a handful of musicians to work out arrangements for the songs they were planning to record. Though Domino toured with a crack band of his own, Bartholomew sometimes preferred to work with local musicians like Herbert Hardesty and Lee Allen on tenor sax, Joe Harris on alto, Ernest McLean on electric guitar, Frank Fields on bass, Earl Palmer on drums, and Bartholomew himself on trumpet. In its day, this studio band was the best of its type, exemplifying the virtues of impromptu riffing and ensemble swing. Since the musicians were attuned to each other, it was easy to work out parts by ear before each session. The band played with a loose precision, creating a limber, irresistibly kicking pulse that made the written charts used by labels like Atlantic sound stiff in comparison.

Most sessions began at around 10:00 in the morning. When Domino was home, the setting was the J&M Studio, the only one in town, run by an engineer named Cosimo Matassa. It was a small room, and Matassa used just a handful of microphones and a rudimentary tape recorder. Since the musicians all played together and eschewed editing and taped overdubs, the recorded sound was largely determined by where the microphones were placed. To bring out the beat, Matassa put microphones near the bass and drums, letting the pianist pound and the horns blow hard in the background. It would usually take about a half hour to assemble all the musicians, arrange the microphones, and warm up. Once down to business, they worked fast. Most songs required only a few takes.

As a veteran recording team with three million-selling records already to their credit ("The Fat Man" in 1950, "Goin' Home" in 1952, and "Goin' to the River" in 1953), Domino and Bartholomew had a clear idea of what they were aiming for. The music was usually uptempo, but never frenzied. The arrangements were simple: the electric guitar and bass doubled up on the same riff, often reinforced by the horns, leaving the drummer free to move around the beat. The accent was on songs that could exploit Domino's relaxed style and mellow Creole patois, which gave his singing a distinctively rural flavor. As Bartholomew explained to blues historian John Broven years later, "we all thought of him as a country-western singer."

On March 15, Domino and Bartholomew were on tour in Los Angeles, where they cut four songs, as usual: "Help Me," "All By Myself," "Oh Ba-a-by," and "Ain't It a Shame." A fruitful session, it produced Domino's thirteenth and fourteenth R&B hits: "Ain't It a Shame" and "All By Myself." Both were strong performances, but it was "Ain't It a Shame," the first to be released, in April 1955, that dramatically changed the singer's status.

Before "Ain't It a Shame," Fats Domino was an anonymous R&B journeyman, not unlike Wynonie Harris. After it, he was a prototypical rock and roll star—and well on his way to becoming an iconic figure of American popular culture, like Fats Waller and Louis Armstrong before him.

A jaunty lyric jointly credited to Domino and Bartholomew, "Ain't It a Shame" featured a rolling bass line doubled by the electric guitar, and Domino's trademark eighth-note piano triplets, hammering home the beat. The main musical novelty was the staccato, stop-time arrangement, which broke up the easy swing of the performance, giving the song a lurching momentum reminiscent of "(We're Gonna) Rock Around the Clock."

Still, there was remarkably little to distinguish "Ain't It a Shame" from the numerous R&B hits Domino had already produced. Why, then, should this particular song have come to be regarded as a pioneering piece of early rock and roll?

Part of the answer lies in the larger cultural context. Domino's recording was released three months after he had been a featured performer at Alan Freed's first Rock 'n' Roll Ball in New York City—and just as the popularity of *Blackboard Jungle* was turning "(We're Gonna) Rock Around the Clock" into a bugle call for juvenile delinquents. With the phrase "rock and roll" on the lips of disc jockeys, industry executives, and cultural commentators, it was easy enough to categorize Fats Domino as an archetypal rock singer— which, by definition, made his music of potential interest to the young white audience that Freed was now attracting in New York City.

Domino's recording of "Ain't It a Shame" entered *Billboard*'s rhythm and blues charts in May, reached number one in June, and stayed on top for nearly three months, becoming one of the year's biggest R&B hits. It was a strong record by a veteran rhythm and blues artist. But in order to explain how Fats Domino's song acquired an even larger cultural resonance, it is necessary to tell another story, about another singer and another small record label, working out of another studio in another part of the South.

Gallatin, Tennessee, is a small town outside Nashville. In the mid-Fifties, Gallatin was well known to music lovers throughout the Deep South as the home of Randy's Record Mart, a mail-order record store that specialized in rhythm and blues and sponsored a black music program every night on WLAC, a powerful station that reached listeners throughout the region. The owner of the record mart, an auburn-haired Southern gent named Randy Wood, also owned Dot Records, an independent label he had started in 1951. Soft-spoken and genial in manner, Wood cut an odd figure among the buccaneers of the independent record business; still, he was one of the most successful.

Dot's first recordings were of country music. Then, in 1952, Wood produced his first pop hit with a vocal group called the Hilltoppers. Shortly afterward, Wood (like Ahmet Ertegun and Jerry Wexler) began to notice that white Southern "cats" were buying a lot of black rhythm and blues records. The fact that he owned Randy's Record Mart gave Wood a rare edge: the store's sales figures offered a good index of the songs the cats wanted to hear.

Like Sam Phillips in Memphis, Randy Wood was an entrepreneur with a vision. He sensed that if only he could find the right white voices to sing the cats' favorite songs, he could make a million dollars. In the same months that Phillips was starting to work with Elvis Presley, Wood hired a stable of straight white pop singers, all homespun vocalists like Patti Page, pure of voice, sweet in manner—and willing to take a stab at singing almost anything.

Wood quickly demonstrated a gift for matching singers with songs. He hired the Fontane Sisters, long associated with Perry Como, and had them belt out a pop cover version of the rhythm and blues hit "Hearts of Stone"; it became a number one best-seller early in 1955. He hired Gale Storm, who was the star of *My Little Margie* on television, and had her sing "I Hear You Knockin'," a rhythm and blues song first recorded in New Orleans by Smiley Lewis and Dave

Bartholomew; Storm's version of the song reached number two on the *Billboard* pop charts, also in 1955.

But Wood's shrewdest gambit of all involved "Ain't It a Shame." Shortly after Domino's recording had been released, Wood handed a copy of the record to a twenty-one-year-old singer named Pat Boone—and helped him turn the song into "a coast-to-coast rock and roll sensation," as the liner notes to Boone's first album put it.

Wood's recipe was simple. Closely following the outlines of Domino's original recording, he had his arranger, saxophonist Billy Vaughn, polish the arrangement, giving the Dot version a big band kick. A chorus scats "bop-a-do-do-wop" during the instrumental break, while Boone croons in his own earnest style, cleanly enunciating the lyrics.

The popularity of Boone's recording (with the song's title changed to "Ain't That a Shame") provoked fresh interest in Fats Domino's quite different version of the song. Boone's record eventually reached number one on the *Billboard* chart of pop best-sellers, while Domino's "Ain't It a Shame" reached number ten, introducing "The Fat Man" to an entirely new audience—and launching a lucrative new phase in Domino's career. Years later, Boone recalled going to see Domino perform at a club in New Orleans. "When he heard I was in the audience," Boone says, "he called me on stage and he said to the crowd, 'I want you all to know something. You see this ring?' He had a big diamond ring on every one of his fingers, and he pointed to the most prominent of his diamond rings and he said, 'This man bought me this ring with this song,' and the two of us sang 'Ain't That a Shame' together."

Although Boone was a native-born Southerner whose father-in-law, Red Foley, was a hillbilly singer renowned for his mastery of country boogie, Boone himself had colorless diction and a creamy voice that owed more to Bing Crosby than to any hillbilly stylist. Boone had started singing in public when he was ten years old, landing his own radio show in Nashville, Tennessee, when he was seventeen, winning a local talent contest the following year, and eventually earning appearances on both Ted Mack's *Original Amateur Hour* and *Arthur Godfrey's Talent Scouts*. At the time, he sang straight pop; he knew nothing about rhythm and blues. Despite his forays onto network television, his declared ambition was to become a high school English teacher. When Randy Wood first played him a rhythm and blues record to cover—it was "Two Hearts" by the Charms, a

Negro vocal group that recorded for Syd Nathan—Boone asked Wood if he had the phonograph running at the right speed. Bothered by the bad grammar of "Ain't It a Shame," Boone made a point of introducing the song in concert as "Isn't That a Shame." He wore argyle socks with white buck shoes, was polite and clean-cut, and took pride in attending an Ivy League school, posing on the campus of Columbia University for his first album cover.

Armed with the same song and tagged with the same label, Pat Boone and Fats Domino at a crucial moment offered the public reassuring images of what rock and roll was all about. Domino was roly-poly, good-humored, and easily pegged as a happy-go-lucky, wide-grinning, loud-laughing, shuffling sort of latter-day minstrel—he was renowned for closing his shows by shoving the piano across the stage while his band blared "When the Saints Go Marching In." Pat Boone was Al Jolson without the burnt cork or emotional intensity, a low-key, clean-scrubbed, deeply pious spokesman for cultural uplift, filtering much of the blues and the rhythm out of rhythm and blues, and turning the new music into a winsome form of family entertainment.

At the same time, Boone's recordings suggested that the new idiom might be boiled down to one simple musical innovation: the use of piano triplets. There they were on Pat Boone's version of "Ain't That a Shame"; and there they would be, again, on Pat Boone's hugely successful 1957 recording of the 1931 hit ballad, "Love Letters in the Sand." It briefly seemed that triplets sufficed to turn any old song into rock and roll, a feat Domino himself accomplished with his 1956 version of the 1940 Glenn Miller hit, "Blueberry Hill."

It is no wonder that Boone and Domino were, apart from Elvis Presley, the two most popular recording stars of the early rock era. Audibly rooted in songs and sentiments from the past, highly stereotyped, their music was designed to give pleasure, not offense. Wholesome exemplars, Boone and Domino together helped ease the new music into the mainstream of American popular culture—where it has been ever since.

"Maybellene"

It was a stomp of a song, with surreal lyrics and a jack-hammer beat, intense, focused, wild, like the car chase the song's lyrics described. Though the music was played by a more or less conventional combo featuring guitar, piano, bass, drums, and percussion, the band's chaotic attack—and the distorted timbres of the electric guitar—violated almost every ideal of musicality held dear by Fats Domino, never mind Pat Boone. Delivered with nonchalant cheeriness, the song seemed without precedent. Chuck Berry's recording of "Maybellene" nevertheless owed its own kind of debt to the past, a debt doubly disguised: by the form of parody; and by the mass-marketing of the parody as a singular example of Alan Freed's trademark music.

"Maybellene," as Berry would later recall, had its roots in an old country fiddle tune called "Ida Red." It was an up-tempo dance tune, with the accents falling squarely on the beat—no syncopation, no blue notes. The lyrics were impromptu, improvised from singer to singer and version to version, often absurd, always punctuated by the same singsong refrain: "Ida Red, Ida Red, I'm plum fool about Ida Red." Roy Acuff recorded the song in 1939, and so did Bob Wills and the Texas Playboys, the country-swing stars. In 1950, Wills revived the song again, this time titling it "Ida Red Likes the Boogie."

In the autobiography he published in 1987, Berry recalls hearing "Ida Red" growing up in St. Louis. Born there in 1926, Berry had been raised by hardworking parents who were prosperous enough to own a radio, which filled the house with every imaginable kind of popular music, from Glenn Miller and Fats Waller to Gene Autry and Bob Wills. While still a teenager, Berry began to fool around with an old acoustic guitar, amusing himself by trying to copy the riffs and solos on popular rhythm and blues recordings. In 1951—after serving time for armed robbery and working at a variety of odd jobs—Berry bought his first electric guitar, hoping to pick up some extra cash by performing at private parties. The new instrument changed his life. "I found it was much easier to finger the frets of an electric guitar," he later explained, "plus it could be heard anywhere in the area with an amplifier. It was my first really good-looking in-strument to have and hold. From the inspiration of it, I began really searching at every chance I got for opportunities to play music."

As the first famous electric guitarist to play rock and roll, Berry exemplified the kind of musical brashness that Leo Fender had inad-vertently helped to flourish. As a latecomer to the guitar, relieved that the amplified instrument was "easier to finger," Berry was con-tent to approximate crudely the rounded tones and fluid tempos of his musical models, the jazz virtuoso Charlie Christian, the blues great T-Bone Walker, and Carl Hogan, for many years Louis Jordan's guitarist. In 1958, for example, Berry took Hogan's opening single-note solo on Louis Jordan's 1946 hit, "Ain't That Just Like a Woman," and banged out a raucous but essentially note-for-note copy of the solo, to use as the opening on his classic recording of "Johnny B. Goode"—thus turning Hogan's few notes into perhaps the most famous single riff in rock and roll history. It is telling—and typical of a salient type of difference between rock and rhythm and blues—that Hogan played with fleet finesse. Berry's rendition was, by contrast, rough and jerky—and also, not coincidentally, wonder-fully easy for anyone to copy.

In 1952, at the age of twenty-six, Berry got his first job working as a musician. Before the year was out, he had also discovered the man who would become his longtime musical soulmate, Johnnie Johnson, a barrelhouse pianist who played a stomping style of boogie-woogie. Settling into a regular gig at the Cosmopolitan Club in East St. Louis, where the laws were looser and the music was hotter, Berry and Johnson worked up a repertoire of blues and careening boogies. To fill out the nightly sets, Berry also worked up some pop and swing tunes. And he started to fool around with a few old country tunes, including "Ida Red."

Since "the Cosmo clubgoers didn't know any of the words to those songs," Berry has recalled, he felt free "to improvise and add comical lines to the lyrics." In this way, he elaborated an entirely new version of "Ida Red," which he called "Ida May," exercising an artistic license that his audience otherwise discouraged. The blues are a highly ritual-ized musical form, and Berry's patrons regarded the form with a cer-tain reverence; but the same patrons couldn't have cared less what Berry did to an old fiddle tune. (Elvis Presley, coming from the oppo-site direction, felt similarly free to fool around with the blues.)

In his autobiography, Berry recalled how his hillbilly repertoire changed his fortunes. "Some of the clubgoers started whispering, 'Who is that black hillbilly at the Cosmo?' After they laughed at me a few times, they began requesting the hillbilly stuff and enjoyed trying to dance to it. If you ever want to see something that is far out, watch a crowd of colored folk, half high, wholeheartedly doing the hoedown barefooted."

That was just the beginning. As Berry's reputation spread, the composition of his audience changed. "Sometimes nearly forty percent of the clients were Caucasian," Berry wrote, adding that the change in his audience produced, in turn, a change in the way he sang: "When I played hillbilly songs, I stressed my diction so that it was harder and whiter. All in all it was my intention to hold both the black and the white clientele by voicing the different kinds of songs"—blues for the blacks, hillbilly for the whites—"in their customary tongues."

One weekend in early May 1955, Berry took a trip to Chicago, carrying with him a homemade tape that contained "Wee Wee Hours," a new blues song inspired by Big Joe Turner's majestic and melancholy "Wee Baby Blue," and also a recording of Berry's most requested hillbilly novelty, "Ida May." During a weekend of South Side club-hopping, Berry met one of his musical idols, the Delta blues star Muddy Waters, who suggested that he bring the tapes to his boss, Leonard Chess.

Like Morris Levy, Leonard Chess had entered the music business by running a nightclub, a jazz room called the Macomba. He got into the recording business as a sideline. Shortly after opening a storefront studio in 1946, Chess had his first race hit with McKinley Morganfield, aka Muddy Waters. In the years since, his company had prospered, recording jazz and doo-wop, as well as most of the Windy City's important blues musicians.

Given the history of the label, Berry assumed that Mr. Chess would be most interested in his own blues material. He was wrong. It was "Ida May" that "struck him most as being commercial," Berry has recalled. "He couldn't believe that a country tune (he called it a 'hillbilly song') could be written and sung by a black guy." Chess told him to "give it a bigger beat," and hastily arranged a recording date for May 21, 1955.

When Berry, Johnnie Johnson, and their drummer arrived at the studio that day, they discovered that Chess had invited two other musicians to join them, bassist Willie Dixon (a songwriter who also scouted blues talent for Chess) and maraca player Jerome Green (who normally played with another new Chess artist, Bo Diddley). They also discovered that Leonard Chess wanted to change the song's name—he thought that "Ida May" sounded too corny. According to Johnnie Johnson, "there was a mascara box laying on the floor in the corner of the studio and Leonard Chess said, 'Well, hell, let's name the damn thing Maybellene.' " Berry, for his part, recalls that Maybellene was *his* idea—it was the name of a cow in his third-grade primer.

The song's lyrics are an odd blend of romance and car racing inspired, Berry claims, by "memories of high school and trying to get girls to ride in my 1934 V-8 Ford." The verse, about the race, and the refrain, about the girl, almost sound like they come from two different songs. It is the music's unrelenting beat—and Berry's distinctive guitar sound—that holds the song together. On the recording, Berry plays with a twangy *"chop, chop, chop,"* using a staccato style that he would develop into his musical calling card.

Quite apart from the exuberance of Berry's high-spirited performance, Leonard Chess had good reasons for focusing on "Maybellene." Since 1952, he had been a business partner with Alan Freed, who managed Chess' most profitable doo-wop group, the Moonglows (and took a cut of the group's song publishing). As Chess well knew, more and more white youngsters were attending Freed's "rock 'n' roll" concerts. He guessed that "Maybellene" might be their kind of song. "The kids wanted the big beat, cars, and young love," Chess remarked years later. "It was a trend and we jumped on it."

Chess and Freed cut a deal—not their first, and not their last. Chess assigned Freed one third of the songwriting credits and royalties for "Maybellene." In return, Freed pushed Berry's record on his radio show. (It took three decades and several lawsuits, but Berry in 1986 finally won back sole ownership of "Maybellene.")

Freed's radio listeners loved the song—and they were not alone. By August, "Maybellene" had entered the *Billboard* charts, rivaling Fats Domino's version of "Ain't It a Shame" as the year's biggest rhythm and blues hit. Berry's debut also broke into the pop top ten, peaking at number five.

On September 2, 1955, Chuck Berry and his trio opened a week-long engagement at Brooklyn's Paramount Theater, as part of Alan Freed's First Anniversary Rock 'n' Roll Show. It had been a year since Freed had begun to broadcast from New York City, eight months since Freed's first Rock 'n' Roll Ball had shown that there was an integrated audience for this music. Freed's September concert featured a variety of currently popular doo-wop groups, from the Harptones to the Moonglows. With the exception of singer Tony Bennett, who quickly withdrew from the engagement after angry young fans greeted him with catcalls—he wasn't a real rock and roller!—the musicians, as always, were all black. The audience, on the other hand, as Berry later recalled, "seemed to be solid white."

In his memoir, Chuck Berry movingly recounts his emotions at meeting his new fans. It was "frightening," he admits, this "multicult audience" (as he calls it)—and it forced Berry to jettison old assumptions. "I was merely playing it by ear and taking in every move made around me," Berry writes, emphasizing the oddity, to him, of the unrestrained white enthusiasm for his music. "I doubt that many Caucasian persons would come into a situation that would cause them to know the feeling a black person experiences after being reared under old-time southern traditions and then finally being welcomed by an entirely unbiased and friendly audience, applauding without apparent regard for racial difference."

At the same time, a thousand miles away, a different kind of racial détente was being staged. In these weeks, Elvis Presley, "the hillbilly cat," had begun to sing the song of "the black hillbilly," adding "Maybellene" to his repertoire. Performing Berry's hit before a solidly white, solidly country audience on *The Louisiana Hayride*, a live country radio show aired on KWKH in Shreveport, Louisiana, Presley and his band played it cool, calm, and fast.

The evidence is plain: despite their disparate backgrounds, Berry and Presley were speaking the same musical language. Rock and roll was still less than a year old; but the new genre had already produced a telling convergence of vernacular idioms, a blend of country and blues styles, raising the prospect of a new musical fusion—and a collective leap into the unknown, "without apparent regard for racial difference."

September 14, 1955:

"Tutti Frutti"

Richard Penniman's leap into the unknown occurred one afternoon in September 1955. The rhythm and blues singer was nearing the end of a marathon recording session in New Orleans, where he had come to record eight songs for an independent record label called Specialty. For nearly two days and eight hours, Richard and his A&R man, Robert "Bumps" Blackwell, had been rehearsing Richard's jump blues repertoire, trying to find the right groove. Despite his recording at J&M with the same crack studio band that Fats Domino used, the sessions weren't going well. The musicians viewed the outsider with some mistrust: at the time, Richard was twenty-two, a journeyman from Atlanta who looked like the queen of the prom, his hair piled high with pomade, his eyes lined with mascara, perfectly pretty.

Richard's singing style was tremulous and intense; he did jump blues and slow blues, all with a trace of churchiness, a hint of the gospel singer's use of shrieks, cries, and melisma. While touring the South with his own band, the Upsetters, "Little Richard," as he billed himself, had perfected a stage show of legendary flamboyance, performing raucous versions of songs made famous by Fats Domino and Roy Brown, singing a handful of original songs as well, banging away at his piano, jumping around the stage, and rolling his eyes at the audience.

But in Cosimo Matassa's studio, Richard's singing was subdued, his showmanship under wraps. In order to insure a professional sound—Penniman could play the piano in only one key—Bumps Blackwell had hired a local pianist, Huey Smith, to accompany him in the studio. This was a mistake. Deprived of his main musical prop, Richard had plodded through a variety of generic tunes, from a lugubrious slow song called "Lonesome and Blue" to a strangely stiff version of Leiber and Stoller's "Kansas City."

Bumps Blackwell was disappointed. He'd come to the Crescent City hoping to cut some really raunchy, gutbucket blues, something to compete with such current R&B hits as "I Got a Woman" by Ray Charles, a wildly secular version of a gospel hymn that the singer and his band had heard on their car radio.

Blackwell was a thirty-seven-year-old veteran of the music business; in the late 1940s, while he was living in Seattle, he had run a local big band that had given a start to the teenaged Ray Charles, and also to Quincy Jones (later renowned as an arranger for Count Basie, a composer for Hollywood films, and a producer for Michael Jackson). Since leaving Seattle, Blackwell had watched with interest as Charles dropped his original cool jazz mannerisms, and developed instead a spiritually charged vocal intensity straight out of the black Baptist church services he had attended every Sunday growing up in Greenville, Florida. Blackwell heard a similar gospel tinge in the tapes that Richard Penniman had sent to the Specialty label earlier in 1955: it was these tapes that had brought him to New Orleans. "People were buying feel," Blackwell later recalled—and "feel" was what he wanted from Little Richard.

In the studio, though, he just couldn't seem to get it. Frustrated, Blackwell adjourned for lunch, and went with Penniman and the other players to the Dew Drop Inn, the place where local musicians met to drink and jam. Spying the club's piano, Richard bounded up to the bandstand. "Awop-bop-a-Loo-Mop a-good Goddam," he shouted, and slammed into a song he'd been using in concert: "Tutti Frutti, good booty/If it don't fit, don't force it/You can grease it, make it easy."

Blackwell was stunned. The feel was right, the music a joy. But the lyrics, with their thinly veiled anal eroticism, had to go.

Time was running out. The musicians and Matassa's studio were booked for only a few more hours. Convinced he could cut a hit song, Blackwell tracked down a young songwriter named Dorothy La Bostrie, had her come down to the Dew Drop Inn, and asked Richard to sing his song so La Bostrie could dash off some new lyrics. At first, Richard refused to cooperate; he was too embarrassed to sing the song again to a woman. La Bostrie, for her part, wasn't sure she wanted to hear the song. Blackwell grew desperate. He asked Richard "if he had a grudge against making money," he later recalled. "I told her that she was twenty-one, had a houseful of kids and needed the money. And finally, I convinced them. Richard turned to face the wall and sang the song two or three times and Dorothy listened."

Richard had composed "Tutti Frutti" in between tours, while washing dishes at the Greyhound bus station in his hometown of Macon, Georgia. "I dreamed I was going to be a star," he later said.

"Everybody in my hometown laughed and made fun. They said this cat is never gonna be no star, he's gonna wash dishes. I couldn't talk back to the boss, so instead of saying bad words I'd say 'Wop Bop a Loo Bop a Lop Bam Boom,' so he wouldn't know what I was thinking."

It's a nice story, but the song's original lyrics suggest another genealogy. As he explains in an authorized biography published in 1984, Richard Penniman had grown up in the segregated South with three strikes against him: he was wild; he was black; and he was gay.

"Richard would holler all the time," one of his brothers later recalled, describing the genesis of the first archetypal voice in rock and roll. "I thought he couldn't sing, anyway, just a noise, and he would get on our nerves hollerin' and beating on tin cans and things of that nature. People around would get angry and upset with him yelling and screaming. They'd shout at him, 'Shut up yo' mouth, boy,' and he would run off laughing all over."

Shunned by his Baptist family and childhood friends, Richard soon enough learned that he could make money by screaming on stage, letting go, and dressing up. In 1947, at the age of fourteen, he left home to join Dr. Hudson's Medicine Show. He stayed on the road, singing with B. Brown and His Orchestra, and performing in drag with Sugar Foot Sam from Alabam, a minstrel show (blacks performing in blackface still being a viable way to make a living in the Deep South).

In Atlanta, Richard met Billy Wright, another gay rhythm and blues singer, then at the height of his popularity. "His makeup was really something," Richard later recalled. "I copied him as far as dressing, the hairdo and the makeup, 'cause he was the only man I ever seen wearing makeup before."

Through Wright, Richard got his first recording date in 1951, which produced a modest local hit, "Every Hour." More recording sessions followed in 1952 and 1953, but Richard earned most of his money on the road, crisscrossing the Deep South, playing in both black clubs and white clubs, refining his live act. By 1954, he had his own band, the Upsetters, and something of a reputation around Georgia, Tennessee, and Kentucky. "We were making a darned good living," Richard later recalled. "One song that would really tear the house down was 'Tutti Frutti.' "

Not every house, though: Richard discovered that "Tutti Frutti" worked best in the whites-only clubs. "He only did 'Tutti Frutti' in white clubs," one old friend has recalled, " 'cause you see, blacks were a little more sensitive than whites." Richard, too, remembers a difference in the crowd's reaction: "White people, it always cracked 'em up, but black people didn't like it that much. They liked the blues."

That is perhaps one reason why Little Richard didn't send a tape of "Tutti Frutti" to Specialty Records when he was looking for a contract. He dreamed of going legit, of becoming a straight blues singer. "Tutti Frutti" was too queer.

It was late in the afternoon when Dorothy La Bostrie finally arrived at the J&M Studios with her bowdlerized new lyrics for Richard's song. By then, there was time for only two takes. For the first time in two days, Richard was asked to play piano. The band bore down. The music didn't swing, it exploded.

The record starts with a bark: "WOMP-BOMP-A-LOO-MOMP ALOP-BOMP BOMP." The band socks out a clipped riff while Richard pummels the keyboard, hammering triplets, and periodically yelps "WOOOOO" in a tremulous falsetto, as if in mock ecstasy. The cleaned-up lyrics are both senseless and trite: "I've got a gal, named Daisy . . ." The saxophones honk, the drummer drives, the singer keeps barking, shrieking, and yelping. It is over in two and a half minutes.

Blackwell had, finally, gotten what he wanted. On September 17, he wrote a letter to his boss, Art Rupe of Specialty Records, comparing "Tutti Frutti" to "Maybellene."

This wasn't rhythm and blues, Blackwell explained, it was rock and roll.

Rupe was nervous. He had been hoping for "a big-band sound expressed in a churchy way"—not a bizarre novelty with a strident beat. Finally he relented, pressing copies of "Tutti Frutti" for distribution. "Actually the reason I picked it wasn't solely for the tempo," he later explained, "it was because of the wild intro, it was different—you know, Be Bop A Lop Bop, all that in front. You didn't hear things like that much on a record"—and that is putting it mildly.

Richard himself was skeptical: "I didn't go to New Orleans to record no 'Tutti Frutti.' . . . I never thought it would be a hit, even with the lyrics cleaned up."

But two months later, the news was out. "I was at home in Macon," Richard has recalled, "when I heard them play it on *Randy's Record Mart,* Radio WLAC out of Nashville, Tennessee. The disc jockey Gene Nobles said, 'This is the hottest record in the country. This guy Little Richard is taking the record market by storm.' "

"Tutti Frutti" started to sell in Richard's home territory, moving briskly in Atlanta and Richmond, Nashville and Charlotte. Once again, Randy Wood watched with keen interest as Richard's song went flying out of his Record Mart. Hoping to duplicate his success covering "Ain't It a Shame," Wood rushed Pat Boone into the studio to record a version for his Dot label. Boone had another pop hit. But for Little Richard—who watched his version climb to number two on *Billboard*'s rhythm and blues charts, and number seventeen on the pop charts—"Tutti Frutti" was the start of a whole new career.

Emboldened by the success of his recording, Richard intuitively grasped the issues at play. Being black and being gay, he was an outsider twice over. But by exaggerating his own freakishness, he could get across: he could evade the question of gender and hurdle the racial divide. "We decided that my image should be crazy and way-out," Richard recalls in his memoir, "so that the adults would think I was harmless. I'd appear in one show dressed as the Queen of England and in the next as the pope."

As the crowd grew whiter, his live shows grew wilder. To warm up the crowd, he had his band, the Upsetters, blow on a riff; the band was like a chorus line, always moving to the beat. At the right moment (his band never knew exactly when), Richard would burst on stage. He wore capes and blouse shirts and beautiful tailored suits, and his long hair was always piled high above his painted eyes as the show began. While the crowd screamed, Richard improvised. One night he might walk on top of the piano. Another night he might wander into the crowd. He'd prance and preen, then jump and holler, egging the audience on, whipping them up, getting ready to play. Suddenly, he'd hit the piano, hammering out triplets, a picture of frenzy, sweat pouring down his face, his head shaking, his hair falling, the music rocking, and then "WOMP-BOMP-A-LOO-MOMP ALOP-BOMP BOMP."

It was a shriek heard round the world, thanks to Alan Freed and Hollywood. Filmed in performance for *Don't Knock the Rock*, Freed's sequel to *Rock Around the Clock*, Little Richard stole the show. Wearing a baggy suit, Richard stood silently after being introduced by Freed—and then tore into "Tutti Frutti." As the camera zoomed in for a close-up, Richard pounded the piano, tossed his head, rolled his eyes, and waved his arms, an image of jubilant anarchy. The song finished, he took an ironically exaggerated bow. Then he tore into "Long Tall Sally," his follow-up to "Tutti Frutti." Arms flailing, he leaned back, kicked his leg onto the piano and shimmied while saxophonist Grady Gaines soloed, blowing his horn from the top of Richard's grand piano.

Don't Knock the Rock produced Little Richard's first top ten hit in England. It also bowled over a lot of young viewers around the world. Here was a creature who seemed to live life at a higher pitch than ordinary mortals, convulsed with energy, screaming at the top of his lungs.

The thrill was infectious. Within a matter of weeks, Elvis Presley added "Tutti Frutti" to his repertoire, performing it on two of his first television appearances, and also recording it for his first album. Other singers followed suit: Bill Haley, the Everly Brothers, and Buddy Holly all tried to sing Richard's songs, usually without much success: his mania defied imitation. In Macon, Georgia, a young local singer named Otis Redding devoted himself to emulating Richard's raspy style, while another local entertainer, James Brown, went his rival one better, by developing a stage show that was tighter—and more histrionic—than anything Richard had yet done.

And half a world away, in Liverpool, England, Paul McCartney—too polite to be wild, but as anxious as any restive adolescent to cut loose and let go—heard Richard yelp "WOOOOO" and found his calling. Like Presley and all the rest, McCartney, too, would study that noise and try to emulate its freedom, by learning how to play and sing rock and roll.

November 1955:

"Why Do Fools Fall in Love"

Little Richard was twenty-three years old in 1955, when he suddenly emerged as a rock and roll star; Fats Domino was twenty-seven; Chuck Berry was twenty-eight; and Bill Haley was over thirty. Frankie Lymon was only thirteen—which made him that rarity among rock performers, a kid the same age as his core audience.

A child of the streets, born and raised in the Sugar Hill neighborhood of Harlem, Lymon hustled money for booze and drugs by bagging groceries at a corner store when he wasn't pimping for prostitutes. Looking for an even bigger score, he also tried his hand at singing, dancing, and playing bongos. In 1955, while still a student in a Harlem junior high, he took the lead vocal on "Why Do Fools Fall in Love," an up-tempo doo-wop recording, released at the end of the year, and promoted with all the muscle the song's part-owner, Morris Levy, could muster. A kid with a cuddly look, he affected Frank Sinatra's cocky attitude, coat slung casually over his shoulder. His voice was waiflike and fragile, his style a matter of openhearted emotion.

The record that made Lymon famous was a doo-wop fluke like "Sh-Boom." It begins with a bass singer scatting alone, "Doom-wop, a doom-wop, doom-wop, ah-doe-doe." Tenors and a baritone join in, scatting "oo-ah, oo-ah," homing in on the song's title line and refrain—"Why Do Fools Fall in Love?"—which they sing in harmony.

The choruses belong to Lymon. He bobs and weaves through the lyrics like a bantamweight boxer. A saxophone with a squeaky reed snakes through a stomping break, accompanied by hand-claps. Lymon flutters into falsetto on the last verse. The lyrics are tough, even cynical, echoing the question raised by the title; but the voice is ingenuous, sweet, innocent. That's the record's charm.

In the months after "Sh-Boom" had galvanized the local music scene, countless street-corner harmony groups had been searching for a memorable phrase, a cool bass line, a thrilling falsetto. Among those searching were two of Lymon's boyish classmates at Stitt Junior High, Sherman Garnes, a bass, and Jimmy Merchant, a tenor. In 1955, the two young students, who were black, invited two Puerto Rican classmates to join: Herman Santiago, a tenor, and Joe Negroni, a baritone. After this ethnically mixed quartet had been rehearsing for several weeks, they added Lymon, the youngest of the lot.

They called themselves the Premiers or, sometimes, the Ermines. They sang in hallways, in school rehearsal halls, and in the streets—all the usual places. Like the other groups in Sugar Hill, they copied the local hits, concentrating on ballads. They had worked up one original song, built around the line "Why Do Birds Sing So Gay?," and also worked up their own arrangement of a neighborhood favorite, "Lily Maebelle," an up-tempo doo-wop tune made popular by an older Sugar Hill group, the Valentines.

The Valentines were led by a singer and songwriter named Richard Barrett, nineteen years old in 1955. A former landscaper who had moved from Philadelphia to New York to seek his fortune in the music business, Barrett had turned the Valentines into one of the most admired doo-wop groups on Harlem's hotly competitive scene. A sharp dresser, Barrett outfitted his group in matching white suits with red hearts sewn on the pockets; he also taught the group rudimentary dance steps, giving the Valentines one of the sharper stage shows of the era. But the Valentines were not Barrett's only source of income. In these months, he was also scouting talent for local record labels, including one run by Morris Levy's old pal, George Goldner.

One night, Barrett ran into Santiago and his group. They impressed him with their version of "Lily Maebelle." Barrett recalls the quintet serenading him on the street outside his apartment; Lymon recalled Barrett overhearing their harmonizing in the hallway of a tenement; still others in the group recall meeting Barrett and the Valentines at a Stitt rehearsal hall. However he first heard them, Barrett arranged an audition with George Goldner, who, at thirty-seven, was looking for ways to sell records to kids half his age.

Renowned within the music business as "the phonograph record's King of Salsa," Goldner (as Jerry Wexler once bluntly summed him up) was "a Jewboy from the Bronx who came downtown to the Palladium, converted to a mambo freak, and married a Latina." In 1948, capitalizing on his love for the mambo bands that played the Palladium, Goldner had founded Tico, which quickly became the most successful independent Latin music label in America. When several of Tico's biggest stars, including Tito Puente and Tito Rodriguez, left to record for RCA at the height of the mambo craze in the mid-1950s, Goldner branched out into rhythm and blues. In 1953, he had started a new label called Rama, which quickly had a national doo-wop hit with "Gee" by the Crows.

In partnership with Morris Levy, Goldner moved to cash in on the fad for rock and roll. In 1955, Goldner and Levy launched still another new label, called (for good luck) Gee. Goldner signed the Valentines, recorded "Lily Maebelle"—and began to use Richard Barrett as his talent scout and musical arranger. (Like most of the other independent record producers, Goldner had no formal musical training.) In later years, Barrett and Goldner together would groom a series of classic early rock and roll acts, including Little Anthony and the Imperials ("Tears on My Pillow"), and the first important girl group, the Chantels ("Maybe").

Goldner was an elegant man. A natty dresser and skilled dancer—he briefly worked as a ballroom instructor—Goldner appreciated, as only a connoisseur can, the sounds and rhythms of New York City's many different kinds of dance music. Like Ahmet Ertegun and Wexler at Atlantic, Goldner cared enough about his craft to rehearse his amateur groups, striving to achieve a certain mood and sound in the recording studio. Besides discovering "Why Do Fools Fall in Love," Goldner would play a role in producing a long series of memorable rock and roll hits, from "Little Girl of Mine" by the Cleftones (in 1956) and "I Only Have Eyes for You" by the Flamingos (in 1959) to "The Chapel of Love" by the Dixie Cups (in 1964).

In the parlance of the record business, Goldner had "ears." He also had a certain genius for hustling. He loved to play fast and loose. Schooled by his friend Morris Levy, he learned early and well the fine art of plying disc jockeys with wine, women, and song, filling hotels with call girls to amuse them, stuffing cash and gifts in their pockets, showing them a famously good time. To this day, Goldner is a legendary rock and roll Robin Hood, almost universally admired by his peers.

He had one tragic flaw: he couldn't control his lust for gambling. In 1957, he retired one set of gambling debts by selling his share of the Tico, Rama, and Gee labels to Morris Levy. Goldner then turned around and started two new labels, Gone and End; in order to retire more gambling debts, he ended up selling his share in both labels to Levy as well. A few years later, when Goldner launched Red Bird Records with Jerry Leiber and Mike Stoller, his illustrious partners jumped ship after discovering Mafia loan sharks circling their joint venture.

In 1955, though, Goldner was on top of his little world, and on the lookout for a hot new rock and roll act, one that would appeal to Alan Freed and his burgeoning local audience of teenage listeners. Goldner was impressed by the Premiers, and particularly by Frankie Lymon—though how Lymon became the group's lead singer is disputed. In one version of the story, Santiago had a head cold on the day of the Premiers' audition for Goldner, so that Lymon was forced to sing his parts—thus becoming the lead singer by accident. In another account, Goldner, impressed with the group's original song, auditioned everyone individually, and then suggested that Lymon take over the lead vocals.

Sometime in the fall of 1955, probably in late November, Goldner and Barrett brought the Premiers into a recording studio to tape two songs with saxophonist Jimmy Wright's quintet. Struck by the unusual youthfulness of the group—the oldest member, Jimmy Merchant, was only fifteen—Wright suggested they call themselves the Teenagers. Shortly after Christmas, the first Gee recording by the Teenagers appeared. Morris Levy had no trouble convincing Alan Freed to plug the record. Within weeks, the Teenagers were being heard on Freed's radio show, performing at Freed's concerts, and bringing down the house at the Brooklyn Paramount.

Richard Barrett outfitted the group with black trousers, white shoes, and matching white sweaters with red Ts—a collegiate look, especially incongruous on Frankie Lymon, who had yet to graduate from the ninth grade. While the group bounced around the microphone, Lymon commanded the stage with the twinkle in his eye and the throb in his voice. He was just a child—as everyone in the audience could see—but he sang with disarming authority. He had an unusual voice: a girlish soprano, it tended to crack and break, a weakness that Lymon knew how to exploit. Before his voice changed, he used his wavering vibrato to deliver his lyrics with an uncertain pitch and yaw that promised romantic shipwreck. The pleasure he took in singing was palpable; and his vocal limitations only enhanced the impression that Lymon was lucky enough to be acting out a fantasy that any kid might aspire to fulfill.

Young singers got the message. Years later, Arlene Smith, who would become a teenage star in her own right as lead singer for the Chantels, recalled the day that Frankie Lymon changed her life: "Alan Freed came on the radio and played Frankie Lymon and the Teenagers singing 'Why Do Fools Fall in Love.' It was a lovely high voice and a nice song. Then Freed announces that Frankie is just thirteen! Well! I had to sit down. It was a big mystery, how to get into this radio stuff. I thought if he could do it . . ."

Ronnie Spector, in her bittersweet memoir of "My Life as a Fabulous Ronette," recounts a similar story: "I was twelve years old when I first heard Frankie and the Teenagers. . . . I fell in love the minute that record came on. I couldn't tell if he was black, or white, or what. I just knew that I loved the boy who was singing that song. I would sit by my grandmother's old Philco every night waiting to hear

him sing 'Why do birds sing so gay?' And when he finally came on—
with his innocent little voice and his perfect diction—my hands got
all sweaty, my toes curled up, and I climbed right under that old box
radio, trying to get as close to the sound as possible."

Lymon's voice and stage manner were innocent—but Frankie Lymon was anything but. As he explained to a reporter from *Ebony* in
1966, "I never was a child although I was billed in every theater and
auditorium where I appeared as a child star. . . . When I was 10, I
made a good living hustling prostitutes for the white men who would
come to Harlem looking for Negro girls. I knew every prostitute in
our neighborhood and I'd get a commission for every customer I
brought them. I was a fresh young kid and some of them thought
I was cute. Sometimes, they'd pay me off with something extra. I
learned everything there was to know about women before I was 12
years old."

Like many child stars before and since, Lymon was too young—
and, for all his hard-boiled bravado, too naive—to appreciate how
fragile his ability to manipulate an audience really was. Unlike
Michael Jackson, who would follow in his footsteps, he was no
prodigy. That was part of his appeal. He was one of the first rock
stars to present himself as Everyman; or, more literally, Everykid.

All this changed with the passage of time. The audience got over
the novelty of a child singing a man's song. The singer got over the
novelty of being on stage. Transformed overnight into a famous and
wealthy man-child, Lymon devoted himself less to music, and more
to the pursuit of physical gratification without measure or limit. He
drank, he did drugs, he chased women. The other group members
came to resent his prominence: he had been, after all, the last to join.
In 1957, after a series of increasingly joyless recordings, the
Teenagers broke up.

Lymon tried to pursue a career as a solo singer. But his voice had
lost its boyish luster. Before he was twenty, his career was finished. In
1968, he died of a heroin overdose in a Harlem apartment. He was
twenty-five years old.

By then, "Why Do Fools Fall in Love" had achieved a kind of pop
immortality. It was one of those rare records that radio stations never
stopped playing. The song became a rock standard. In 1964, the
Beach Boys recorded a beautiful version for their album *Shut Down,
Volume Two*. Two decades later, the song became a hit again, this
time for Diana Ross.

Since there was money to be made every time the song was played, the anthem that so powerfully evoked a fantasy of eternal youth produced one of the most melancholy of adult scenes, a growing mountain of legal briefs and lawyers' bills. In 1955, the five Teenagers, ranging in age from thirteen to fifteen, had been "persuaded" to sell "Why Do Fools Fall in Love" to George Goldner for $50. But when the song's copyright was eventually filed, it listed Frankie Lymon and Morris Levy as co-authors. As the years passed, and the song's popularity endured, three women appeared, each claiming to be Lymon's widow, challenging Levy's song credit, and asserting her right to inherit Lymon's song royalties; meanwhile, the two members of the Teenagers who were still alive filed lawsuits of their own, alleging that *they* were the ones who had been defrauded of their rightful royalties.

The case dragged on for years, in part because almost all of the crucial facts were in dispute. According to one account, the first version of the song, titled "Why Do Birds Sing So Gay," had been written by Herman Santiago and Jimmy Merchant, using the words of a poem given to them by a neighbor of Sherman Garnes; in this account, the title was changed at the behest of George Goldner. Levy's lawyers naturally stressed *his* role in revising the song. Lymon's widows, for their part, claimed that *he* had composed the song, using material from a cynical essay he had written for school, titled "Why Do Fools Fall in Love?," about the unhappy marriages and common-law relationships in his neighborhood. ("We had to come up with an original tune right away and I got the idea of putting music to the essay I had written," Lymon told *Ebony* in 1966. "It took me about two hours to work up the song.")

In 1991, a judge handed down a ruling. He declared that Morris Levy had played no part at all in composing the song; and neither had Frankie Lymon. "Why Do Fools Fall in Love" rightfully belonged to Herman Santiago and Jimmy Merchant. And thirty-six years after the fact, the two surviving members of the old group, Teenagers no more, got to enjoy a last fling with fame when newspaper and television reporters converged on them to record their reaction to the verdict.

The sight was touching. There were Santiago and Merchant, two men old enough to know just what they had won, and old enough, too, to know how much they had lost, laughing with joy and singing with pleasure, rehearsing for anyone who would listen the melody of the song that, all those years ago, George Goldner and Richard Barrett had handed to the pint-sized hipster with the pixie smile: the first rock idol to be, for better or worse, a real teenager.

December 19, 1955:

"Blue Suede Shoes"

A thousand miles from Harlem, a world away from the street corners of Sugar Hill, a different kind of rock and roll, rooted in country idioms rather than rhythm and blues, had slowly been taking shape. The place was Memphis, the key player Elvis Presley— not that many people outside the mid-South noticed. Throughout most of 1955, Presley remained a largely regional phenomenon, his influence a matter of the impression he made in his live appearances, his commercial impact limited to the field of country music. Alan Freed in these months refused to play Presley's records, explaining that he "really sings hill-billy, or country-and-western style."

There were multiple ironies at play. Elvis Presley, after all, was no hillbilly. Before Sam Phillips had begun to work with him at Sun Records, Presley evinced scarcely any interest at all in country music. Still, because he was white and because he was performing with guitar and bass accompaniment, the most obvious way to market him was as a country singer. That is why Presley ended up playing a country music show at Overton Park on July 30, 1954. And that is why Presley's first professional manager, Bob Neal, was a country music veteran, familiar with country music venues.

Outside Memphis, Presley was a hard sell. A lot of country disc jockeys thought his records sounded too "black." As Sam Phillips discovered to his chagrin, a lot of rhythm and blues disc jockeys, unlike his friend Dewey Phillips, thought that his records sounded too "white." (The mystery of what, exactly, gives a piece of music a particular racial hue has yet to be rationally explained.)

On October 2, 1954, Presley had gotten his first shot at the big time when Sam Phillips succeeded in booking him as a guest on the Grand Ole Opry radio show, beamed to half the country from WSM, a clear-channel radio station in Nashville. He chose to sing his souped-up version of Bill Monroe's "Blue Moon of Kentucky." Though Presley was mortified at the prospect of offending Monroe, a longtime Opry regular, the great mandolin player was supportive: Monroe, after all, had launched his own career on the Grand Ole Opry with a souped-up version of Jimmie Rodgers' classic (and jazz-tinged) "Mule Skinner Blues."

Jim Denny, the Opry's manager, proved less tolerant. After hearing Presley, Denny chose not to exercise the Opry's option for a return visit: in his view, Presley wasn't really a country singer at all.

Several weeks later, after another stream of phone calls stressing, again, the indisputable fact that Elvis was a "white boy," Sam Phillips managed to get the singer booked on yet another country music showcase, *The Louisiana Hayride,* the Opry's only real rival.

On October 16, 1954, the night Presley made his debut on the *Hayride,* the following exchange, surprising only because it so bluntly sums up the musical facts of the matter, occurred between Presley and the *Hayride*'s emcee, Frank Page:

"I'd like to know how you came up with that rhythm and blues style," asked Page. "Because that's all it is."

Presley: "Well, sir, to be honest, we just stumbled upon it."

Page: "You're mighty lucky, you know. They've been looking for something new in the folk music field for a long time now. I think you've got it."

So did a growing number of fans and musicians. Slowly but surely, Presley's unusual brand of music began to influence up-and-coming local acts, none more powerfully than Carl Perkins—one of the first country pickers directly influenced by Presley, and the first man to write a song successfully emulating his style.

In 1954, when Perkins, then twenty-two, first heard "That's All Right" and "Blue Moon of Kentucky," he was working at the Colonial Bakery in Jackson, Tennessee, with a part-time job on the side, playing country music with his brothers Jay and Clayton—they billed themselves as the Perkins Brothers Band. Carl played electric guitar and sang most of the leads, in a style modeled after his first musical hero, Hank Williams; Clayton played stand-up bass, and Jay played acoustic rhythm guitar as well as handling some vocals in the gruff style of Ernest Tubb.

The Perkins Brothers were representative of the main trend of postwar country music. Throughout the 1930s, most country songs had been rooted in tradition and filled with pious sentiment—it was a music that was "morally good," as one of the Carter Family's old concert posters proclaimed. But after the war, a new style, called "honky-tonk," had captivated country listeners, allowing a new strain of realism to appear in songs about fast living and hard drinking. The dreamy ardor of "The Tennessee Waltz" was out, the searing intensity of Hank Williams' "Lovesick Blues" was in; and as the title of Williams' song suggests, much of honky-tonk owed its emotive charge to the use of stylistic devices borrowed from jazz and the main currents of the African-American blues tradition. (They called it "honky-tonk" because that is where the music was commonly played: in the roadhouses, or honky-tonks, dotting the South, places with a bar for drinks, stools for drunks, and a hardwood floor for dancing.)

As postwar country music evolved, it developed in two contrasting directions, both epitomized in the work of Hank Williams, the greatest of the honky-tonk singers of the early Fifties. On the one hand, Williams wrote wailing laments, songs of melancholy and heartbreak; but he also knew how to play music with a beat, performing country boogies and up-tempo dance novelties like "Jambalaya." As the country music historian Rich Kienzle has written, these two strands of the genre faithfully expressed the oscillations in mood at a typical honky-tonk, where "patrons swung between wrenching depression over lost or unrequited love and liquor-fueled cockiness and occasional violence."

Carl Perkins—unlike Elvis Presley, who didn't drink—knew a lot at first hand about honky-tonks. When the Perkins Brothers Band worked, it was in local bars and dance halls, playing the hits of Hank Williams and Lefty Frizzell and Ernest Tubb. "I would mix beer with whiskey," Perkins later wrote of his honky-tonk days, "and, with soul on fire, I'd stand on the table tops striving for the attention I thought my music deserved."

Then, one day in 1954, Perkins heard a new record on the local country radio program. "The first time I heard Elvis was when my wife was in the kitchen," Perkins later recalled: "and she said, 'Carl, that sounds just like y'all.' "

It's true that Elvis shared the same instrumentation with the Perkins Brothers Band: electric lead guitar, acoustic rhythm guitar, and bass. It was also true—and this impressed Perkins deeply—that Presley recorded for a small company just seventy-five miles down the highway from Jackson, Tennessee. Perkins had already tried, without success, to peddle tapes of his original songs to RCA and Columbia in faraway New York City. Now, he decided, he would contact Sam Phillips.

At first, Phillips wasn't interested. He was too busy trying to market Presley.

Perkins wouldn't give up. A month later, he coaxed his brothers into packing their instruments and making the trip to Memphis. They drove straight to the Sun studios at 706 Union Avenue, and walked right in. Marion Keisker, as usual, was behind the front desk. She gave Perkins the brush-off. Desperate, Perkins and his band waited outside. Time passed. Finally, Sam Phillips pulled up in a Cadillac. "Sam later said he felt sorry for me," Perkins recalled. "He said I looked like I would have died if he hadn't listened to me. And I might have."

As Sam Phillips quickly grasped, about all that Carl Perkins had in common with Elvis Presley was the composition of his band and the color of his skin. Presley at heart was a dreamy balladeer, a vocalist who preferred the rapturous joy of gospel songs to the moping laments and mid-tempo bounce of honky-tonk, a teetotaling pop stylist with a knack for singing the blues and scarcely a hint of country influence: in conversation, he may have sounded like a hillbilly, but when he sang, he sounded more like Dean Martin than Hank Williams. In this respect, "I Forgot to Remember to Forget," the song that finally, in August 1955, turned Presley into a national country star, was an anomaly—the only hard-core honky-tonk song that Elvis Presley ever recorded.

Perkins, by contrast, was country to the core. "He was a tremendous honky-tonk picker," Sam Phillips recalled years later. "He had this feel for pushing a song along that very few people had. . . . But I was so impressed with the pain and feeling in his country singing, though, that I wanted to see whether this wasn't someone who could revolutionize the country end of the business."

In October of 1954, when Sam Phillips did his first session with Perkins, it was to record two songs: a straight country-western ballad for one side, with a country dance tune for the other. Eight months later, Phillips followed up by releasing a similar pair of songs. With Presley still recording for Sun, Phillips was less than eager to push Perkins in the direction of rhythm and blues.

Perkins was growing impatient. Thrilled by Presley's sound, and able to play a mean country boogie himself, he yearned to record something different. "I stood backstage many times," Perkins recalled, "watching Elvis stir audiences with music with a beat. I was longing to throw away my ballads and join him."

In the fall of 1955, Carl Perkins finally found a way to do just that. One night playing in a honky-tonk, Perkins chanced to see a dancer get mad with his date for scuffing up his blue suede shoes. The incident struck him instantly, since only days before, Johnny Cash, another struggling local performer and Sun recording artist, had suggested that Perkins compose a song about blue suede shoes. Later that night, unable to sleep, Perkins jotted down the words for a new song, carefully (mis)spelling the title: "Don't Step on My Blue Swaed Shoes."

The pretext was shoes; but the subtext was Elvis Presley. And with "Blue Suede Shoes," Carl Perkins finally convinced Sam Phillips to let him make the leap from country to "music with a beat."

Not that Phillips needed much convincing. On November 15, requiring a large amount of cash in order to prevent Sun from going bankrupt, Phillips had sold Elvis Presley's contract to a partnership formed by RCA records, Hill & Range song publishers, and "Colonel" Tom Parker, a onetime carnival barker and country-western impresario who had just become Presley's exclusive manager. With Presley gone, Perkins became the most logical Sun artist to follow in his footsteps.

Like Phillips, Perkins had grown up in rural poverty. Like Phillips, too, he would in later years remember visiting a local black oracle, an aging sharecropper who sat on his front porch, picking guitar, singing the blues, handing the music down. Whether or not the South was ever so densely populated with such musical missionaries, the stories carry a certain biblical weight. Phillips recalls receiving the gift of the blues from a neighbor named Uncle Silas Payne; Perkins got his gift from Uncle John Westbrook. "It was his inspiration," Perkins has said, "that let me know what it was I wanted to do for the rest of my life."

By the end of 1955, Sam Phillips had sound business reasons to bring out the blues strain in Perkins' music. Thanks to Fats Domino, Chuck Berry, and Little Richard, rhythm and blues was hot in the pop marketplace; and thanks to Elvis, string-band music with a blues feel was hot in the country field. Having just escaped his creditors and been handed a handsome sum of money in addition, Phillips was in a position, as never before, to promote a pop record—all he had to do was find the right song.

On December 19, several weeks after composing "Blue Suede Shoes," Perkins and his band arrived in Memphis for their third Sun recording date. Besides "Blue Suede Shoes," Perkins brought three other songs to the session: a laid-back boogie called "Honey Don't," a honky-tonk novelty called "Tennessee," and a sad-sack country ballad, "Sure to Fall." Those involved recall a long but relaxed day of work, starting in the afternoon and stretching far into the evening.

After recording a low-key, almost diffident first take of "Blue Suede Shoes," Phillips set to work suggesting changes: "I told Carl that [singing] 'Go Man Go' [in the first verse] made it sound too country. 'Go Cat Go' made it into something altogether different and new"—and of course pitched the lyrics directly at the same white "cats" that Ahmet Ertegun and Randy Wood had been trying to reach in different ways with the Chords and Pat Boone.

Besides changing the lyrics, Perkins and the band revised the end of the song, closing with a boogie vamp ("blue blue blue suede shoes"). As the session progressed and the liquor flowed, the music got tougher, harder, looser. Perkins was no virtuoso; he sounded as homespun as he looked; but he played with passion, and on the final version, he sang "with soul on fire."

Sam Phillips could feel it. Jettisoning his country strategy for marketing Perkins, Phillips shelved the session's two honky-tonk songs, and paired "Blue Suede Shoes" with "Honey Don't," slipping advance copies of these songs to Dewey Phillips and other local disc jockeys. Released on January 1, 1956, the record was an almost instant hit on country radio stations, crossing over within weeks, becoming a hit on pop radio stations, and then—astonishingly enough—on rhythm and blues radio formats, too. On March 17, Carl Perkins became the first country artist to reach the national rhythm and blues charts. Shortly afterward, "Blue Suede Shoes" became the first Sun recording to sell more than one million copies.

By then, it was clear that rock and roll was a way to make money in the music business. It was also clear that rock and roll as a genre, was, as *Billboard* said of "Blue Suede Shoes," a "mongrel music." A mélange of vernacular styles, the genre combined aspects of jump blues and Tin Pan Alley pop with country and gospel and fiddle hoedowns from long ago and far away. A cacophonous style of dance music, aimed more or less self-consciously at a growing mass of mostly white teenagers, it was still a music made mostly by blacks. But Carl Perkins heralded a revolution. For another kind of history—this time, cultural as well as musical—was about to be made by the original "Hillbilly Cat," Elvis Presley.

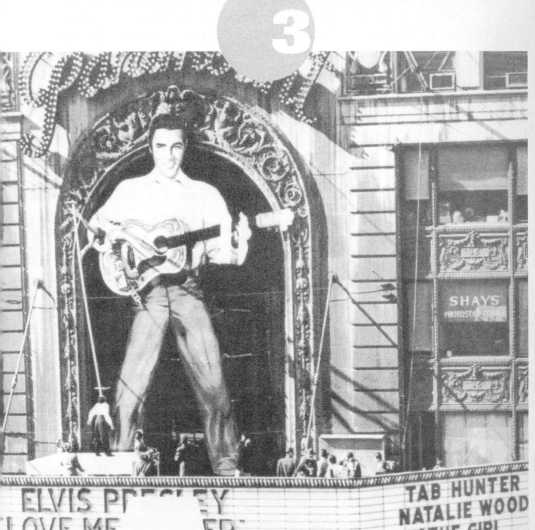

3

A Shook **Up**

ELVIS PRESLEY
"LOVE ME TENDER"
THURS NOV... ...ARAMOUNT

TAB HUNTER
NATALIE WOOD
IN "THE GIRL
HE LEFT BEHIND"
PARAMOUNT

SHAYS
PHOTOSTAT

Elvis From the Waist Down

Although its lasting cultural significance—if any—remained unclear, rock and roll by the spring of 1956 was ubiquitous.
Strains of the "Big Beat" (as some now dubbed it) could be heard on
radio, in film, on recordings. Only one mass medium in the United
States had yet to register fully the force of the new musical style—
and that was television.

These were the years when America's three major television networks—CBS, NBC, and ABC—had finally emerged, for better or
worse, as the nation's most powerful arbiters of aesthetic taste and
political judgment. By 1956, there were tens of millions of TV sets in
the United States, far more than in any other country. The networks
fed programming to affiliates located coast to coast, uniting the nation as radio had the previous generation. Successful programs ran
the gamut: in 1955–1956, the hits included quiz shows (*The $64,000
Question*, the year's top-rated program), screwball comedies (*I Love
Lucy*), and—above all—a wide array of variety shows, sometimes
aimed at kids (*Disneyland*), sometimes aimed at adults old enough to
have seen the same routines in vaudeville. At the dawn of the television era, in the late Forties, the most popular variety hour of the
week belonged to Milton Berle, the host of *The Texaco Star Theater*.
In the early Fifties, the format's leader was Arthur Godfrey—it was
on *Arthur Godfrey's Talent Scouts* that Pat Boone had made his television debut. But by 1955, Godfrey and Berle had both been eclipsed
by *The Ed Sullivan Show*, which for an hour every Sunday night featured a dizzyingly indiscriminate array of jugglers and movie stars,
opera divas and Borscht Belt comics, crooners, animal acts, and
Shakespearean actors—almost anyone (or anything) regarded as able
to entertain viewers for a few minutes.

As 1956 began, media tip sheets were buzzing about a fresh new
face from Memphis, a Southern boy with a funny look and a wild
way of singing. His name was Elvis Presley, and he made his television debut quietly, on January 28, 1956, appearing on *Stage Show*, a

program hosted by two veteran big band leaders, Jimmy and Tommy Dorsey. At first, few people noticed; *Stage Show* was not widely watched. But his first TV appearance coincided with the release of his first recording for RCA, a dour blues lament, "Heartbreak Hotel," that would shortly turn Presley's world upside down—and change the face of American popular culture.

Recorded at RCA's studios in Nashville, Tennessee, on January 10, 1956, two days after Presley had turned twenty-one, "Heartbreak Hotel" was a stark performance, with a walking bass line, a smoky blues piano part, and a strident but effective electric guitar solo. Inspired by a news story about a suicide who had left a note saying "I walk a lonely street," the lyrics strained for Gothic effect. Presley delivered them with heartfelt conviction, in a heavily echoed, highly stylized wail, full of garbled gospel devices, as if the lovelorn singer no longer had the will to live (never mind enunciate clearly). It became the prototype for a new genre of morbidly self-pitying rock songs (a genre that flourished well into the Eighties and Nineties, thanks to the moping mood evoked in popular songs by bands like New Order, the Smiths, and the Smashing Pumpkins).

From the start, Presley's new manager, Tom Parker, was angling to break his client nationally. In Cleveland, he had the support of disc jockey Bill Randle, who was also playing Presley's records on a Saturday afternoon network radio show. In New York and Los Angeles, he got even more crucial help from Abe Lastfogel, head of the William Morris Agency, and Harry Kalcheim, his associate, though it was Parker himself who got Presley onto *Stage Show.*

Presley was scheduled to appear on the Dorsey show for four Saturday nights in a row, with an option for two more appearances if the show wanted him back. The day before his debut, RCA released "Heartbreak Hotel" as Presley's sixth single. But for the first *Stage Show,* on January 28, Presley did two other tunes, neither of them then available on record, a medley of Joe Turner songs, and a version of Ray Charles' "I Got a Woman." For the second show, on February 4, he did "Baby, Let's Play House," his fourth single (originally released on Sun), and a version of Little Richard's "Tutti Frutti." It was only on the third show, after "Heartbreak Hotel" had started to get exposure on the radio, that Presley finally debuted his new recording on television.

When he wasn't in a New York City television studio, Presley was on the road, playing one-nighters from St. Louis to Tampa, gradually expanding his base of operations beyond the mid-South. While Presley hit the hustings, Bill Randle kept plugging "Heartbreak Hotel" on his various radio shows. Randle's support, together with the *Stage Show* appearances, for the first time made Presley credible as a mainstream performer. At the same time, "Heartbreak Hotel" was selling briskly enough to reach the *Billboard* chart of Best Sellers in Stores—the first time that one of Presley's recordings had accomplished this feat. With this new evidence of his growing popular appeal, the Dorseys invited Presley back for two more appearances on *Stage Show,* on March 17 and March 24.

Each time, he sang "Heartbreak Hotel." Each time, sales of the recording snowballed.

That exposure of a song on television could dramatically spur record sales had been shown in 1954, when an unheralded singer named Joan Weber became an overnight sensation after her version of the song "Let Me Go Lover" was featured six times on *Studio One,* a prestigious drama showcase on CBS-TV. The arithmetic was compelling: one performance on TV could reach more people in an evening than a year of performing live at clubs and concert halls.

Pulling out all the stops, Abe Lastfogel asked a favor from one of his prominent clients, "Mister Television" himself—Milton Berle. He asked the old trouper to let the young Presley sing "Heartbreak Hotel" on his April 3 show. Though he was in the twilight of his television career, Berle still had an audience. And for the first time, on April 3, 1956, large numbers of Americans, having finally heard "Heartbreak Hotel" on their radios, tuned in to see Presley sing the song on television.

A little over two weeks later, on April 21, Presley's recording jumped to number one—and there it stayed for two months, the most widely heard song in America. It was in these weeks that "Elvis" became a household name—at least in those households where people paid attention to what was reportedly being talked about in every other household in America.

On June 5, 1956, in the midst of the national hubbub over the new singing phenomenon, Presley paid a return visit to *The Milton Berle Show.* By now, Elvis was the talk of the town, even in normally unflappable New York City. As a result, an unusually large number of influential cultural commentators were primed to pay careful attention, many of them for the first time. And this is what they saw:

Presley appeared with his hair slicked back in a ducktail, wearing a baggy light jacket, dark pants, and white socks. His face cocked in a nervous grin, he faced the camera without a guitar, his customary prop. When his small band (electric guitar, bass, and drums) began to play, he grabbed the microphone. His left hand fluttering, he began to gyrate wildly. He was singing a song about a hound dog, the same song Jerry Leiber and Mike Stoller had written for Big Mama Thornton. In the mouth of Big Mama, "hound dog" was a figure of speech for a gigolo. In Presley's mouth, the phrase meant nothing. He looked—and sounded—ridiculous.

That was the point: the singer was cracking a good-natured musical joke.

Midway through the song, Presley and his band cut the tempo in half. To a striptease beat, Presley did a bump and grind, lurching back and forth with the microphone, knock-kneed, quivering with mock emotion.

The studio audience reacted with stunned delight. Three nights before, at a concert in Oakland, California, music critic Ralph J. Gleason had watched in fascination as the singer had turned the same stunt, whipping an audience of mainly teenaged girls into a collective state of erotic frenzy. "It was the first show I'd seen that had the true element of sexual hysteria in it," he recalled years later. "He'd slap his crotch and give a couple of bumps and grinds and half grin at the insane reaction it produced each time."

On the Berle show, Presley's act was over in a flash—less than three minutes of music sandwiched between the usual variety of jugglers and clowns.

The fallout from Presley's burlesque, however, lasted for weeks.

The pundits weren't laughing. Leading the pack was Jack Gould, the respected television critic for *The New York Times*. "The conscience of the industry," as he was sometimes called, Gould was constantly trying to stiffen the resolve of craven television executives by blasting the networks for their mindless commercialism, and doling out favorable reviews to shows that he felt had some redeeming social merit.

Elvis wasn't Jack Gould's cup of tea. "Attired in the familiar oversize jacket and open shirt which are almost the uniform of the contemporary youth who fancies himself as terribly sharp," Gould huffed, "he might possibly be classified as an entertainer. Or, perhaps quite as easily, as an assignment for a sociologist." To Gould's ear, "Mr. Presley has no discernable singing ability." He sang "in a whine," with all the finesse of an amateur crooning an "aria in a bathtub." His only skill was anatomical: "He is a rock-and-roll variation of one of the most standard acts in show business: the virtuoso of the hootchy-kootchy," a specialist in the sort of gymnastic exhibition "that heretofore has been primarily identified with the repertoire of the blonde bombshells of the burlesque runway."

Traveling, as always, in a herd, the mainstream critics rallied to the flag of good taste. (Decades later, in one symptom of rock and roll's lasting cultural impact, the same sorts of critics would have disparaged, in unison, the very idea of "good taste.") "He can't sing a lick," declared a reviewer for the *New York Journal-American*; even worse, added the same reviewer, Presley indulges in "the weirdest and plainly planned, suggestive animation short of an aborigine's mating dance."

"He gave an exhibition that was suggestive and vulgar," chimed in the *Daily News*; this "kind of animalism," the critic chided, "should be confined to dives and bordellos."

Within days, politicians had piled on. "Rock 'n' roll has its place," Congressman Emanuel Celler conceded, at least "among the colored people." But white folk had better watch out: "The bad taste that is exemplified by the Elvis Presley 'Hound Dog' music, with his animal gyrations which are certainly most distasteful to me, are violative of all that I know to be in good taste."

It is a rare event that can trigger this kind of reaction. And in order to understand why, it is useful to recall the broader context.

In the United States, the Fifties were the heyday of the nuclear family—a mythical, and intensely moralized, object of cultural (and commercial) concern. Ideally, moms took care of meals while dads brought home the bacon. Everyone was supposed to smile and be happy, cheered by the endless acquisition of fabulous new labor-saving devices—roll-on deodorants, electric can openers, frozen TV dinners. Kids, in turn, could glory in fabulous new frivolities: Sugar Frosted Flakes, Davy Crockett hats, cartoons on TV, not to mention *Mad* magazine and rock and roll records.

But for teenagers, and particularly for teenage girls, these were not the best of times. As Anne Stevenson, an acute historian of the era, has remarked, "Middle-class teenage Americans in the 1950s subscribed to an amazing code of sexual frustration. Everything was permissible to girls in the way of intimacy except the one thing such intimacies were intended to bring about. Both partners in the ritual of experimental sex conceded that 'dating' went something like this: preliminary talking and polite mutual inspection led to dancing, which often shifted into 'necking,' which—assuming continuous progress—concluded in the quasi-masturbation of 'petting' on the family sofa, or, in more affluent circumstances, in the back seat of a car. Very occasionally, intercourse might, inadvertently, take place; but as a rule, if the partners went to the same school or considered themselves subject to the same moral pressures, they stopped just short of it."

It was no mean feat to maintain this code of teen sexual etiquette, particularly in the context of the popular culture of the Fifties. The obligation to remain abstinent had to contend with Marilyn Monroe, *Playboy* magazine, and—after June 5, 1956—with the putative concupiscence of Elvis Presley.

The people handling Presley were simultaneously elated and alarmed. The publicity was priceless. But they were walking a fine line: under the prevailing terms of the culture industry's tacit contract with civil society, titillation was okay, but really lewd behavior was taboo. The publicist for Presley's record label, Ann Fulchino, artfully reminded journalists of one key difference: "Elvis is the equivalent of a male strip teaser," she said, "with the exception that he doesn't take his clothes off."

Colonel Parker worried that the controversy could spoil the plans he had carefully laid to have his singer follow in the footsteps of Bing Crosby and Frank Sinatra. If all went well, Presley would become a family entertainer, at home on stage and screen.

A complex struggle over the Presley image—and hence over the cultural meaning of rock and roll—unfolded quickly in the weeks that followed. At the center of this struggle, and in critical respects no longer in control of his destiny, was Presley himself.

He had to be stunned. Throughout the winter and spring, he had watched as his career had suddenly taken off, propelled by his first number one hit recording, "Heartbreak Hotel," and by his series of television appearances on *Stage Show* and then on *The Milton Berle Show*. Now, there was a risk, however slight, that his momentum might be slowed. And all because of a musical joke!

As it happens, Presley had first discovered "Hound Dog" in April, during a two-week stint playing the Venus Room at the New Frontier Hotel in Las Vegas as an accompanying attraction for bandleader Freddy Martin, renowned for jazzing up classical warhorses like Tchaikovsky's Piano Concerto in B Flat. It proved to be a tough crowd: the pseudo-sophisticates who loved Freddy Martin hated the "Hillbilly Cat." To kill time between sets, Presley and the members of his band sampled the other acts then playing in Vegas, which included (in addition to one of Elvis' personal idols, Liberace) a sextet from Philadelphia called Freddie Bell and the Bellboys. A jump combo loosely modeled on Bill Haley and the Comets, Bell and the Bellboys had recorded virtually nothing, though in 1955, an obscure small label, Teen Records, had released one of their trademark spoofs, a send-up of Big Mama Thornton's "Hound Dog" complete with vulgar beat and mock drum fusillades.

Like Presley, the Bellboys were new to Vegas, fresh from the Midwest, where they had built their reputation in nightclubs. But unlike Presley, who had bombed with the big rollers, the Bellboys had become bona fide stars on the Strip. They would spend most of 1956 working the lounge at the posh Sands Hotel, building up a reputation as one of the hottest nightclub acts of the year (and also earning themselves a cameo role in the film *Rock Around the Clock*).

"We stole it straight from them," Presley's guitarist, Scotty Moore, later recalled: "He already knew it, knew the song [presumably from Big Mama Thornton's recording], but when we seen those guys do it, he said, 'There's a natural.' We never did it in Las Vegas, but we were just looking on it as comic relief, if you will, just another number to do onstage."

As their giggles and laughter will attest, the small audience assembled to see Presley and his band perform "Hound Dog" live on the Berle show got the joke. But after the controversy in the press, Tom Parker wasn't inclined to take any chances the next time around; and neither was comedian Steve Allen, the host of the television show that Presley was next booked to play.

Nobody, of course, wanted Presley to drop "Hound Dog." Plans were already under way to have him record the song, and the controversy almost guaranteed a large audience for Allen's upcoming show, scheduled to air on July 1, 1956. The trick was to imbue Presley's performance with some semblance of "good taste"—that is, to drain the song of its disturbing erotic overtones. "You can rest assured," said Steve Allen, "I will not allow him to do anything that will offend anyone."

Allen's strategy was simple. His network, NBC, told the press that Presley would be appearing in black tie and tails—and singing to a dog!

Presley was a dutiful young man. As his biographer Peter Gural-nick puts it, "Elvis was fresh-faced and eager to please, pure plastic-ity in an informational age that required a protean hero." He wanted to be a trouper, if only to show people like Steve Allen that he had a real future as an all-round entertainer. In April, he had taken a screen test for Paramount. He was poised to make the transition to larger-than-life fame and easy money that, in 1956, Hollywood alone could offer (though Presley's impact would soon enough change the rules of the game). Elvis Presley, in short, had good reason to become the willing butt of any jokes that Steve Allen wanted to crack.

But he wasn't happy about it. He was stung by the New York crit-ics. On June 26, shortly before his appearance on the Allen show, his anger boiled over in an off-the-cuff interview (one of his last):

"Did you see the show?" he asked a reporter in Charlotte, North Carolina, referring to his television appearance on the Berle show. "This Debra Paget is on the same show. She wore a tight thing with feathers on the behind where they wiggle most. And I never saw any-thing like it. Sex? Man, she bumped and pooshed all over the place. I'm like Little Boy Blue. And who do they say is obscene? Me!"

In a touching gesture indicative of a more innocent era, Presley in-terrupted this tirade to flirt with the waitress, fingering her lace slip when she brought him a cup of coffee. "Aren't you the one," she asked.

"I'm the one, baby!"

He turned back to the reporter, ready to nurse his sense of hurt again: "The colored folks been singing it and playing it just like I'm doin' now, man, for more years than I know. They played it like that in the shanties and in their juke joints, and nobody paid it no mind 'til I goosed it up. I got it from them. Down in Tupelo, Mississippi, I used to hear old Arthur Crudup bang his box the way I do now, and I said if I ever got to the place where I could feel all old Arthur felt, I'd be a music man like nobody ever saw."

Did Elvis Presley ever manage to "feel all old Arthur felt"? How would we know? And what were the relevant feelings about? Sexual freedom? Suffering? Being hopelessly misunderstood?

Presley's appearance on *The Steve Allen Show* on Sunday night, July 1, went smoothly. As planned, he sang "Hound Dog" in a tux, and even agreed to kiss the pooch that served as his stage prop. Pres-ley's handlers were relieved.

The next morning, when the singer arrived at the RCA Victor studios to record "Hound Dog," he was met by fans carrying picket signs. "We Want the Real Elvis," read one—and "The Real Elvis" they would soon enough get (a fact not lost on the record company, which would subsequently release the results of this recording session in an extended-play disc entitled *The Real Elvis*).

Defying Steve Allen and every other uptight arbiter of good taste, Presley and his band methodically turned "Hound Dog" into a shocking burst of noise. As he ended up recording it, the song wasn't a joke anymore. With drummer D.J. Fontana's machine-gun fills and Presley's snarling vocal, it sounded more like a prison riot.

America got the message—and so did the world. "Hound Dog" went on to overtake both "The Tennessee Waltz" and "Rock Around the Clock," becoming the biggest hit record of the Fifties, and selling more than seven million copies.

Elvis would become the "King of Rock and Roll," a cultural monarch universally recognized by his first name only.

And last but not least, the arbiters of good taste, led by America's most popular TV variety host, Ed Sullivan, would admit defeat, welcoming Presley into the mainstream of American popular culture.

Years later, Jerry Leiber, who had written "Hound Dog" with his partner Mike Stoller, looked back in wonder at what had happened, still amazed that a singer of such raw talent, singing a song of such little musical value, could have become an Olympian figure of post-war global culture.

"You could say this guy is a monumental cosmic success," mused Leiber. "Maybe what he wanted to do was more important. Maybe Coca-Cola is more important than Eugene O'Neill—maybe in the final countdown of America that's what's more important."

As the arbiters of "good taste" intuitively understood, these were the stakes in the rock and roll revolution. For after Elvis, only a fool would venture to say with confidence which was more important: *The Emperor Jones* or "Hound Dog."

March 25, 1957:

Ricky Nelson Impresses His Girlfriend

By the spring of 1957, rock and roll in many respects had already achieved its definitive form. *Blackboard Jungle* had put into play the key cultural values, glorifying rebellion, delinquency, youthful disorder. Fats Domino and Chuck Berry and Little Richard had defined, in broad strokes, the parameters of the new musical style, with its driving beat, teen-oriented lyrics, and mixed-up stew of jazz and pop and blues and gospel and country influences. And after Elvis, the picture was complete. Rock now had a commanding celebrity: one dominant figure, exciting awe, reverence—and imitation.

Celebrities in postwar America played a role once reserved for the heroes of mythic sagas: they offered models of how to live. Elvis had grown up wanting to be the next Robert Mitchum. Like many young Americans in these years, he turned instinctively to Hollywood for clues about how to dress, how to walk, how to sneer, how to look cool and act sexy. But Elvis himself was changing the rules of cultural reference. And in 1957, a boy who already was a Hollywood star set out to become the next Elvis Presley.

"I was going with this girl at Hollywood High School," Ricky Nelson recalled twenty years later. "I remember taking her home one night and she didn't really like me that well"—which is a little hard to imagine, since he was, after all, one of the most famous teenagers in America, thanks to his weekly appearances, playing himself, on *The Adventures of Ozzie and Harriet,* a televised comedy series.

"I was taking her home and driving down Laurel Canyon and Elvis's record came on the radio. She did this whole thing about Elvis and I thought I have to say something. So I said, 'Well, I'm going to make a record.' She laughed. She thought that was real funny. I thought right then I'm going to make a record. If it's just one record, I'm going to hand it to her and say, 'Now laugh.' "

It is hard to distinguish fact from fantasy in this story. Nelson certainly repeated it countless times; so maybe it is true. But the driving force behind Ricky Nelson's decision to cut a record was almost certainly not his girlfriend, but rather his father—a cunning veteran of the pop music business.

In 1957, Ozzie Nelson was at the peak of his powers as a Renaissance man of the entertainment industry. A former bandleader, Ozzie had become a popular radio personality in the 1940s, working in tandem with his wife (and former band vocalist), Harriet. Since 1944, the two of them had been staging a weekly make-believe version of their everyday lives, first on radio, then, starting in 1952, on television. Using a set modeled, with meticulous realism, on the Nelson family's actual living room, Ozzie helped to set new technical standards for the production of a television series, employing some of Hollywood's ablest cameramen; along with Desi Arnaz and Lucille Ball, he also helped to establish a new genre: the family situation comedy.

Fascinated by the new medium, Nelson developed a flair for sight gags that disrupted, with a wink, the air of realism that the show otherwise assiduously cultivated. In one early episode, for example, Ozzie offered his older son, David, a basketball while his wife, Harriet, sitting in an easy chair, looked on; crossing in front of Harriet to take the ball, Ozzie quipped, "Hold it up a little son, you're blocking your mother's face"—which he was, though only from the perspective of the camera (and home viewer).

Ozzie presented his family as the very image of the American Ideal at mid-century: four happy white folk, prosperous and fun-loving, but wholesome, kindhearted—and never, ever lustful, or morbid-minded. In 1950, *Look* magazine published an article on the family shortly before the Nelson show made the transition to television. Photos showed Harriet sunbathing at the side of a swimming pool while Ozzie helps his two young boys, David and Ricky, practice somersault dives. Underlining this bucolic image of suburban bliss, the headline proclaimed "Ozzie and Harriet . . . They Never Leave Home." As the article explained, "Broadcasting a weekly radio show is no trick for the Nelsons. The whole family just plays itself." "These days," Harriet told the reporter, "cottage economy has all but disappeared. If modern kids are sassy, lack responsibility, treat home strictly as a stopover between dates, and have no respect for earning money, it may be because the old-time ties that bound have been broken. With the Nelsons they have become a firm anchor to happiness."

At the time, countless Americans were prepared to take a claim like this at face value. Jack Gould—the *Times* critic who had panned Presley for "Hound Dog"—had nothing but praise for *The Adventures of Ozzie and Harriet.* "A bright new hit has come to television," he reported in 1953. "The show is fine family fun"—and the family itself, he assured readers, "are as realistic as the neighbors down the street and, in playing themselves on the screen, they are staying in character."

It was a lie, of course. Far from being the easygoing, stay-at-home dad that the show depicted, Ozzie Nelson was a monomaniacal, domineering, rarely-at-home dad, a real all-American workaholic. The nation's youngest Eagle Scout at the age of thirteen, the elder Nelson had been an honor student and star quarterback at Rutgers, subsequently taking a law degree before becoming a bandleader in the Thirties. A compulsive perfectionist, he controlled every detail of the family program.

Ricky, too, was not quite what he seemed on TV. A sullen adolescent with a wild streak, he hung out with some of the teen hipsters who attended Hollywood High, smoking marijuana on the sly. At the same time, he rebelled against his parents in ways that any kid could, if he wished, imitate easily: by donning a black leather jacket, affecting an air of sovereign disdain—and disappearing at home into his room, to listen to his favorite rock and roll records.

He had become an aficionado of what, after Presley's success, was called "rockabilly"—rock and roll sung by Southern hillbillies. The first and greatest rockabilly star was Carl Perkins, whose "Blue Suede Shoes" exemplified the genre. And the record label that came to represent rockabilly at its best was Sun records in Memphis, home to a variety of hard-rocking Southern stars, from Johnny Cash with his stately baritone to Jerry Lee Lewis and his frantically pumping piano. High school friends recall young Nelson making frequent forays to Hollywood's biggest record store, Wallach's Music City, in quest of the latest vinyl singles with the bright yellow Sun label.

Like millions of other American teenagers in these months, Ricky Nelson used rock and roll as a kind of fashion accessory, one element in a larger transformation of his look, changing everything from the style of his hair to the way that he walked. His father, meanwhile, doubtless monitored developments on the home front with an eye to their implications for the TV show. He may have deplored the company his son kept at Hollywood High—he certainly said he did—but he also could appreciate the need to incorporate some elements of his son's rebellious new style into the character Ricky was playing on TV, if only to maintain the show's vaunted veneer of realism.

Elvis Presley's television appearances had shaken up more than the music business. When Presley joined Ed Sullivan for a show aired on September 9, 1956, the Sullivan show posted a staggering 43.7 Trendex rating—a figure said to indicate that it had reached precisely 82.6 percent of America's television audience. Moreover, if a popular musician could boost television ratings, by 1956 it was already clear that the formula could also be reversed, and that television exposure could open new markets for an aspiring musician. That power was confirmed by Tommy Sands, who debuted a song called "Teen-Age Crush," on the January 30, 1957, *Kraft Television Theatre*. After being featured in *Singing Idol,* a television play loosely based on the Presley phenomenon, Sands' recording of "Teen-Age Crush" shot into the *Billboard* charts, turning a make-believe singing idol into a bona fide pop star. It is no wonder, then, that Ozzie Nelson should have supported Ricky's fantasy of making a record, just like Elvis— if, in fact, the notion of making a rock record was really Ricky's idea in the first place.

On March 25, 1957, with "Teen-Age Crush" one of America's topselling records, Ricky Nelson entered a recording studio for the first time in his life. With his father supervising—as he would throughout the early stages of Rick's career—the sixteen-year-old boy cut three songs. Ozzie had arranged for him to work with a crack group of studio professionals, including veteran rhythm and blues drummer Earl Palmer, who had only recently left Cosimo Matassa's studio band in New Orleans (where he had recorded with Fats Domino and Little Richard) for the greener pastures of Sunset Strip.

The session focused on two songs, both suited to the boy's modest ability and bland voice. One was "I'm Walking," a jaunty new Fats Domino tune that the band played crisply and young Nelson sang stiffly. But the song destined for even greater success was a piece of fluff called "A Teenager's Romance," an earnest ballad with a lyric largely inspired by "Teen-Age Crush." "It was scary," Rick later recalled. "I had gone straight from singing in the bathroom to the recording studio. There was nothing in between."

Three weeks later, in an episode broadcast on April 10, Ricky Nelson made his television debut as a singing idol. Dressed in a tuxedo and looking dreamy, he mimed "I'm Walking," singing along to the record.

The response was overwhelming. Bags of mail poured into the television network. Copies of the recording went sailing out of shops. Overnight, a sixteen-year-old amateur with virtually no previous musical experience had become the latest example of rock and roll's commercial clout.

When *The Adventures of Ozzie and Harriet* returned to the air for another season in the fall of 1957, Ricky closed the first show by singing two new songs. His first album, *Ricky*, released in November, climbed to the top of the *Billboard* charts. A series of popular singles followed, turning Nelson into one of the era's best-selling male singers. A generation grew up with his televised image as a weekly presence. With his cleanly styled pompadour, he became Presley's kid brother, the rock star as a model of decorum and restraint. When he sang ballads, he shut his eyes. When he did rockabilly, he stood still. He was all voice and no body—an impression reinforced by his deliberate omission of songs that conveyed even the slightest hint of lust.

Yet despite the artificial constraints on his repertoire imposed by his father's overarching vision of the image his son should project as a member of the ideal American family, Ricky's voice—this surely was the secret of his appeal—*felt* real. Limited though his vocal range was, Nelson worked with what he had. His affection for rockabilly was genuine. And he sang with conviction, conveying a quiet yearning, a cool passion, the sorts of sentiments that most kids watching at home had reason to envy. Besides, he had a very fine band of musicians who backed him up, a rock and roll powerhouse that could outplay even Elvis Presley's fabled trio of Scotty Moore, Bill Black, and D.J. Fontana.

The key was guitarist James Burton, a country picker with jug ears and a broad grin. Only one year older than Ricky, Burton was already a veteran musician by the time he arrived in California in 1957. A native of Shreveport, Louisiana, he had been only fifteen years old when he became the staff guitarist on *The Louisiana Hayride*, the radio show where Elvis Presley was a featured artist in 1955. By the time Burton turned eighteen, he had already created one of the signature rock guitar solos, on the song "Suzie-Q," a hit in 1957 for Dale Hawkins. Thanks to the guitarist's regular television appearances with Ricky on *The Adventures of Ozzie and Harriet*—and thanks as well to the many stunning examples of his artistry on Nelson's early albums—James Burton became one of the new music's first models of virtuosity, admired by aspiring electric guitarists as different as Jimmy Page (later of Led Zeppelin) and John Fogerty (later of Creedence Clearwater Revival).

As for the girlfriend whose cold shoulder supposedly provoked this saga, Rick Nelson in later years made a point of recalling how he relished his moment of triumph. "This friend of mine drove her up to the house and said,'Well, she would really like to see you.' And I said, 'Oh, really? Oh, sure.' So I remember walking out the front door and she was sitting in the car. I sat down and he got out and let us talk. She goes, 'Why don't you ever call me or see me? Why don't we go out anymore?' And I said,'You know, I've been real busy recording. I'll try and call you.' And that was another rush. It was one of those great moments, you know, those ego things. I got up to walk out of the car and I said, 'I'll call you some-time.' "

In his private life, rock and roll functioned for Ricky Nelson much as it functioned for the rest of his generation. Embedded in an ostensibly defiant pattern of gestures, the music and its idols offered a focus for fantasies of youthful revolt and sexual mastery—a ritual representation of potentially unruly impulses.

Yet when properly packaged, in songs sung by a wholesome kid just like other wholesome kids, rock and roll could escape the implication of anarchy conjured up by *Blackboard Jungle* and Elvis Presley's gyrating hips.

Then rock and roll could seem as cute, and as innocuous, as the character Ricky Nelson played every week on *The Adventures of Ozzie and Harriet*—a dream date, good enough, and safe enough, for anyone's daughter.

August 5, 1957:

American Bandstand

Though the popularity of singing idols like Ricky Nelson confirmed the purchasing power of the American teenager, the wants and needs of this new breed of consumer remained uncertain. The teenager had first been seriously studied by G. Stanley Hall, the founder of American child psychology, who in 1904 published a pioneering study, *Adolescence*. Since then, a variety of social scientists had tried to get a grip on those between the age of twelve and twenty. Widely regarded as volatile and unstable, teenagers, in the eyes of the experts, were caught between infantile impulses and mature inhibitions, driven to orgies of passion and despair by the onset of generally unrequited and often uncontrollable sexual desires. Subject to wild mood swings, teenagers oscillated unpredictably (and paradoxically) between aimless rebellion and a craven conformism, or "pack-running," as Robert Lindner labeled it in *Rebel Without a Cause*. In another prominent study, the Harvard sociologist Talcott Parsons boiled the teenager down to three defining traits: "compulsive independence"; "compulsive conformity"; and "romanticism: an unrealistic idealization of emotionally significant objects."

One thing was clear: for the first time in history, America's teenagers, no matter how compulsive or unrealistic, had money to spend. In a 1956 survey, *Scholastic* magazine's Institute of Student Opinion calculated that there were thirteen million teenagers in America, with a total income of $7 billion a year, and an average income of $10.55 a week—a figure close to the average disposable income available to an average American *family* just fifteen years before. Even more significant, according to Eugene Gilbert, the head of Gilbert Youth Research (the first research group specializing in teens), the money at the disposal of adolescents was psychologically free in a way that the money of adults was not: "The adult market is a depression-conscious market," explained Gilbert: "Young people, on the other hand, have never known a nonprosperous world. What the adult considers a luxury, young people consider a necessity, to keep pace with today's living."

Unburdened by adult scruples, unashamed to purchase commodities that would aid and abet the pursuit of idle pleasures, America's teenagers became pacesetters in postwar popular culture, their volatile tastes monitored ever more closely by entrepreneurs and corporations avid to meet their needs. The music business was among the first to be regulated, in this market-driven manner, by the presumptive tastes and wishes of teenagers. In 1956, *Billboard* reported that "more money was spent on records than at any time in history"—and that most of the money was being spent by teenagers. "The consumer—the kid with the 89 cents in his pocket—is ready and willing to lay his cash on the line for what he likes. Those who won't give him what he wants may be well-intentioned, but they will lose out to someone who will."

Laissez faire is a French term for license: it entails letting someone do something without restrictions or interference. In an economy organized, like that of the United States, around the principle of laissez faire, the new class of young consumers was rightly approached with a measure of fear and trembling, since the teenager behaved like a fickle sovereign, unimpeachable in his demands. Others, perhaps older and wiser, might react with horror at the shameless idiocies that ensued. But for anyone in the business of catering to adolescent customers, what mattered was not moral goodness or a refined taste for beauty, but rather the ability to discern, and then gratify, the young monarch's whims, no matter how crazy or crass—as the career of Richard W. Clark nicely illustrates.

On Monday, August 5, 1957, at 3:00 in the afternoon, it was Mr. Clark who introduced a new daily television show called *American Bandstand* to a national audience. On the screen appeared a dance floor crowded with kids, framed by a cutout map of the United States. "Hi, I'm Dick Clark," the show's genial host said. "Welcome to *American Bandstand*. You and I have got an hour and a half to share together with some of my friends here, lots of good music, and our special guest stars."

The format was simple. Aired every weekday between 3:00 and 4:30 P.M., the show featured kids dancing to records with a beat, guest stars miming their current hits, and the host exchanging small talk with members of the teen audience. Clark's manner was low-key, suave, unmenacing—a "junior executive type," as *This Week* magazine put it in November 1958. Looks, for once, did not deceive. Clark was, above all, an entrepreneur. "I listened to the kids," he remarked years later, recalling his early days in the music business. "I knew that if I could tune into them and keep myself on the show I could make a good deal of money."

Bandstand had started as a local show, aired weekdays on the ABC network's Philadelphia affiliate, WFIL. An up-and-coming radio and television broadcaster, Clark had inherited *Bandstand* in 1956, when his predecessor was fired in a sex scandal. After restoring the show's good name by exploiting his own aura of clean-cut respectability, Clark, then twenty-seven, began to lobby executives at ABC, urging them to broadcast the show nationally, as a way to reach the teen audience. "It's no secret that the young people in this country are the single most powerful element," Clark explained to a reporter from the *New York Post* in 1958. "They control our taste in music, in the arts, and they even influence what we wear."

At the network, programmers were wary but interested. "We had a feeling that the teenage market had never before been successfully reached by network programming," said ABC programming vice president Ted Fetter a year after the show had gone national: "Dick Clark has proved it's a lucrative market."

In order to tap this market, Clark worked hard to keep his product clean. Simple censorship was not only difficult, it was undesirable. Teen viewers wanted to see performers like Presley and Little Richard, and network officials had trouble drawing a line. (Asked why NBC had decided to air Little Richard's leering performance of his hit "Long Tall Sally" on one of the network's variety shows, a censor pleaded ignorance: "How can I restrict it when I can't even understand it?")

Clark for his part established a measure of ad hoc control by recruiting an informal "committee" of recurrent dancers, the "regulars," to anchor the broadcast. Appearing day in and day out, the regulars provided continuity, in addition to policing the program's code of conduct. Boys were required to wear jackets and ties. Girls were encouraged to wear simple skirts and blouses; slacks, shorts, low-necked gowns, and tight sweaters were all prohibited. Impulsive or overtly demonstrative behavior was grounds for expulsion: waving to the cameras was forbidden, and so was chewing gum. Only kids between the ages of fourteen and eighteen were allowed into the studio—an upper age limit that prevented soldiers and sailors from spoiling the show's carefully cultivated atmosphere of puppy love. Though blacks were not barred from the set, they were few and far between; as a veteran of the show confided to the *New York Post* in 1958, "it is station practice to allow eight or nine colored kids at a time—and not to focus the camera on them." With his slicked-back hair and bland good looks, Clark for his part offered the younger generation a respectable new self-image: "Even rock 'n' roll," reported the *Post,* "loses its switchblade set association."

Within months of its national debut, *American Bandstand* was reaching more viewers than any other show on daytime television. Both adults and teenagers developed "a kind of soap opera attachment to us," as Clark put it, lured by the on-screen sparks between regulars like fourteen-year-old Kenny Rossi and fifteen-year-old Arlene Sullivan. Most of the kids, like Rossi, were third-generation Italian-Americans, and something about their working-class background (most came from South Philadelphia) and winsome ethnicity tapped into America's ongoing fascination with the figure of the bel canto singing idol (Frank Sinatra, who had become the first teen music idol in the Forties, was also an Italian-American of working-class origin).

The regulars were encouraged to bring new dance steps to Clark's attention. As it happened, most of the show's trademark steps originated with black students in one of Philadelphia's integrated high schools, where whites learned how to do the dances. As John A. Jackson tartly puts it in his authoritative history of *American Bandstand,* "Dick Clark's task was to excise the controversial body movements from the black-inspired dances introduced on *Bandstand,*" just as Vernon and Irene Castle, famed white popularizers of the tango, had done two generations earlier with dances like the fox-trot (a step, and a tempo, first devised by W.C. Handy, the black composer of "The Memphis Blues," "The St. Louis Blues," etc.).

Clark became skilled at introducing cleaned-up versions of the coolest new black dances, which he then promoted in conjunction with upbeat new songs, often specially recorded just for this purpose (sometimes by white artists, sometimes by black). In this way, *Bandstand* introduced America to the Bop, the Stroll, and the Twist through songs like "At the Hop" (a number one pop hit in 1958), "The Stroll" (number four in 1958), and "The Twist" (number one twice, in 1960, and again in 1961).

A great many of these dances were free-style and athletic, performed without the partners touching. Presented in a context that stressed playful revelry, the gyrations that had scandalized older critics when they saw Presley in action seemed now, paradoxically, to be a welcome form of sublimation (again, not unlike ballroom dancing two generations earlier). "So furious is the rate of the dancing, which is mostly rock 'n' roll, that it is inconceivable that any dancer would have an ounce of energy left over to invest in any kind of hanky-panky whatsoever," marveled a writer in the *New York Herald Tribune.* In a similar vein, an official in New York's police department publicly praised Clark for providing teenagers with "a tranquilizing pill."

From a radically different perspective, writing a decade later as an advocate of Black Power (and armed insurrection), Eldridge Cleaver analyzed the phenomenon in subtler, and more ambiguous, terms. "The Twist was a form of therapy for a convalescing nation," Cleaver declared in *Soul on Ice,* explaining how white folk were struggling to reclaim "their Bodies again after generations of alienated and disembodied existence. . . . They were swinging and gyrating and shaking their dead little asses like petrified zombies trying to regain the warmth of life, rekindle the dead limbs, the cold ass, the stone heart, the stiff, mechanical, disused joints with the spark of life. This spectacle truly startled many Negroes, because they perceived it as an intrusion by the Mind into the province of the Body, and this intimated chaos; because the Negroes knew, from the survival experience of their everyday lives, that the system within which they were imprisoned was based upon the racial Maginot Line and that the cardinal sin, crossing the line—which was in their experience usually initiated from the black side—was being committed, *en masse,* by the whites." If one is willing to accept the gist of Cleaver's analysis (and Norman Mailer, for one, hailed his book on publication), then Dick Clark in these years had, in effect, become an unwitting accomplice to race treason, winning vast numbers of new recruits for a mass movement of "white Negroes" in revolt, however unconsciously, against old racial barriers and sexual taboos.

Clark himself, though, rarely missed a chance to link rock and roll to old-fashioned American values—and old-fashioned styles of entertainment. "Today rock 'n' roll is—let's face it—*the basic form of American popular music,*" Clark declared in a "guest column" distributed to newspapers in the summer of 1958. "What I'd like to suggest here is that r'n'r has become today what swing was in the '30s—a universal form of music within which almost all tastes can be satisfied."

As if to underline the reassuring continuity between the swing and rock eras, Clark made a point of scouring the South Philly neighborhoods near the *Bandstand* studios, in search of young Italian crooners. In the previous generation, mainstream popular music had been dominated by Italian-American vocalists—Sinatra and Perry Como were the most famous, but South Philly had produced its share of stars, from Al Martino and Mario Lanza to Eddie Fisher and Buddy Greco. Intuiting that his viewers would welcome a younger version of these matinee idols, Clark kept his ears open for local unknowns, and also for national stars who might bridge the stylistic gap between Sinatra and Presley. The singers he thus promoted gave *Band-*

stand a distinctive musical profile, associated with names like Paul Anka, Frankie Avalon (born Francis Avallone), Bobby Rydell (born Bobby Ridarelli), Fabian (born Fabiano Forte), Dion DiMucci, and—perhaps the most musically talented of the lot—Bobby Darin (born Walden Robert Cassotto). All of them were cute, young, and thrilled to be at the center of attention; they all liked rock and roll, but also sang traditional pop songs. Whenever Dick Clark's touring live revue, the "Caravan of Stars" appeared in concert, he made sure, as he recalls, that the show "always closed with a white romantic teen idol."

By his own admission, Clark had no personal interest in music at all, never mind rock and roll. When he was booked as a guest on Edward R. Murrow's long-running *Person to Person* television show, he was told that they would want to ask about his record collection. Clark didn't have one. In a panic, as he later recalled in his memoirs, he phoned up friends in the record industry and asked them to supply him with hundreds of empty record jackets—the substance of the "collection" depicted on Murrow's national broadcast.

Despite his patent lack of interest in music, Clark had an enviable knack for capitalizing on the latest trends. He could scarcely have been in a better position to determine what these trends were. As *Billboard* reported in March 1958, the popularity of *American Bandstand* had turned Philadelphia into a mecca for music men: "Record manufacturers, music publishers, promotion men and artists flock into this city daily and the 30th Street Station of the Pennsylvania Railroad is like an annex to the Brill Building"—the symbolic nerve center of Tin Pan Alley in Manhattan. Every afternoon, the visitors converged on the WFIL studios located at 46th Street and Market, trying to hustle songs onto the *Bandstand* play list. "According to the gossip," *Billboard* reported, "Clark owns a piece of every record he plays, whether it be the artist, the copyright, the label, or even the distributor who hands him the record." As Clark himself later recalled, "it was like the early days of the movie business—there was nothing mysterious about making records, the trick was to give the teen-age record buyers what they wanted to hear."

On weekends, Clark auditioned discs at the local dances, or "hops," that he hosted, deciding whether to add new recordings to the *Bandstand* playlist. As the TV show took off, Clark shrewdly made investments in a variety of different music-related concerns, from pressing plants and publishing companies to management firms and one record label, Jamie (best known for its popular guitarist Duane Eddy—an artist relentlessly plugged by Clark). When a *Billboard* reporter in 1958 asked about the propriety of these investments, Clark shrugged the question off. "If a man knows what's good for him—what side his bread is buttered on—and he's intelligent and honest with himself, then there's nothing wrong with it at all."

It is easy to be cynical about what Dick Clark achieved, if only because *Bandstand* was a calculated ploy by a largely detached businessman. By the time he turned thirty, Clark was a millionaire—one of the first, though hardly the last, produced by the popular enthusiasm for rock and roll.

But what Clark took lightly, his audience and many of his regular performers did not. "Life could be a dream," the Chords had sung in 1954—and for more than one young person, *Bandstand* was a dream come true.

Years later, Connie Francis—the first of the female teen rock idols—recalled the moment when she first heard her recording of "Who's Sorry Now" being played on *American Bandstand:* "Well, the feeling was cosmic, just cosmic! Right there in my own living room it became Mardi Gras, kickoff at the Super Bowl. The ruckus I raised was startling enough to tear thirty-odd ravenous Italians from their mountainous portions of manicotti, and everyone knows that's no mean feat."

Even more surreal—and vicariously satisfying to the audience at home—was the fame of the show's cast of teenage regulars. Recalls former *Bandstand* dance star Ed Kelly: "The craziest part of it was that many of us became these instant celebrities, yet none of us really had any *talent*. Sure, some of us were okay dancers, and some of us were cute and acted nice on camera, but is *that* a talent that deserves getting thousands and thousands of adulatory letters each week, and getting written up in *16* and *Teen* and getting your own columns in those magazines, and having your own fan clubs across the country and getting offers from recording and film studios? Gimme a break."

Here was one key to the fascination with *Bandstand* to a kid watching at home: if Ed Kelly could make it, why not me? The *Bandstand* regulars were not children of privilege like Ricky Nelson, nor were they children of poverty like Frankie Lymon. No, the regulars on *Bandstand* were ordinary and *white,* kids little different, really, from the millions who watched at home and then dressed like the regulars, danced like the regulars, and dreamed of winning fame like the regulars (thus confirming Talcott Parsons' point about "compulsive conformity").

By producing a show that facilitated a dream of renown beyond measure or merit, Clark played a pivotal role in transforming the shared experience at the heart of rock and roll. More than a genre of popular music, it now defined a classless and ostensibly color-blind "universal form"—the product of the coldest sort of commercial calculation, true, but also embodying a not ignoble vision, of an America transformed, of Mind and Body, Black and White, dancing the same dance, moving to the same beat, as kids, en masse, joined in their own brand of Dionysian revelry, watered down and trite, but genuinely uplifting all the same.

October 21, 1957:

Jailhouse Rock

Unlike previous forms of vernacular music, from jazz and blues to gospel and country-western, rock and roll from the start was manufactured with the help of a variety of technological gimmicks, propped up with electronic prostheses, and then disseminated, in more or less controlled contexts, through every available mass medium: radio, recordings, film, television, newspapers. No matter the superficial impression some listeners had of a kind of musical anarchy, rock and roll by 1957 could scarcely have survived apart from a large and growing cast of managers, publicists, directors, arrangers, and a new breed of audio fixers, able to airbrush away almost any sonic blemish.

This mode of production transformed, in turn, the ways in which the music actually came to be made. In an earlier era, vernacular musicians had learned how to play by performing with others (even if, by the 1920s, many musicians also learned how to play by copying what they heard on recordings and on the radio). Wynonie Harris' career—from vaudeville to barnstorming—was typical of the apprenticeship served by musicians of the older generation.

But it bore no resemblance at all to the careers of many of the new rock stars. At the age of sixteen, with no previous musical experience and no claim to musical literacy other than the discriminating taste he showed in placing the coolest rockabilly recordings on a turntable, Ricky Nelson was handed fame on a platter—and this kind of story became increasingly common. Many of the young singers who first became famous on *American Bandstand*—Fabian is only the most notorious—had no real gifts, apart from moxie and a pretty face.

It didn't matter. The resources of modern recording technology were deftly deployed to dress up weak voices; and Dick Clark's practice of having his television guests mime, or "lip-synch," their songs, meant that no one on the show really had to sing: they had only to synchronize their lips to their own prerecorded vocals.

In this respect, as in so many others, Elvis Presley was a transitional figure. A singer of undeniable talent, he had never served a serious apprenticeship as a performer, never worked extensively with older and more seasoned musicians until he was nineteen and had already cut a record. It was, in part, Presley's sheer inexperience that explained the explosive freshness of his style: understanding in only the most inchoate and tentative terms the orally transmitted traditions of the forms of music that he would inherit, and renew—gospel, bel canto ballad singing, rhythm and blues—he was free to find, and elaborate, a voice that was truly his own.

By 1957, he had come of age on stage. Ironically, the better he got at performing, the less he got to do it. The problem was the tumult he now routinely provoked. "Girls screamed and hundreds of flash bulbs popped," reported the *St. Louis Post-Dispatch,* describing a show early in 1957. "Presley clung to the microphone standard and staggered about in a distinctive, distraught manner, waiting for the noise to subside a bit."

The noise rarely stopped. And the risks kept mounting. It was not so much the possibility of injury to his star that worried Colonel Parker. It was, rather, the possibility, indeed the likelihood, that sooner or later some underage girl would break through the barriers protecting his boy and entice him into performing some unspeakable act. In such an event, if the public at large, still assumed to be reflexively Puritanical, ever found out—and with the press paying close attention, it surely would—Presley's image as an eligible bachelor would be tarnished, his career possibly ruined, and so also Parker's livelihood.

Parker had cut his teeth hawking patent medicines at carnivals before he moved on to manage top country acts like Eddy Arnold and Hank Snow. His idea of industriousness was to stand outside a hall where Presley was playing and hawk glossy photos of his star at a 100 percent markup. (One wonders what he would make of the market in memorabilia surrounding a contemporary rock concert, where the sale of T-shirts and programs accounts for a huge percentage of an act's total gross.)

Behaving like a barker outside a freak show, teasing customers into paying for a quick peek, Parker jealously limited access to his attraction. He reckoned, rightly in the short run, that the less people actually saw of Elvis, the more they would want mementos bearing his likeness, which by 1957 included, besides records in Elvis picture sleeves: Elvis belts, Elvis scarves, Elvis skirts, Elvis jeans, Elvis lipstick, Elvis charm bracelets, Elvis statuettes, Elvis fan magazines, Elvis bola ties—the list of Elvis junk seemed endless. According to *Variety,* it was the largest merchandising effort ever aimed explicitly at teenagers.

But what, exactly, would keep these consumers hungry for more? For guidance, Parker, like Presley, instinctively fell back on older models, figures like Al Jolson, Bing Crosby, and Frank Sinatra—pioneers of popular singing who had sustained their careers for years.

In March of 1956, after a screen test hastily arranged just as Presley was achieving fame with "Heartbreak Hotel," Presley was signed to appear in a period potboiler set in the Civil War South, released at the end of the year under the title *Love Me Tender,* to tie in with Presley's recording of the movie's theme song of the same name. He also signed a long-term, though nonexclusive, contract with Hal Wallis—a veteran producer of films ranging from *Little Caesar* (1930) to *Casablanca* (1942), but by the Fifties a specialist in slick musical comedies with breezy plots and lots of upbeat song and dance routines. Wallis had made a fortune on his films earlier in the decade with Jerry Lewis and Dean Martin, a Presley favorite; following a similar formula, he would make equally profitable films for Presley, including his second and fourth feature films, *Loving You* (1957) and *King Creole* (1958), and also his most popular later film, *Blue Hawaii* (1961).

As Presley began to concentrate on his acting career, he cut back on live appearances. After doing well over 200 shows in 1955, and more than 100 the following year, in addition to eleven appearances on television, he did only twenty in 1957, in addition to *one* TV show—his last for several years.

For most people, the only place actually to *see* Presley—to behold his body in motion—was in a movie theater on a big screen. In effect, Parker was banking on the Hollywood pros to keep the image of Presley constantly fresh in the public mind, though he did not surrender control completely. He had refused to sign an exclusive contract with Hal Wallis because that producer's preferred approach to musical comedy risked ignoring the very things—the wildness, the sexiness, the air of sullen aggressiveness—that had gotten everyone excited about Presley in the first place.

When Presley's third feature film, *Jailhouse Rock,* was assigned to Richard Thorpe, a sixty-one-year-old veteran most renowned for cranking out his pictures on a tight schedule, the director was allowed to develop and shoot a script that played to the dark side of the Presley mystique.

In the film, Presley appears as Vince Everett, a happy-go-lucky singer stuck behind bars after punching out, and inadvertently killing, an obnoxious bully in a barroom brawl. Made callous by his experience in prison, where he is brutally whipped, the film's hero funnels his aggressive energies into his music, deciding to try a career in show business after his release. A raw talent, Everett reaches a discerning audience of teenagers, who force the music business to take him seriously—and, at the same time, allow the singer to show the heart of gold behind his tough facade.

It was the kind of film role that Presley had long coveted. "You can't be a rebel if you grin," Presley had explained to a reporter in 1956: "I've made a study of poor Jimmy Dean. I've made a study of myself, and I know why girls, at least the young 'uns, go for us. We're sullen, we're brooding, we're something of a menace."

The songs written for *Jailhouse Rock* toyed with this persona. The coveted commission to write the songs fell to Jerry Leiber and Mike Stoller. Ironically, despite Presley's global success with "Hound Dog," neither man had ever met the singer before. For that matter, neither man particularly cared for his singing. But in a six-hour burst of creativity, they got the job done. The ex-con's spiritual redemption was expressed through Leiber's lyrics for "Treat Me Nice" (in which Vince Everett comes across as truculent but vulnerable), "I Want to Be Free" (plaintive), and "(You're So Square) Baby I Don't Care" (tender and ecstatic).

The first step in making the movie was to record the key songs. Years later, in an interview with Presley's biographer, Peter Guralnick, Leiber and Stoller recalled their surprise when they finally met Elvis at the soundtrack recording sessions on April 30, 1957. "We thought we were the only two white kids who knew anything about the blues," Stoller said. "We thought he was like an idiot savant," agreed Leiber, "but he listened a lot. He knew all of our records."

Even more surprising to Stoller was Presley's relaxed approach in the studio: "The thing that really surprised us was that there was no clock"—a harbinger of things to come. Instead of banging out a series of takes with professional precision, Presley loosened up with gospel songs, experimented with different arrangements, and patiently ran through new material in the studio, looking for the right song, the right sound, the right feel. By the standards of journeymen like Wynonie Harris or Fats Domino, Presley was a bumbling amateur, making up his music as he went along. Thanks to the unprecedented scale of his popularity, Presley was able to do just that, working to his own clock, and setting a precedent for other popular rock stars, forced by the limits of their talent and experience to grope uncertainly toward a satisfying performance, letting free time, intuition, and sheer luck take the place of seasoned musicianship.

There is a scene in *Jailhouse Rock* that deliberately echoes what had first happened to Elvis in 1954 at the Sun studios in Memphis: the sudden, accidental discovery of a God-given gift for song. But the secret of Vince Everett's metamorphosis—and also of Elvis Presley's cultural balancing act—was perhaps best conveyed in the film's big production number, an intricately choreographed performance of "Jailhouse Rock," Leiber and Stoller's title song. The lyrics are droll, even faintly mocking (not unlike "Riot in Cell Block #9," the song skit that Leiber and Stoller turned into a 1954 hit for the Robins, the vocal group that eventually became the Coasters). And the staging of the song underlined its satiric detachment. Working in front of a skeletal set evoking two levels of cell blocks, Elvis improvised a series of moves that were elaborated and amplified by a large cast of professional dancers. Spontaneous in feel, spectacular in execution, the film's treatment of "Jailhouse Rock" validates rock and roll on something close to its original terms, while at the same time integrating its aura of menace into a classical piece of Hollywood stagecraft.

Jailhouse Rock premiered on October 21, 1957, at a time when the teen music marketplace was clogged with imitations of the kinder, gentler Elvis on display in *Love Me Tender* and *Loving You*. But when smartly wrapped up in a package like *Jailhouse Rock*, even images of sullen youth could be highly rewarding. Elvis Presley figured in three of the top twenty films of 1957: *Love Me Tender* (number ten, originally released in November 1956, grossing a cumulative $4.5 million at the box office), *Loving You* (number nineteen, released in July 1957, grossing $3.7 million), and *Jailhouse Rock* (number fifteen, grossing $3.7 million by the end of the year). Low-budget films like *Rock, Pretty Baby; Don't Knock the Rock;* and *Rock, Rock, Rock!* also returned handsome profits.

By 1958, the long-term implications of these facts were just beginning to dawn on filmmakers. The taste of kids was going to play a large role in calling the shots in Hollywood, as it already did on Tin Pan Alley. A front page headline in *Variety* put it this way: "Film Future: GI Baby Boom." One of the experts that *Variety* quoted, Arno H. Johnson, vice president and senior economist for the J. Walter Thompson Company, predicted that "the growth of the 'teen market' is bound to make itself felt in many areas, but nowhere is it of greater significance than in the film field, both in terms of audience potential and as a guide to motion picture content. Not only are these the future homemakers, but they represent the 'restless' element of the population, the people who don't want to stay home and watch TV and who are still immune to any sophisticated disdain of run-of-the-mill screen offerings."

In other words, kids wouldn't care about a crappy film, they wouldn't know any better (being immune to "sophisticated disdain"—a great way to describe the discerning exercise of judgment).

But Mr. Johnson was right. And thanks to the mind-boggling mediocrity of almost all of his highly profitable films, Elvis Presley not only squandered the best years of his creative life on drivel and kitsch—he also can take credit for accelerating what one historian has aptly called "the juvenilization of American movies," from *Blackboard Jungle* to *Star Wars,* and beyond.

October 15, 1958:

"Lonely Teardrops"

For African-Americans in the pop music business, the Fifties in the United States were the best and the worst of times. The market for pop music performed by black musicians had never been bigger. But it was a bitter fact that rock and roll, originally just one more euphemism for black music, had quickly become a label applied largely to stars who were white, teenaged, and often untalented, while performers who were black, mature, and often richly gifted were left languishing on the threshold of rock and roll stardom, making money, certainly, sometimes quite a lot of it, and enjoying a measure of fame, too, but rarely earning the kind of lucrative adulation showered on Elvis and Ricky Nelson. One indication of the new pop pantheon and its racial composition is the pitifully small number of recordings by black artists to reach the top of the *Billboard* pop charts at the dawn of the so-called rock and roll era, from the start of 1955 to the end of 1958. There were only six: three by the most successful vocal group of the era, the Platters ("The Great Pretender" and "My Prayer" in 1956, "Twilight Time" in 1958); one by Sam Cooke ("You Send Me" in 1957); one by Johnny Mathis ("Chances Are," 1957); and one by Tommy Edwards ("It's All in the Game," 1958).

Still, change was in the air, and not only in the world of popular music. Under the pressure of a gathering protest movement, galvanized, in part, by a 1954 Supreme Court ruling that segregated institutions were unconstitutional, America's complex and subtle version of apartheid was under assault as never before. And in show business itself, after decades of slow but steady integration made possible by the popularity of black minstrelsy, vaudeville, ragtime, blues, and jazz, and led by enterprising innovators like Bert Williams, Eubie Blake, W.C. Handy, James Reese Europe, Ethel Waters, Bessie Smith, Louis Armstrong, Duke Ellington, the Mills Brothers, Cab Calloway, Count Basie, Billie Holiday, Ella Fitzgerald, Lionel Hampton, the Ink Spots, Louis Jordan, Nat Cole, Dizzy Gillespie, and Miles Davis, black musical artists were visible as never before, despite the forms of racial discrimination that still existed.

In 1956, Nat "King" Cole became the first African-American to headline a TV network variety series, *The Nat "King" Cole Show*, which ran through 1957. In these years, Cole loomed large as a model for black musicians who wanted to cross over, and win mainstream acceptance from the larger white public. Like Bing Crosby and Frank Sinatra, Cole was a versatile entertainer, willing to smile and clown, but unwilling to suppress his native intelligence. First renowned for his enviably soft touch as an improvising pianist, he played beautifully with jazz giants like Lester Young, the tenor saxophonist. With his trio in the Forties, he invented a fleet form of jump blues, which he played and sang with finesse as well as good humor. By the start of the Fifties, he had made the transition to pop singing, delivering definitive renditions of classic songs as different (and as harmonically demanding) as "Stardust" by Hoagy Carmichael and "Lush Life" by Billy Strayhorn. Cole's mere presence on television, like his life in Hollywood, was proof positive that popular music offered one way for black people to fulfill a classic American dream: by dint of talent and hard work, to strike it rich.

In the fall of 1958, a young black songwriter named Berry Gordy, Jr., was nursing a dream of his own. A native of Detroit and onetime boxer, Gordy, then twenty-nine, already had a couple of hit songs to his credit. His father was a successful small businessman who had honored the patron saint of black enterprise by opening a Booker T. Washington Grocery Store; in addition, he had operated plastering, carpentry, and printing businesses. But unlike his older siblings, Berry Jr. had refused to help his father with the family businesses. An avid jazz fan, he kept looking for ways to exploit his love of music. In 1953, he opened a record shop dedicated to jazz, the 3-D Record Mart, a venture that failed two years later, in part because the vogue for rhythm and blues and rock and roll had all but destroyed the local market for jazz.

Finding a salaried job on one of Ford's assembly lines, Gordy nurtured his musical ambitions by composing pop ditties while bolting chrome onto luxury cars. He had read in a magazine that "you could get your songs written up on sheet music by paying $25," he recalled in a later interview. "I got a song of mine written up called 'You Are You.' I had been inspired very much by seeing a movie with Danny Thomas. . . . Doris Day was in it, and I wrote this song for Doris Day after seeing the movie."

Gordy never did get a song to Doris Day. But he did get one of his songs to Jackie Wilson, a virtuoso vocalist and Detroit native who was also a former boxer. In 1957, when Gordy first met him, Wilson was twenty-three years old, and hoping to launch a new career as a solo artist. Though he had cut his teeth on church music, and had a mesmerizing approach to singing rhythm and blues, he cared most of all about delivering the most wrenching imaginable version of "Danny Boy," a song that he featured for years as a showstopper in his live act (he also recorded the song no fewer than three times). An unabashed showman, Wilson wowed crowds with his operatic range, his acrobatic dance steps, and his flirtatious stage manner. After every show, his manager would line up ladies outside his dressing room, and then lead them in one by one to meet the star. "Wilson would kiss all the women, especially the ugly ones," one witness marveled years later, "because he knew if he did they'd be with him forever."

Wilson had broken into show business as a singer with a vocal group, the Dominoes. The group recorded for Syd Nathan, and at first featured Clyde McPhatter on vocals. Though the Dominoes had topped the *Billboard* rhythm and blues charts in 1951 with the bawdy "Sixty Minute Man," the group's leader and chief arranger, Billy Ward, was a schooled musician with refined taste: recording risqué blues was not his recipe for long-term success. And as soon as he could, Ward broke away from Nathan's vulgar formulas.

Taking Wilson under his wing as a replacement for McPhatter when he left the Dominoes to go solo, Ward appreciated the hybrid nature of his new protégé's gifts. He steered Wilson toward impassioned, pseudo-operatic renditions of current pop hits. In 1953, a cover version of Tony Bennett's "Rags to Riches" that featured Wilson at his most florid reached number two on the *Billboard* rhythm and blues charts; but Ward still longed to find some way for the Dominoes to make the big leap, from inner-city venues to mainstream respectability.

Leaving the King label, Ward moved with Wilson to Decca, a major record label, where the Dominoes recorded a lachrymose version of "St. Therese of the Roses" with orchestral accompaniment. In 1956, this recording became the biggest hit yet for Ward and the Wilson-led Dominoes, crossing over to the pop audience, and eventually reaching number thirteen on the *Billboard* chart of pop best-sellers.

By that fall, when Ward and his group played Las Vegas, Wilson had worked up a medley to honor the pop singing sensation of the hour, and one of Wilson's new favorites: Elvis Presley. As it happens, Presley, in Vegas on vacation, caught Wilson's act—and was so impressed that he went back to hear him four nights in a row. (In December 1956, Elvis, in an impromptu recording session at the Sun studios horsing around with Carl Perkins and Jerry Lee Lewis, can be heard imitating Jackie Wilson imitating himself singing "Don't Be Cruel"—an imitation that he, in turn, would incorporate into his rendition of the song on *The Ed Sullivan Show* in January of 1957.)

It was shortly after his stay in Las Vegas that Wilson met Berry Gordy, and selected one of his songs, "Reet Petite," for his first solo recording session, for the Brunswick label, a subsidiary of Decca. Written in a stuttering, stop-and-start style, Gordy's song recalled "Don't Be Cruel" and "All Shook Up," two Presley hits written by another black songwriter, Otis Blackwell. As if to underline the connections, Wilson turned his recording of "Reet Petite" into a virtual parody of Elvis Presley's vocal mannerisms; but he executed them so brilliantly, with such pleasure and finesse, that one can only share in the singer's obvious delight. In later years, Wilson made no bones about his debt: "I'd have to say I got as much from Elvis as he got from me."

On October 4, 1957, shortly after "Reet Petite" had been released, Wilson became one of the first black artists to be featured by Dick Clark on *American Bandstand*. If Clark was right—if rock and roll had in fact become "the basic form of American popular music"—then aspiring pop stars like Wilson would need to tailor their music to the teenage audience for *American Bandstand*. It was Berry Gordy's genius to sense what types of songs this audience would buy. Along with a handful of other black songwriters—Otis Blackwell, Chuck Berry, and Sam Cooke were the most important—Gordy worked at delivering a musical product that would reflect "the sound of Young America," as the motto of his Motown record label later put it.

Gordy and his black songwriting peers came at the challenge of rock songwriting from an angle opposite to that of self-styled white hipsters like Jerry Leiber and Mike Stoller. While Leiber and Stoller prized blues feeling, street-smart lyrics, and a gritty vocal delivery, Gordy aimed to make music that could pass for white. (It is no wonder that when Leiber and Stoller first heard Gordy's music, they were unimpressed. "At first we thought it was white bread," Leiber has recalled. "We said, 'Man, those are white teenage stories. What does that have to do with black culture?' ")

Throughout 1958, Jackie Wilson was the main vehicle of Gordy's ambition. Working with his older sister Gwen and her boyfriend Roquel "Billy" Davis (who published under the exotic and faintly swashbuckling nom de plume Tyran Carlo), Gordy honed his lyrics to express a certain "teen feel," that necessary but ineffable ingredient in most successful rock and roll hits. The crafting of such songs was a new game, with only a few serious players in these early years. In New York City, often working on Tin Pan Alley in, or near, the Brill Building, there were a handful of young, mostly white composers catering to the same market, led by Bobby Darin ("Splish Splash," 1958), Doc Pomus and Mort Shuman ("Teenager in Love," 1959), and Neil Sedaka ("Oh! Carol," 1959), who were joined later by Carole King and Gerry Goffin ("Will You Still Love Me Tomorrow," 1960), and Barry Mann and Cynthia Weil ("Uptown," 1962). The trick was to draft a sketch for a *record,* not just a song, making the lyrics simple and the melody instantly memorable, leaving plenty of room for the musicians, singers, and in-studio technicians to improvise an apt signature sound for the final recorded product. As Gordy came to appreciate, "Reet Petite" had been simultaneously too hip and too square: its lyrics were rife with street slang that a great many white teens couldn't fathom, while the brassy sound of its big-band arrangement was a throwback to swing-era conventions. (By the Nineties, the problem of translating ghetto English into a form fathomable to white teens had long since vanished, the last obstacles having been removed by the international vogue for rap and hip-hop.)

Gordy followed "Reet Petite" with "To Be Loved," a keening ballad, sung by Wilson with stirring passion and arranged by his record label's pop-oriented conductor with bombastic precision. Still, it was only on his fifth song for Wilson that Gordy finally found the formula he would exploit for the next decade, producing an unprecedented series of best-selling records with a variety of different black artists. Recorded on October 15, 1958, the song was called "Lonely Teardrops." It became Jackie Wilson's signature—and Berry Gordy's passport to a long and lucrative career in pop music.

It was recorded at the first of Wilson's sessions to be supervised directly by Gordy and Roquel Davis—and as one witness later recalled, jaws dropped when the featured artist sauntered into the Detroit studio. The local players had never seen anyone like Wilson, as one witness later recalled: "What a sight: His perfected 'do and his shimmering shirt unbuttoned to the navel. Diamond rings and gold chains. Major flash and personality."

Mining the same vein of adolescent self-pity expressed by "Heartbreak Hotel," Gordy's lyrics for "Lonely Teardrops" were almost a parody of "teen feel." On the demo (a reference recording, to show what the song should sound like), Gordy's friend Eddie Holland (later renowned as a songwriter in his own right) had sung the words slowly, with bluesy emphasis. As Gordy and the musicians worked together with Wilson in the studio, the tempo of the arrangement picked up. A white vocal group improvised a perky introduction, chanting "shooby-doo-wop" and also adding an ersatz gospel-style answering vocal on the chorus: "say you will." The accompaniment was sparse: just a rhythm section, beefed up with a baritone saxophone and a banging tambourine, to add bottom and brightness— two hallmarks of Gordy's later productions. The upbeat arrangement was designed to exploit one of the latest dance fads being pushed by Dick Clark on *American Bandstand,* something called the "cha-lypso," a kind of cha-cha done to a modified calypso beat. The musical foundation was relatively simple, and it left plenty of room for Wilson to show off his full range of vocal tricks. Dick Jacobs, his A&R man in these years at the Brunswick label, described the final effect accurately: "Jackie Wilson opened his mouth and out poured that sound like honey on moonbeams, and it was like the whole room shifted on some weird axis."

"Lonely Teardrops" was the first in a series of top ten hits for Jackie Wilson. For several years, he enjoyed success as a teen idol marketed to the *Bandstand* crowd. His live shows became legendary, inspiring the stagecraft of Michael Jackson, among others.

Berry Gordy, by contrast, walked away from "Lonely Teardrops" determined to make his mark in the music business in some more profitable way. With "Lonely Teardrops" on top of the charts, Gordy was still broke: Wilson's white manager, Nat Tarnapol, had cut himself the lion's share of the song-publishing royalties, robbing Gordy of income.

Gordy resolved to start his own record company. His parents after all had long preached the gospel of self-reliance according to Booker T. Washington: work hard, make a better product, and people will buy it. He would make a better product—and keep the profits for himself.

In his memoirs, Gordy includes a telling passage about his thinking in these crucial months. "I realized this was not just about good or bad records," he writes, "this was about race. In the music business there had long been the distinction between black and white music, the assumption being that R&B was black and Pop was white. But with Rock 'n' Roll and the explosion of Elvis those clear distinctions began to get fuzzy. Elvis was a white artist who sang black music. What was it? (a) R&B, (b) Country, (c) Pop, (d) Rock 'n' Roll or (e) none of the above." Gordy's answer to his own quiz is unequivocal, and mildly surprising: after Elvis, argued Gordy, if a record sold a million copies, it was "Pop," period, and never mind the old distinctions between black and white: " 'Pop' means popular and if it ain't that, I don't know what is. I never gave a damn what else it was called."

In the months that followed, Gordy formed a family of corporations, and took dead aim at the teen market that Dick Clark had demonstrated was one place to sell a million copies of a record. The names of Gordy's labels—Motown, Tamla, Gordy, Soul—would, in time, become synonymous with American pop. A generation of white kids would grow up dancing to the records that Gordy made, and a generation of young black musicians such as Smokey Robinson, Mary Wells, Marvin Gaye, Diana Ross, David Ruffin, Martha Reeves, and Michael Jackson would all learn from a master how to follow in the footsteps of Jackie Wilson—the first of the black teen idols.

November 22, 1959:

Payola

What came to be known as "the payola scandal" summed up the paradoxical status in America of rock and roll as the Fifties drew to a close. The rise of rock had created a booming new market for pop music. But the resistance to the style remained fierce, not least from critics inside the music industry.

Tin Pan Alley professionals had cause to worry. Under the new musical dispensation, there was no need for arrangers, orchestras, conductors, schooled players who could read music; there was scarcely a market anymore for sheet music, once the backbone of the music business; and there was certainly no demand for old-fashioned pop singers, who usually lacked the immunity to standards of musical taste essential to carry off a convincing rendition of a typical rock and roll tune. For just this reason, the legendary *Lucky Strike Hit Parade,* a staple on radio and television since 1935, was canceled in the spring of 1959.

At the same time, unease about the vices of the new music ebbed and flowed alongside anxiety over the fate of America's still growing mass of teenagers. With the Cold War at its height, a diffuse but widely shared sense of moral crisis was deepened by fears that the national culture was vulnerable to sabotage. Government officials worried publicly about Communist infiltration; and in cities and towns, citizens mobilized to prevent the addition of fluoride to local water supplies. It was in this context—of pandemic paranoia about secret plots to poison the public—that rumors, adroitly manipulated by the old-guard American Society of Composers, Authors and Publishers (ASCAP), began to spread about "payola," the practice of giving a disc jockey money or gifts in exchange for playing a record. By associating rock and roll with corrupt business practices, the rumors suggested that a shadowy conspiracy lay behind its otherwise inexplicable popularity.

At first, the rumors were largely confined to the music industry, as ASCAP waged a turf war with its upstart rival, Broadcast Music Incorporated (BMI), a competing trade association (and collection agency) for composers and music publishers that, not coincidentally, had cornered most of the writers active in the fields of country-western, rhythm and blues, and rock and roll. When the rest of America finally heard the allegations, the news came as a shock. On November 22, 1959, *The New York Times* carried the headline on page one: "Alan Freed Is Out in 'Payola' Study."

The day before, the man who had popularized the term "rock and roll" had been fired from his job as a disc jockey for WABC radio after refusing to sign a statement that he had never taken money or gifts to promote a record. And this was just the start of Freed's troubles. The next day, Freed lost his job as host of the television show *The Big Beat.* Two days later, he was served with a subpoena issued by the New York district attorney. Shortly afterward, congressional investigators called Freed and several other prominent rock disc jockeys, including Dick Clark, to testify the following spring before a House Commerce subcommittee investigating corrupt practices in the music industry.

The symbolism of a subcommittee hearing was hard to miss. The 1950s had begun with a witch hunt conducted by Senator Joseph McCarthy, who adroitly used the powers of Congress to subpoena and publicly grill a variety of suspected subversives, in the process ruining lives and wrecking careers. More recently, Congress had conducted a highly publicized probe into the rigging of certain television quiz shows (including *The $64,000 Question*), destroying still more reputations—and placing the mass media and its impact on the nation's moral fiber at the top of the cultural agenda.

In November of 1959, as the congressional hearings on the quiz show scandals wound down and the latest allegations about payola in rock and roll spread, John Steinbeck, a cranky populist tribune and the revered author of *The Grapes of Wrath*, addressed a jeremiad to the nation's leading liberal, Adlai Stevenson, a two-time Democratic presidential candidate. "HAVE WE GONE SOFT?" Steinbeck angrily asked in his open letter. "If I wanted to destroy a nation I would give it too much and I would have it on its knees, miserable, greedy, and sick . . . on all levels, American society is rigged. . . . I am troubled by the cynical immorality of my country. It cannot survive on this basis."

Perhaps not. But America's music business had not only survived, it had flourished in an atmosphere of generalized greed and bribery. The "rigging" of publicity for a song in exchange for cash or gifts was a practice dating back to the 1890s, when the unprecedented sales of the sheet music for Charles Harris' ballad "After the Ball"— more than five million copies were sold—revealed that the mass-marketing of music could be a very lucrative business. By the 1930s, it was customary for so-called song pluggers to pay for the debut radio performance of a song, and also for the song publisher to foot the bill for a debut recording. Star vocalists and bandleaders routinely cut deals with the song publishers to share the boodle. The pluggers became adept at selling songs, giving gifts, and doing favors, like picking up the tab for a band's arrangements. In 1935, fearful that envelopes stuffed with cash were replacing the personal touch, pluggers in America even formed a fraternal organization, called Professional Music Men.

It was thus business as usual on Tin Pan Alley when Alan Freed, after arriving in New York in 1954, began to ask for, and receive, publishing credits, cash, and various gratuities. A nonchalant paragon of "cynical immorality" (to borrow Steinbeck's phrase), Freed was so deeply imbued with the ethos of the industry that he didn't have the faintest idea what the uproar over payola was all about. On Saturday, November 28, 1959, when he arrived at the WNEW television studios for the final broadcast of his *Big Beat* show, Freed was mobbed by reporters and sobbing teenagers. After comforting his fans ("Now don't cry"), he talked to the press. Payola "may stink but it's here and I didn't start it," he remarked. He saw nothing wrong, he said, with taking money from aspiring artists in return for giving them airtime. He saw no harm in getting paid for services rendered as a consultant to record labels. Nor did he see any problem with accepting a gift, "whether it ranged from a bottle of whiskey to a Cadillac." Once, he recalled nostalgically, "a man said to me, 'If somebody sent you a Cadillac, would you send it back?' I said, 'It depends on the color.'"

For the grand finale of *The Big Beat,* Freed invited a number of old cronies and veteran song pluggers to join him in front of the cameras. They presented Freed with a scroll, stating their appreciation for his friendship. He shrugged: "Payola, payola, that's all we've been hearing. These are the nicest guys in the business."

It is symptomatic of their respective personalities that Dick Clark, in a similar jam, behaved completely differently. The same week that Freed was summarily fired from WABC radio and also lost his *Big Beat* television show, the ABC network gave Clark a choice: either give up his outside interests in the music industry, or lose *American Bandstand.* Clark hardly skipped a beat: he gave up his outside interests.

He was giving up a lot. By then, he had a financial stake in several music publishers, a record-pressing plant, an artist management firm, and three record companies. He owned several song copyrights. He had a share in a toy company that made a stuffed cat that could spin 45 rpm discs, the Platter-Puss.

In a way that Alan Freed's career never had, Dick Clark's position hinged on his personification of mainstream American values. For the past year, he had written a weekly newspaper column, offering advice to teenagers, retailing prim maxims and platitudes. If his image of integrity were successfully impugned, he would lose one of his most bankable assets.

With his reputation on the line, Clark seized the initiative in a prepared statement that he delivered before the congressional subcommittee on April 29, 1960. Acknowledging the outside financial interests he had so assiduously cultivated in his three years as host of *American Bandstand,* Clark explained that he had been hedging his bets, prudently aware that "television can be an extraordinarily fickle medium." Handed "a unique opportunity"—to turn his "expert knowledge" of popular taste into a steady source of income— Clark had only done what any red-blooded American would have done under the same circumstances. It seemed unjust to cast aspersions on an entrepreneur who, having "followed normal business practices under the ground rules that then existed," was remarkable only for his acumen and good judgment. "I was surprised to learn," said Clark sweetly, "that some people were apparently shocked to hear that I made 30-some thousand dollars from a $125 investment in Jamie records. Believe me, this is not as unusual as it may seem. The music industry is the only business I have any personal knowledge of where a man can invest less than $500 and profit by as much as $50,000 to $100,000 from one single record. . . . I think this probably explains why there are over 2,000 record companies in existence."

Clark implied that the congressmen should praise, not bury him. After all, as he reminded the subcommittee, by broadcasting *American Bandstand,* he was performing an important public service: "I seek to provide wholesome recreational outlets for these youngsters whom I think I know and understand." Still, Clark in his concluding remarks went out of his way to be conciliatory: If, after gathering its evidence, Congress wanted to create new ethical standards for the music business, "I am glad to have participated."

By the time the public outcry over payola had died down, Dick Clark had secured his fortune and his future, while Alan Freed was a broken man. (He died in 1965 of medical complications caused by years of heavy drinking.)

But even before Freed was laid to rest, a revealing metamorphosis had occurred. Among serious rock fans, Clark became a figure of fun. A sharp salesman, he was thought to epitomize a commercial ethos that was somehow alien to rock and roll (a claim that required a heroic suspension of disbelief, combined with an ignorance of the historical facts).

In disgrace, Alan Freed, by contrast, loomed larger than ever. He became a martyr, a mythic hero. Tough, cynical, worldly, unafraid to throw his weight around, he represented for some an ideal way to do business. And it was Freed's ethos, of the vulgar outlaw, that would for better or worse mark the music's distinctive moral economy, inspiring a number of wayward disciples, from the producer Phil Spector to the British manager Andrew Loog Oldham, who taught the Rolling Stones how to turn buccaneering behavior into a badge of cultural honor—another lasting legacy of the rock and roll revolution.

May 12, 1960:

Elvis Comes Home

The symbolism alone left an impression (however mis-leading) of historic moment. The "Sultan of Swoon" and the "King of Rock 'n' Roll." Sinatra and Presley. Two generations of pop music royalty, on stage together!

They had never met before; they would never share a stage again. They had little in common, either culturally or musically. But the commercial logic of a joint television appearance had been irresistible, particularly to Sinatra, who used the occasion of a TV special to welcome Presley back to America after his two years of military service at a base in West Germany.

At the age of forty-four, Sinatra was a musical colossus who towered over his peers, epitomizing a great tradition by offering nonpareil renditions of songs that, in his hands, became canonic. Implicitly commenting on the paucity of good new popular music, he drew most of his repertoire from the Broadway shows, movie musicals, and Tin Pan Alley tunes composed between 1925 and 1950 by the likes of George Gershwin, Jerome Kern, Cole Porter, and Rodgers and Hart, all giants of the musical theater, America's distinctively hybrid form of light opera and musical comedy mixed with minstrelsy.

The twenty-five-year-old Presley, by contrast, despite selling a great many more records than Sinatra since 1956, had yet to prove his mettle as an all-round entertainer worthy of appearing in the same ring with the old master. (Presley also had a more intangible disadvantage. At the time, he lacked the aura of supernatural grace created by undergoing a media ritual of death and resurrection; he was too young to have experienced the kind of early fame, sorry decline, and midlife renaissance that Sinatra had already undergone— and that Presley, too, would capitalize on after 1968.)

The Sinatra special marked Presley's first live public appearance in nearly three years. Since being drafted into the army in the fall of 1958, he had not been able to make any new films or recordings. The Sinatra television special would be the American public's first indication of whether the King still ruled his Kingdom or whether he'd lost ground to rivals like Ricky Nelson.

In the context of the continuing uproar over payola, the show took on added significance. In the minds of many, rock and roll now had a taint of corruption. The luster of early stars like Frankie Lymon and Carl Perkins had badly faded. By 1960, Little Richard had retired from secular music to sing gospel, and Chuck Berry, convicted on a morals charge, was in jail. Though rock and roll now effectively functioned as the basic form of American popular music, this was not an outcome welcomed by Sinatra or the best singers of his generation. Its long-term prospects as a distinctive musical idiom were by no means clear.

As the date of Presley's discharge from the army approached, the press was filled with feature stories and contests keyed to Presley and his return. Although Presley had yet to record any new songs, his label, RCA Victor, received advance orders for one million copies of his next recording, whatever it was and whenever it might appear.

On March 3, 1960, the plane flying Presley home landed at Fort Dix in New Jersey. On March 6, he was officially discharged from the army. A limousine whisked him from the base. A few hours later, he embarked on a train trip back home to Memphis. Recording studios were booked and a script was readied for a new film, *G.I. Blues*. And arrangements were finalized for Presley's appearance on Sinatra's TV special.

If nothing else, the summit meeting demonstrated how money, when combined with the prospect of an attentive mass public, could sweep aside a declared commitment to preserving the good, the true, and the beautiful. Only a few years earlier, after all, Frank Sinatra had denounced Elvis Presley and everything he stood for. "His kind of music is deplorable, a rancid-smelling aphrodisiac," declared Sinatra.

There was some irony in this stance. As a crooner in the Forties, Sinatra had earned his sobriquet by concocting a musical aphrodisiac of his own, sending bobby-soxers into swoons of ecstasy. Still, Sinatra was unimpressed by (or unaware of) the similarities between Presley's early career and his own. The music itself, in its aggressive simplicity, left him aghast. "It fosters almost totally negative and destructive reactions in young people," he pontificated in a magazine article about rock and roll in 1957. "It is sung, played and written for the most part by cretinous goons."

Cretinous goons were presumably bad—but the promise of high television ratings was obviously good. By the spring of 1960, Sinatra had established his stature as a singer of classic popular songs; he had also established himself as a box office draw in Hollywood; but there was one medium he had yet to conquer, despite trying, and that was television. With much fanfare, he had signed a three-year, $3 million contract with ABC-TV in 1957. But the results had been disappointing. A weekly *Frank Sinatra Show,* which aired in the 1957–1958 season, was a dud. After that series was canceled, ABC tried to recoup its investment by airing periodic specials hosted by Sinatra. But these, too, had been flops.

At the time, Sinatra's longtime associate, songwriter Sammy Cahn, told *The New York Times* that Sinatra was determined to make a splash on television. Money was no object. He recalled sitting with Sinatra one day, "wondering about the next show. Suddenly, out of left field, Frank said, 'What about Elvis Presley?' "

The effective answer to that question, of course, depended neither on Sinatra nor Presley himself, but rather on Presley's domineering manager, Colonel Tom Parker. Eager though Parker was to get his client back in the public eye, he wasn't about to sell his boy cheap. For three songs and six minutes of his time, he insisted, Elvis would cost $125,000. Presley's fee—the largest yet for a guest appearance on television—prompted Sammy Cahn to quip that "you should make in a year what Frank is losing on this show."

The show was taped on March 26 in Miami, in the Ballroom at the Hotel Fontainebleau, where Sinatra was currently performing. For moral and musical support Sinatra had invited Joey Bishop, Peter Lawford, and Sammy Davis, Jr. On Presley's behalf, the Colonel had demanded 400 tickets to the event; on the day of the taping, he convened a meeting of Presley fan clubs to give the tickets away.

As the time for the taping drew near, the hotel lobby was filled with blasé socialites awkwardly rubbing shoulders with starry-eyed rock fans on a mission, casing the joint, looking for ways to crash through the cordon of guards and policemen assigned to protect their King. By the time the throng was admitted to the Ballroom, the Elvis fans were in a frenzy. When their hero made his entrance in an army uniform, the screams began.

The format was simple. Elvis would be welcomed home by Sinatra and his Rat Pack. He, in turn, would sing both sides of his long-awaited new recording, "Stuck on You" and "Fame and Fortune." Sinatra and friends would then bring Elvis up to date on what he'd missed while he was away—this turned out to include a lot of songs that they'd made famous. For a grand finale, there would be a duet with Sinatra and Presley in formal attire.

The duet revolved around a gimmick. Each man would sing one of the other's signature songs in his own signature style. Nelson Riddle's orchestra provided sleek, swinging support to Sinatra on "Love Me Tender." Presley, by contrast, was forced to groan his way through a cheesy arrangement of "Witchcraft," complete with piano triplets—still the simplest way to turn any song into "rock and roll."

As an exercise in musical humiliation, this was just about perfect. Presley sounded lost. Not that his fan club cared: every time he groped for a note, they screamed and moaned.

As a piece of family entertainment, on the other hand, the show was hard to fault. It was easygoing, tongue-in-cheek, and utterly forgettable—just the sort vacuous variety show that Elvis had inadvertently disrupted four years before with his gyrating, striptease send-up of "Hound Dog" on *The Milton Berle Show.*

Shortly after the taping, Sinatra and Presley both headed into recording sessions. Sinatra produced *Nice 'n' Easy,* by no means his finest album, but a very good one that became the biggest hit of his long career, remaining at number one during a nine-week run that was rivaled only by Presley's concurrently popular soundtrack album for the film *G.I. Blues.*

Presley, for his part, returned to Nashville on April 3 to cut a new batch of songs, twelve in all. It was, perhaps, the single most remarkable recording session of his career.

In the studio, surrounded by familiar musicians—Scotty Moore on guitar, Floyd Cramer on piano, D.J. Fontana on drums, the Jordanaires on harmony vocals—Elvis staked his own claim to his own version of the American popular songbook, moving with ease from old-fashioned ballads to raw country blues, even demonstrating his mastery of romantic schmaltz.

His repertoire included not just the up-tempo rhythm and blues of Clyde McPhatter's "Such a Night," but also a beautifully earnest rendition of "I Will Be Home Again," a sentimental ballad by the Golden Gate Quartet from the Forties, and an equally earnest version of "Are You Lonesome To-night?," a song made popular in 1927 by Vaughn Deleath (the first woman to sing on radio) and by Henry Burr (a balladeer who had made his first recordings in 1903).

The session's high point was even more improbable. Several months before, Freddy Bienstock, a representative of the music publishing house Hill & Range, had overheard Presley singing "There's No Tomorrow," an English language version of "O Sole Mio" made popular in 1950 by Tony Martin. In order to secure the publishing rights for his own company (which had invested in Presley, and had a claim on his repertoire), Bienstock commissioned a new set of lyrics, using the old Neapolitan melody as the basis for "It's Now or Never."

In the course of this marathon dusk-to-dawn session, Presley had already sung raunchy rhythm and blues, and sweetly crooned treacly ballads. But singing "It's Now or Never," he reached for, and hit, a new level of melodramatic intensity in his music, nailing every high note, summoning an impassioned persona and an operatic range to rival the most perfervid pop arias of a Mario Lanza (never mind Jackie Wilson or Tony Martin).

But what did it all mean, this warm embrace of the maudlin by the once and future King of Rock and Roll?

Despite the breathtaking virtuosity of Presley's rendition of "It's Now or Never," his recording lacked the subtlety, class—the sheer musicality—that graced the Sinatra session that produced *Nice 'n' Easy*. In some ways, Presley was more of an anachronism than Sinatra himself. "Are You Lonesome To-night?" was a throwback to the kind of bathetic ballad singing perfected by Al Jolson.

The paradox went deeper still. Elvis Presley sounded *at home* with these two songs. The lyrics were corny; the singer's commitment was tangible.

His easy identification with the most old-fashioned of the pop songs offered a telling contrast to the way he approached his blues material. Unlike Sinatra, Presley had a feel for down-home blues. He loved to listen to the music, and ever since Sam Phillips had suggested that he sing it, it had formed a part of his musical birthright. But Elvis never quite shed the old edge— of anxiety, of nervous energy, of tittering raunchiness—that had marked even his first, exhilarating blues records for Sun five years before.

Take "Reconsider Baby," a performance that is often cited as a high point of Presley's April 3 session. The song had been composed, and first recorded, by the jump blues singer and guitarist Lowell Fulson in 1954, in a rendition that beautifully joined jagged electric guitar fills and Fulson's smooth vocal delivery with accompaniment from a tight combo that featured saxophonist Choker Campbell (whom Berry Gordy would later employ to lead the road band for Motown's touring shows).

Presley's version was cut at the end of the all-night marathon session. Compared to Fulson's tight jump band, Presley's pickers sound stiff, wooden, tired enough to coast on blues mannerisms.

Employing the hoarsest of his protean voices, Presley sings with obvious affection. He plays with the lyrics the way he toyed with "Hound Dog." But he's *outside* this music, not inside the way he was a few hours earlier, when he recorded "It's Now or Never." And when Elvis mutters, "Play the blues, boys," the performance teeters on the brink of parody—the kind of unconscious parody that would become all too familiar from the *faux* passion of later white blues rockers.

As a new decade began, the once and future King of Rock and Roll was thus glorying in the range of his musical gifts, belting out good-natured blues and bombastic ballads. Even more striking, his heart was in the ballads.

If Elvis was the King, then this new music must be a part of his Kingdom. But if "Are You Lonesome To-night?" and "It's Now or Never" were now to be regarded as rock and roll, one might well wonder what, if anything, distinguished Presley's new music from old-fashioned pop.

In 1960, an honest answer might have been: very little.

4

Glad All Over

Brian Epstein Enters the Cavern

At the peak of his fame, writing his memoirs in 1964, Brian Epstein, the provincial impresario whose unswerving faith in his musical ministry had helped turn Liverpool, England, into the promised land for style-conscious teenagers everywhere, recounted the epiphany that changed his life—and also the world (such being the newfound significance widely imputed to rock and roll in the wake of "I Want to Hold Your Hand").

As he told the story in his "autobiography" (in fact, a long-form press release, concocted largely by his publicist, Derek Taylor), it happened like this:

On Thursday, November 9, 1961, Epstein, the twenty-seven-year-old scion of a locally prominent Jewish family, dropped by the Cavern, a small basement coffee bar in downtown Liverpool. At the time, Epstein was managing the region's largest retail outlet for phonograph records, the North End Music Store on nearby Whitechapel Street. The Cavern was around the corner, but (so the official version goes) Epstein had never visited it before. He was coming on this particular day to see a local band, his curiosity having been piqued by a teen customer's keen interest in obtaining a German import recording of the band accompanying an expatriate English singer.

"I arrived at the greasy steps leading to the vast cellar and descended gingerly past a surging crowd of beat fans to a desk where a large man sat examining membership cards. He knew my name"—since Epstein had arranged for a free pass—"and he nodded to an opening in the wall which led into the central of the three tunnels which make up the rambling Cavern.

"Inside the club it was as black as a deep grave, dank and damp and smelly and I regretted my decision to come."

He doubtless felt out of place. As one of his former associates has recalled, "he was a handsome but slight young man with a patrician air about him. His wavy brown hair was kept perfectly trimmed and combed. He was usually dressed in a hand-tailored suit, Turnbull and Asser shirt, and a silk foulard about his neck. His imperious manner and elegant dress made him seem older than he was."

His music of choice was classical. He preferred more elevated social circles. It is no surprise that he should have suffered a momentary pang of regret at venturing into the Cavern. Still, he was a businessman on a business trip. He began to take mental notes.

The crowd was overwhelmingly teenaged, and consisted mostly of girls with beehive hairdos. The club's sound system was blaring the latest hits from America. The visitor tried to strike up a conversation: "I started to talk to one of the girls. 'Hey,' she hissed. 'The Beatles're going on now.' "

There were four of them: two guitarists, a bassist, and a drummer. Electric guitars chiming, the drums pounding, the noise echoing, the quartet tore into songs made famous by the likes of Fats Domino, Chuck Berry, Little Richard, Elvis Presley. Rhythm guitarist John Lennon, twenty-one years old and the band's nominal leader, stood stiffly, stared blankly, and screamed his heart out. Paul McCartney, nineteen, the band's co-leader and bassist, smiled and bobbed and radiated goodwill. George Harrison, eighteen, the lead guitarist, kept to himself. Pete Best, the twenty-year-old drummer, looked cute.

"I eased myself toward the stage," recalled Epstein, "past rapt young faces and jigging bodies and for the first time I saw the Beatles properly.

"They were not very tidy and not very clean"—roughly dressed, one imagines, in their regular outfit: black turtlenecks, black leather pants, black leather jackets. Playing the part of rock and roll beatniks, they were hoods without the customary gobs of greased-up hair: with the exception of the drummer (who was still mimicking Elvis), they sported "French cuts" with blow-dried bangs—an arty (and androgynous) touch.

"I had never seen anything like the Beatles on stage," Epstein recalled. "They smoked as they played and they ate and talked and pretended to hit each other. They turned their backs on the audience and shouted at them and laughed at private jokes."

After the band had finished their set, the emcee welcomed Mr. Epstein to the club, and the shopkeeper made his way to the bandstand to introduce himself. It was Harrison, the quiet guitarist, who first extended his hand: "Hello there. What brings Mr. Epstein here?"

For the rest of his short life—Epstein would die in 1967, whether a suicide or the victim of an accidental barbiturate overdose has never been determined—the man who discovered the Beatles relished retelling this particular story. Whatever the facts of the matter, the story has the ring of mythic truth. Epstein in the Cavern evokes Orpheus in the Underworld, and also Stanley in search of Livingstone, plunging into the heart of a dark continent. That this particular dark continent happened to be a *coffee bar* was equally evocative. After all, Britain's first rock Svengali, the legendary Larry Parnes, was said to have discovered Tommy Steele, Britain's first native rock star, in the 2 I's coffee bar in London's Soho in 1956; and Parnes, like Epstein, had gone on to manage a stable of artistes, mainly proletarian bad boys repackaged with pretty Presley-style haircuts and moody stage names like Marty Wilde and Billy Fury (subtlety wasn't at issue here), producing a flock of teen idols who doubled as adoring ephebes for Mr. Parnes, who kindly invited several of the lads to live as house guests in his magnificent London mansion. It was a lifestyle that Brian Epstein in the fall of 1961 had every reason to envy.

An academic failure who had also dropped out of the Royal Academy of Dramatic Art, Epstein had finally found a niche for himself in the family business, which consisted of a chain of furniture and record stores. For the past several years, by methodically tracking the whims of his customers, he had turned the family-owned NEMS store into a highly profitable retail outlet.

He was prosperous. But he was also bored. He felt a desperate need to make a new beginning.

Shortly before his visit to the Cavern, Epstein had spent six weeks in Spain at the behest of his mother, who was worried about his mental health. Throughout the summer, her son had been unhappy and depressed. He was drinking too much. Driving recklessly, he had smashed up his car more than once. Above all, he was living in fear, worried that a blackmailer he had helped send to prison would, upon his release in September, reveal the secret that he had thus far shared with only a handful of his closest friends: that he was a homosexual.

The Beatles offered him hope. He began to think about changing the shape of his life. Building on his experience in record retailing, he could become the band's manager. He could make them stars. In return, they could make him money. Perhaps they could even make him happy: following in the footsteps of Larry Parnes, he, too, might be able to build a stable of grateful teen idols, leather-clad bad boys personally in his debt.

There certainly were plenty of leather-clad bad boys to be found in

Liverpool (which had already produced the toughest stud in Parnes' stable, Billy Fury). A rough-and-tumble port city, Liverpool had never fully recovered from World War II. Rubble still scarred the landscape, a reminder of the German blitz, and unemployment ran high, leaving plenty of kids with time to kill.

Perhaps that is one reason why the city sported so many rock and roll bands. By the fall of 1961, there were hundreds of them, appearing regularly in dozens of clubs and coffee bars. The thriving local scene supported a fortnightly journal called *Mersey Beat,* which ran ads for the clubs and stories on the bands. The editor, Bill Harry, had gone to school with John Lennon, so of course he championed John's band. But the paper also chronicled the comings and goings of Gerry and the Pacemakers, Johnny Sandel and the Searchers, Rory Storm and the Hurricanes, the Merseybeats. Willy-nilly, these amateur bands had forged a style of their own, playing American rock hard and fast, with a relentlessly pounding beat, jangling guitars, and keening vocal harmonies.

The repertoire of the Beatles was typical. Learning the songs from records (since none of them could read music), they spiced their set with hits currently popular in the States, as well as a few ballads and even some sentimental show tunes ("Till There Was You," "Falling in Love Again"). But the heart of their act was vintage rock and roll, the songs made famous by Elvis Presley, Chuck Berry, Little Richard, Carl Perkins, and Buddy Holly. Connoisseurs of rock song form, their repertoire featured no less than eleven songs written by Jerry Leiber and Mike Stoller ("Kansas City," "Hound Dog," etc.).

Because of the stress on primal rock and roll, and the rough-and-ready way the old songs were sung, the "Mersey Beat" of the Beatles and their Liverpool rivals was a world apart from the milder sounds then popular in England. The year's biggest single hit in Britain was Elvis Presley's cloying version of a German folk tune, "Wooden Heart," complete with tuba oom-pahs, and possibly the most insipid record Presley ever made (which is saying something). The most popular British album of the year featured songs from the *Black and White Minstrel Show,* an unembarrassed throwback to the racial stereotypes of another era that was hugely popular on the London stage and also on British television. Rock and roll was perversely hard to hear, since the airwaves in England were controlled by the state, and the British Broadcasting Corporation refused to play anything held to be too vulgar. In any case, most of England's home-grown rock stars, taking their cue, as always, from Elvis, and led by Cliff Richard, the most popular Elvis clone of them all, were busy making insipid records of cloying ballads.

The Beatles weren't insipid. They were clever, ironic, acerbic. They played hard-core rock and roll. And they took pride in mocking the pieties of popular music.

In the first issue of *Mersey Beat* (dated July 6–20, 1961), John Lennon contributed a typically sardonic little essay "on the Dubious Origins of Beatles": "Once upon a time there were three little boys called John, George and Paul, by name christened. They decided to get together because they were the getting together type. When they were together they wondered what for after all, what for. So all of a sudden they all grew guitars and fashioned a noise."

In fact, John Lennon had first met Paul McCartney on July 6, 1957, at a church picnic. At the time, Lennon was about to turn seventeen, and McCartney was just fifteen. The gist of what happened was simple: after they had been introduced, McCartney showed Lennon how to tune a guitar, and wrote out the words for two classic rockabilly songs, Eddie Cochran's "Twenty Flight Rock" and Gene Vincent's "Be-Bop-a-Lula." His rock and roll bona fides thus confirmed, McCartney was invited to help the older boy form a new band.

Shortly afterward, Lennon and McCartney added George Harrison, an equally earnest student of early rock and roll. For nearly two years, this threesome, augmented by a shifting cast of friends, performed informally. In the spring of 1960, they regularly played on Friday afternoons at Liverpool College of Art, where Lennon was completing a third year of education.

The art school context was crucial to the band's emergent attitude and sense of style. In the postwar period, Great Britain had created a unique network of schools like Liverpool College of Art. Here boys and girls with poor academic credentials and no other professional prospects were able to learn the commercial arts in a low-key atmosphere of bohemian experimentation. In this setting, Lennon, McCartney, and Harrison were free to make music without having to work at pleasing anyone. Like jazz trumpeter Miles Davis, they played with their backs to the audience, refusing to feign civility, let alone enthusiasm, and taking a perverse pride in flouting the conventions of show business. Lennon and his friends also dabbled in beat poetry, reading Ginsberg and Ferlinghetti and Corso. They learned how to cut an ironic figure by looking like Elvis Presley, using vulgar rock hairstyles to stand out from the art school crowd (just as they would later use an arty French-cut hairstyle to stand out from the rock crowd).

In 1960, shortly after Lennon had left art school, the newly christened Beatles, named in (punning) honor of Buddy Holly's band, the Crickets, turned professional. Hired after auditioning in Liverpool for Larry Parnes and Billy Fury, the band embarked on their first tour outside the city, accompanying the one and only Johnnie Gentle. Their next trip was on their own, to Hamburg, Germany, where they stayed for nearly four months, honing their skills. In the months that followed, they split their time between Liverpool and Hamburg, and also made their first trip into a recording studio, in Germany, to accompany the expatriate English singer Tony Sheridan.

Though Lennon and McCartney by then were already composing together, they rarely performed their own songs live. The patrons preferred the songs of Chuck Berry and Little Richard. The Beatles obliged, stripping the old songs of any lingering traces of subtlety, and driving them home with casual aggression, delivering the lyrics (if it was Lennon singing) in a hoarse, grainy voice of pure wounded pride.

Besotted though he was by the nervous energy of classic rock and roll, Lennon played with grim determination. Just listen to the version of Gene Vincent's "Be-Bop-a-Lula" that the Beatles sang at the Star Club in Hamburg, Germany (during a live set taped in 1962). Vincent had sung his piece of good-natured gibberish with a smile and a leer, his band playing with quiet finesse—his drummer used brushes. The Beatles blow up the song. The drummer pounds mindlessly. Lennon's vocal is harsh, adamant, seductively self-absorbed, as if to say (as one witness later recalled): "I'm going to have a bloody good time, hope you'll join me."

Since every issue of *Mersey Beat* ran news about the Beatles; since Brian Epstein's record store sold the magazine; since the second issue of *Mersey Beat* had trumpeted the Beatles on the cover, with a photo and bold headline; and since Brian Epstein himself had been contributing a regular column to *Mersey Beat* starting with the third issue—for all of these reasons, it seems certain that Brian Epstein had heard of the Beatles well before his pilgrimage to the Cavern on November 9.

At least one Liverpool veteran remembers seeing Epstein at a Beatles show in June, standing in the shadows, staring intently, clapping wildly. Still another witness, who worked at the NEMS store, swears that Epstein in these same months would often gaze longingly at a photo of the band, torn from the pages of *Mersey Beat:* a reverie of young lads in leather.

However the connection was first made, it was at this intersection—between the band's alienated look and the impresario's longing gaze—that a new kind of rock and roll sensibility took shape. It was, in a word, a matter of *camp:* a new way of seeing the world, in terms of artifice and exaggerated style. To look at rock in this way involved, among other things, the ironic embrace of kitsch; a theatrical flair for witty masquerade; the seductive packaging of deadpan images of revolt and marginality; and, above all, the projection of ambiguous erotic fantasies with a wink—as Susan Sontag remarked in her famous essay on the topic, "the androgyne is certainly one of the great images of Camp sensibility."

In the photo reportedly admired by Epstein, the band's look was rough, enigmatic, defiantly aloof. The picture had been taken in Hamburg by a young German artist and photographer named Astrid Kirchherr. A bohemian devotee of French existentialism and modern art, she had given the group their first French cuts, and helped them pick their black-on-black leather outfits. She had then shot the group with their instruments in a variety of industrial wastelands. Her photos left an impression of dreamy disaffection, as if a band of aspiring delinquents had wandered by accident onto the set of a film by Antonioni. The settings were artfully cold, the poses sullen, coy, sexy.

Brian Epstein reacted with rapture. The closer he got, the more excited he became. Back at the record shop after introducing himself to the band at the Cavern, all he could talk about was the Beatles, as one of his employees later recalled: "He ranted and raved about them to anyone who would listen. They were wonderful, he said, just wonderful. The music was the best he ever heard of any beat group, loud and crazy and driving, and they were so much fun to watch, there was something infectiously happy about them."

The night after his lunchtime visit to the Cavern, Brian Epstein ventured out to see the Beatles again. He was a man obsessed (though it would be several weeks before the band formally consented to have him become their manager).

The venue on the night of November 10 was the Tower Ballroom in New Brighton. The Beatles were headlining a show packaged by a local promoter named Sam Leach, who aspired to do for Liverpool what Alan Freed had done for Cleveland with his Moondog Coronation Ball—put the Big Beat on the city's musical map. Besides the Beatles, the bill featured Rory Storm's band, along with Gerry and the Pacemakers (another quartet that Epstein would eventually manage).

Operation Big Beat, as Leach called it, turned out to be one of the largest rock shows in Liverpool yet. By eleven o'clock, the Tower Ballroom was packed. Nearly 4,000 people filled the hall.

One by one, the bands took their turn on stage. At the ballroom taps, the ale was flowing. Gangs roamed the room, looking for trouble. While waiting to perform, Paul McCartney was nearly hit by a hurled table.

It was after 11:00 when the Beatles took the stage. The crowd surged forward. While Brian Epstein looked on, the band began to play. The girls began to shriek. Sam Leach, aware of the crowd's volatility, held his breath.

"That night," Leach later recalled, "was when Beatlemania began."

Almost no one noticed. In Liverpool, the newspapers ignored the event. For the Beatles themselves, little had changed. They were still a provincial band, far from the limelight of London, let alone New York City.

Brian Epstein, though, had found his calling. As he would famously snap at a skeptical record label executive a few months later, "These boys are going to explode. I am completely confident that one day they will be bigger than Elvis Presley."

He had a job to do—and a world to convince.

1961–1962:

Robert Johnson: King of the Delta Blues Singers

Without fanfare or publicity, his first album appeared in 1961. The music was strikingly out of place and out of time, particularly in a year when the best-selling album in America was Elvis Presley's *Blue Hawaii*. Still, as one critic has aptly remarked, *King of the Delta Blues Singers* turned Robert Johnson into "a sort of invisible pop star."

The album consisted of sixteen songs, several with starkly evocative, even apocalyptic titles: "Hellhound on My Trail," "If I Had Possession Over Judgment Day," "Me and the Devil Blues." The songs had been recorded in 1936 and 1937. Robert Johnson had been dead for a generation. In 1961, no photographs of him were known to exist. A mysterious and elusive figure, he was—literally—invisible. He nevertheless became a pop star: minor, perhaps, but highly influential just the same.

In his own lifetime, a total of twelve recordings had been released. With the exception of the first one, "Terraplane Blues," none of them had sold well, even in Johnson's home region, the mid-South. From the start, the quality of his music was nevertheless recognized, if only by fellow blues singers, as well as by a handful of respected writers and record collectors.

After the appearance of *King of the Delta Blues Singers*, Johnson's reputation steadily grew. His music was heard, and imitated, by a coterie of prominent young musicians. Among the cognoscenti, his album became a badge of hip taste: in the photo on the cover of Bob Dylan's *Bringing It All Back Home* (1965), the Johnson album is prominent among the emblematic pieces of bohemian bric-a-brac on display. What people like Dylan took away from Johnson's life and work became the source of a tacit ethos, silently transmitted, internationally shared, creating a new mythic measure of what rock and roll could *be*, quite apart from the example of Elvis Presley.

But who *was* Robert Johnson? In an era when worthless teen idols were routinely ballyhooed, Robert Johnson was a mystery, unknown, remote, accessible only through his music. The most storied of the classic Delta bluesmen, his legend had its roots in a failed quest to find him.

The search had begun in 1938. In December of that year, John Hammond was staging the first of his "Spirituals to Swing" concerts at Carnegie Hall (it was this concert that would introduce the jump blues of Big Joe Turner to New York listeners). Hammond was the first important jazz critic and record collector to become an impresario and record producer in his own right, serving as a role model for Ahmet Ertegun when he started Atlantic Records a decade later. An avowed socialist despite his pedigree (his mother was a Vanderbilt), Hammond in the 1930s was committed to advancing the cause of "the people" through a suitably classy presentation of suitably populist strains of music. In an announcement for the Carnegie Hall concert printed in the *New Masses* (a weekly that was an avowed cultural organ of the nation's "class-conscious workers and revolutionary intellectuals"), Hammond promised a program of "American Negro music as it was invented, developed, sung and played by the Negro himself—the true, untainted folk song, spirituals, work songs, songs of protest, chain gang songs, Holy Roller chants, shouts, blues, minstrel music, honky-tonk piano, early jazz and, finally, the contemporary swing of Count Basie." The list of featured artists included Robert Johnson.

A few months before, Hammond had gone to work for Columbia Records, and had chanced upon Johnson's masters, transcriptions of all of his original recordings, many of them still unissued at the time. Transfixed by Johnson's music, Hammond was convinced that he had found an archetypal troubadour—the purest, most powerful (and most authentically populist and proletarian) blues singer in the Deep South.

A call went out. John Hammond wanted to bring Robert Johnson to Carnegie Hall. In Texas and Mississippi, the music men who had first found and recorded Johnson made inquiries. Piecing together information from a variety of itinerant informants, they learned that Johnson had died just weeks before, under uncertain but sinister circumstances.

One search was over. But another was just beginning. In these same months, Hammond played Johnson's unreleased masters for a young friend of his, the Harvard-educated folklorist Alan Lomax. Though he was only twenty-six, Lomax was already a seasoned student of American folk music. In 1934, he had accompanied his father, John, editor of the first major anthology of American folk song, on a trip to the South to record indigenous musicians in the field. Their express purpose had been "to find the Negro who had had the least contact with jazz, the radio, and with the white man." On that trip, they had visited the Louisiana State Penitentiary at Angola, where they had discovered Huddie Ledbetter, aka Leadbelly, whose release they secured, and whom they subsequently took on a well-publicized tour of Harvard and other college campuses: *Life*, a weekly magazine, covered the phenomenon under the headline "Bad Nigger Makes Good Minstrel."

Leadbelly's tour naturally compromised the authenticity of his claim to be "the Negro who had had the least contact with jazz, the radio, and with the white man." Robert Johnson's recordings, on the other hand, suitably esoteric as they were, suggested someone who came closer to embodying that elusive (and implicitly revolutionary) ideal. Even better, he was dead: so his work would forever remain untainted by contact with "the white man" (never mind that Lomax, like Hammond, was white). But the fact of his death only added urgency to the riddle that now haunted Lomax: who *was* Robert Johnson—who had he been?

In 1941, Lomax headed south, in search now of a ghost. He did not return to New York empty-handed. Assembling evidence and following clues from Memphis back to the Mississippi Delta, Lomax was able to locate Robert Johnson's mother. He discovered Son House, one of Johnson's mentors. And he found one of Johnson's most talented disciples, McKinley Morganfield, later famous as Muddy Waters, who in 1941 was still living on a plantation (he moved to the South Side of Chicago two years later).

From these sources, a legend began to take shape. Some friends said that he'd been shot by a jealous man; others swore that he'd been poisoned by a woman. In his death throes, they said, he crawled on all fours and barked like a dog—the victim of a voodoo curse. In later years, Son House hinted that Robert Johnson had sold his soul to the devil—to House, this was the only conceivable explanation for the man's musical genius.

John Hammond and Alan Lomax first talked about compiling an album of Robert Johnson's music in 1939. But the project was shelved, and evidently forgotten. The rugged beauty of Johnson's recordings, well known by reputation, was rarely experienced firsthand.

Then, in the Fifties, in a paradoxical counterpoint to the simultaneous craze for rock and roll, an international fad for "folk" music took off, stalled, then took off again, finally creating a small but impassioned new market for Robert Johnson's rough-hewn style of music.

In America, the fad had begun in 1950, when the Weavers, led by Pete Seeger, one of Lomax's musical friends and political allies, turned Leadbelly's "Goodnight Irene" into a lushly orchestrated exercise in sentimentality. As a writer remarked at the time in *Billboard*, songs like "Goodnight Irene" and "Tennessee Waltz" were of a piece; the Weavers, like Patti Page, demonstrated the popular appeal of "a bright, homey, simple, folksy melody sort of tune."

This first wave of the America folk revival fell apart in 1951, after the Weavers were prominently mentioned in an FBI publication, *Red Channels: Communist Influence on Radio and Television*. Meanwhile, in England, folk music independently came into vogue in 1956, when the singer Lonnie Donegan took yet another Leadbelly song, "Rock Island Line," and performed it with spirited artlessness, accompanying himself on acoustic guitar. Donegan called his brand of music "skiffle," a term originally used in the late 1920s to describe blues played by so-called jug bands, consisting of guitar, harmonica, kazoo, jug, washtub bass, and washboard drums. It was, in fact, skiffle that John Lennon was playing in 1957 at the church picnic where he first met Paul McCartney.

At first glance, rock and roll and folk music might seem utterly incompatible. Where rock and roll was designed to be popular, folk music evoked a reverie of pastoral populism, untainted by vulgar commercial calculations; where rock and roll was loud and highly amplified, folk was performed on acoustic instruments, an audible emblem of its populist authenticity.

Still, as John Lennon intuitively understood (since his skiffle band performed Elvis Presley songs), rock and folk had some crucial ingredients in common: both genres welcomed, indeed highly prized, the creativity of frank amateurs; both rock and folk were do-it-yourself formats that inspired many listeners to start bands of their own; finally, both rock and folk were simple enough musical forms that even teenagers could, without much practice, successfully approximate the sounds they heard on their radios and record players.

In 1958, the folk fad had resumed in America, and proceeded to blossom, this time fueled by the popularity of the Kingston Trio, a clean-cut (and impeccably apolitical) vocal group. The Kingston Trio wore starched, striped short-sleeve shirts, strummed acoustic guitars quietly, and sang plangent Appalachian ballads with the same kind of deadpan intonation and colorless diction that Ricky Nelson had brought to rockabilly. Across America, guitar sales soared, as aspiring folk singers joined the ranks of aspiring rock guitarists. And by 1961, when Robert Johnson's first album was belatedly released (thanks, in part, to the continuing interest of John Hammond), there was, at last, a demonstrable market for music that was ostensibly pure, archaic, uncommercial. Out of time, Robert Johnson could at last come into fashion.

For almost everyone who bought *King of the Delta Blues Singers*—the point needs stressing—this was *new* music. In some ways, it was more novel, because more exotic, than anything else readily available in record stores around the world. There had been folk song reissues before, of course, on small American labels like Folkways and RBF, but one had to make a special effort to search them out. There had similarly been blues reissues before, but nothing as raw as *King of the Delta Blues Singers*—and certainly nothing as drenched in romance and mystery.

"The voice sings," Rudi Blesh wrote in 1946, offering the first of countless purple encomiums, "and then—on fateful descending notes—echoes its own phrases. . . . The high, sighing guitar notes vanish suddenly into silence as if swept away by cold autumn wind. Plangent, iron chords intermittently walk, like heavy footsteps, on the same descending minor series. . . . The notes paint a dark waste-land, starless, ululant with bitter wind, swept by the chill rain. Over a hilltop trudges a lonely, ragged, bedeviled figure."

For want of a photograph, the album's cover was a painting. It showed an isolated, featureless black man hunched over his guitar, casting a long shadow over an equally featureless ground the color of parched sand. "Robert Johnson is little, very little more than a name on aging index cards and a few dusty master records in the files of a phonograph company that no longer exists," the album's liner notes began. "A country blues singer from the Mississippi Delta . . . Robert Johnson appeared and disappeared, in much the same fash-ion as a sheet of newspaper twisting and twirling down a dark and windy midnight street."

Once music has been preserved on recordings, the sounds become available, in principle, to any listener anywhere. When the music thus preserved represents the orally transmitted heritage of an other-wise inaccessible milieu, the effect, paradoxically, is to open up for cosmopolitan appreciation, and imitation, what had been previously segregated, what had been self-contained: the legacy of an organic community of musical craftsmanship. In this way, the Beatles could master from afar a regional American idiom like rockabilly. It was in this way, too, that a new generation of British rock and roll musi-cians came to study, and copy, a music so tortured in its timbres, and so tormented in its poetic imagery, that Johnson's recordings made

Another R & B band, The Animals
rivaled Stones global popularity.

"Blue Suede Shoes" sound like "Three Blind Mice"—a simpleminded nursery rhyme.

"I don't think I'd even heard of Robert Johnson when I found the record," Eric Clapton recalled years later. "It was probably just fresh out. I was around fifteen or sixteen," and Clapton's apotheosis as the first widely celebrated demigod of the rock guitar was five years in the future: "It was a real shock that there was something that powerful. . . . It all led me to believe that here was a guy who really didn't want to play for people at all, that his thing was so unbearable for him to have to live with that he was almost ashamed of it. This was an image that I was very, very keen to hang on to."

A similar scene occurred in the spring of 1962, when Keith Richards, then nineteen, visited a fellow rhythm and blues enthusiast named Brian Jones, then twenty—together with Keith's friend Mick Jagger, they would shortly begin to play together as the Rolling Stones. "I'd just met Brian," Richards later recalled, "and I went round to his apartment—crash pad, actually, all he had in it was a chair, a record player, and a few records, one of which was Robert Johnson. He put it on, it was just astounding stuff. . . . To me he was like a comet or a meteor that came along and, BOOM, suddenly he raised the ante, suddenly you just had to aim that much higher."

What Johnson represented to art school students like Clapton and Keith Richards was, to start, a matter of music: a complexity of affect conveyed by guttural vocals, kinetic countermelodies, and a rhythmic attack so relentlessly choppy that, on a recording like "Walkin' Blues," the singer and his guitar achieve a feeling of raw urgency rarely matched by later bands playing with amplified instruments. A model of impassioned artistry, a song like "Walkin' Blues" was also a perfect expression of (among other sentiments) unrequited love; desolation and abandonment; and the untrammeled freedom of a young man unafraid to leave his "lonesome home." For a generation bored by the complacency and comfort of middle-class life, Johnson's songs held out the image of another world—one that was liberated; fearful; thrilling.

It was a music of apparently brute honesty. But as countless later homages would prove, if Johnson's basic sound was imitable, the impression of brute honesty was not. As Greil Marcus remarked in *Mystery Train*, perhaps the first major study of rock as a cultural form, "all of Eric Clapton's love for Johnson's music came to bear not when Clapton sang Johnson's songs"—for example, "Ramblin' on My Mind" in 1966 (with John Mayall), or "Crossroads" in 1968 (with Cream)—"but when, once Johnson's music became part of who Clapton was, Clapton came closest to himself: in the passion of 'Layla' " in 1970 (with Derek and the Dominos).

There was, finally, a certain Gothic beauty about Johnson's legend, which insured that the legend itself became an influence in its own right. By reputation a diabolical and doomed figure, he had died for his art. That creative freedom required a pact with the devil was, of course, a romantic cliché, as well as a major theme in Goethe's *Faust,* Nietzsche's philosophy, and Baudelaire's poetry. But with Johnson's example in mind, the mystique surrounding evil in modern thought acquired a concrete new meaning, transforming the significance of blues borrowings within rock culture.

For Elvis Presley, the blues had been a matter of elemental sensuousness, the kinds of passions that could be routinely evoked by a journeyman like Arthur Crudup: "if I ever got to the place where I could feel all old Arthur felt, I'd be a music man like nobody ever saw." As Elvis proved, one could be "a music man" like Crudup and still embody the virtues of patriotism and a pious reverence for traditional family values.

For Keith Richards and Brian Jones, by contrast, the blues had now to be visibly rooted in "Sympathy for the Devil." Thus was born what has become one of the corniest motifs in subsequent blues-oriented rock and roll, a fascination with evil routinely exploited by so-called heavy metal bands like Black Sabbath in the 1970s, Van Halen in the 1980s, and Metallica in the 1990s. As one academic has solemnly summed up the "discursive practice" of these latter-day rock and roll bands, "Running with the Devil means living in the present, and the music helps us experience the pleasure of the moment. . . . Freedom is presented as a lack of social ties: no love, no law, no responsibility, no delayed gratification."

That such sentiments almost certainly travesty Robert Johnson's life and work does not change the lines of cultural descent connecting Johnson's "Hellhound on My Trail" (recorded in 1937) with Van Halen's "Runnin' With the Devil" (1978); or, for that matter, the parallel lines of cultural descent connecting the gangster folk music of Leadbelly with the gangsta rap of N.W.A. (for "Niggers With Attitude"—compare "Bad Nigger Makes Good Minstrel").

Thanks to the growing influence of country blues, and specifically of Johnson's example, unruliness, already a key component of the rock ethos, acquired the kind of cultural legitimacy Norman Mailer had prophesied in his essay "The White Negro": the cachet of frankly expressing raw desires, deep emotional truths, specifically those too violent for civil society, too ugly for fine art—too danger-ous to be condoned.

September 4, 1962:

"How Do You Do It?"

From the start, three things set the Beatles apart. One was the furious energy with which they resurrected "original style rock 'n' roll music," as one British newspaper called it, playing with a beat so big and old-fashioned it sounded brand new. Another, sub-tler asset, which took a longer time to blossom, was the intelligence and dedication with which John Lennon and Paul McCartney jointly pursued the craft of popular songwriting.

But in many ways the most important aspect of their idiosyncratic style, a tacit tribute to the band's art school origins and bohemian pretensions, was the spunky determination with which, at unex-pected moments, they defied the showbiz conventions, demanding instead the right to create their own kind of art in their own kind of way—as if rock and roll was an art!

"These four boys who are superb instrumentalists, also produce some exciting and pulsating vocals," wrote Brian Epstein on December 8, 1961, trying to pitch the group to one of the big labels in London. "This is a group of exceptional talents and appealing personalities." Less than a month after his visit to the Cavern, and even before he had a formal contract to manage the band, Epstein was ardently wooing potential suitors. His passion was doubtless instrumental in landing the band a quick audition, on January 1, 1962, for Decca—a major British label.

For the occasion, the band, at Epstein's behest, selected a conser-vative cross section of their repertoire. They included three original compositions by Lennon and McCartney: "Like Dreamers Do," "Hello Little Girl," and "Love of the Loved." But apart from doing

Chuck Berry's "Memphis," and Buddy Holly's "Crying, Wishing, Hoping," they ignored "original style rock 'n' roll music." Instead, Epstein had the band demonstrate their versatility by singing an impressively wide array of material, from "Take Good Care of My Baby," a current *American Bandstand*–type hit, to "September in the Rain," a standard associated with Guy Lombardo, more recently revived by the great jazz singer Dinah Washington.

Apart from Lennon and McCartney's "Hello Little Girl," the most striking performances came on two songs associated with the Coasters. A vehicle for the songwriting talents of Jerry Leiber and Mike Stoller, the Coasters were the most theatrically sophisticated black vocal group of the Fifties. They specialized in painstaking renditions of mordant skits, what Leiber and Stoller called "three-minute playlets." Built around teen themes, delivered in a droll black vernacular, and often blending harsh and bluesy timbres with witty lyrics, these playlets were generally arranged so that each member of the group had to use his distinctive voice to bring a different mood, or character, to life. For the Decca audition, the Beatles sang "Searchin'," the first and funkiest of the big Coaster hits (in 1957), and "Three Cool Cats," a more whimsical (and esoteric) song from 1959. On both songs, the Beatles demonstrated their own love of comic irony, and also a profound understanding of Leiber and Stoller's musical theatrics. The Coasters were, in effect, the first rock group to dramatize successfully the disparate vocal personalities of each of its separate members: a talent that Lennon, McCartney, Harrison, and (later) Ringo Starr would perfect as well.

Apparently unimpressed by the tongue-in-cheek burlesque evoked by the Beatles imitating the Coasters, Dick Rowe, the A&R executive at Decca, decided to pass. So did executives at nearly every other record company in London. It was only by a stroke of luck that a tape of the Decca audition finally landed on the desk of George Martin, an A&R man best known as a specialist in comedy, having produced the original cast recording of *Beyond the Fringe*, as well as two hit albums for Peter Sellers.

Though he, like everyone else, was unimpressed by much of what he heard, Martin was nevertheless struck, as he later recalled, by "an unusual quality of sound, a certain roughness that I hadn't encountered before. There was also the fact that more than one person was singing"—especially on the Coasters material—"which in itself was unusual."

A provisional contract with Parlophone, the label that employed Martin, was drawn up, and the Beatles were invited to another audition, this time on June 6 at the EMI studios on Abbey Road. Meeting the band for the first time, Martin was impressed by "their engaging personalities," and also by their personal hygiene: "they were all quite clean."

Brian Epstein had worked hard to polish the band's manners. Taking his cues from Larry Parnes, who liked to dress up his rock and roll bad boys, Epstein had outfitted the Beatles in lounge suits with pencil-thin lapels and matching ties. Preaching the virtues of organization, Epstein prepared a neatly typed playlist, specifying the songs the group would audition.

Opening with a medley that showcased each of the group's three singers in turn (Paul, John, and George), the band ran through a variety of songs similar to those performed for Decca in January: Coasters material again, show tunes ("Over the Rainbow," "Till There Was You"), covers of current American rock and roll hits (McCartney doing Bruce Channel's "Hey! Baby," Lennon singing the Shirelles' "Baby It's You"), plus more goofy versions of old songs, among them "The Sheik of Araby" and "Your Feet's Too Big," a jazz novelty popularized by Fats Waller in 1939.

"Frankly, the material didn't impress me," George Martin later recalled—"least of all their own songs. I felt that I was going to have to find suitable material for them, and was quite certain that their songwriting ability had no saleable future!"

Lennon and McCartney had a quite different estimate of their songwriting ability. By then, the two of them had already served a lengthy apprenticeship. Besides a handful of instrumentals, the Lennon-McCartney songbook in these early years featured material written in an unusually wide variety of styles: "Hello Little Girl," which they had first performed in 1957, was inspired by a 1940s pop song that Lennon remembered his mother singing to him; "Like Dreamers Do," also dating from 1957, was a Latin-flavored ditty reminiscent of Paul Anka's "Diana"; "The One After 909," again from 1957, was a rockabilly train blues, in the style of Carl Perkins; "I'll Follow the Sun," from 1959, was a wistful ballad with a beautifully proportioned melody line; "Love of the Loved," from 1960, was still another ballad with unconventional chords; "I'll Be on My Way," from 1961, was written in the style of Buddy Holly and sung in the manner of the Everly Brothers, who had applied the piquant

195

"How Do You Do It?"

harmonies of country music to the simple teen themes of songs like "Bye Bye Love," creating a bittersweet vocal sound that the Beatles made their own. Last but not least, there was "Hold Me Tight," also from 1961. An up-tempo rocker built around a boogie riff and a dramatically unconventional modulation between major and minor keys, "Hold Me Tight" was written in one style alone—that of John Lennon and Paul McCartney.

At their June 6 audition, Lennon and McCartney had performed seven of their own songs: the three played at the Decca audition, plus four new ones: something called "Pinwheel Twist," plus "Love Me Do," "P.S. I Love You" and "Ask Me Why." Of variable quality, none was a masterpiece. The wistfully Latin-tinged "Ask Me Why," one of Lennon and McCartney's first homages to Berry Gordy's Motown style of songwriting, offers, as one critic has cruelly but accurately remarked, "pastiche without substance." "P.S. I Love You" has a shapely tune but lyrics devoid of the wit on display in the song's namesake, a pop standard composed by Johnny Mercer with Gordon Jenkins. "Love Me Do," finally, is a dirge: a meager melody with minimal harmony and perfunctory lyrics, it lumbers along to a plodding, choppy beat enlivened only by a plaintive harmonica riff (inspired by a similar riff on "Hey! Baby").

At this point, it is worth emphasizing, no one expected Lennon and McCartney to make a career out of composing. Certainly no one expected them to *sing* their own songs.

On the contrary. In the early Sixties, it was customary for rock and roll acts to record songs written by somebody else. That, after all, is how Elvis Presley had done it. It was how the music business had been run for a century. Songwriters wrote, and singers sang—a division of labor that helped to maintain a certain (often minimal) standard of professionalism.

It was only natural, then, that George Martin should turn to a professional songwriter for help. Some months before, an associate had sent Martin a demonstration recording of a song called "How Do You Do It?" With its facile wordplay and perky beat, it had the sound of a surefire hit. "He *knew* it was a number one hit," Paul McCartney later recalled, "so he gave us it on a demo. . . . We took it back to Liverpool and said, 'What are we gonna do with this, he's our producer, we'll have to do it, we'll have to learn it.' " And so they did, working up their own arrangement of the song, and making it a part of their live act.

George Martin, meanwhile, journeyed to Liverpool to see the Beatles at the Cavern. It was a revelation. For the first time, Martin could appreciate the power of the group at its most grimly determined: "The rock-and-roll gyrations of Tommy Steele and Cliff Richard were clinical, anemic, even anesthetic, compared with the total commitment of the Beatles."

Afterward, Martin made a crucial decision: he would not try to sweeten the group's sound. As he asked rhetorically, years later, in his autobiography, "Why do that? Why not keep them as they were? It hadn't been done before—but then, I'd made a lot of records that hadn't been 'done before.' Why not experiment in pop as I had in comedy?"

On September 4, 1961, the Beatles arrived at the EMI studios with a new drummer, Ringo Starr, and a stubborn wish to have one of their original songs released as their first single, no matter what George Martin might think.

In the afternoon, the band rehearsed six songs, including "How Do You Do It?," "Love Me Do," and yet another new Lennon-McCartney composition, "Please Please Me." Like "Love Me Do," "Please Please Me" at this stage was a rock and roll dirge. McCartney recalls that it was meant to be "a Roy Orbison–type song"—a romantic melodrama punctuated by portentous chords and sung at a snail's pace: " 'Come on, *ching ching;* Come on, *ching ching;* Come on, *ching ching;* Come on, *ching ching;* Please pleeeeaaase me!' It's very Roy Orbison when you slow it down."

Martin, though he was now listening with open ears, wasn't bashful about making suggestions. A rare kind of chemistry began to develop in the studio. Unlike Sam Phillips or most of the other important pioneering rock and roll producers, George Martin was a trained musician; before joining the staff of Parlophone, he had studied oboe and composition; in addition to comedy albums, he had recorded jazz, cabaret, and the pop balladry of Shirley Bassey and Matt Monroe. Another A&R man with this kind of background might simply have rejected Lennon and McCartney's latest song out of hand. But not George Martin.

"He was a super-sympathetic guy," recalls Paul McCartney. "He was never a cultist about jazz or serious music. . . . And it wasn't as if we were young nitwits and yobs, and that he wasn't interested in our opinion. It was exactly the opposite."

Bending his taste to their talent, Martin used his trained ear to edit

"Please Please Me," inviting Lennon and McCartney to conceive the song in different terms. "He thought it was too much of a dirge," recalls McCartney, "and probably too like Roy Orbison. So he cleverly speeded us up, and we put in the little scaled riff at the beginning"—played by Harrison on a pealing twelve-string electric guitar.

Setting aside "Please Please Me" to give the band more time to work on it, Martin in the evening had the Beatles record "How Do You Do It?," and then moved on to "Love Me Do." By the end of the night, rough mixes of both songs had been completed.

For the Beatles' debut, Martin still wanted to release "How Do You Do It?" Lennon and McCartney disagreed vehemently. "They said they wanted to record their own material," Martin later wrote, "and I read the riot act. 'When you can write material as good as this, then I'll record it.' "

Lennon and McCartney were adamant. "We came back to George," recalls Paul McCartney, "and said, 'Well, it may be number one but we just don't want this kind of song, we don't want to go out with that kind of reputation. It's a different thing we're going for, it's something new.' "

And it *was* something new: a sound, still in the midst of being formed, that combined, as if miraculously, virtually every ingredient of vintage rock and roll—the sullenness and sweetness, the aggression and nostalgia, the country plaintiveness and the bluesy bravado, the disarming amateurishness and the painstakingly acquired craftsmanship—all of this, brought to life by a band of buffed-up British beatniks for whom rock and roll was what country blues had been to Robert Johnson, what jump blues had been to Wynonie Harris: a way of life, a free life, "an only life."

On September 11, the Beatles returned to the EMI studios on Abbey Road. They cut a new version of "Love Me Do," and rerecorded "P.S. I Love You." They also tried out their new up-tempo arrangement of "Please Please Me." Still not satisfied with "Please Please Me," Martin and the band selected the other two songs for their debut.

On October 5, 1962, Parlophone released the first single by the Beatles.

It was not a hit. Largely ignored in London, "Love Me Do" sold briskly in the North, where the Beatles had built a following (and where Brian Epstein, it was assumed, had instructed his family chain of stores to order the record in bulk). On the chart compiled by the most authoritative source, *Record Retailer,* "Love Me Do" only reached number seventeen, a showing that Martin, for one, considered disappointing.

The Beatles thus began their recording career quietly, an inadvertent result of their refusal to release a more conventional and predictably commercial sort of song. George Martin, after all, had been right about "How Do You Do It?" In March 1963, the Beatles' arrangement of the song became a number one hit for Gerry and the Pacemakers (who, in addition to being managed by Epstein, were produced by Martin).

Not that Lennon and McCartney cared. By then, their career had been well and truly launched by "Please Please Me," performed as a furious blast of "original style rock 'n' roll music."

Finished on November 9, their recording of the song was released on January 11, 1963, as the band's second single. By the end of February, "Please Please Me" was a number one hit, and Lennon and McCartney were on their way, and on their own terms.

And that was how the Beatles did it: by singing their own song, exulting in an unbridled energy, and communicating a mood of joyous glee—the sound of youth triumphant.

April 28, 1963:

Andrew Loog Oldham Enters the Crawdaddy Club

The tip came from journalists at one of England's music weeklies. At the Crawdaddy Club, a "magnet for jazz beatniks," located in the London suburb of Richmond, "the hip kids," it was said, were gyrating "to the new 'jungle music.' " The savage sounds were made by a new combo—the Rolling Stones.

His interest piqued, a baby-faced London publicist named Andrew Loog Oldham set out for the suburbs on a Sunday evening, April 28. The Crawdaddy Club was packed, as it had been for weeks, ever since the Stones had drawn the attention of London's smart set. A local reporter had described the scene a few days earlier: "Save from the swaying forms of the group on the spotlit stage, the room is in darkness. A patch of light from the entrance doors catches the sweating dancers and those who are slumped on the floor, the long hair, suede jackets, gaucho trousers and Chelsea boots."

Oldham, though only nineteen, was already a veteran of the British pop scene. During the winter, he had worked as a freelance press agent for Brian Epstein, watching a kind of history being made. He was standing in the wings when the Beatles first mimed "Please Please Me" on Britain's premier televised pop music showcase, *Thank Your Lucky Stars*. Broadcast in the dead of winter, the show hit home: suddenly, it seemed as if every pop fan in England had warmed to the Beatles. By February, "Please Please Me" was the country's best-selling record. And Andrew Loog Oldham, striking out on his own, had resolved to find a beat group of his own, to manage, to publicize, to exploit.

The Rolling Stones at the time were a sextet. Their leader, Brian Jones, twenty-one, was a dedicated collector of records, with a refined taste for down-home black music from America. A student of classic blues form, he knew how to use a steel slide to produce ghostly sounds on his electric guitar, and he was equally adept at blues harmonica. The band's musical heart, Brian was also its visual focus: after seeing the Beatles on *Thank Your Lucky Stars*, he had let his hair grow in a great billow, with bangs down to his eyebrows.

The other members of the band varied in talent and visual interest. Mick Jagger, nineteen, then still a student at the London School of Economics, was a grotesquely mannered singer with thick lips and a demeanor on stage that was faintly disturbing: twitching to the music, he flopped like a fish out of water. His jug-eared friend Keith Richards, also nineteen, was by comparison an image of composure: though he sometimes helped Mick with vocal harmonies, his metier was elemental electric guitar riffs, played with blazing authority.

The rest of the band stayed mostly in the background: Ian Stewart, a friend of Brian Jones, was a capable boogie-woogie pianist; Bill Wyman, twenty-six, played bass; and Charlie Watts, twenty-one, was, along with Jones and Richards, the band's most accomplished musician: an unabashed jazz fan, he had a knack for playing swing time and jump blues, talents rarely found in young rock and roll drummers.

Together less than four months, the Rolling Stones specialized in "unrepressed R&B," as the Crawdaddy Club advertised it. Keith Richards adored imitating Chuck Berry's guitar licks. Brian Jones had a similar flair for emulating Elmore James, the single most important slide guitarist of the postwar period. The band's tutelary spirit was Robert Johnson; but since his aura of cursed creativity was at this point beyond their grasp, they had to content themselves with learning how to play in the more streamlined style of Johnson's greatest postwar disciple, Muddy Waters, one of whose songs, "Rollin' Stone," gave the band its name.

That the Rolling Stones were savvy about American R&B did not, in itself, interest Andrew Loog Oldham. That their sound could be called *"unrepressed,"* on the other hand—that was a quality to conjure with.

"It was always the sex in rock 'n' roll that attracted me," Oldham once explained. "The sex that most people didn't realize was there. Like the Everly Brothers. Two guys with the same kind of face, the same kind of hair. They were meant to be singing together to some girl, but really they were singing to each other."

Blessed with a fertile imagination and an equally fertile sense of how to publicize "sex," Oldham had two principal ambitions: to live his life near famous people and to become a famous person in his own right.

As a twelve-year-old rock and roll fan, he had spent his spare time at Soho's storied 2 I's coffee bar, hanging out with other aspiring teen idols. Dropping out of school at the age of sixteen, he talked his way into a job working with dress designer Mary Quant, an art school graduate and pioneering British tastemaker who had transformed British fashion by mass-marketing bohemian looks. Working his way from Kings Road to Fleet Street, Oldham next joined a public relations firm, breaking into the music business by writing press releases and courting journalists for teen idols and their Svengalis, including (briefly) the great Larry Parnes. His connections let him hang out with England's self-styled clique of "New Aristocrats," people like the model Jean Shrimpton and the photographer David Bailey: "I was where I wanted to be—around stars."

On the night of April 28, the Stones played with scholarly restraint, seated in a ring on bar stools, looking very cool, very arty, very pure—very "authentic." "There was no production," Oldham recalled. "It was just the blues roots thing . . .'Here I am and this is what I'm playing.' Even so, I knew what I was looking at. It was sex."

Or, as another seasoned observer summed up the impresario's moment of vision: "Here were his ready-made homunculi. He looked at Jagger as Sylvester looks at Tweetie Pie."

Oldham hastened to introduce himself. He doubtless rehearsed his credentials. He had worked with Larry Parnes, Brian Epstein, the Beatles.

The Beatles!

Scarcely two weeks before, the Beatles had dropped by the Crawdaddy Club to catch the Stones in person. Off stage, the two bands had chatted about songwriting and played records for each other. Brian had asked for, and gotten, an autographed photo, which he subsequently displayed for all to see, as a kind of votive offering. Appreciating the fervor of these fellow rhythm and blues enthusiasts, the Beatles invited Brian and the other Stones to attend their first major concert in London, at the Royal Albert Hall, where they were headlining a "pop prom" four nights later.

On the evening of April 18, Brian, Mick, and Keith arrived at the back entrance to the Royal Albert Hall. Mistaken for one of the Beatles, Brian was mobbed by young women. He was beside himself. "This is what we *like*," he stammered to Mick and Keith: "This is what we *want!*"

These were boom days for beat music in Great Britain. The week that Oldham met the Stones, "How Do You Do It?" by Gerry and the Pacemakers was on top of the British charts. Poised to replace it was "From Me to You," the Beatles' third single. Meanwhile, *Please Please Me,* the debut album by the Beatles, issued on March 22, was settling in for a long stay on the British album charts.

Oldham moved fast. By the end of April, he had negotiated a contract to manage the Stones. He then told the band to get rid of Ian Stewart: his hair was too short, his build too stocky, his look too plain.

The next step was to secure a recording contract. In this venture, Oldham had an ally: the avidity with which every record company in England was looking for the next Beatles. Decca, the label that had let the Beatles slip away, was especially keen: "Things got so bad," one executive later recalled, "that if a boy with a guitar had just walked along Albert Embankment past our office, the whole A&R staff would have rushed out to sign him up."

In the first week of May, Decca's most infamous A&R executive, Dick Rowe, aka "The Man Who Turned Down the Beatles," took a trip to Liverpool to judge a talent contest, and perhaps discover the next Beatles. One of the other judges turned out to be George Harrison. Evidently taking pity on Rowe, Harrison confided that there was a new band that he ought to hear—the Rolling Stones.

Rushing back to London, Rowe drove straight to the Crawdaddy Club. "As I had turned down the Beatles earlier," Rowe later explained, "I didn't want to make the same mistake again."

Sensing Rowe's desperation, Andrew Loog Oldham drove a hard bargain. Decca could have the Stones. But Oldham would retain ownership of the recordings, and also have control over key aspects of production and marketing.

On May 10, 1963, Oldham and the Stones made their first stab at cutting a hit single. They were, as Mick Jagger later put, "a bunch of bloody amateurs, ignorant as hell." For all his big talk, Oldham had never produced a record. And despite the band's newfound lust for fame, the Stones were still, at heart, a folk blues band. Combing through their record collections for material that was suitably authentic, yet plausibly commercial, they came up with two songs: "Come On," an obscure song that Chuck Berry had recorded the year before, and "I Want to Be Loved," an even more obscure song, recorded in 1955 by Muddy Waters.

Despite the reverence with which Brian Jones and the other Stones regarded Muddy Waters, their version of "I Want to Be Loved" raises the specter of burnt-cork minstrelsy in a way that the music of the Beatles, and Elvis Presley before them, had not. When Elvis sang "Good Rockin' Tonight," or the Beatles sang "Twist and Shout"—a new addition to their repertoire, and the song most frequently aired from their first album—they made the material their own, singing it in their own style, with a nervous edge, perhaps, or (in the case of the Beatles) a frenetic sensuality, but without mannerism. One can argue that the Beatles' version is better than the original version by the Isley Brothers.

No such argument is possible about the Rolling Stones' version of "I Want to Be Loved." It is a minor example of Waters' finest band at work, a sextet with the incomparable Little Walter on harmonica, Jimmy Rogers on guitar, and Otis Spann on piano. The song is played by the band at a jaunty lope; Waters sings with a smile, enunciating the lyrics, about unrequited passion, in his own Delta dialect. It is the dialect ("ask" pronounced as "axe") that Mick Jagger most assiduously mimics; the song's rather modest palette of emotions is beyond him entirely.

Of course, the Rolling Stones would do better in the future. On "Mona (I Need You Baby)," which they recorded in 1964, the Stones rendered Bo Diddley's famous syncopated beat with more drive and élan than Bo Diddley himself. And thanks to Brian Jones' eerie slide-guitar playing, the Stones' version of "Little Red Rooster," also from 1964, bears comparison to the quite different version recorded by Howlin' Wolf in 1961. True enthusiasts, the Stones played a leading role in educating young listeners about artists like Howlin' Wolf, who was invited by the Stones to join them on a television show in America that marked his first nationally broadcast performance.

But what really put the Rolling Stones over at the start was not music in any case. It was hairiness, it was slovenliness—it was *ugliness*.

With the Stones' debut single slated for release early in June, Oldham lined up interviews for the band with some of Britain's leading teen magazines: *Boyfriend, Rave, Fabulous, Valentine.* "We bite our fingernails because we're so hungry," Brian Jones deadpanned. "We don't eat regularly. Sometimes when we're starving we go down the road and buy a ready-cooked chicken, bring it home, pull it to bits and eat it, but days go by and we forget to eat again." Added Keith Richards: "The last time I had my hair cut was June last year." *Beat Monthly* described them as "five wild beatmen," with "wild haircuts or should I say hairnotcuts!"

On July 7, the band made its debut on *Thank Your Lucky Stars.* The show's host introduced them with a joke: a delegation from the hairdressers' union wanted to see them. During the broadcast, a TV executive pulled Oldham aside and advised him to "get rid of that vile-looking singer with the tyre-tread lips." Jagger's preening also rang alarm bells. The British papers reacted with indignation: the Stones, one critic sniffed, "had gone way beyond the Beatles' acceptable boundaries." Unlike the Beatles, who were then in the midst of charming a nation, "the Stones were the louts who kicked it in the bollocks."

This was priceless. And Oldham and the Stones weren't done yet. In September, Oldham, following the example of Larry Parnes, moved both Keith Richards and Mick Jagger into his Hampstead flat. Emulating Alan Freed and another of his heroes, Phil Spector, Oldham decided, in his words, to behave like "a nasty little upstart tycoon shit." He took pride in throwing his weight around, acting capriciously, traveling with sinister bodyguards, and generally reveling in his ability to perform acts of gratuitous cruelty.

The image of the band, in Oldham's eyes, revolved around Jagger and Richards. Instead of Brian Jones, Mick would be the visual focus: a figure of blues burlesque, an icon of camp sensuality. Keith would be his ambiguous sidekick. Together, they would be two boys like the Everly Brothers, singing songs of love, perhaps to some girl, perhaps to each other.

Carefully nurturing the Stones' nascent infamy, Oldham took the traditional formula for showbiz success and inverted it. Instead of cleaning them up and making them look "presentable" according to the conventions of polite society, he let the boys in the band keep their hair shaggy, their teeth crooked, their posture a slouch; he let them mutter and curse and behave unpleasantly; he let Jagger look effeminate, let him flutter his eyes and wave his arms in a rubber-legged parody of impassioned feeling; and, of course, he let the band concentrate on "unrepressed R&B," even as he urged them to write their own songs, just like Lennon and McCartney, one result being, in due time, "(I Can't Get No) Satisfaction"—a minor milestone in the musical expression of unabashed, unashamed, unconcealed sexual lust. In all of these ways, the Stones were able to exploit bohemian images of freedom and rebelliousness, a trick that Mary Quant had already turned in the rag trade. Feeding the press stories of mayhem and mischief, Oldham generated lurid headlines, among them the famous "Would You Let Your Daughter Go With a Rolling Stone?"

This was some kind of breakthrough. Taking traits widely regarded as repulsive, if not morally repugnant, Oldham seduced the media, provoking them into saturation coverage of outrageous behavior (much of it either exaggerated, or simply untrue).

The effect was perverse and paradoxical, as Oldham doubtless intended: those in the know were invited to invert the terms of judgment. Bad was now good. And vice versa. This was not Orwellian. This was fun!

That it was also a form of nihilism scarcely mattered, least of all to Oldham and the Stones. It was irritating, of course, to have an undeserved reputation for dirtiness; Brian Jones was in fact so compulsive about keeping his hair clean that Keith and Mick had nicknamed him "Mr. Shampoo." Still, the band played along, however grudgingly, for reasons any working stiff could understand.

Bill Wyman, the Stones' senior statesman, tells a relevant story. In the summer of 1963, during the first push to produce a public image of the Stones as grungy slackers, Wyman was accosted on a train by a prim stranger, who began to rant about "long-haired yobs who shouldn't be allowed in public places."

"I stared at him," Wyman recalls, "and said quietly, 'I'm getting paid for looking like this. What's your excuse?' "

November 11, 1963:

BEATLEMANIA!

There have been moments in modern times—and their rarity has only made their occurrence more striking—when an art-work has provoked an enthusiasm so profound, so widely shared, and so intoxicating that, to those swept up in it, life seems suddenly full of new possibilities, new prospects, new cultural horizons. At times like this, it may even seem as if an artist has been graced with supernatural powers, and that his works can be held up to "Life, as the prophetic mirror of its Future," as the composer Richard Wagner once put it. The works of such artists then appear to embody nothing less than a new spirit, heralding the advent of a whole new world.

Such, for example, was the import of Wagner's opera in Bismarck's Germany. And such, for better or worse, was the impact of the Beatles on the 1960s.

"This isn't show business," John Lennon remarked in December 1963, shortly after the idolatry of his band had become a source of shared wonder. "It's something else. This is different from anything that anybody imagines"—and different, certainly, from anything that Brian Epstein or John Lennon had ever imagined.

That the Beatles should have functioned as demigods to a generation was, after all, unplanned, unforeseen, and finally unprecedented. More than songs or singing, they offered the world themselves—not as a "total artwork" meant to serve as a "prophetic mirror," but rather as a spontaneous representation, at first quite unconscious, of a new kind of culture, a "counterculture" as it would later be called: a culture of prescriptive youthfulness, committed not to reason or beauty or sober good taste, but rather to whimsy, freedom, and fun, the crazier the better.

An inadvertent by-product of the usual ballyhoo, the phenomenon of the Beatles—their importance as a cultural touchstone—only became clear over the course of a few hectic months, starting in the spring of 1963. In the months that followed, fascination with the Beatles, at first confined to young British fans of popular music, breached the normal barriers of taste, class, and age, transforming their recordings and live performances from events of strictly parochial interest into a matter of much wider public import. Before it was all over, the growing popular passion for the band had produced an explosion of shared sentiment that spread convulsively: from Liverpool to London; from aspiring rock musicians like Brian Jones to the faceless rock fans who paid attention to their aspirations; from England to America; from the margins of pop music to the heart of the mass media; and from the centers of global culture to the periphery, finally embracing virtually everyone in the world—and transforming even those who, starting the process, imagined they were in command of it.

Only seven years later, John Lennon would speak of the Beatles as a kind of "dream," a myth, a puerile fantasy that he, personally, had outgrown: "I don't believe in Beatles." That the mania for the Beatles invested them with a pseudo-religious aura in these years is hard to dispute. Still, to this day, it is difficult to say why, or what the intensity of belief was finally about—if anything.

It had begun with "Please Please Me"—music that was rough yet sweet, crisply harmonized, aggressively performed. It had quickly become a matter of the band's look—faintly exotic, androgynous, utterly unexpected. And by the spring of 1963 in England it had become, as well, a matter of the band's collective persona. Unlike the English Elvis clones, with their lacquered good looks and empty prattle, the Beatles seemed like four characters in search of a play, figures from a waking dream, bursting with inventiveness and wit.

Ray Coleman, at the time an editor at *Melody Maker*, the hippest of England's music weeklies, has recalled how even jazz snobs warmed to the Beatles in the spring of 1963, thanks largely to John Lennon and his gift for improvised wordplay. "Most pop stars before John had a problem sustaining a conversation beyond the bland talk of their latest record and their narcissism. Lennon single-handedly stood that credo on its head. In his speech alone, pop music grew up."

Where Lennon was acerb and ironic, the rest of the band was just plain funny. "The Beatles made me laugh immoderately," recalls Maureen Cleave, the first reporter from a British daily newspaper to be bowled over by their unrehearsed antics. "They all had this wonderful quality—it wasn't innocence, but everything was new to them."

So it seemed as well to photographer Dezo Hoffmann. Sent to Liverpool on assignment for the weekly *Record Mirror,* Hoffmann, a veteran used to the self-conscious posturing of pop icons from Charlie Chaplin to Marilyn Monroe, found himself floored: "They were so fresh, so full of vitality and fun and so honest."

In April of 1963, Hoffmann spent a day in Liverpool shooting the band in a variety of locations, from the Cavern Club to the barbershop where the boys had their bangs trimmed. Most memorable of all was a sequence of shots taken at a local park picked by McCartney. After letting the lads horse around with his photo equipment, Hoffmann asked them to leap in the air with arms akimbo. It was this icon of playful whimsy that appeared, fittingly enough, on the picture sleeve of the extended-play disc containing "Twist and Shout"—the band's signature song in these heady months.

Recorded in February and featured on the band's debut album, released in March, "Twist and Shout" had quickly become the Beatles' trademark raver, their showstopper, the song they invariably used throughout these months to climax their short but exciting sets (which, at Epstein's behest, had been streamlined and pared down to twenty-five minutes). They had picked up the song from a recording made by the Isley Brothers. A black vocal group, the Isley Brothers had first won notice in America in 1959 with a recording called "Shout," an outlandishly perfervid simulation of a gospel sing, replete with meaningless call-and-response lyrics. In 1962, the Isleys had resurrected the formula, toned it down, and applied it to a trashy novelty called "Twist and Shout," a lyric meant to cash in on the Twist, a dance craze launched by Dick Clark on *American Bandstand.* Ignoring the graceful ease of the Isleys' rendition, John Lennon sang "Twist and Shout" with grim, almost ferocious determination. Shouting—literally—at the top of his lungs, Lennon turned the song into a shrieking catharsis; it is no wonder that, in 1970, he would be drawn into the orbit of Arthur Janov, a psychologist who preached the therapeutic value of what he called "the primal scream."

If nothing else, a scream that is primal will cut through a lot of ambient noise. In the summer of 1963 (a time when the Rolling Stones were still just starting to roll), the sound of the Beatles was both ubiquitous and, among the smart set, an indispensable ornament of hip taste. In England, the album that featured "Twist and Shout," *Please Please Me,* rose to the top of the British album charts, and remained there for thirty consecutive weeks. The extended-play recording that featured "Twist and Shout" (and also Dezo Hoffmann's jump photo) sold tens of thousands of copies in its own right. And the band's third single, "From Me to You," eclipsed even the sales of "Please Please Me" and "Twist and Shout," remaining at number one for seven weeks.

Never before had a musical act enjoyed this level of popularity in Great Britain. Never before had a record been so keenly anticipated as the Beatles' next single.

"She Loves You" was released on August 23—and instantly set a definitive musical stamp on what the British press, with good reason, would soon be calling "The Year of the Beatles."

Anarchic in feel and informal in structure, the recording cleverly reprised the wild exuberance of "Twist and Shout." A celebration of old-fashioned rock and roll, "She Loves You" also conjured up the good-natured sweetness of "Ain't It a Shame," the chaotic verve of "Tutti Frutti," the joyous aggression of "Hound Dog." Famous for its exuberant refrain—"yeah yeah yeah"—it became equally famous for its falsetto "WOOOOO," a mock-ecstatic device copied from Little Richard, also used by the Beatles in "Twist and Shout," and sung in concert by McCartney and Harrison, who would shake their mop-tops in unison, a cue for the crowd to shake and shriek along. Number one for four weeks in September, and then again for two weeks at the end of November, "She Loves You" became the best-selling recording of the 1960s in England—the unofficial anthem of an era.

As the Beatles continued to crisscross the country, the crowds at their shows began to mushroom. The band was the toast of British teens—and, increasingly, the talk of their parents. In one way, at least, they were a throwback to an older era. Since Britain still boasted relatively few television sets, radio was still an important national medium. The BBC routinely aired a number of performances taped live in their studios. In 1942 and 1943, at a time when World War II had put a halt to the distribution of new recordings, Frank

Sinatra had become the first major teen idol on the basis of live radio broadcasts in America; in 1963, the Beatles accomplished something similar in England. Between March 1962 and June 1965, the Beatles were featured on fifty-two BBC radio programs. And throughout the summer of 1963, from June through the end of September, they hosted their own series of radio shows, *Pop Go the Beatles*, singing the songs they had written, and also singing the vintage Fifties rock and roll songs they loved, by Chuck Berry, Little Richard, Carl Perkins, and Jerry Leiber and Mike Stoller.

By that fall, the music of the Beatles had become a constant companion in the lives of a great many people in England. But most of them had never laid eyes on the band. That changed on October 16, the night the Beatles performed on Britain's top-rated TV show, *Val Parnell's Sunday Night at the London Palladium*.

Fifteen million people tuned in to watch—the largest audience in the history of British television. Paul McCartney and George Harrison went "WOOOOO" and shook their heads. John Lennon shrieked "Twist and Shout." Ringo Starr looked animated and cute. Screams echoed from the fans inside the theater, while outside a crowd of several hundred more fans pressed against a police cordon, chanting "We Want the Beatles." By the next day, virtually everyone had heard the news. "Siege of the Beatles," ran one typical tabloid headline: "What a Sunday Night at the Palladium!"

A week later, the band flew to Sweden for a week of concerts. On their return to Heathrow Airport on October 31, they were mobbed by countless screaming kids. The scene was captured and dutifully broadcast by the British press corps, out in force. "We were amazed," said Paul McCartney a few weeks later, "because although we had had several No. 1's in the record charts, teenage interest had only been on the normal, pop level."

For the Beatles, however, life on a "normal, pop level" was now over. Brian Epstein was elated but alarmed. He didn't want anyone hurt. He certainly didn't want his boys associated in any way with "hooliganism." In his autobiography, he deplored the rioting and vandalism typical of rock and roll "in the days of Bill Haley and 'Rock Around the Clock.' . . . Yet though the Beatles' music is rock and roll, though it is as exciting and stimulating as the mid-fifties version, it has remained remote from savagery."

Keen to have the band project a wholesome image, Epstein over the summer had negotiated a spot for the Beatles on a prestigious variety show staged annually for the royal family. Filmed on Monday, November 4, for broadcast the following Sunday, the 1963 *Royal Variety Performance* featured Marlene Dietrich and Tommy Steele, in addition to the Beatles, who were the seventh act on a nineteen-act bill.

But of course the Beatles by now had become the main event. Once again, the press appeared in force. Once again, reporters watched to see what these wonderfully wacky lads would do next, running in a pack that reinforced the mood of carnivalesque excitement the Beatles now provoked without even trying.

In the days leading up to this appearance, the most important one yet in the eyes of their manager, Epstein had asked his favorite Beatle how he expected an audience of lords and ladies to respond to "Twist and Shout." "I'll just ask them to rattle their fucking jewelry," John Lennon had shot back—and with the expletive deleted (to Epstein's great relief), it was a line that Lennon actually used.

It remains one of the most celebrated single sentences ever uttered by a rock star. The audience tittered; the press applauded; and all of England smiled.

The air of festive good feelings around the Beatles now became generalized, while the members of the band were left to cope as best they could with the discrepancy between their private sense of self and the band's happy-go-lucky corporate persona. Lennon, for example, was deeply ambivalent about fame, as well he might be, given the bohemian art school milieu that had shaped his ambitions. A deeply cynical, even bitter young man, he nevertheless became an object of universal affection, and a target on stage for stuffed animals and plush dolls: "Although all the Beatles are 'fab' in every way and form," one fan wrote Lennon, "you are the 'fabbest' of them all. I love you, John, so much that I bought you this cuddly toy, which is what I think of you as."

Fleet Street was beside itself. The *Daily Mirror*, in its headline on November 11, the day after the Royal Variety show had aired, coined a name for the new sentiment that now seemed to grip all of England: BEATLEMANIA! "You have to be a real sour square not to love the nutty, noisy, happy, handsome Beatles," declared the *Mirror:* "The Beatles are wacky. They wear their hair like a mop—but it's WASHED, it's super clean. So is their fresh young act."

What the educated British elite now discovered came as a shock. Unlike previous teen idols, the Beatles were articulate. They were funny. They had wit, irony, attitude. They even seemed intelligent!

On November 22, Parlophone released *With the Beatles*, the second album by the band, and the first to be planned as a coherent program of music, without any help from a current hit single. A demonstration of the band's musical versatility, the album also featured a striking black-and-white photo on the cover, showing the faces of the four Beatles in half shadow, looking almost somber, and certainly looking serious.

Consisting of fourteen songs, the album featured eight new original compositions. "All My Loving" was a joyous romp with a bright walking bass line and a beautiful guitar solo, played by Harrison in the rockabilly style of Carl Perkins. McCartney crooned "Till There Was You" with the beguiling directness of Peggy Lee, one of his favorite singers, while Lennon sang "You Really Got a Hold on Me" with a sweet sincerity worthy of Smokey Robinson, the song's composer and one of Lennon's idols. From their repertoire at the Cavern, the band resurrected Chuck Berry's "Roll Over Beethoven." But the climax came at the end, with a blast of John Lennon at his most feral, this time shouting out a version of a Berry Gordy song, "Money," so vehement and so aggressive that it made the original (released in 1960 by a singer named Barrett Strong) sound effete by comparison.

As if the new album was not enough, a week later, on November 29, Parlophone released two more new songs by the Beatles, as their fifth single: "This Boy," a ballad as delicately wrought as anything the Everly Brothers had ever sung, and "I Want to Hold Your Hand"—the song that would shortly make the Beatles famous around the world.

Cleanly recorded with propulsive hand-claps, "I Want to Hold Your Hand" had starker dynamic contrasts than "She Loves You," with a serene bridge leading abruptly back into an agitated expression of sexual longing ("it's such a feeling that my love, I can't hide!"). The piquancy of the vocal harmonies, like the freedom you could feel in the unorthodox chord changes, gave the song an irresistible aura of novelty. Roughly hewn yet utterly self-assured, the record had an aggressive confidence that hadn't been heard in pop music since Elvis Presley's breakthrough in 1956.

But the Beatles' breakthrough in 1963 differed from Presley's in one crucial aspect: from the start, the tribunes of elite culture bestowed their blessings. On December 27, the *Times* of London solemnly declared the Beatles to be "the outstanding English composers of 1963." Gingerly acknowledging the most vulgar aspects of the group's overwhelming popularity—the screaming fans, the media hype, the "handbags, balloons, and other articles bearing the likenesses of the loved ones"—the anonymous author (a musicologist later identified as William Mann) consecrated their *music* by describing it in the most recondite of terms: "Harmonic interest is typical of their quicker songs too, and one gets the impression that they think simultaneously of harmony and melody, so firmly are the major tonic sevenths and ninths built into their tunes, and the flat-submediant key-switches, so natural is the Aeolian cadence at the end of 'Not a second time' (the chord progression which ends Mahler's *Song of the Earth*)."

This may well be the first time that anyone had the audacity to compare, without irony, a rock and roll musician and an Olympian figure like Gustav Mahler—a token of cultural prestige. Not that John Lennon (who had composed and sung "Not a Second Time") especially cared, knowing little about Mahler, and less about Aeolian cadences: "To this day," Lennon admitted in an interview in 1980, "I have no idea what they are. They sound like exotic birds."

Meanwhile, Brian Epstein had flown to New York, trying to drum up publicity for the band's new single and upcoming visit. Several weeks before, Epstein had arranged to have the Beatles follow in the footsteps of Elvis Presley by headlining *The Ed Sullivan Show,* America's version of *Val Parnell's Sunday Night at the London Palladium.* By chance, Sullivan and his wife had been in London at Heathrow on October 31. "There must have been 50,000 girls there," Sullivan recalled, "and I later found out they had prevented Lord Home and Queen Elizabeth from taking off." Suitably impressed, Sullivan introduced himself to Epstein, and secured the Beatles for three shows the following February.

As Epstein explained to a reporter from *The New Yorker* several weeks later, shortly before their first trip to America, "They have tremendous style, and a great effervescence, which communicates itself in an extraordinary way. . . . They are genuine. They have life, humor, and strange, handsome looks."

Despite the Sullivan booking, Epstein still had plenty of reason to worry about the band's prospects in the U.S. Earlier in the year, Capitol, the American record label owned by EMI, the multinational that also owned Parlophone, had passed up every one of its options to issue the Beatles' records. As a consequence, Epstein and George

Martin had been forced to lease "Please Please Me," "From Me to You," and "She Loves You" to smaller, independent labels in America. Not one had been even a modest success.

Dick Clark, at the time still a tastemaker, recalls airing "She Loves You" when it was first released in America, in September 1963. Largely because the option on this particular Beatles record had been picked up by an old friend and former business associate, Clark decided to feature the disc on the "Record Revue" segment of *American Bandstand*. After hearing the record, a jury of three randomly selected Philadelphia teenagers was asked to rate it. "It's all right, sort of like the Everly Brothers and Chuck Berry mixed together," said the first juror: "I'll give it a 77" (out of a possible 100—a mediocre mark). "It's not all that easy to dance to," sneered the second reviewer, "I give it a 65." "It doesn't seem to have anything," said the third kid; "the best I can give it is a 70." Clark then showed everyone a photo of the four lads with the funny haircuts. The kids all snickered.

That was before news of Beatlemania began to filter out of England, along with pictures of girls in ecstasy.

While he was in New York, Epstein convinced Capitol not only to release "I Want to Hold Your Hand," but also to launch it with a lavish ad campaign. News of the frenzy surrounding the band overseas had reached America, provoking curiosity and giving the publicists at Capitol something to work with, in addition to the band's upcoming appearances on *The Ed Sullivan Show*.

Printing millions of stickers, Capitol papered New York and Los Angeles with the news that "The Beatles Are Coming." The actress Janet Leigh was photographed in a Beatle haircut. Capitol even tried, without success, to bribe a cheerleader into holding up a card saying "The Beatles Are Coming" during the pageantry at the Rose Bowl, a nationally televised sports event.

Such publicity ploys became moot once people heard "I Want to Hold Your Hand." Capitol released the record the day after Christmas. Within three days, 250,000 copies had been sold. By January 10, sales had topped one million. In New York City, the disc was reportedly selling 10,000 copies an hour—though who was keeping count?

There has never been anything quite like Beatlemania, either before or since. Listeners in the nineteenth century may have swooned to the artistry of Franz Liszt—but that was before modern media made it possible for millions of people to swoon as one. Subsequent rock stars, for example, Michael Jackson in 1984, have certainly sold more records than the Beatles—but without the music getting under people's skins, or provoking anything like a collective swoon.

With the Beatles, by contrast, the popular reaction, in America, as it had been in England, was sharp, profound—and enduring. It was as if a large segment of the population had fallen suddenly, and hopelessly, in love—the feeling of shared pleasure was that intense. At Carnegie Hall, where the Beatles did a couple of shows on their first visit to America, a journalist saw a young girl turn to her two friends and exclaim, "God! It's the greatest catharsis I've ever had!"

Performing in front of a studio audience of 728 people, many of them teenagers invited specifically to shriek and scream for the cameras, the Beatles made their live American television debut on Sunday, February 9, 1964. *The Ed Sullivan Show* that night was seen by an estimated 73 million people: at the time, the largest audience, by far, in the history of television.

Unlike Elvis Presley in 1956, the Beatles received generally respectful notices, however grudging. Television critic Jack Gould, writing in *The New York Times,* carped that the show was an "anti-climax." But the same paper's music critic expressed almost unqualified admiration, in terms that anyone properly cultured might appreciate: "The Beatles are directly in the mainstream of Western tradition. Their harmony is unmistakably diatonic."

Leaving little to chance, Epstein had paid a claque of fans in New York City to besiege the airport, and then stake out the hotel where the band was staying, waving placards and creating a photogenic hubbub. He had also organized saturation coverage of the trip, hiring Albert and David Maysles to shoot footage, some for a planned documentary film, some for a television special in England, and some simply for the private use of the Beatles (who were preparing to make their first feature film, with the working title *Beatlemania*).

Unlike Tom Parker, who had kept the press at a distance from Elvis Presley, Brian Epstein, by now confident of the boys' winning personalities, treated the media as allies, granting them easy access. Wherever the band went, they were shadowed by reporters and the film crew. As they traveled from New York to Washington, D.C., and then flew on to Miami, the bloated entourage reinforced the atmosphere of hysteria, as reporters and disc jockeys and photographers moved freely in and out of limousines and hotel rooms, grabbing quotes and taking pictures. The images of that trip, widely broadcast at the time, have, in retrospect, an almost touching innocence: the frenzy of the crowds, the glee of the media, the joy of the band, not yet jaded by the wages of fame.

In its cover story—the first that a serious, mass circulation magazine in America had ever devoted to a rock and roll act—*Newsweek* recounted the band's visit to the British embassy. While they were in Washington, they had attended a party thrown by the British ambassador, Sir David Ormsby-Gore: "At one point, Sir David, confused about the names, asked John if he was John. No, John said, he was Fred. Then, pointing to George, he said: 'He's John.' Sir David started to address George as John. 'No,' George said, 'I'm Charlie,' and, pointing to Ringo, said 'He's John.' The game worked so splendidly it was repeated several times. As the Beatles were leaving, Ringo turned to the unsettled ambassador and inquired: 'And what do you do?' "

Like boys on an endless lark, the Beatles in these days seemed able to send up everything—even themselves.

George: "We're rather crummy musicians."

Paul: "We can't sing; we can't do anything, but we're having a great laugh."

So why Beatlemania?

John: "Why not?"

And how does it feel to put on the whole world?

Ringo: "We enjoy it."

Paul: "We aren't really putting you on."

George: "Just a bit of it."

John: "How does it feel to be put on?"

For all the joshing, the Beatles weren't a joke—least of all to John Lennon (no matter how many disparaging remarks he would later make about the band after it had broken up in 1970). Shortly after returning from America, Lennon had a characteristic, and revealing, dustup with a British journalist named George Melly. A former jazz singer turned pop music critic, Melly, like Lennon, was a native of Liverpool with a caustic wit and a blunt personality; later in the decade, his book *Revolt Into Style,* on the pop arts in England, would famously argue that in pop music, "what starts as revolt finishes as style—as mannerism."

At a party for Lennon, Melly did not shrink from taking a jab at Lennon's vanity. Implying that the Beatles had already sunk into mannerism, he declared that Lennon, despite his fame and wealth, had made music that was manifestly inferior to that of the black American singers he admired.

"He turned on me with sublime arrogance," Melly later recalled. "He'd admit no such thing. Not only was he richer but better too. More original and better."

The episode captures perfectly the cocky belligerence—and creative determination—with which Lennon and the other Beatles took their popularity to heart. The adulation they received only reinforced the pride they took in their craft, creating a form of vaulting ambition all but unprecedented in rock and roll.

That spring, shortly after returning from their trip to America, the Beatles took time off from touring to make their first movie. Shot on a low budget and a tight schedule, *A Hard Day's Night* shrewdly exploited the excitement that now surrounded the band wherever it went. Pioneering a mixed genre—the director, Richard Lester, called it a "fictionalized documentary"—the film dramatized "an exaggerated day in the life of the Beatles." The script, by Liverpool writer Alun Owen, depicted the pop process with startling candor, tearing away the veil of glamour, and showing a band being pushed around by its managers, trapped as well as exalted by its fame.

Featuring seven new songs by Lennon and McCartney, the film revolved around a make-believe television broadcast, which allowed Lester to choreograph the rapture of the fans, reproducing what TV viewers in England and America had seen on the Parnell and Sullivan shows. There was an almost magical scene of the band running free in a park, clowning and leaping about and acting as carefree as they had looked in Dezo Hoffmann's photo on the sleeve of "Twist and Shout." There was a fake press conference with new ad-libs improvised by the band (Q: "How do you find America?" A: "Turn left at Greenland."). There was a mad dash through a railway station, another mad dash into a limousine, scenes replete with real fans running wild in a real frenzy (scenes that were easy to stage, since frenzied fans routinely ferreted out every location where the film was being shot).

Premiered in London on July 6, *A Hard Day's Night* soon enough made its way into cinemas around the world, communicating the wit of the band, the adoration of the fans, the sheer exuberance of the moment—and bringing the glad tidings, of Beatlemania, to viewers around the world.

"Although we did it in a light way, I still feel there is a serious purpose to the film," Richard Lester remarked years later, reflecting on what he had hoped to accomplish. "The Beatles told everybody, 'You can do anything you damn well like.' Just go out, and do it. There's no reason why you can't."

At first glance, this may seem a banal sentiment. But as Lester well knew, in a country like England, where the prospects of young people had long been circumscribed by caste and class, Beatlemania was anything but banal. As Lester put it, "the Beatles sent the class thing sky-high; they laughed it out of existence." John Lennon was not by upbringing a member of the working class; in England in 1964, he became a working-class hero.

In the United States, on the other hand, the band's impact was different. In America, the prospects of young people had long been circumscribed not by class, but rather by an openhearted eagerness to want whatever one was supposed to want, to do whatever one was supposed to do, to *be* just like everyone else.

In America, it was this timid conformism that the Beatles laughed out of existence. The stars of *A Hard Day's Night* made the cookie-cutter teen idols of *American Bandstand* seem fake and meretricious by comparison. A new sort of festive spirit took shape, unafraid, even proud, of what before would have seemed alien, idiosyncratic, unacceptable.

Evidently on an island unto themselves, nourished by the apparently inexhaustible love of their fans, the Beatles as they appeared in these months offered one image of utopia in the Sixties. Affluent, unattached, carefree, they were able to act out before a mass audience a surreal saga of triumph and conquest, achieved as if without effort—as if life, in the prophetic mirror of their music and persona, could become a permanent vacation.

LET GO! HAVE FUN!

Such were the imperatives of the new age dawning—and the party had just begun.

July 25, 1965:

Dylan Goes Electric

It was on a meandering, month-long trip from New York to San Francisco in quest of America, by way of Harlan County, Kentucky (to meet coal miners), Hendersonville, North Carolina (to speak with the poet Carl Sandburg), New Orleans, Louisiana (to celebrate Mardi Gras), Dallas, Texas (to see the place where President Kennedy had been shot), and Denver, Colorado (to look up the folk singer Judy Collins), that Bob Dylan experienced, again, the rush of musical excitement he had first felt, years before, in high school, listening to Little Richard.

It was February 1964. Dylan, twenty-two, was the most widely admired young folk singer and songwriter in America, thanks to "Blowin' in the Wind"—a song of wistful longing and defiant hope, sung the previous summer at the civil rights March on Washington led by Dr. Martin Luther King, Jr. On the road, Dylan meant to consort with the ghost of Walt Whitman, the muse of Allen Ginsberg, the wayward spirit of Jack Kerouac—and also the diverse democratic vistas represented by the anonymous and common folk he sought out everywhere he went: the miners in Kentucky, fireworks salesmen in South Carolina, college students in Georgia, revelers on the streets of New Orleans.

In search of America, he discovered something else, as well, blaring from his car radio: the Beatles.

"We were driving through Colorado," Dylan later recalled, "we had the radio on and eight of the Top Ten songs were Beatles songs. In Colorado! 'I Want to Hold Your Hand,' all those early ones. They were doing things nobody was doing. Their chords were outrageous, just outrageous, and their harmonies made it all valid. You could only do that with other musicians"—and Dylan at the time was performing by himself. "It started me thinking about other people"—about forming his own rock and roll band.

Perish the thought! This, after all, was *Bob Dylan*, folk singer, the purest of the pure, a young man who had won fame by singing rustic ballads and topical broadsides, the darling of America's intellectual left, the rightful heir of Woody Guthrie, a musician fabled for his unwillingness to compromise with the moneychangers and image merchants. To the old lions of the folk scene, people like Alan Lomax and Pete Seeger, unrepentant radicals who had survived the McCarthy era and still dreamed of using the folk revival as a vehicle for social change, the Beatles were one image of sin—thieves of authentic black music, singing mindless songs of their own, promising the emptiest sort of "fun."

Bob Dylan, on the other hand, had grown up, like John Lennon and Paul McCartney, with Elvis Presley and Chuck Berry and doo-wop rhythm and blues. While still in high school, in Hibbing, Minnesota, he had formed a rock band. By the time he was seventeen, he was writing his own songs, including an earnestly raucous homage to Little Richard. The home recordings that survive from this period—of him singing Little Richard's "Jenny, Jenny," and Robert and Johnny's dreamy "We Belong Together"—suggest that he (like Lennon and McCartney) preferred his rock and roll raw. "When you hear a good rhythm and blues song," he remarked to his best friend in Hibbing in 1958, on one of these home tapes, trying to sound *very* cool, "chills go up your spine"—and that is a visceral quality that his own best music would always try to convey.

"Now, at a certain time the whole field got taken over into some milk, you know—into Frankie Avalon, Fabian and this kind of thing," Dylan remarked in a 1966 interview, explaining how his musical taste had evolved: "So everybody got out of it. . . . But nobody really lost that whole thing. And then folk music came in as some kind of substitute for a while, but it was only a substitute. . . . Now it's different, because of the English thing." Born Robert Zimmerman in 1941, he was shaped by many of the same currents that had formed British musicians like Lennon and Keith Richards. In the fall of 1959, when he went off to college at the University of Minnesota in Minneapolis, he discovered a bohemian student milieu similar to what Lennon had found at the Liverpool College of Art and Richards at Sidcup College of Art: a world of cheap wine, beat poetry, and coffeehouse music, mainly jazz and folk, a scene that, in America, had blossomed in 1958 after the Kingston Trio's breakthrough hit, "Tom Dooley," reminded a new generation what folk music was all about—songs that sounded primordial, sung simply, with plain acoustic accompaniment.

It was at college that Robert Zimmerman turned himself into "Bob Dylan," folk singer. He created an alter-ego first by mimicking

Woody Guthrie, the archetypal "working-class minstrel" of the 1940s, an Okie who seemed drawn straight from the pages of John Steinbeck's *Grapes of Wrath,* a hobo and migrant laborer who embodied the romance of the road, of the West, of the uncorrupted proletarian. For the next two years, Dylan almost obsessively identified with Guthrie. He would listen to Guthrie's famous Dust Bowl ballads endlessly, mastering his Oklahoma twang, mimicking his artless, almost deadpan vocal style, admitting to one Minneapolis friend that he was "building a character."

By 1961, when Dylan left school for Greenwich Village, he had developed a very compelling act. "Mr. Dylan's voice is anything but pretty," wrote *The New York Times'* Robert Shelton that fall in the first significant review that Dylan received: "He is consciously trying to recapture the rude beauty of a Southern field hand musing in melody on his porch." When he wasn't on stage or in the streets, Dylan spent endless hours listening to records, taking special pleasure in whatever sounded alien and idiosyncratic. "Folk music," he remarked in a 1965 interview, "is the only music where it *isn't* simple. It's weird, man, full of legend, myth, Bible and ghosts . . . chaos, watermelons, clocks, everything."

It was this sense of strangeness and out-of-time otherness that Dylan first reached for in his music. He stalked the streets of the Village with a spiral notebook in his hand, jotting down ideas and observations about everything from the poetry he was reading to animals in the street or a newspaper headline, beginning to work up new songs of his own. At the same time, he became actively involved in a little mimeographed magazine called *Broadside,* which Pete Seeger and some friends, inspired by the reawakening student left and civil rights movement in America, had started up to publish new topical songs.

Signed to a recording contract at Columbia Records by John Hammond (who was something of a legend in his own right by then), Dylan proved exasperating and erratic in the studio. It was his songs, not his singing, that first made him famous. For his second album, released in the fall of 1963, he showcased a number of the tunes that he had been publishing in *Broadside:* "Masters of War," "A Hard Rain's A-Gonna Fall," and, the song that became his signature, "Blowin' in the Wind." Meanwhile, Dylan's manager was peddling his songs to other artists, including Peter, Paul and Mary, one of the more frankly commercial folk acts that had sprung up in the wake of the Kingston Trio. In the summer of 1963, Peter, Paul and

Mary released a pretty version of "Blowin' in the Wind"; the record took off, selling over one million copies in America, and also becoming a hit in England.

Dylan's first major performances in England, in the spring of 1964, came at the height of Beatlemania. The British journalist Ray Coleman recalls interviewing Dylan for *Melody Maker*, and striking up a conversation about the Fab Four. "He referred to a song whose title he could not remember. . . .'You know,' he said, 'that song about dope?' I must have looked even more baffled than I felt. It transpired that Bob believed the real words, 'I can't hide, I can't hide,' at the end of one chorus [of "I Want to Hold Your Hand"], were 'I get high, I get high.' "

After a show at the Royal Festival Hall in London, Dylan, as he always did in those days, made a public exit. For the first time in his career, he was mobbed. Fans swarmed around him, grabbing at his clothes and hair—the first sign that he, like the Beatles, could inspire a pseudo-religious sort of frenzy. In England, at least, he was already regarded as a pop star, a sex symbol, a sybaritic prophet—all rolled into one! For the young man who would have been Woody Guthrie, a world of new possibilities now beckoned.

Within a matter of months, Dylan began to turn his music inside out. In June 1964, shortly after returning from his trip to England, he recorded a number of new songs in a marathon session that would be his last for many years as a strictly solo artist. Most of them were love songs like "It Ain't Me Babe"; but unlike the love songs of Tin Pan Alley, or of rock composers like Berry Gordy or Lennon and McCartney, Dylan's featured unromantic and sometimes inscrutable lyrics that were involuted, hermetic, yet seething with an undefined, faintly intoxicating sense of self-righteous rage. Of the new songs, there was only one, "Chimes of Freedom," that was more or less "political," but it, like the love songs, offered a whorl of fantastic imagery. In notes that Dylan composed for the back cover of *Another Side of Bob Dylan,* he underlined the change. "You tell me about politics," he wrote, "an I tell you there are no politics . . . i know no answers an no truth/for absolutely no soul alive/i will listen t no one/who tells me morals/there are no morals/an i dream alot."

The style was clumsy, the sentiments an almost embarrassing mélange of romantic clichés and pulp existentialism. But once the sentiments, set to a howling beat, were groomed for the top ten, the clumsiness of the style scarcely seemed to matter. Dylan had reinvented himself first as a hobo minstrel, then as a troubadour of dissent. Reaching out to a wider audience still, he was about to become a rock and roll Rimbaud.

When it came, the metamorphosis was abrupt, surrounded by controversy, and greeted in some quarters as a scandal.

In April 1965, Dylan released a raucous and bluesy single, "Subterranean Homesick Blues." A modest success in America, it became Dylan's second top ten single in England, confirming his surprising status there as a rock star rivaled only by the Beatles and Rolling Stones. In May 1965, the month that he released *Bringing It All Back Home,* his first album with electric band accompaniment, Dylan knocked the Beatles off the top of the British album charts. (In the United States, by contrast, Dylan did not have a number one album until *Planet Waves* in 1974.)

In the months that followed, as he barnstormed across England (a tour shot by D.A. Pennebaker and edited into the film *Don't Look Back*) and America, Dylan became one of the most storied figures in rock and roll history, completely transforming the music and its expressive possibilities in the minds of those who played it and those who listened to it.

Dylan's image in those days had just as much impact as his music. A tangled aureole of hair crowned a pale and wraithlike figure. Dylan's face seemed frozen in a scowl. The growing unpredictability of his live performances—and his frequently glazed, impassive gaze—fueled speculation about drug use. At the time, Dylan did nothing to dispel the speculation. "Being a musician," Dylan said, expressing a conviction that would soon enough become widely shared among other rock and roll musicians, "means getting to the depths of where you are at. And most any musician would try anything to get to those depths." Try *anything*—that was the message. And around the world, a large and growing audience was ready to listen.

What they heard was, in many ways, singularly odd. Dylan was no musical virtuoso. He had deliberately stamped out any hint of smoothness in his singing style, preferring a timbre the texture of sandpaper. Technically, he was a singer of limited gifts, with a narrow range and slurred enunciation. His concerts were often sloppy. On his recordings, instruments were out of tune, arrangements a clutter. And some of his memorable songs and lyrics sounded equally helter-skelter. "Like a Rolling Stone"—his breakthrough rock and roll hit in America, released in July 1965—was "really vomitific in its structure," Dylan explained to a journalist. "It seemed like it was twenty pages, but it was really six. . . . You know how you get sometimes."

The voluble lyrics to a song like "Rolling Stone" lie dead on the printed page. What matters is Dylan's *voice*: the poetry of the song depends on it. There is, for example, the way that he pounces on a phrase like "How does it FEEEEEL?"—turning the question into an insult. The song cannot be separated from the singer—in that sense, "Like a Rolling Stone" is rock and roll through and through, closer in spirit to "Tutti Frutti" than to "We Shall Overcome."

By the summer of 1965, Dylan's new vocal approach was all but fully formed. As Dylan remarked some years later of his concerts in this transitional period, "This is what made me different. I played all the folk songs with a rock and roll attitude." He shouted his lyrics helplessly, like a sailor at the helm of a storm-pitched ship. Though he was still performing by himself throughout the spring, his guitar playing on the newer songs, like "Gates of Eden," "Mr. Tambourine Man," and "It's Alright Ma (I'm Only Bleeding)," had a hypnotic rhythmic propulsiveness, while his singing had a febrile, exalted, almost uncanny quality, as if Dylan's songs were singing him. An unnatural apparition giving voice to pell-mell rhymes, Dylan seemed like a medium for somebody else's messages. "I am just a voice speaking," he said in a 1966 interview. "And anytime I'm singing about people, it's like my voice is coming out of that dream."

Dylan's concerts came to resemble a kind of séance, often punctuated by tumult. This was something radically new in the world of pop music. Rock fans were accustomed to going to concerts to be near an idol, to jump up and down, perhaps to scream—that is what now routinely happened when the Beatles or the Rolling Stones went on tour, because that is what everyone expected a rock concert to involve. Folk music concerts of course were different—reverent students thoughtfully hung on every word. What Dylan in 1965 managed to do was to blast himself free from the intellectual complacency of the folk scene while daring the rock fans to *listen*. His music was full of surprise—and the disembodied, sometimes vehement way in which it was sung made it seem like a revelation that could only be received by the most faithful and fervent of disciples.

Still, it was with some trepidation, one imagines, that Dylan prepared to issue a more formal, and irrevocable, declaration of musical independence from his old friends at the Newport Folk Festival in

July of 1965. Even though "Like a Rolling Stone" was already blaring from Top 40 radio stations coast to coast, on its way to becoming the biggest rock hit of Dylan's career, the doyens of the folk scene, and the men who ran the festival—Alan Lomax and Pete Seeger prominent among them—doubtless expected Dylan to do what he had done the previous year: to appear on stage by himself, alone with his acoustic guitar, and then to make the crowd feel righteous by singing properly topical broadsides like "Blowin' in the Wind" or "The Times They Are A-Changin'."

From the time the festival began, a buzz was in the air. When was Dylan coming? What would he play? What would he sound like?

After he arrived, the tension only mounted. Instead of the Bob Dylan of the 1964 festival—who had worn blue jeans and a work shirt, in the customary folk singer's gesture of solidarity with the working class—the Bob Dylan of 1965 arrived with shades on, wearing a puff-sleeved dueling shirt with op-art polka dots, very pop, very provocative.

He chose to rehearse with a group of musicians who had never played with him before: this was his first foray into performing live with amplified instruments. The band included the drummer and the electric bass player from the Paul Butterfield Blues Band, an amplified Chicago blues group, and also the Butterfield band's lead guitarist, Mike Bloomfield. Like Butterfield, Bloomfield was white—and that spelled more trouble. A number of the festival elders, Alan Lomax for one, took it as an article of faith that the blues belonged to black folk—not white boys.

When Dylan and his makeshift rock band shambled onto the stage at Newport on the night of July 25, 1965, they launched into "Maggie's Farm," one of the electric blues pieces that Dylan had recorded for *Bringing It All Back Home*.

Jeers floated from the crowd: "Play folk music!" "Sellout!" Irate at the sheer volume of the sound, Pete Seeger was, as he later admitted, "ready to chop the microphone cord." After singing two more songs, Dylan abruptly left the stage, as did his band. The jeering intensified. Finally, in an apparent effort to mollify the crowd, Dylan returned by himself and sang two more songs in his customary "folk" style.

In retrospect, it is hard to see what the fuss was all about. A film was made of this performance, and it shows a poorly rehearsed band led by a wobbly singer. (As one member of the film crew recalls, "it was obvious that he was stoned, bobbing around the stage, very Chaplinesque, really.")

But any strictly musical account misses the drama of the moment. The use of electric instruments, turned up LOUD, was an act of aggression. And it worked. Hurling imprecations and threats at Dylan and his crew backstage, Lomax and Seeger went wild—a demonstration of the kinds of raw emotions that a rock and roll musician, if he wished, could stir up.

He could irritate and enrage. He could provoke an argument, cause a furor. He could polarize a tight-knit subculture like the folk community, making of his music an art form that demanded for its sincere reception something like the shock of conversion.

And that is one of the ways in which Bob Dylan became a new kind of rock and roll hero. Like Zarathustra, Nietzsche's holy fool (and like Ziggy Stardust, David Bowie's holy rock fool a decade later), he would dramatize a different way to live. A poet and a prophet, he would write out of his own life, with no apparent regard for the pieties prevailing in society. In the spirit of Rimbaud, he would make himself "a *seer* by a long, gigantic and rational *derangement of the senses*," exploring "all forms of suffering, love, and madness," exhausting "all poisons in himself," extracting only their "quintessences" through the systematic use of intoxicants, and concentrating the force of his personal revelations in a music of delirious immediacy.

It didn't take long for Dylan's new style to hit home. As the Beatles and every other rock musician with artistic pretensions understood immediately, it was the end of "yeah yeah yeah" and the start of something else—a new kind of music, made for a new kind of listener.

October–November 1965:

Rubber Soul

Bob Dylan singlehandedly showed the Beatles a new way
to fashion themselves. He did this through the way that he sang, the way that he wrote songs, the scruffy and offhand way that he played

harmonica and guitar. Even more, though, he did it through the edge in his voice, the defiance in his gaze, the breathtaking freedom of his actions both on stage and off.

His influence, in short, was a matter of attitude.

George Harrison was the first of the Beatles to pay attention. In 1963, with the band in the grip of Beatlemania, Harrison bought Dylan's second album, the one with "Blowin' in the Wind" on it, and played it for his mates. McCartney, impressed, duly bought the first Dylan album, the one with all the songs about death and the cover photo of a baby-faced, avowedly Chaplinesque tramp wearing a corduroy cap. As it happened, John Lennon owned a cap of the same style; and as he fretted out loud, with a reporter present, "Paul bought a Bob Dylan record, and he was wearing this exact cap on the cover. He even had the button open like mine. Everybody will think I copied it from him."

Never mind the intelligence and idiosyncrasy of Dylan's wordplay—Dylan's *look* was reason enough for jealousy. A rival and a natural model in the eyes of Lennon, Dylan was a paragon of bohemian chic, someone who represented everything that Lennon still silently aspired to: artistic integrity, musical honesty, the priceless cachet of being hip, not with screaming teenagers, but with serious adults—poets like Allen Ginsberg, artists like Andy Warhol, political leaders like Martin Luther King, Jr.

On the night of August 28, 1964, the Beatles and Bob Dylan met face-to-face for the first time. The place was a hotel room in New York City, the occasion a post-concert get-together, organized after the Beatles had finished an outdoor show at the Forest Hills Tennis Stadium in front of 16,000 fans—many of them screaming teenagers.

Eagerly awaited, Dylan made a grand entrance, sweeping past a roomful of people waiting patiently to see the Fab Four—reporters, photographers, radio announcers, Peter, Paul and Mary, the Kingston Trio (for some reason, folk singers were drawn to the Beatles).

Ushered into the inner sanctum, Dylan and his entourage were formally introduced to John, Paul, George, and Ringo, who were seated at a table, finishing a room-service dinner. Brian Epstein asked the visiting bard what he wanted to drink.

"Cheap wine," came the reply.

Since Epstein stocked only fine wine, plus Scotch to mix with Coke for the band, an assistant was sent out for a jug. While he was waiting, Dylan was offered a hit of "speed"—since their days in Hamburg, the Beatles kept themselves up by using amphetamines. Turning down the pill, Dylan offered to roll a joint.

Sheepishly, the band admitted that they had never tried marijuana.

Dylan was floored. What about that line in their song? "Love that one, man," McCartney recalls him saying: "I get high, I get high, I get high." He was still laboring under the misapprehension that "I Want to Hold Your Hand" was a delphic ode to dope.

The band was eager to make up for lost time. Blinds were pulled, drapes drawn, doors bolted shut. Given the green light, Dylan began to roll joints. After issuing brief instructions about how to inhale, he lit one and passed it to Lennon. Reluctant to plunge right in, Lennon passed it on to Ringo—"my royal taster," he nervously joked. Ringo puffed away, while Dylan rolled and passed out more joints.

As the pot kicked in, the band became giddy. Ringo began to laugh, and the others began to laugh, too. "I'm so high," Brian Epstein exclaimed, "I'm on the ceiling!"

"It's as though we're up there," Paul agreed, pointing at the ceiling—"up there, looking down on us!"

Excited by a flood of sudden thoughts, McCartney, as he has recalled, scrambled around the room looking for a piece of paper and a pencil "because I discovered the meaning of life that evening and I wanted to get it down. . . . And I went into a little room and wrote it all down, 'cos I figured that, coming from Liverpool, this was all very exotic and I had to let my ordinary people know, you know, what this was all about: like if you find the meaning of life, you've got to kind of put it about. Mal"—the Beatles' road manager—"handed me the little bit of paper the next morning after the party and on it was written, in very scrawly handwriting: THERE ARE SEVEN LEVELS. Till then we'd been sort of hard scotch and Coke men. It sort of changed that evening."

Change it certainly did—for McCartney; for the Beatles; and for the global youth culture that the Beatles now embodied, if only symbolically.

Up till then, rock and roll had been primarily a music of revelry, a medium for lifting people up and helping them dance their blues away. Under the combined influences of marijuana and Bob Dylan's unkempt persona, the Beatles would turn it into something else again: a music of introspective self-absorption, a medium fit for communicating autobiographical intimacies, political discontents, spiritual elation, inviting an audience, not to dance, but to *listen*—quietly, attentively, thoughtfully.

The first thing to change was the texture of the Beatles' recorded sound. Starting with "Eight Days a Week," "She's a Woman," and "I Feel Fine," all recorded in October 1964, the band began to toy with different technical tricks in the studio, expanding their palette of musical colors, creating new kinds of artificial sounds: for "Eight Days a Week," they improvised a fade-in to the song; for "I Feel Fine," they worked with distorted sonorities and deliberately produced feedback; and for "She's a Woman," they built an entire song around a boldly melodic bass line. The experimentation continued, as Lennon created an entirely acoustic, folk feel for "You've Got to Hide Your Love Away," while McCartney helped George Martin overdub an austere string quartet onto "Yesterday," a ballad of classic proportions, instantly recognized as such. (In 1992, British composer Peter Maxwell Davies declared "Yesterday" to be his favorite Beatles song, "because it demonstrates the generosity of spirit in Paul McCartney's melodies and their exemplary, instinctive technical know-how.")

Serious as their newfound dedication to sound was, a rediscovered taste for whimsy was another by-product of their new drug of choice. "Let's have a laugh" was their private code for "Let's go get stoned." On February 14, 1965, the same day that McCartney recorded "Yesterday," he also recorded "I'm Down," a raving parody of Little Richard, delivered with blithe abandon. At the end of the first take of "I'm Down," McCartney, audibly pleased with his performance, mutters "plastic soul, man, plastic soul"—a phrase that, slightly changed, would become the title of the Beatles' next album, *Rubber Soul*.

A farewell to innocence, the album is (like Dylan's appearance at the Newport Folk Festival earlier in the year) a declaration of independence.

It has a number of contrasting facets. Some of the songs are comic playlets, including the opening track (on the original British version of the album), "Drive My Car," a facetious vignette that recalls Lennon and McCartney's youthful admiration for Leiber and Stoller. As if to honor the self-deprecating irony of the album's title, this song, like others, incorporates a riff borrowed from a black American soul hit—in this case, the model is Otis Redding's "Respect." But the riff is so cleverly concealed, in a song structure so idiomatically distinctive, that it is virtually unrecognizable, functioning as an inside joke, rather than a generic gesture.

And this was just the beginning of an album that sums up everything the Beatles had thus far brought to rock and roll, as well as offering a preview of where they were taking it—off the road, and into the studio.

For the preceding two years, as popular adulation for the band had continued to grow uncontrollably, the group had adhered to a tight schedule of touring, recording, and shooting films. Their fame had forced them into playing larger and larger venues, where the roar of the crowds routinely canceled out the sound of the music, creating within the band a growing contempt for the ritual of performing. "It's like we're four freaks being wheeled out to be seen, shake our hair about, and get back in our cage afterwards," John Lennon remarked at the time.

He was among the first, though certainly not the last, to remark on the strange vacuity of the live rock concert, once the shows had reached a certain scale, and the performers had provoked a certain level of frenzy: "I reckon we could send out four waxwork dummies of ourselves," said Lennon, "and that would satisfy the crowds. Beatles concerts are nothing to do with music, any more. They're just bloody tribal rituals."

Studio work was an escape. And for the first time in two years, the band now demanded a decent interval of time off in which to write and rehearse songs for a new album, their sixth to be released in England—and the first real indication of how profound Dylan's impact had really been.

Largely recorded in one month, between October 12 and November 11, 1965, *Rubber Soul* was simultaneously witty and weighty, arty and folky, ironic and sincere—and altogether more impressive than any previous album by the Beatles or, for that matter, virtually any previous album by any other rock and roll act.

Consisting of fourteen songs, all of them new compositions, the album explored an unusual variety of textures and moods. The exotic instrumentation included sitar, the Indian instrument (used on "Norwegian Wood"), and bouzouki, a mandolinlike Greek stringed instrument (used on "Girl"). Distorted timbres dominate "The Word," the band's first ode to love as a universal panacea, while acoustic instruments and plush vocal harmonies characterize "Michelle," McCartney's loving parody of a French cabaret song.

Throughout, McCartney plays electric bass with a melodic freedom and rhythmic daring rivaled only by his model and main inspiration, James Jamerson, a mainstay of Berry Gordy's Detroit studio band, who played on most of the era's hits by the Supremes, Four Tops, and Temptations.

But if any one song exemplifies the newfound sophistication of the Beatles' songwriting on *Rubber Soul,* it is "In My Life." A collaborative effort, its lyric, by Lennon, is set to a melody, largely composed by McCartney (though in retrospect, no one could agree on the details of who had written what). "It was the first song I wrote that was consciously about my life," Lennon later recalled. It started out as a set of words, without music, cataloguing the places Lennon had passed by on the bus he rode as a child from his home into downtown Liverpool. "I wrote it all down, and it was so *boring.* So I forgot about it and laid back, and these lyrics started coming to me about friends and lovers of the past."

More powerfully than any Beatle lyric before it, "In My Life" communicates a melancholy mood of yearning, a sentiment that is also conveyed by McCartney's vaulting melody line. After rehearsing and then recording a usable basic track of the song on October 18, Lennon asked George Martin to add "something baroque-sounding here." Martin came up with a clever pastiche, recording a piano part at half speed, and then playing it back at full speed, in this way simulating the sound of a harpsichord.

From the moment it was released (on December 3, 1965), it was obvious to anyone listening—and that was millions of people—that *Rubber Soul* presented, in George Martin's words, "a new, growing Beatles to the world. For the first time we began to think of albums as art on their own, as complete entities."

But it was not just artistry that the album intimated. Halfway round the world, in the crash pads of the Haight-Ashbury in San Francisco, *Rubber Soul* was avidly received by local poets and folk singers and protesters and the district's scattered bands of born-again beatniks and dope fiends. Listening intently and staring at the album art, people noticed the fun-house photo on the cover, the biomorphic lettering of the title, the line "I get high" in one of the songs on the American version of the album ("It's Only Love"—the line was yet another inside joke, this one aimed at Dylan). And in the Haight, as throughout the bohemian world of students everywhere, in art schools and colleges and universities, people wondered.

Could it be—was it possible—that the Beatles, too, were getting *stoned?*

Years later, McCartney put the moment into perspective. "The main thing," he insisted, "is that people were getting high, that's the main thing. It was the shift from drink to pot in fact—that's really all it was."

Meanwhile, the man who had turned on the Beatles keenly followed their career, even composing an inscrutable parody of "Norwegian Wood" called "4th Time Around." To say that Bob Dylan was ambivalent about the Beatles doesn't quite do justice to the caustic closing lines of "4th Time Around": "I never asked for your crutch/Now don't ask for mine."

McCartney recalls a pilgrimage to see Dylan in London a few months after *Rubber Soul* had come out. "Oh, I get it," McCartney recalls Dylan saying. "You don't want to be cute anymore!" And McCartney, in retrospect, has agreed: "That summed it up. That was sort of what it was. The cute period had ended."

And the strange period was just starting.

5

Break on **Through**

The Acid Test

As midnight approached on December 4, 1965, kids came pouring out of the Civic Auditorium in San Jose, California. Homeward bound, they had just seen a show by the Rolling Stones. Standing outside, waiting, were a handful of people, each one wearing face paint and what looked like a Halloween costume: there was a cowboy, a clown, a Victorian dandy. Fanning into the crowd, the painted and costumed people—the "Merry Pranksters," they called themselves—pressed leaflets into outstretched hands. Each piece of paper was unique, a homemade work of art in mixed media, crayon, and colored pen:

CAN *YOU* PASS THE ACID TEST?

A dare that dangled the promise of adventure, the leaflet gave directions to a nearby house. Dozens of fans, in search of "Satisfaction" (as Mick Jagger had just put it in song), took the handbill and lit out for the territory.

Their destination was a run-down place filled with more folks dressed in funny clothes, all of them already high on "acid"—the medium for the evening's promised "test."

Acid was local slang for lysergic acid diethylamide, or LSD-25. A mind-altering drug first synthesized, by accident, in 1938, it was a chemical compound of great potency but uncertain value. After the war, it was explored first by researchers interested in its psychotomimetic properties—that is, its power to induce mental states thought to resemble those experienced by schizophrenics. Some psychiatrists hoped it might help in therapy. Researchers for the U.S. Army, meanwhile, investigated its suitability as a weapon for chemical warfare.

At the same time, a handful of daredevil spirits, having had the drug in various sets and settings—some in therapy, some as unwitting subjects of army research—concluded that LSD was no ordinary drug. It was, rather, an elixir that opened the doors of perception, revealing something wondrous: the essence of reality, or being, or nothingness (before such wonders, language failed).

Evangelical in their passion, the proponents of LSD prophesied the dawning of a new era of alchemical soulcraft. The patriarch of the group was Aldous Huxley, British-born and bred, a raffish critic of modern society, the author of satiric novels and also of *Brave New World,* a celebrated dystopia. A man preoccupied with the mysteries of the mind, Huxley sought out states of altered consciousness, experimenting with various Eastern religious practices and also with mind-altering drugs like LSD and mescaline (a natural substance chemically related to LSD). He eloquently detailed his experiences with mescaline in *The Doors of Perception* (1956), a book that enthralled a small but influential audience of poets, writers, and daredevil social scientists. Among Huxley's readers was a young professor of psychology at Harvard named Timothy Leary, who, having stumbled onto LSD by accident, quickly became an enthusiast, touting its virtues to anyone who would listen, convinced (as the patrician Huxley never was) that this marvelous new chemical means of enlightenment should be put in the hands of anyone who wanted it.

Last but not least, and more radical still, was a West Coast Mr. Hyde to Leary's Dr. Jekyll, a writer named Ken Kesey. Large, athletically imposing, and blessed with a superabundance of animal energy, Kesey was the author of a widely praised first novel, *One Flew Over the Cuckoo's Nest* (1962), written under the influence of mescaline. Since then, Kesey had invested almost all of his energy in staging, in order to film, a virtually nonstop, LSD-fueled happening, a mind-bending circus that roamed the land in a bus painted in swirls of garish color with an ad hoc cast of freelance lunatics and genuine artists, including (sometimes) the young Robert Stone, later renowned as a novelist, and also the old Neal Cassady, the real-life prototype for Dean Moriarty, the fictional hero of Jack Kerouac's classic beat novel, *On the Road,* which, in part, had inspired Kesey to launch his Dionysian odyssey to ports more or less unknown.

It was Kesey and his friends, the Merry Pranksters, who had organized the happening in the old house in San Jose. As kids began to arrive, Kesey and his gang offered each one some LSD. This was their ticket to the Acid Test.

In preparation, the house had been carefully booby-trapped by Kesey and his co-conspirators. There was a movie projector and a light machine, and tape recorders and a kind of mechanical drum that went "boom," and there were microphones scattered around everywhere to pick up odd sounds and bits of conversation, which were then relayed to a mixing board and sent out to loudspeakers arranged throughout the house, so that as people wandered they would hear strange voices drifting in and out of focus. Various musical instruments—flutes, horns, guitars—were scattered about, and people were encouraged to pick one up and make some noise.

In the main room, finally, there was a bunch of dedicated musicians, a real rock and roll band, most of them younger than the Rolling Stones, but trying to play the same sort of music: pop with a "black" twist, that is, high-strung variations on blues and dance hits originally made popular by African-American singers, for example: Martha and the Vandellas ("Dancing in the Street," from 1964), Howlin' Wolf ("Good Morning Little School Girl," 1959), and Cannon's Jug Stompers ("Viola Lee Blues," 1928). The singers hooted and hollered, mangling the songs with cheerful gusto, leaving plenty of room for the lead guitarist to take off on long, meandering solos, joined by the bassist, who played a lot of different notes, as if he were soloing at the same time, too. The band stretched out the beat, sometimes losing it, sometimes letting it snap back into place, offering its own highly amplified form of rubbery jubilation (most of them were in the midst of taking Kesey's Acid Test, too).

Formerly known as the Warlocks, the band was called the Grateful Dead. There were five of them. The bassist, Phil Lesh, twenty-five, was a former guitar player, and also a trumpeter, blessed with perfect pitch, it was said, though it was hard to know, given the surrounding cacophony. The rhythm guitarist, Bob Weir, eighteen, was unseasoned but full of teen spirit. Bill Kreutzmann, nineteen, the drummer, worked hard at playing with the big kind of beat needed to imitate the Rolling Stones. Ron "Pigpen" McKernan, twenty, the band's burly organist, chain-smoked, drank hard, and did his best to look menacing, clad in biker denim and wearing a headband. The group's lead guitarist and tutelary spirit, Jerry Garcia, twenty-three, was by contrast a beatific bear of a man whose eyes lit up as he played; a former banjo picker and onetime jug-band leader, he had shocked his folk music friends by ditching his banjo and jug, picking up an electric guitar, and deciding to form a rock band after seeing the Beatles in *A Hard Day's Night*.

Since no recordings survive of the Grateful Dead performing at their first Acid Test, one must conjure with the evidence of "Viola Lee Blues," the sole marathon blues number included on their first album (released in the spring of 1967). Only distantly modeled on the slap-happy sound of the song as recorded by Cannon's Jug Stompers, a band that featured banjos, harmonica, and kazoo, the Dead's version began with everybody singing (sort of) several choruses of the song—vocal harmony was not the group's forte. One of the oldest items in the Dead's repertoire, the album version of "Viola Lee" is nearly fifteen minutes long (in concert, it would likely have been longer still). Most of the song, in their hands, consists of a sequence of rollicking instrumental solos, starting at a relaxed lope and speeding up, with the band pushing hard, Garcia flying over the frets, and Pigpen hurling himself into a roller-rink orgy of simpleminded riffs. Forget about swing or even keeping proper time: these boys were aiming at ecstasy.

Years later, the man who would become the band's manager, Rock Scully, recalled his first impression. "Everybody followed Jerry," Scully said. "They had to because Jerry was rushing," playing songs faster and faster, "because he was high on acid. Bill Kreutzmann was trying to keep up with him and Phil had only been on the bass for a couple of weeks so he was doing his best to keep up and make the sound presentable, but in the middle of an Acid Test, it didn't much matter. . . . You know how you can sometimes see what people are thinking? Garcia was either thinking that there were insects on his guitar or that it had done a Salvador Dali drip over his wrist and now was melting over his hand."

While the band played on, the people in the audience, high on acid, began to undulate and wobble. With the pulse of the music expanding and contracting to accompany the ebb and flow of Garcia's playing, the dancers were forced to follow. Scully, in his memoir, marshals improbably mixed metaphors to evoke the sensation: "We inhale and exhale . . . as if to the great collective heartbeat of an invisible whale. We are all under the hypnotic spell of this ghostly pulse. Whoever these guys are, they are uncannily tuned into the wavelength of the room. They hover over the vibe like dragonflies."

While the band played and the crowd wobbled, a strobe light flashed. At the house in San Jose, motion pictures were projected from Kesey's work in progress, shots of the psychedelic bus, of people getting high, of the goofy things these stoned freaks had chosen to film: feathers, beads, broken glass, clouds, weird piles of junk strangely decorated. Cups of Day-Glo paint with brushes were scattered round the house, allowing newcomers to splash colors as the spirit moved them. When the band paused for a break, Neal Cassady took over, speed-rapping (he popped amphetamine like candy), doing breathless verbal riffs, dancing in the strobe light, shredding his clothes.

Kesey had come up with the idea for the Acid Test after taking the measure of two formative experiences. The first was a party in the woods he'd thrown the previous summer for members of the Hell's Angels motorcycle club, a gang of brutal bikers who struck Kesey's fancy. He'd served a lot of beer and handed out a lot of acid. Behold, the lions had become as lambs—an impressive feat, given the gang's sinister reputation.

Kesey's second formative experience occurred a few weeks later, in September, when he resolved that he and the other Pranksters should make a special effort to go see the Beatles.

Like a lot of other people around the world, Kesey and his friends had been partying throughout the summer to songs from *Help!*, the first album the Beatles had recorded after entering their own phase of psychedelic experimentation. (Things moved fast in these years. By the time *Help!* was recorded, in the spring of 1965, Lennon and Harrison had been turned on, not just to pot, but also to acid, by their dentist, of all people, who had distributed LSD at a dinner party.)

Listening to *Help!*, it was obvious, Kesey and his friends agreed: the Beatles were getting high! It was obvious, too, that Kesey and his pals should not only see the Beatles, they should *welcome* them, show them a good time, perhaps even coax them into coming out to join them at one of their acid orgies, another wild party, just like the one they had thrown for the Hell's Angels.

There was one problem. No one knew how to reach the band. No matter! All things were possible, provided one trusted to chance, went with the flow—and let Kesey's skill at seizing the moment work another miracle.

In the event, Kesey did manage to procure a row of seats to the sold-out show. He did get the Pranksters out of the house and into the bus.

But once the Pranksters had gotten inside the Cow Palace, they froze.

They were surrounded by screaming girls and menacing cops. From a distance, the musicians on stage looked like ants. No one could hear anything. Mortified by the situation, Kesey signaled a retreat. Mission unaccomplished, the Pranksters went home.

It was still a great notion, said Kesey. They just needed a better way to introduce LSD into the rock subculture.

His solution was the Acid Test.

Kesey had located a free house, and advertised the party at the Stones show. He had hired his own band, the Dead, and drawn on the generosity of a newfound friend and fellow acid evangelist, a young chemist named Augustus Owsley Stanley III, to offer anyone who came to his party a hit of pure LSD, still a legal drug (in the United States, criminal sanctions for the possession of LSD were enacted, hastily, only in the following year).

This wasn't show business, this was tinkering with souls. Under the pressure of the psychedelic experience, after all, some people were bound to fall apart: Kesey had seen it happen before, on the bus—and that was with people he knew fairly well. Nobody knew who they were inviting after the Stones show. One of the strangers might go nuts, or get violent, not that Kesey or the Pranksters seemed to care: they acted as if caring, and taking care, were obsolete aspects of a castrating ego.

Still, nobody flunked the first Acid Test. And by the time dawn broke on the morning of December 5, 1965, a number of Kesey's newfound flock were happily roaming the streets of San Jose, blinking and naked, born again.

And the test wasn't even finished!

Later that day, as Rolling Stones bassist Bill Wyman has recounted, Kesey, leaving nothing to chance, journeyed down the coast to join some of the Stones at a party after they had finished their American tour with a show, one of their biggest yet, at the Los Angeles Sports Arena. Armed with tabs of Owsley acid, Kesey trawled the room for takers.

Bingo!

Brian Jones was willing. And so was Keith Richards. The dada evangelist added two more converts to his cultural crusade.

And that is how an era of anarchy, experiment, and the great new beginning was well and truly launched by Ken Kesey, the Merry Pranksters, and the Grateful Dead.

A week later, they all convened again, to stage still another Acid Test, this one in San Francisco. This time, though, the big draw wasn't the drugs—it was the band. "We always thought of the Grateful Dead as being the engine that was driving the spaceship that we were traveling on," one of Kesey's friends, Ken Babbs, recalled years later. "Once the Grateful Dead got the engine cooked up and running, that became the motor driving the thing."

For the Bay Area, it was the start of a new scene. While Kesey laid plans to turn his Acid Tests into a regular event, other impresarios moved fast to copy the formula. Within weeks, new psychedelic ballrooms had opened up in Berkeley and in San Francisco, presenting light shows and rock bands playing in open spaces where people could undulate as one. And within a matter of months, the music made by new bands like the Grateful Dead, and by old bands like the Beatles and the Rolling Stones, would fulfill Ken Kesey's wildest fantasies, producing a global explosion of interest in LSD—and bringing to a mind-boggling climax the cultural revolution that Alan Freed and Elvis Presley had started ten years before.

February 8–13, 1966:

Andy Warhol, Up-Tight

Around the world in the mid-Sixties, everywhere people were listening to rock and roll, "everything went young"—and time seemed to accelerate. So remarked Andy Warhol, one of the era's most prominent architects, in his memoir *POPism: The Warhol '60s.* "I could never finally figure out if more things happened in the sixties," Warhol wrote, "because there was more awake time for them to happen (since so many people were on amphetamine), or if people started taking amphetamine because there were so many things to do that they needed to have more awake time to do them in."

Warhol, for one, needed a lot of "awake time" in his busiest decade. A relatively obscure commercial artist when the Sixties began, Warhol quickly developed reputations in a variety of fields. He was an artist, he was a filmmaker, he threw great parties, and he had New York City's hottest hangout, the Factory, which doubled as his studio. And in February 1966, he branched out yet again, presenting a musical event that, by design, turned Warhol into the most consequential rock and roll Svengali since Brian Epstein and Andrew Loog Oldham.

The show was billed as "Andy Warhol, Up-Tight." The posters promised "Rock 'n' Roll, Whip Dancers," and "Film-maker Freaks." The music was made by a new band called the Velvet Underground, who were joined on stage by a variety of glamorous figures, pretty boys and girls, dancing with themselves, gyrating with whips, miming kinky sex—a little bondage, a little discipline. Behind the band flickered silent images from two experimental films, projected side by side simultaneously. Midway through the evening, a young woman ran down the aisle with a handheld camera, a blinding light, and a microphone, to record the answers to outrageously intimate questions: "Is your penis big enough?" "Does he eat you out?"

The band was painfully loud. It consisted of five musicians, all but one dressed entirely in black. An androgyne drummer, twenty-year-old Maureen Tucker, played standing up, with tom-tom mallets. She was flanked by two impassive young men: Sterling Morrison, twenty-three, an electric guitarist, and John Cale, twenty-five, who played the electric bass as well as his main instrument, a viola wired for amplification. One of the singers, Lou Reed, twenty-three, wore high-heeled boots, played an electric guitar, too, and sang with histrionic precision, enunciating every syllable in a monotonic whine. The one dressed in white, and the visual focus of attention, was another vocalist, a stunning German beauty named Nico (her real name was Christa Päffgen), at twenty-seven the oldest member of the group; with studied composure and a vacant gaze, she projected an image of blank despair, a lost Teutonic soul, her voice like a foghorn, creating a mood of calm foreboding. With instruments blaring, the singers sang simple songs with hard-edged titles: "Venus in Furs"; "Heroin"; and another song about junk, "Waiting for the Man."

By the time of the Up-Tight revue, the show's producer, Andy Warhol, was one of the most storied—and controversial—figures of the age. As much as any one person, he personified the idea of "Pop," his term for a kind of camp alchemy in which the mundane was suffused with supernatural potential—and mass-marketed commodities were transformed into artifacts of sublime and singular beauty. Long a journeyman illustrator on the fringes of the New York art world, Warhol had become famous in 1962 for his paintings of Campbell's soup cans, his wooden replicas of Brillo boxes, and his silkscreens of various celebrities and movie stars, including Elvis Presley. Struggling to get beyond the lyrical aspects of painting prized by abstract expressionists, Warhol produced images that conveyed an aura of disquieting detachment, cheerfully turning his art into a branded commodity in its own right.

In the spring of 1965, Warhol held a press conference in Paris to announce that he had retired from painting. "Art just wasn't fun for me anymore," he later explained. "It was people who were fascinating and I wanted to spend all my time being around them, listening to them, and making movies of them."

He bought a camera and started to shoot films, eschewing editing and offering his actors only a minimum of direction. Enthralled by the banal and the ordinary, he shot a short film showing Nico weeping, another short film of someone else sleeping, still another showing only a guy's face while getting a blow job; not to mention *Empire,* an eight-hour epic film capturing the play of light on the Empire State Building, filmed from one camera placed on a tripod a certain distance away. (In these years, Warhol also bought a tape recorder and started to record conversations; by the time he died, his archive contained approximately 6,000 hours of audiotape.)

If nothing else, Warhol's new career was a fabulous pretext. Filming people left the impression that Warhol could create a star—just like Louis B. Mayer in Hollywood! Half in jest, half in earnest, he began to build a repertory company, including a handful of aspiring actors, plus a lot of ordinary people whom Warhol found amusing. He couldn't always pay them, so he let them hang out at his studio, the Factory.

Pretty soon, friends and business partners began to frequent the Factory, just to see who was hot. They were a motley lot of lost souls, desperate for recognition: drag queens, fashion models, black sheep from Brahmin families, aspiring artists "too gifted to lead 'regular lives,' " as Warhol once put it, but "too unsure of themselves ever to become real professionals."

Warhol adored them all—or, to be more precise, he loved the purity of their desperation, the pathos of their narcissism. "When you were around them," he later explained, "you forgot you had problems of your own, you got so involved in theirs. They had dramas going right around the clock, and everybody loved to see them through it all. Their problems made them even more attractive." These were Warhol's "superstars."

He set some ground rules. Junkies and speed freaks couldn't shoot up in the studio. But apart from that, Warhol pretty much left his "superstars" alone. He took them as they were, and encouraged them to do whatever they wanted. Everyone turned to him for emotional support, which he dispensed in measured doses.

As Warhol himself conceded in *POPism,* "the big social thrust behind the Factory from '64 through '67 was amphetamine." In order to keep up his own productivity, Warhol popped pills; but almost everyone else was a purist, retreating to a staircase outside the Factory to shoot up Methedrine. The most powerful of the amphetamine class of synthetic stimulants, often used in conjunction with psychedelics, which heightened the sensation of onrushing mental alertness, and narcotics, which counteracted the irritability produced by prolonged use, Methedrine (the leading brand of methamphetamine) produced its most potent effects when administered intravenously.

Since meth made users paranoid, suspicion became pandemic at the Factory. But since the drug also gave users unlimited energy, the Factory was also generally an up, fun place to be. "People in the Factory knew the zaniest people," Sterling Morrison recalled years later. "Whenever I went there, it always had this kind of visceral tingle. . . . There was always this feeling that something incredible was going to happen, something really exciting or fun or new. You didn't know what corner it was going to come from. And you could sit by languidly and wait for it to happen. Wait for someone to burst out of the elevator and say, Quick, come on, let's go. And zoom, you'd go, and be gone."

Long before Morrison and the other members of the Velvet Underground had become a part of his scene, Warhol was a connoisseur of rock and roll. To help him "completely remove all the hand gesture from art and become noncommittal, anonymous"—one of his declared goals—he developed a routine of painting "with rock and roll blasting the same song, a 45 rpm, over and over all day long. . . . The music blasting cleared my head out and left me working on instinct alone." His favorite song was "Sally, Go 'Round the Roses" by the Jaynetts, one of the strangest American hit recordings of the early Sixties, a swirl of eerily distorted instruments and sultry girls' voices, singing, over and over again, a childish ditty. He recalled getting together with a few other artists, including Jasper Johns, Claes Oldenburg, and Walter De Maria, to play in an informal downtown rock band of their own. Gerard Malanga, the Factory's unofficial "talent scout" in these years, had been a dancer on *The Big Beat,* Alan Freed's TV show. In the early Sixties, Warhol often took his entourage out to Brooklyn, to see the rock and roll package shows that disc jockey Murray the K staged at the Fox Theater. His interest in the scene heightened after the Beatles hit. Warhol found the androgynous new British rock stars endlessly fascinating, and some of them found him fascinating, too. Mick Jagger, like the rest of the Rolling Stones, was a frequent guest at the Factory; he had first met Warhol in 1963, through a mutual friend of the fashion photographer David Bailey (who had shot the early album photos for the Rolling Stones).

In the fall of 1965, Warhol and his coterie were invited by a veteran Broadway producer to help him launch a new nightclub. It sounded like brilliant fun. Amused by the possibilities, Malanga set out to discover a suitable rock band; he wanted to help turn Andy into the next Brian Epstein.

Shortly before Christmas in 1965, Malanga brought Warhol and some friends to the Cafe Bizarre in Greenwich Village, to hear the band he had selected. A quartet at the time, consisting of Reed, Cale, Morrison, and Tucker, they had taken their name, the Velvet Underground, from the title of a pulp pornography paperback. ("Here is an incredible book. It will shock and amaze you. But as a documentary on the sexual corruption of our age, it is a must for every thinking adult.")

As Malanga would later tell the story, the musicians didn't at first recognize the silver-haired man in the dark glasses and black leather jacket, though the café was virtually empty at the time. The band played a set of such screeching ugliness that idle talk was impossible. But when Malanga got up and began to dance in his black leather pants with his whip, "eerily mirroring the Velvets' style with his sinuous, mesmeric movements, which resembled a cross between the Frug and an Egyptian belly dance," any doubts vanished: Andy Warhol had found his Beatles.

"The Pop idea," Warhol later remarked, "was that anybody could do anything, so naturally we are all trying to do it all." It was in keeping with Warhol's emergent Pop aesthetic of can-do amateurism that he should become the manager of a rock and roll band. Besides, he had a lot to offer. The Velvet Underground could star in one of his movies. They could be the house band at his stylish parties. And they could join in the city's hippest happening, staged every day on the floor of the Factory.

Not that they were merely pawns in Warhol's current portfolio of art projects. They had ideas of their own, especially John Cale and

Lou Reed, collaborators as serious about their songwriting, and as fortuitously matched, as Lennon and McCartney. Reed, born Louis Firbank in 1942, had grown up within earshot of Manhattan, in a solidly middle-class and mainly Jewish suburb on Long Island, with the primary focus of his fantasies the doo-wop ballads and keening teen pop he heard broadcast nightly by Alan Freed. He formed a band in high school and, at the age of fourteen, had his first song released on a record ("So Blue" by the Shades, on the Time label). Cale was meanwhile growing up in Great Britain, and preparing for a career in classical music; a violist of prodigious talent, he had first come to the United States in 1963 on a scholarship to study at Tanglewood with Franco-Greek composer Iannis Xenakis, an early and influential proponent of electronic music.

At the time that Reed and Cale met, early in 1965, Cale was playing the viola in the Dream Syndicate, an ensemble led by La Monte Young, a musical dadaist who had made his New York debut with a "Piano Piece for David Tudor," a score supplied with the following set of instructions: "Bring a bale of hay and a bucket of water onto the stage for the piano to eat and drink. The performer may then feed the piano or leave it to eat by itself."

Reed, by contrast, was trying to find some entree into the pop music business. By the time he graduated from college (Syracuse, Class of '64), he was sufficiently accomplished as a musician to land an entry-level job as a contract composer at Pickwick Records in New York City, writing generic teen fodder with titles like "Sneaky Pete" and "The Ostrich," a song meant to launch a new dance craze (it didn't). At the same time, he tried his hand at his own brand of "folk-rock," adding amplification and a big beat to poetic lyrics like those of Bob Dylan, composing tunes like "Heroin" and "Venus in Furs"—songs of no value to his employers at Pickwick Records.

Cale was fascinated by the alien musical world that Reed inhabited, and impressed as well by his connoisseur's taste in drugs. As a member of La Monte Young's ensemble, Cale was asked to sustain a note on his viola for two hours at a stretch. To focus the minds of the players and to perfect their capacity for entranced concentration, Young kept his coterie supplied with copious quantities of drugs: hashish, LSD, pot, opium.

Reed had different poisons of choice: pot and booze and the usual downers (like Seconal), but also heroin; and, above all, speed—his passport to the metabolic frenzies that daily peopled Warhol's Factory. "Amphetamine doesn't give you peace of mind," Warhol remarked in *POPism,* "but it makes not having it very amusing."

That Lou Reed lacked peace of mind was obvious from the songs that he wrote. "Lou was very full of himself and faggy in those days," Cale later recalled. "We called him Lulu and I was Black Jack." Fueled by a steady diet of booze, barbiturates, and amphetamines, Lulu and Black Jack set to work to make music that was "amusing." With the help of Sterling Morrison, an old classmate of Reed's, Cale began to rearrange the songs while Reed refined his style of singing.

The starting point was Reed's infatuation with Bob Dylan. But Reed, unlike Dylan, was a hard-boiled prose stylist; and Cale had no musical interest in either the blues or traditional folk ballad forms, the two main stems of Dylan's style. In a demo of "Heroin" recorded sometime in the summer of 1965, Morrison strums an acoustic guitar while Reed croaks the lyrics and blows a harmonica, emulating Dylan's sound on "Mr. Tambourine Man." It is Cale who adds tension and surprise to the performance by the way in which he plays his viola—an instrument that, by its sonority alone, seems jarringly out of place. Playing with an astringent, sometimes harsh aggressiveness, Cale improvises an accompaniment that is occasionally agitated, but more often catatonic—bowing his instrument to sustain a piercing drone.

It took endless hours of rehearsal and practice, but by the end of 1965, the harsh simplicity of Cale's approach had been fully absorbed by Reed, Morrison, and the drummer, Maureen Tucker, the last musician to join. On stage, they used only amplified instruments, cranking up the volume so loud that Cale's viola sounded like a buzz saw. Discarding his Dylan mask, Reed perfected a new style of vocal delivery, very fey, very declamatory, carefully enunciating every syllable, even when the words were inaudible.

The Velvets at the time were living together in the West Village. As Warhol recalls in *POPism,* the place "looked just like a stage set. The living room was raised and there were long mirrors on both sides of the door. . . . And then there was the heating system—a fifteen-foot gold dragon built onto the ceiling with flames from the heater shooting out of the mouth. . . . John Cale used to sit in the front room for days and days with his electric viola, barely moving."

When Warhol agreed to manage the band, at the end of December 1965, he stipulated one condition. They had to add a singer, a girl whom he'd just "discovered."

Nico had been in New York for several months, working as a fashion model and consuming large amounts of amphetamine ("They used to give it to us to stay thin"). A bleached German blonde with a Lotte Lenya accent and an otherworldly aura, she had spent the war years with her grandfather, a railwayman, and made a point of telling her New York friends that she had seen, at the age of six, cattle cars filled with human beings—the death trains. After leaving Germany as a young woman, she had drifted listlessly from scene to scene: in Rome, she'd joined the cast of *La Dolce Vita,* and at Fellini's behest took acting lessons, though without success; in Paris, she'd become a fashion model, and worked for Coco Chanel, until Coco's unwanted sexual advances forced her to flee; in London, she'd bedded Brian Jones of the Rolling Stones, and he'd helped her make her first recording, a folk-rock song, produced by Andrew Loog Oldham. Nico wore this history on her face, and she poured it into her songs. She sounded like a melancholy moon goddess.

Countless photographs survive of Nico and the Velvets performing in Up-Tight at the Cinematheque in February 1966, and, later that spring, in "The Exploding Plastic Inevitable" (as Warhol renamed the revue) at the Dom in the East Village; and then at a variety of different venues around the country. But the photos fail to record the almost excruciating dullness of the shows. The films that were projected were aimless by design, and the gyrations of the "whip-dancers" more campy than exciting. The light show consisted of polka dots projected in different colors over the stage. The roar of the band was unmodulated and unrelenting, an exercise in deliberate monotony—which was, after all, another one of Warhol's most cherished ideals. "The more you look at the same exact thing," he once explained, "the more the meaning goes away, and the better and emptier you feel."

It is sometimes said that the Underground were a "cult" band "undone by circumstance, reviled by the love-and-peaceniks, exiled from the mainstream"—and greeted with "almost total rejection." So says the critic David Fricke in an essay for a comprehensive anthology of Velvet performances that was issued in 1995. But he is mistaken. When *The Velvet Underground and Nico,* their first album, was finally released, early in 1967, nearly a year after it was recorded, the timing was right, the minds of a great many younger listeners were wide open, and the band had an instant impact. Aficionados of cutting-edge pop admired the bold cover, designed by

Warhol: against a plain white background, it showed only the artist's name, in the lower right-hand corner, and, in the center, a bright yellow banana with a discreet arrow directing the beholder to "peel slowly and see" (the banana was a sticker that peeled off to reveal the pink flesh of the phallic fruit). The "banana album" went on to sell enough copies to appear on *Billboard*'s chart of the best-selling albums in America (it peaked at number 171, and stayed on the chart for thirteen weeks).

This will seem a paltry feat only if one chooses to compare the Velvet Underground to the Beatles or the Rolling Stones. But a more relevant comparison is with La Monte Young—a demanding experimental composer who has *never* had a recording appear on a *Billboard* chart, and whose music, to this day, remains all but unknown.

By joining forces with Andy Warhol and Lou Reed—and by helping to make music that could be successfully marketed to large numbers of people as a rock and roll art project—John Cale went his mentor one better. Escaping from the avant-garde ghetto, Cale succeeded in bringing his own crusading brand of minimalism to the world at large: first with the Velvet Underground, and then in a series of desolately beautiful albums he arranged for Nico.

So this music, too, became a part of the cultural form first named by Alan Freed: an art of apathy, built around repetition, droning sonorities, and the promise of forbidden pleasures. And because what the Velvet Underground and Nico played *was* rock and roll, and not a pure "art" music, tens of thousands of kids around the world heard this music. From David Bowie in the 1970s to Sonic Youth in the 1980s to Pavement in the 1990s, rock acts aiming to challenge and provoke were moved to emulate the Velvet Underground's dark style and minimalist sound. It took time, but as the twentieth century drew to a close, the evidence was clear: For better or worse, the Velvet Underground had become Andy Warhol's greatest hit—the most influential rock band since the Beatles.

June 1, 1967:

Sgt. Pepper's Lonely Hearts Club Band

In the late winter of 1966, not long after Ken Kesey had conducted his first Acid Tests, the wildest episode yet in the adventure of the Beatles was launched, at least symbolically, in an avant-garde art gallery and bookstore. Located in Mason's Yard, in central London, near the hottest pop club in town, the Scotch of St. James, the shop was called Indica—in honor of "cannabis indica," a strain of marijuana, and a shared enthusiasm of the shop's cross section of customers, the rock stars and East End artists and stylish West End aristocrats who in these months defined "swinging London" (as *Time* magazine labeled it).

Besides literature on drugs, Indica carried a discerning selection of beat writing and weird art, which instantly established the shop's tone as quirky and cutting edge: typical was one work, described by an early visitor, consisting of "handbags, lumps of cement, pieces of machinery, and odd scraps of miscellaneous bric-a-brac all glued together on a canvas"—and available for purchase, at a cost of 200 pounds. The wares on display reflected the tastes of Indica's three youthful partners: Barry Miles, John Dunbar, and Peter Asher. Miles, who stocked the books, knew and admired a number of American poets and writers, including Allen Ginsberg and William Burroughs; Dunbar, a graduate of Churchill College, Cambridge, and also married at the time to pop singer Marianne Faithfull, filled the gallery with artworks that reflected his fondness for Warhol pop art and prankish neo-dadaism; while Asher had bankrolled the venture with some of his earnings from Peter and Gordon, a rock duo that had achieved global success in 1964, largely thanks to recording a Lennon-McCartney song, "World Without Love." (Asher's sister, Jane, was Paul McCartney's girlfriend at the time.)

In addition to helping out Peter and Gordon, Paul McCartney also helped out with Indica, designing flyers to advertise the shop, and also designing its wrapping paper. Even before the store was open to the public, McCartney had become its first prominent customer, buying books like *Gandhi on Non-Violence* and *Drugs and the Mind.*

In March 1966, a few weeks after Indica had opened, McCartney brought John Lennon by. As Barry Miles has recalled, Lennon "professed to be looking for a book by someone named Nitz Ga." After an awkward effort to clarify the request—Lennon was deeply insecure about his intellectual pedigree, and ready to lash out at any hint of academic snobbery—Miles went off to hunt down a copy of something by the German philosopher Friedrich Nietzsche. When Miles returned, Lennon was paging through a book he had found called *The Psychedelic Experience.*

First published in 1964, and written by Timothy Leary in collaboration with Ralph Metzner and Richard Alpert, *The Psychedelic Experience* was meant to help novices prepare to take LSD as a tool of spiritual enlightenment. To this end, the manual instructed users to recite a variety of passages more or less paraphrased from *The Tibetan Book of the Dead,* for example: "That which is called ego-death is coming to you. This is now the hour of death and rebirth." In their general introduction, the authors offered an even simpler piece of advice: "Whenever in doubt, turn off your mind, relax, float downstream."

Intrigued, Lennon purchased a copy of both *The Portable Nietz-sche*—the book that Miles had found for him—and *The Psychedelic Experience.* Once home, he decided to put Leary's manual to the test. He'd taken acid only once before, and that trip had not been a happy one. Game to try again, Lennon took to heart Leary's advice—and found the inspiration, not only for a new song, "Tomorrow Never Knows," but also for a whole new way of *making* music: by whim, on impulse, with a little help from drugs, and a lot of help from electronic gimmickry.

"Tomorrow Never Knows" was a psychedelic tone poem, evoking the singer's "ego death" with tape loops that swooped and swirled behind Lennon's vocal like a flock of vultures. As musicologist Ian MacDonald has justly remarked, this recording, "in terms of textural innovation, is to pop what Berlioz's *Symphonie fantastique* was to 19th-century orchestral music"—a challenge, an inspiration, a revolutionary innovation in the arrangement of prerecorded sound. Released on August 5, 1966, as the last song on *Revolver,* the Beatles' seventh album, "Tomorrow Never Knows" set the musical stamp on London's giddiest cultural season since the end of the war, a summer of tangerine trees and marmalade skies, at least for those in the know about the mind-altering ecstasies of LSD and cannabis indica.

The Beatles, however, had been booked by Brian Epstein on yet another grueling round of concerts. This tour started at the end of June with shows in Germany, proceeded to Japan, and then finally on to the Philippines, where the band had to brave an angry mob after "snubbing" President Marcos and his wife by failing to attend a party Mme. Marcos had given in their honor. After a brief respite in the U.K., the tour resumed with dates in Canada and the United States. Most of the new material from *Revolver* was, like "Tomorrow Never Knows," impossible to reproduce on stage. In the studio, McCartney and Lennon were testing the limits of their artistry: on stage, they felt like puppets pantomiming music, prisoners of their own fame, trapped by the blind idolatry of their fans, who screamed so loudly that the band could scarcely hear itself play. When the tour ended (in San Francisco, on August 29), all four Beatles privately agreed that they would never tour again.

Returning to England, they took a vacation, their longest break yet since becoming the most famous band in the world. Ringo Starr relaxed with his family. George Harrison, who had recently met the sitar virtuoso Ravi Shankar at a dinner party, flew to India to study with him at his Himalayan retreat. McCartney, donning a disguise, trekked across France to test what it would feel like to live, as he once had, anonymously, without the burden of fame (he concluded that being famous wasn't so bad after all). And John Lennon, caught in a crumbling marriage, lapsed into a chronic state of passive aggression, reinforced by constant trips on LSD—a regimen broken by seven weeks on location in Spain, playing the part of a cockney soldier in Richard Lester's new antiwar film, *How I Won the War.*

Early in November, as the Beatles regrouped to go back into the studio to record their next album, word leaked out that the most famous band in the world would no longer be available for live bookings. And insiders were also quietly warned that the next album was going to be a long time coming.

Executives at the band's parent record company, EMI, weren't thrilled. The received wisdom was that a pop music act should regularly tour and issue new music if it wished to produce a steady stream of revenue. But there wasn't much that EMI could do. And so George Martin, still the band's producer, and soon to double as their resident voice of reason, was left to cope, as best he could, with perhaps his toughest assignment yet: "to give them as much freedom as possible in the studio, but to make sure that they did not come off the rails in the process."

Apart from the acid-fueled innovations on "Tomorrow Never Knows," the music that the Beatles now began to create had little real precedent in the history of popular music. Slowly, almost indolently, one senses from the various accounts, the Beatles returned to the recording studio—but with no definite plan, and no fixed timetable. Since this, after all, was the Beatles, the most popular musical act in the world, executives at EMI gnashed their teeth—and gave them virtually free run of their Abbey Road studios. If one of the boys had a flash of inspiration, he had only to pick up the phone and ask for studio time.

They sometimes kept George Martin and his staff waiting for an hour or two before ambling into the studio at, say, ten o'clock in the evening. Once they got down to work, McCartney relied on Martin to help him orchestrate and arrange the music, while Lennon got in the habit of issuing vague orders for the creation of evocative sounds (he once asked Martin to make a song sound like an orange). In these months, McCartney and Lennon were exasperating, arrogant, imperious—and, spurred by a variety of startling new albums, including *Blonde on Blonde* by Bob Dylan, *Pet Sounds* by the Beach Boys, and *Fifth Dimension* by the Byrds, they were also single-mindedly dedicated to making the most mind-boggling album in the history of rock and roll.

Years later, while making a television documentary about *Sgt. Pepper,* George Martin, still marveling at the beauty of the results, asked McCartney, in all seriousness, "Do you know what caused *Pepper*?"

"In one word," answered McCartney, without skipping a beat, "drugs. Pot."

Since the lads in front of the fatherly Martin had kept their bad habits to themselves, taking breaks to smoke in secret, the producer was incredulous: "No, no. You weren't on it all the time."

"Yes, we were," replied McCartney. "*Sgt. Pepper* was a drug album."

So off to work they set, happily dazed and confused—and fascinated, as never before, with improvised wordplay, abstract sounds, and the chance results of deliberately induced prodigies of intoxicated reverie.

The first track set the tone for everything that followed. While he was in Spain, Lennon had pieced together a new song, "Strawberry Fields Forever." On the demonstration tape of the song he made at home, singing in his most plaintive monotone, accompanying himself only on acoustic guitar, he seems, as Ian MacDonald has remarked, "to have lost and rediscovered his artistic voice, passing through an interim phase of creative inarticulacy reflected in the halting, child-like quality of his lyric. The music, too, shows Lennon at his most somnambulistic, moving uncertainly through thoughts and tones like a momentarily blinded man feeling for something familiar."

The lyrics in the song in fact did allude to something familiar, a Liverpool park that Lennon had called Strawberry Fields, where he had been able as a child to run free, playing hide-and-seek with his chums (a far cry from his current fate as a miserably married Beatle). George Martin has recalled instantly appreciating the unfeigned pathos of the new song, telegraphed in the line that Lennon chose to open the first version of the song, finished after nine hours of work on November 24, 1966: "Living is easy with eyes closed."

Striking though this first version was (in 1996, it was officially re-leased on volume two of the Beatles' *Anthology*), it did not satisfy Lennon. He may have been uncomfortable with the naked vulnera-bility of the singing, recorded straight, without any of the sonic tricks (multitracking, plus various brands of deliberate distortion) that he had come to count on to disguise the blemishes in his voice. Four days later, Lennon recorded the song again, starting with the chorus ("Let me take you down") instead of the verse, and asking Martin to modify drastically the sound of his voice, overdubbing and slowing it down by manipulating the speed of the tape recording it, in order to make it sound slightly warmer—and much, much stranger.

Still Lennon was not satisfied. The new version was uncanny in its poignance—but the music still, as it stood, was unlikely to blow minds.

The next day, on November 29, the group recorded the song again, this time with the intention of producing a more lushly orches-trated version. Pleased with the basic track, Lennon and McCartney in the days that followed oversaw the recording of additional musical elements, piled on like icing on a cake. Harrison appeared one evening with a svarmandal, an Indian instrument that sounded a lit-tle like a zither; unable to play it properly, he spent hours retuning the strings so that he could produce a glissando by plucking each string in turn, as a harpist would pluck the strings of a harp. Martin cooked up an obbligato for four trumpets and three cellos. Ringo created a tape loop of crashing cymbals, and then Martin turned the loop upside down, played it backward, and added the resulting *woosh* of sound to the sonic frosting. Lennon dubbed on another layer of vocals, another piano track, and, finally, a coda of impromptu stoned tomfoolery, featuring incoherent vocal whoops from Lennon and an outburst of free drumming from Ringo. And so it went.

It was now nearly Christmas, and still "Strawberry Fields Forever" was unfinished. Lennon remained torn between the relative simplicity of the slow early version, and the more baroque orchestral version that he had been working on ever since. Unable to choose, he blithely instructed Martin to splice the two versions together. As a trained musician, Martin was flabbergasted. "Brilliant," he shot back. "There are only two things wrong with that: the takes are in two different keys, a whole tone apart; and they have wildly different tempos."

Lennon scarcely cared. He had a relatively short attention span, and, unlike McCartney, wasn't especially eager to learn more about the technical details involved in making, and appreciating, a complicated piece of music. (Martin, in his memoirs, recalls, with scarcely concealed horror, the night he asked Lennon to sit through a recording of Ravel's Suite No. 2 from *Daphnis and Chloé*, one of his favorites pieces of classical music. When the piece was done, Lennon turned to Martin and said "I couldn't really understand the tune." When Martin protested that Ravel had written an absolutely gorgeous sustained melody, Lennon said, "Yes, but I'd forgotten how the beginning was by the time we got to the end.")

Swallowing his doubts, Martin went back to the drawing boards with his EMI staff of engineers, to see if they could do their master's bidding ("When it came right down to it," Martin once admitted, "we were all their minions"). The staff rigged up a Rube Goldberg contraption to vary the frequency of the tape playback. Luck was with them. By dropping the speed and pitch of the orchestral version, and speeding up the slower version of November 29, they were able to splice the two together.

Presto! Nearly four weeks and more than fifty-five hours after they had begun, the Beatles had produced a new piece of music. And even George Martin had to admit that the result was impressive. With pride, he once described "Strawberry Fields" as "a complete tone poem—like a modern Debussy."

If an argument is to be made for the creative value of serendipity in music—and the case for rock and roll as a form of art in part depends on it—then "Strawberry Fields" offers convincing evidence. As Ian MacDonald (a trained composer himself) has put it, "Here, The Beatles show that technical shortcomings, far from constraining the imagination, can let it expand into areas inaccessible to the trained mind. Heard for what it is—a sort of technologically evolved folk music—'Strawberry Fields Forever' shows expression of a high order." It was certainly expression of a higher musical order than that of its distant precursor, Patti Page's music box version of "Tennessee Waltz."

Still, it was only one song. Worried by the amount of time spent in the studio, and concerned as well by a rumor circulating that the Beatles were about to break up, Brian Epstein begged George Martin to speed up the pace of work on the album—and also pleaded with him to release a new single in the meantime.

This put Martin in a bind. By the time Epstein made his request (at the start of 1967), the Beatles, according to Martin, had five more or less mind-blowing songs either complete or near completion: "Strawberry Fields," "When I'm 64," "Penny Lane," "A Day in the Life" and "Good Morning, Good Morning"—a blast of old-fashioned, feral rock and roll, and perhaps John Lennon's most vitriolic composition yet. The album that Lennon and McCartney were now in the midst of making promised to become a suite of songs loosely linked by autobiographical themes as well as the conceit that they were all being performed by a fictional group, Sgt. Pepper's Lonely Hearts Club Band. "Strawberry Fields" and "Penny Lane" were the heart and soul of this musical project. To his regret ("it was the biggest mistake of my professional life"), George Martin nevertheless submitted to Epstein's pressure by letting him give EMI both of these songs, to rush into release as a new single.

With the completion of the next album now further complicated (the band had taken pride, since *Meet the Beatles,* in trying to fill each new album with all-new recordings), the Beatles went back to work. Amateurs they may once have been; lazy they were not. The Abbey Road studios had been turned into their private playground. They now proceeded to generate more songs using the ad hoc methods pioneered on "Tomorrow Never Knows" and "Strawberry Fields Forever."

On January 31, 1967, while taking a break from filming a promotional clip for "Strawberry Fields," John Lennon wandered into an antique shop and discovered a poster advertising "Pablo Fanque's Circus Royal": "LAST NIGHT BUT THREE! Being for the BENEFIT OF MR. KITE (late of Wells's Circus) and MR J. HENDERSON, the celebrated somerset thrower!" Under pressure to produce a new song, Lennon bought the poster, hung it on the wall of his home studio, took some LSD, sat down at his piano, and began to write a song inspired by the poster. (In general, members of the band did acid in private, limiting themselves to pot at the actual recording sessions.)

By February 17, Lennon had a rough draft ready of the new song, "Being for the Benefit of Mr. Kite." He phoned Martin to book time in the studio that evening. Arriving with a sheet of lyrics and the chords, he played the song for Martin and the band, accompanying himself on acoustic guitar. The group then spent the night working out the music, coming up with a preliminary arrangement that featured a hand-pumped harmonium. "I'd love to be able to get across all the effects of a really colorful circus," John explained to Martin. "The acrobats in their tights, the smell of the animals, the merry-go-rounds. I want to smell the sawdust, George."

Since he was by now familiar with such musically vague but programmatically precise instructions, Martin, instinctively assuming the role of a psychotherapist, asked Lennon to elaborate on his associations. Lennon mentioned his love for the music used on a children's television program. Martin thought of the little organ in Walt Disney's *Snow White*. Swapping hunches in this way, the two men eventually agreed that Martin in the morning should seek out and then make a recording of an old-fashioned steam organ of the sort once used on circus carousels.

After a day of research into the location of such an instrument, Martin concluded that finding and fixing up a real steam organ would cost too much time and money. Instead, Martin decided to collect *recordings* of classic steam organs.

At first, the recordings seemed useless. Almost all of them were of military marches. Stumped, Martin dipped into his bag of musical tricks and created a hurdy-gurdy-style arrangement scored for harmonium and several different kinds of conventional organs recorded at different speeds, and modified on playback, to create the impression of a ghostly carnival fairway.

Still, you couldn't smell the sawdust. At wit's end, Martin, entering uncharacteristically into the aleatory spirit of the *Sgt. Pepper* saga, took out scissors and tape. After tape-recording several passages from the steam organ recordings, he instructed his engineer to cut the tape into tiny pieces, throw the pieces up into the air, and then randomly splice the pieces back together. The sound this produced—a swirling crazy-quilt of circus music, mixed into the other sounds like a dash of fairy dust—is one of the most magical touches on an album filled with them.

Work on *Sgt. Pepper* dragged on into the spring of 1967, as the Beatles made it plain that their quest for perfection would not end with the music. Thinking about the cover, Paul McCartney had an idea. He recalled how, as a boy, he would go into downtown Liverpool to buy a new album and then lose himself in looking over the jacket on the bus ride back. Rock, after all, works on many different levels: not just as a public performance, but also as a private means of escape, a silent preoccupation. Organized as a whole, the songs on *Sgt. Pepper,* crammed as they were with spectacular new sounds, but also with odd, sometimes barely perceptible effects, extended an open invitation to daydream. It was music to get lost in—and as McCartney intuited, the music deserved a jacket to match: "The whole idea was to put everything, the whole world into this package; that's why we got Peter Blake in."

A graduate of the Royal College of Art, Blake in 1961 had produced a renowned *Self-Portrait With Badges,* showing himself gazing blankly, looking forlorn and frumpy, clutching an Elvis Presley fan magazine, his jacket decorated with dozens of pins and buttons, the largest displaying a picture of Presley at his most glamorous. In the years since, Blake had worked extensively in collage, using postcards, pinups, and other junk that, by the standards of conventional fine art, belonged in a dustbin. By rescuing and rearranging this junk, he magnified its potential to produce nostalgia, a bittersweet yearning for a lost world of childlike innocence. Since much of the music on *Sgt. Pepper* embodied similar aesthetic impulses, Blake seemed a brilliant choice to design the album cover.

With the costs of *Sgt. Pepper* still escalating, and with no firm date yet set for releasing the album, Brian Epstein was feeling pressure again from executives at EMI. When Sir Joseph Lockwood, the head of the company, learned that Blake's cover would cost fifteen hundred pounds, an unprecedented sum for packaging a pop album, he blew up: "*Fifteen hundred pounds!* I can hire the London Symphony Orchestra for that!" In the heat of the moment, Sir Joseph evidently forgot that the Beatles had in fact already hired a symphony orchestra, to play (at McCartney's suggestion) a mere twenty-four bars of music—the spiraling crescendo of sound used to bring to a climax "A Day in the Life."

Of course, the Beatles got their way. And after more than half a year of work, the finishing musical touches were applied to the album on April 21. EMI, keen to recoup its mammoth outlay, geared up its publicity staff to saturate the world market with teasers and posters and proclamations that the Beatles were back, with a brand-new, mind-blowing album of music, on sale in June.

On May 12, a British radio station aired the album in its entirety; on May 20, the BBC followed suit, omitting "A Day in the Life," which had been banned on the grounds that it encouraged a permissive attitude toward drug taking. (One can only imagine what the censors thought the rest of the album was about.)

A few days later, Brian Epstein invited a select group of journalists and tastemakers to join the Beatles for a listening party. A lavish spread was laid out, and champagne flowed freely while *Sgt. Pepper* was played over and over again at full volume. "The boys were in fine fettle," a reporter told his readers on May 27: "Lennon won the sartorial stakes with a green flower-patterned shirt, red cord trousers, yellow socks and what looked like cord shoes. His ensemble was completed by a sporran [a fur-covered pouch usually worn with a kilt]. With his bushy sideboards and National Health specs he resembled an animated Victorian watchmaker. Paul McCartney, sans moustache, wore a loosely tied scarf over a shirt, a striped double-breasted jacket and looked like someone out of a Scott Fitzgerald novel."

In the annals of rock history, there has never been anything quite like the way that *Sgt. Pepper* was now received by its audience. Released on the Parlophone label on June 1 in England and on the Capitol label on June 2 in America, it was, in the minds of many, a monumental event. In cities like London and Los Angeles, fans queued outside record stores to snap up a copy. In the first weeks alone, EMI sold millions of copies of the album, making it the most popular album yet released by the Beatles—and thus, by definition, the best-selling album in the history of rock and roll till then.

Throughout that summer, the sound of *Sgt. Pepper* was ubiquitous. Everywhere one went, from Los Angeles to London, from Paris to Madrid, from Rome to Athens, snatches of the album drifted out of open windows, faded in and out of consciousness as cars passed by, came in and out of focus in tinny tones from distant transistor radios, the songs hanging in the air like a hologram of bliss. That music this wondrous and original should have been created by four young men with no formal training astonished everyone.

"In a way," George Martin remarked years later, "*Sgt. Pepper* is a utopia." One had only to listen, relax, float downstream. With an open mind (no matter how one chose to open it), *anyone* could feel its spirit—of creativity, of play, of blissful joy. Just as everything had changed for John Lennon after his trip to the Indica bookstore and gallery, everything was going to change for the world as a whole. Writing with Olympian authority in the *Times* of London, the theater critic and cultural commentator Kenneth Tynan declared *Sgt. Pepper* to be "a decisive moment in the history of Western civilization."

That was an illusion, of course. But that is how it really felt.

June 16–18, 1967:

Monterey Pop

By mid-afternoon on Friday, June 16, 1967, every highway leading into the seaside resort of Monterey, California, was clogged with cars full of long-haired kids dressed in funny costumes, armed with incense, and primed to party at the first great congress of youth united by the music of the Beatles and the use of mind-altering drugs. Billed as "The Monterey International Pop Festival," it promised a weekend of revelry featuring many of the Bay Area's top psychedelic rock bands, including the Grateful Dead. A whole afternoon would be devoted to a sitar recital by Ravi Shankar. The Byrds from Los Angeles would appear, as would The Who from England, and also the American expatriate Jimi Hendrix, a guitarist who was the new darling of London's rock scene.

The festival staging area, a county fairgrounds, held some 7,500 seats, and there was an adjacent field within earshot. Reserved seats cost $6.50 for each of the three evening shows, while access to the field cost only $1.00. Although the concerts included the hippest of the new rock bands, the Holy Trinity was missing in action: the Beatles had stopped touring, two of the Rolling Stones were facing drug charges in England after a marijuana bust, and Bob Dylan was still recuperating from a motorcycle accident suffered the year before.

The tickets for reserved seats had sold out quickly. Nobody knew how many people would make the trip to Monterey just to sit on the lawn. But at least 50,000 people came—at that point, the largest gathering ever for a rock and roll concert.

Monterey Pop, D.A. Pennebaker's film about the event, opens with a scene that nicely captures the balminess of the moment. As the crowd is filing into the fairground on Friday afternoon, the camera focuses on a sunny young woman. Off-camera, one of the film crew asks her what she expects to happen. "Haven't you ever been to a Love-In?" she replies, incredulous. Her off-camera interlocutor says no. There is pity in her smile: "God!" (She sighs, and takes a deep breath.) "I think it's gonna be like Easter and Christmas and New Year's and your birthday all together, you know, hearing all the different bands, you know, just like I've heard a lot of 'em, but all at the same time it's just gonna be too much, I mean, the *vibrations* are just gonna be *flowing*, everywhere!"

In the weeks leading up to the festival, there had been a mounting drumbeat of publicity for the event, most of it spurred by larger concerns about the psychedelic subculture that had blossomed in the Bay Area. Scarcely six months earlier, the American media had discovered the existence of a new breed of teenage rebel, "the hippie," at a new kind of public gathering: the world's first "Human Be-In," held in Golden Gate Park on January 14, 1967. Organizers of that event had vowed to "shower the country with waves of ecstasy and purification," by staging what amounted to an outdoor Acid Test. Local rock bands, led by the Grateful Dead, had been the big draw; but the real show had turned out to be the crowd, "a wild polyglot mixture" (as one veteran newspaperman described the scene) "of Mod, Paladin, Ringling Brothers, Cochise and Hell's Angel Formal." Incense burned, bells tinkled, balloons floated. People dropped acid, smoked pot, danced to the music, and hugged on the grass. "We are primitives of an unknown culture," one of the organizers, the beat poet Gary Snyder, had declared on the eve of the Be-In, explaining how the event was meant to promote a "new ethics and new states of mind." Fascinated by the character of the crowd, its pacific spirit and its irresistibly photogenic look, *Newsweek* magazine had run a sympathetic story, describing "a love feast, a psychedelic picnic, a hippie happening."

Hoping to stage a "hippie happening" of their own, the organizers of the Monterey International Pop Festival had papered psychedelic enclaves throughout California with posters inviting people to come to the show, not just to hear music, but to "be happy, be free"—and "dress as wild as you want to." One of the organizers, thirty-two-year-old John Phillips, a singer-songwriter in the Mamas and the Papas, at the time a hugely popular American folk-rock vocal group, had also written and produced a new song (for an old friend, Scott McKenzie), "San Francisco (Be Sure to Wear Flowers in Your Hair)," which spread the news even more widely, over the world's radio airwaves.

But hippies were not the only ones lured by the promise of "Music, Love and Flowers" (in the words of the festival's motto). From L.A. and New York came a host of businessmen, executives from major record labels, their eyes peeled and ears open, searching for fresh talent. Just below the stage, two special seating areas had been set aside, one for reporters from around the world, the other for the music industry executives, who were asked to contribute $150 a seat for the privilege. There was also a film crew prowling the grounds, working on a planned television special under the direction of Pennebaker, who favored shooting as unobtrusively as possible, in order to catch the moment in its unguarded immediacy.

Besides John Phillips of the Mamas and the Papas, there were several other key figures who personified the vision behind the festival. One was Derek Taylor, the veteran press agent who had worked for Brian Epstein and the Beatles before immigrating to L.A. and becoming a convert to the new lifestyle. That spring, Taylor had flown to San Francisco to help drum up support from the local bands, and also to secure the cooperation of Chet Helms, a key figure, whose participation would guarantee that hard-core hippie acts like the Grateful Dead wouldn't boycott the event.

With hair down to his waist, and a beard down to his belt, Helms looked every bit like the LSD evangelist that he was. A onetime amphetamine addict born again as an acid freak, Helms had brought the glad tidings of the Bay Area's new rock culture to the hipsters of swinging London in the winter of 1967. More than an enthusiast, he was also an impresario, operating one of the area's key ballrooms, the Avalon, where stoned kids could undulate as one under flashing strobe lights and blobs of colored light, grooving to the sounds of the latest stoned bands.

"There are only three significant pieces of data in the world today," Helms quipped in these months: "The first is, God died last year and was obited by the press. The second is, fifty percent of the population is or will be under twenty-five. . . . The third is that they got twenty billion irresponsible dollars to spend."

While Helms was highly visible from the festival stage, introducing many of the Bay Area bands, the most important figure behind the scenes was Lou Adler. A veteran of the music business who seemed older than he really was (thirty-two), Adler had composed the song "Wonderful World" for Sam Cooke in 1960, and then moved to L.A. to coordinate West Coast operations for a stable of New York songwriters who worked on the model of Jerry Leiber and Mike Stoller, churning out finely crafted big-beat ditties with heartfelt lyrics pitched at teenagers (one of these writers, Carole King, would go on to become a huge star in her own right by recording the 1971 album *Tapestry* for one of Adler's record labels). Moving from song plugging into record production, Adler had started his own label, Dunhill, in 1964, just as the Beatles broke in America. Taking heed when Bob Dylan declared that "The Times They Are A-Changin'," Adler had helped turn the Mamas and the Papas into one of the most popular folk-rock acts in America. It was Adler who had helped Phillips conceive and organize the festival as a *benefit*: demonstrating their aversion to the money-grubbing culture of their elders, the bands would play for nothing. Other expenses would be covered by selling film rights to a television network, ABC (that was why Pennebaker was there). Everybody would win—the kids, because they'd get to see a great show; and the performers, since they'd get priceless exposure, not least from the international press corps, eager to catch up on America's newest youth fad.

Despite the presence of Helms on the festival staff, a number of the Bay Area bands had their doubts. Some adamantly refused to donate their services to network television, a modern-day Moloch in their minds: the Grateful Dead, among others, would not let Pennebaker film their performance. The entire event was in fact shrouded in ambiguity. On one level, the pop festival was, as advertised, a latter-day Be-In, a gathering of the new hippie tribes and some of their favorite bands. But on another level, Monterey Pop was an unusual, and brilliantly orchestrated, new kind of rock talent showcase.

Adler had no trouble at all in convincing his peers of the event's value. Among those sitting in the $150-a-seat section were Goddard Lieberson and Clive Davis from Columbia Records (which would sign several artists featured at Monterey, most notably Big Brother and the Holding Company). Mo Ostin, the head of Warner Brothers Records, was there to see the Grateful Dead, who a few months before had negotiated an unprecedented contract that guaranteed the band unlimited studio time. Jerry Wexler, who was also there, representing Atlantic Records, would later say that he "missed the boat at Monterey," by failing to snap up any "hippie musicians." Still, he did succeed in using the festival, with financial help from Atlantic, as a promotional vehicle to advance the career of Otis Redding, a black singer revered by connoisseurs like Brian Jones and Mick Jagger, but still largely unknown, even to fans of the Rolling Stones.

Redding was one of the performers prominently featured in *Monterey Pop*. Ultimately rejected by executives at ABC (who reacted with horror to the footage of Jimi Hendrix), Pennebaker's documentary film was eventually distributed in theaters around the world, forming the only impression most people have of what happened at Monterey.

Despite the scenes that featured Hendrix, the film softened much of the festival's hard musical edge, in part because the director was unable for contractual reasons to show a number of the most experimental hippie bands. Still, Pennebaker did manage to evoke a trance-like mood through a prolonged, rhapsodically edited climax, which shows Ravi Shankar, the Indian grand master of the sitar, playing barefoot surrounded by a sea of flowers. (There were flowers everywhere that weekend, since the organizers had spared no expense, flying in 100,000 orchids from Hawaii.) A superbly gifted, highly disciplined virtuoso, anchored within a complex musical tradition that he had made his own, Shankar was the odd man out throughout the festival. Cherished for his open-minded willingness to appear in such a setting, he was also the only musician who demanded, and finally received, a fee for performing. He was also perhaps the only prominent performer at Monterey who played his set straight, if one discounts the possible effect of secondhand hemp smoke.

By cutting back and forth between Shankar on stage, and images of hippies swaying beatifically in the crowd, Pennebaker subtly established one of the enduring images of the moment, evoking a bucolic and cosmopolitan utopia, a world of benign liberty, happy nonconformity, and miraculously nonpossessive individualism, an egalitarian city-state where the dancers with the face paint freaking freely in the crowd were now as much the stars as anyone making music up on the stage.

In reality, matters were more complicated, not least for those San Francisco musicians without a recording contract. For them, Monterey amounted to an unpaid audition in front of a bevy of music business big shots. The anxiety in the air never wholly dissipated, though God knows the guardian angel of the Bay Area acid enlightenment did his level best: Augustus Stanley Owsley III had come with a big batch of specially made LSD—"Monterey Purple," he called it, giving away tabs to any musician who asked.

As the weekend unfolded and the good vibrations grew, a great psychedelic haze rolled in over the crowd like fog off the ocean.

There was royalty in attendance. Like a king at a carnival, Brian Jones floated through the crowd wearing several layers of scarves and robes, periodically dipping into his deep pockets to fish out another pill to pop, indifferent to whether it was speed or acid or a barbiturate ("Let me see," he remarked to one local musician who was astonished by the spectacle. "Left side is up, right side is down"). Much of the time, Jones was accompanied by his old consort Nico, who looked radiant, and who had flown in with Andy Warhol (just a few weeks before, *The Velvet Underground and Nico* had belatedly been released).

Meanwhile, rumors kept sweeping the crowd that the Beatles were coming. The rumors were false; but even in absentia, the Beatles were everywhere. *Sgt. Pepper* was played constantly, wafting out of the concession booths dotted around the perimeter of the grounds. Festival staffers sported badges with a motto lifted from the *Pepper* album: "A splendid time is guaranteed for all." And on Saturday night, David Crosby, on stage to perform with the Byrds, paused to read aloud a few words just printed in *Life* magazine: " 'I believe,' " Crosby read, pausing for dramatic effect, " 'if we gave LSD to all the statesmen and politicians in the world, we might have a chance at stopping war.' That's a quote from Paul McCartney!" Everyone cheered.

The Byrds were in the midst of a sloppy set, by no means an uncommon occurrence at the festival. Still, before it was all over, there would be two unforgettable performances, one preserved only on audiotape, the other filmed as well, that would later stand out as defining moments of what, after 1967, would be widely regarded as the purest and most authentic kind of rock and roll.

The first such performance came from Big Brother and the Holding Company on Saturday afternoon. A shambling hippie quintet consisting of a drummer, a bass player, and two electric guitarists, the band was fronted by a genuine pop-music anomaly: an unglamorous girl. Her name was Janis Joplin, she was Texan by birth, and at the age of twenty-four she pitched every song at the most extreme imaginable level of emotion.

What Joplin did was not *sing*, exactly. She shrieked. She screamed. At one moment, her caterwauling sounded like the cries of a cornered animal; at other times, she seemed transcendental, possessed, in the grip of a demon.

It was mesmerizing to watch someone of modest technical means who nonetheless held nothing back. That had been part of rock's charm from the start: hearing whether a kid like Frankie Lymon would actually hit his notes. But Lymon and the down-home doo-wop groups had never *shrieked*. It was largely thanks to Joplin that amateurish shrieking became a valued emblem of heart and soul among a large and influential number of subsequent rock and roll vocalists, including, later, Johnny Rotten of the Sex Pistols and (an even finer Joplin disciple) Kurt Cobain of Nirvana.

Poor Janis Joplin. After rehearsing obsessively in the weeks leading up to the festival, she had just given the best show of her life—only to remember that the cameras had caught none of it! (Her manager was one of those refusing to do business with Lou Adler and ABC.)

Backstage, Joplin burst into tears. After a quick powwow with the festival organizers, she was permitted to stage an encore performance for Pennebaker's cameras the following night. By then, the edge was gone, the demon of uncontrollable desire somehow dissipated. Singing again the histrionic high point of the Saturday show, "Ball and Chain" (an R&B song previously associated with Big Mama Thornton, of "Hound Dog" fame), Joplin was good—but not great. And that would always be a problem for rock's amateur shriekers: without much in the way of raw talent or acquired finesse to see them through, they were at the mercy of the moment. Hysteria is hard to fake.

This was never an issue with the second defining performance given at Monterey, this time preserved for posterity on film as well as on audiotape.

Late on Sunday evening, the last night of the festival, after a long evening that had featured sets from Big Brother, The Who, and the Grateful Dead, all leading up to a projected grand finale with the Mamas and the Papas, it was the turn of guitarist and singer James Marshall Hendrix, age twenty-four, to stake his claim to rock and roll glory. American by birth, he was unlike the Bay Area hopefuls for three reasons: he was black; he was already a big star in England; and—most important of all—he was a seasoned musician who knew his instrument inside-out. He had been playing professionally since 1962. And he had learned how to woo a white audience at the feet of a master, Little Richard, who had taught him by example the value of flamboyant showmanship.

Jimi Hendrix (his stage name) was, like the great alto saxophonist Charlie Parker, a musician of pure genius. He heard sounds on his instrument, and translated them into skillfully improvised music, with a fluency and artistry that belied his lack of formal schooling. Unlike Parker, he had gone into exile in search of his own voice. In the fall of 1966, he emigrated to England, to work under the tutelage of Chas Chandler, a fledgling British manager who, at the age of twenty-eight, was a veteran of the golden age of Beatlemania, having played bass in the Animals, an R&B band that briefly rivaled the Rolling Stones in global popularity. With Chandler's help, Hendrix had produced three hit singles in England, the most popular of which, "Purple Haze," was a blues-drenched ode to LSD. Booked onto a package tour with other British rock stars popular at the time, and inspired by the Who's showstopping act in which guitarist Pete Townshend in a frenzy of feigned passion smashed up a guitar, Hendrix went Townshend one better: he ended his performances by making out of his guitar a burnt offering, kneeling over it with mock reverence, pouring lighter fluid on the instrument, setting it aflame— and *then,* in a frenzy of feigned passion, smashing the instrument up.

(This stunt, which shocked Ravi Shankar and stunned the hippies at Monterey, had its origin in the aesthetic theory of Gustav Metzger, Pete Townshend's favorite tutor at Ealing Art College. Metzger advocated what he called "auto-destructive" works of art, for example, the "action painting" he created by spraying acid on a sheet of nylon. As Metzger explained them, such works were meant to evoke the apocalyptic prospects opened up at Hiroshima—and also to evade the cash nexus. Nobody could buy or collect Metzger's artworks—an anticapitalist aspect of his project that Townshend and

Hendrix both failed to duplicate, since their auto-destructive stunts proved to be easily marketed and hugely profitable in the form of live entertainment.)

Monterey was the first chance Jimi Hendrix had to show his erstwhile compatriots everything he could do, as a musician, and also (like Little Richard before him) as an absolutely outrageous, over-the-top, good-taste-be-damned *freak*. In his memoirs, Jerry Wexler recalled bumping into Hendrix shortly before he went on stage. "I'd known Jimi since his backup days," Wexler wrote: "There he was, however, a veteran of the soul circuit, in crazy feathers and psychedelic regalia. He looked at me, almost apologetically, knowing I knew where he came from. 'It's only for the show,' he whispered."

But what a show! Hendrix came out wired on acid and primed to blow people's minds. The previous afternoon, the festival had featured a parade of pasty-faced white boys struggling, generally without success, to sound as bad and as "black" as the Rolling Stones. Against this backdrop, when Hendrix opened his set with a piece of classic Delta blues, Howlin' Wolf's "Killing Floor," it was almost a taunt. Hendrix toyed with the licks, playing with effortless abandon, as surely a grand master of his chosen tradition and instrument as Ravi Shankar. Laying out the musical turf he intended to make his own, Hendrix ranged widely, from the primitive rock classic "Wild Thing" to Bob Dylan's anthem of the hour, "Like a Rolling Stone." His instrument howled and raged into the night, but Hendrix himself looked serene, as amazed as anyone by the sound he was producing. And at the end of his set, when he sent his Fender up in flames, the bonfire did not seem gratuitous. It seemed rather a gesture of innocent gratitude, a burnt offering to the unknown pagan gods who had blessed this harvest of creativity, and granted one man-child a moment of rare bliss.

Several months later, writing in *Esquire* magazine, Robert Christgau, one of the first prominent young critics to be hired primarily to cover the world of rock and roll, filed a story about Monterey. Though excited to have seen an event of evident historical significance, Christgau had reservations. The "Love Crowd," as he called it, had shown little more musical taste than the kids who rated records for Dick Clark. They loved Janis Joplin and Jimi Hendrix, but they also loved Buddy Miles, who was cheered mightily for a heavy-handed and interminable drum solo.

Furthermore, as Christgau noted, there was the strange matter of how black music came across at the festival. As he well knew, the problem didn't lie primarily with the festival organizers, who had tried without success to get some of Berry Gordy's Motown stars to perform, and had also asked Chuck Berry.

No, the problem was the audience itself. The members of Christgau's "Love Crowd" behaved like Mailer's "White Negro." Like the hipsters of the Fifties, the hippies of a decade later worshipped black musicians as fantasy objects, preferring those artists who seemed to be expressing a riot of uninhibited emotions. One word that Robert Christgau used was blunt, and to the point: the crowd, he wrote, reacted to Otis Redding as if he were a "Superspade." And Jimi Hendrix was in the same boat. In this case, Christgau didn't need to speculate: he simply quoted a review of the festival that had appeared in the hippest of Manhattan's alternative weeklies, the East Village *Other*: "Jimi did a beautiful Spade routine."

Monterey Pop marked a turning point, and on many different levels. Despite the prominent parts played by black musicians like Otis Redding and Jimi Hendrix, the festival confirmed the fact that "real" rock and roll had become (in a way that Ahmet Ertegun and the executives at Atlantic Records were quick to appreciate), either *real* "White Negro" music—that is, music made by whites (like Janis Joplin) trying to sound "black"—or just plain white music (the Bay Area bands were overwhelmingly white). Christgau put it this way: "White rock performers seem uncomfortable with contemporary black music. Most of them like the best of it or think they do, but they don't want to imitate it, especially since they know how pallid their imitation is likely to be. So they hone their lyrics and develop their instrumental chops and experiment with their equipment and come to regard artists like Martha & the Vandellas [one of Berry Gordy's popular groups], say, as some wondrous breed of porpoise, very talented, but somehow . . . different."

At the same time, Monterey Pop marked the arrival of rock and roll as a mature form of show business. The lighting was professional, and so was the stage crew that handled the transition between acts. A new and sophisticated system of amplification allowed the bands to play for an audience numbering in the tens of thousands; gone were the days (only a year or two earlier) when a band like the Beatles could not hear itself for the roar of the crowd. John Phillips and Lou Adler, who were used to traveling first-class, also set a new standard for creature comforts: from now on, bands on tour could expect to be wined and dined and supplied with copious amounts of whatever drugs were necessary to summon the muse.

Above all, Monterey Pop accelerated the integration of even the hardest rock and roll into the mainstream of the global music business. Gazing out over Monterey's crowded festival grounds, the executives from the New York City labels could see for themselves that what Chet Helms had said was true: the kids might be stoned out of their minds, but they had lots of "irresponsible dollars to spend." And after that "Summer of Love," as the press came to call it, rock and roll was no longer a genre of popular music.

In effect, whether it was "White Negro" music, or experimental hippie music, or even a music performed by blacks, rock and roll now *was* popular music—the only kind that really mattered.

June 7, 1968:

"Sympathy for the Devil"

In the spring of 1968, the world was burning—and the Rolling Stones were busy living up to one of their own ironic adages: "What else can a poor boy do?/But sing for a rock and roll band?" They posed that rhetorical question in "Street Fighting Man," a song they wrote and recorded that spring. About the contemporary explosion of confrontational politics, it was also a song about their own escape *from* the streets and into a world of radical fantasies that existed only in the music they made. But the global turmoil that gave the Rolling Stones an occasion for creating their enduring musical image of turmoil, was, for thousands of young people around the world in these wild months, an urgent reality, and anything but ironic in its implications.

It was an age of courage and folly, of darkness and light, hope and despair. An American officer in Vietnam had declared that he had to "destroy a village to save it." "Burn your money," urged a leaflet distributed by young American radicals, hoping to win over runaways and hippies. "Burn your houses and you will be set free." In the United States, a large part of the nation's capital, Washington

D.C., went up in smoke after the assassination in April of civil rights leader Martin Luther King, Jr. And throughout May, while the Stones were singing about street fighting, young people were doing it, taking to the streets of Paris and Prague, London and Rome, New York and Mexico City, and fighting with police, in increasingly violent protests against a variety of evils: the U.S. war in Vietnam, the Soviet domination of Czechoslovakia, an authoritarian regime in Mexico, and, in France, where the most famous slogan was "all power to the imagination," the sheer emptiness of modern life.

For those rock fans around the world who had been filled with dreams of a peaceful (if drug-laced) new beginning, the world had never looked crazier. What had been presented in artifacts like *Sgt. Pepper* as an introspective ceremony of innocence, promising an inward journey of creative rebirth with the help of various mind-altering chemicals, now threatened in more than one place to erupt into a very public, and very bloody, civil war, pitting young against old, hippies against cops, radicals against the state.

That spring, amid the tumult and shouting, even Mick Jagger found himself swept along by the outpouring of political emotion. In April, he joined thousands of demonstrators at a rally outside the American embassy in London to protest the war in Vietnam—and then escaped back into the studio, to continue working with his band on an album of music befitting "primitives of an unknown culture" (as Gary Snyder had put it the year before, on the eve of the Be-In in Golden Gate Park).

Two months later, Jagger and the other Stones were joined in the studio by a camera crew supervised by French director Jean-Luc Godard. He was shooting a new movie. They were finishing their next album.

The Stones had something to prove. The album they had released six months earlier, *Their Satanic Majesties Request,* had been a pale imitation of *Sgt. Pepper.* But the Rolling Stones couldn't compete with the Beatles on their own musical ground. The portentousness of the Stones' songs on *Their Satanic Majesties Request,* and their psychedelic idealism, had been laughable. The band that had made a fortune by looking ugly and being bad had a hard time pretending they had suddenly become peace-loving flower children. And with their next album, the Stones were looking to regain what they still regarded as their rightful place, on the cutting edge of musical fashion.

From this point of view, appearing in a film by Jean-Luc Godard amounted to a major coup.

At the time, the thirty-seven-year-old Godard was the most controversial of contemporary filmmakers. In movies such as *Two or Three Things I Know About Her* (1966) and *Weekend* (1967), he had left far behind the narrative naturalism of *Breathless* (1959), lavishing his artistic intelligence instead on the elegant representation of everyday objects—billboards, steam shovels, the bubbles in a coffee cup—combining cerebral harangues about the evils of capitalist society with fluid shots of any odd thing that struck his fancy.

He wished to reinvent the marriage of sound and image: nothing more, nothing less. To attain his goal, Godard set about trying to destroy every received idea about film. "I want to make the film as simply as possible," he announced shortly before he began work on *One Plus One* in June of 1968. "What I want above all is to destroy the idea of culture. Culture is an alibi of imperialism. There is a Ministry of War. There is also a Ministry of Culture. Therefore, culture is war." (In those days, grandiose non sequiturs were an acceptable form of expression, especially for artists at a loss for words that might adequately convey their revolutionary vision.)

Godard had agreed to shoot his next film in swinging London—but only if he could have either the Beatles or the Rolling Stones as his stars. The Beatles were unavailable. But the Stones—in search of fresh cultural capital after squandering their prestige on *Their Satanic Majesties Request*—jumped at the chance to be directed by the great Jean-Luc Godard, never mind the script.

In fact, there was no script. Like the Stones, Godard was now in the habit of acting on impulse and intuition. He made up the script as he went along. In the end, this is what viewers got:

A narrator off camera tells us he is waiting on the beach for "Uncle Mao's yellow submarine" (an allusion to the well-known Beatles song on the album *Revolver*). For the duration of the film, we hear this narrator from time to time reading from a make-believe pulp novel, a piece of pornography filled with flaring loins, heaving thighs, and the names of sundry political figures of the day, from Che Guevara, the international icon of guerrilla warfare, to Richard Nixon, on the verge of succeeding Lyndon Johnson as President of the United States.

Shots of the Stones rehearsing and recording at Olympia Studios thread in and out of a sequence of vignettes: black power militants in a junkyard, mouthing revolutionary clichés and brandishing

weapons; a primly allegorical Eve Democracy, shot in a primly allegorical lush green forest, numbly assenting to a series of windy
propositions uttered by a solemn interlocutor ("A man of culture is
as far from an artist as a historian is from a man of action"); the proprietor of a seedy newsstand stocked solely with porn, blankly reciting passages from Hitler's *Mein Kampf*; and so on. By the time the
movie mercifully ends, it has become clear that the title, *One Plus
One,* is ironic. Nothing adds up—with one exception.

By chance, Godard captured on camera the evolution in the studio
of "Sympathy for the Devil," in more ways than one an apt emblem
of the strengths, and weaknesses, of rock and roll as a medium of political expression in these years.

The part of the film that features the Stones opens with guitars being strummed lazily by Mick Jagger, Keith Richards, and Brian Jones
(at the time in their mid-twenties, though looking rather older,
thanks to the increasingly visible ravages of their drug abuse). At this
preliminary stage, they are trying out "Sympathy" as a slow blues.
But the song sounds plodding. Presented as a kind of pseudo-folk
song, one can't help but notice the strained seriousness and deep
moral confusion of the lyrics, which cast Mick Jagger as a dapper
Lucifer, singing a jaunty tune about a mixed bag of abominations:
the crucifixion of Christ, the Russian Revolution, the Holocaust, and
the 1963 assassination of President Kennedy.

Sometime later, as Godard's cameras reveal, the mood of the music
had changed. "Sympathy for the Devil" had evolved into a samba.
And Jagger, against the odds, had begun to imbue the lyrics with a
sense of dread and foreboding. No longer pretending to belt the
blues with his typical leer, he rides over the band, shouting out the
words, "calling his children home" with a carefree abandon that Big
Joe Turner might understand.

Midway through this improvised process, on June 5, Robert
Kennedy, the former President's younger brother, who was then in
the midst of campaigning for the presidency himself, was gunned
down in Los Angeles. On June 7, back at work in the studio, the
words to Jagger's song were revised: "Who killed the Kennedys?"
Jagger now asked, before giving his own glib retort: "After all, it was
you and me." A chorus joined in, chanting "oo-oo" with deranged
glee. The music lifted off. By the time we see Jagger overdub his final
vocal, the song sounds eerily committed—and quite unlike any piece
of rock and roll before or since.

Godard's record of this event leaves a viewer with two distinct artifacts to ponder, both of them quintessential expressions of their era, both of them sharing certain key features. The song, like the film, was the result of an ad hoc process. Both are works saturated with images of violence. Both are trying to come to grips with the vortex of events outside their frames. But there the similarities end.

Since appearing as the keynote song on the album *Beggar's Banquet,* released in the late fall of 1968, "Sympathy for the Devil" has become one of the most celebrated items in the classic rock songbook, often admired, still frequently heard on radio stations—and widely appreciated as an emblem of its era. Godard's handiwork, by contrast, suffered a fate that was far harder to bear, a by-product of a falling out between the director and his producer.

Once the film was finished, the producer wanted to highlight the Rolling Stones. Godard wanted to provoke insurrectionary thoughts. The producer, who held the purse strings, was adamant. Given Godard's stature, this was a big deal. Godard surprised the producer by showing up at a London preview of the film; after punching him in the nose, Godard called upon the audience to demand its money back, and donate it, instead, to a worthy cause; those who would not comply, he declared, were "bourgeois fascists."

After a long and acrimonious dispute, two versions were prepared for theatrical release in 1970: one, the director's cut, entitled *One Plus One,* the other, the producer's cut, entitled *Sympathy for the Devil.* By then, Godard's volatile mix of politics and avant-garde filmmaking had become passé. Most people simply ignored the film. Among film buffs as well as rock fans, it survives primarily as a curio of a time, long gone, when rock and roll superstars embarked eagerly on collaborations and experiments with the most avant-garde and daring of contemporary artists.

Still, the limitations of *One Plus One* reveal a great deal about the limitations of the prescriptively youthful ethos of anarchic creativity that rock bands like the Beatles and Stones had done so much to make fashionable. Perhaps because he was not all that youthful, either in years or in temperament, Godard's film has an unpleasant odor of self-hatred about it. By identifying with young people in rebellion and ostentatiously renouncing "the man of culture," he had wanted, so he said, to liberate pent-up energies. But that project, in practice, proved as self-defeating as the idea of destroying a village in order to save it. The studied amateurism of *One Plus One,* like the deliberately atavistic din of the Sex Pistols a decade later, drove the artist into a dead-end. The formless, more or less deliberately thoughtless pursuit of crude impulses, once it became a routine, did not release any energy at all. It was simply dull.

The song sung by the Rolling Stones on camera, by contrast, was fire and brimstone—the only outburst of palpable feeling in Godard's film. It helped, no doubt, that the music, unlike Godard's cinematography, adhered to a clear and fairly traditional formal pattern. In the early months of 1968, Mick Jagger and Keith Richards had deliberately simplified their songwriting, hoping to recapture the primal energy of elemental rhythm and blues. Pleased with one of the first songs to come out of this new phase in their career, they had earlier in the year rushed into release "Jumpin' Jack Flash," an archetypal, riff-based, guitar-driven rock and roll tune, recorded straight up, without any pretense of mind-altering magic.

"Sympathy for the Devil" was more venturesome musically—diabolically frenzied sambas weren't standard fare with the Stones. But Keith Richards' electric guitar solo on the original studio version was indicative of the band's renewed stress on clearly focused expression. He plays his stark licks roughly, as if clawing at the strings. The effect is visceral, and violent.

The audience for the song, famously, was not bored. But the story of "Sympathy for the Devil" does not properly end in June 1968, when the band finished mixing the master tape released on *Beggar's Banquet*. Nor was it Jean-Luc Godard who captured the greatest version of the song on film.

The legend of the Rolling Stones, so cleverly launched by Andrew Loog Oldham, only received its definitive form at an outdoor concert held on Friday, December 5, 1969, at a speedway not far from San Francisco, in Altamont, California.

Planned at the last minute, it was meant to be a hippie festival in the spirit of Monterey (and the even more widely publicized Woodstock festival, which had attracted half a million more or less peaceful kids almost four months earlier). The bill for Altamont boasted the Grateful Dead and the Jefferson Airplane and a new "supergroup," as it was called, Crosby, Stills, Nash and Young, all in addition to the Stones, on tour in the States for the first time in three years. To provide security for the musicians, the organizers had hired, for $500 worth of beer, a bunch of Hell's Angels. Ever since Ken Kesey had invited the motorcycle gang to one of his outdoor LSD bashes, the bikers had been widely regarded as noble savages, barbarians, perhaps, but the best imaginable guardians to police the gates of Eden. As at Monterey, a splendid time was guaranteed for all.

The Stones may have been lulled into a false sense of complacency by their own experience with a British contingent of self-described "Hell's Angels" at a free concert they had given at Hyde Park in London in August to honor their fallen comrade, Brian Jones, who had drowned in his mansion's swimming pool in July (likely a victim of too much booze and drugs). The British "Hell's Angels" were in fact more noble than savage, sweet guys who dug American biker gear. But like a fairy-tale spell slowly lifting, dream time was drawing to a close at the Altamont Speedway.

As thousands of hippies huddled against the gathering night, disorder in the audience turned to violence. The local constabulary, drunk and high, was getting rough. When people shoved, they shoved back. Some of the Angels began to restore law and order by wading into the crowd with weighted pool cues to bludgeon suspected miscreants. Other Angels preferred to mete out their rough justice even more swiftly, taking aim at troublemakers with their bikes at full throttle, smashing limbs and breaking bones.

The organizers tried to restrain the Angels and failed. They resorted to wan prayers and a theatrical truism: the show must go on.

In the gathering gloom, the Stones took the stage. As events unfolded, they were faithfully recorded by a camera crew, making yet another unblinking rock and roll documentary. The directors of this film were Albert and David Maysles, the two brothers who had filmed the Beatles on their first visit to America. On that tour, they had gotten priceless footage of fans screaming with glee. On this tour, they would get equally priceless footage of fans screaming in horror.

Fully aware of the ominous atmosphere that now gripped the vast speedway, fully understanding the potential for violence, since one of the members of the Jefferson Airplane had shortly before been knocked unconscious by a member of the "security" crew, Mick Jagger stepped into the limelight and began his act.

Dancing like a dervish, he went through the motions, feigning toughness, visibly frightened—a pusillanimous poseur.

Between songs, Jagger watched from the stage as a motorcycle was overturned by the roiling crowd, heightening the rage of the Hell's Angels nearby. "Oh dear," he said, speaking directly into his microphone, his mincing tone dripping with irony, "someone's motorbike fell over."

The show continued. Directly in front of the stage, a fight broke out between the Angels and the audience. Jagger rode the frenzied samba beat of "Sympathy for the Devil." As the melee continued, the Stones started another song, "Under My Thumb." An eighteen-year-old black man surged toward the stage for a closer look. An Angel grabbed him and stabbed him with a knife. The teenager pulled a gun and struggled free, trying to escape back into the crowd. While the band played on, members of the "security force" chased after the wounded boy, caught him, and before he was able to fire a shot, beat him to death.

In one stroke, the Rolling Stones had resurrected their old image of ugliness, and added to it something new: an aura of real evil. Despite some tough questions raised by reporters who covered the event, the episode sealed their mystique, and forever linked the song "Sympathy for the Devil" to the death at Altamont. Sowing the wind, the Rolling Stones had reaped the whirlwind. Like Robert Johnson, it was said, the Rolling Stones had sold their soul to the devil. That was one reason why critics on both sides of the Atlantic now hailed the Stones as the world's greatest rock and roll band.

In some ways, perhaps they were. Yet "Sympathy for the Devil" told another story as well. A hostage to the happenings at Altamont, it was sometimes hard not to hear it as an inadvertent requiem, a paradoxical lament, for a cultural experiment gone sour.

In practice, after all, the formless pursuit of crude impulses had turned out to be more than dull: it was potentially lethal. And if "Sympathy for the Devil" was, finally, a clever piece of pop music marred from the start by the fake bravado of its lyric, the corpse buried after Altamont was just as real as the corpse of Brian Jones, just as real as the bodies left wounded or lifeless after the street fighting of May 1968 in Paris and Mexico City: portents of a potentially murderous descent into psychic as well as social chaos that became, through the music and myth of the Rolling Stones, an even more ominous feature of the cultural form first named by Alan Freed.

1970–1971:

What's Going On

Long after rock bands like the Beatles and Rolling Stones had grown used to whiling away long hours in expensive recording studios, toying with sounds and song forms at whim, most black artists remained stuck in an earlier mode of musical production, doing piecework to order and punctually punching out new music, often under relatively primitive conditions. As it had been for years, the process was largely controlled by sharp businessmen, savvy songwriters, and experienced producers who left little in the way of creative license to the featured artists, even at those companies, like Berry Gordy's Motown family of labels, that were black-owned and operated.

In the decade after breaking into the rock and roll business with Jackie Wilson, Gordy had methodically mastered the art of manufacturing and bringing to market "the sound of young America," as his company liked to brag. Working with a crack band of studio musicians and a staff of prolific in-house songwriters, Gordy had assembled the most consistently popular lineup of black musical talent in the history of the recording industry, including (in the order that Gordy produced the first of their best-selling records): Smokey Robinson and the Miracles ("Shop Around," 1961); the Marvelettes ("Please Mr. Postman," 1961); Mary Wells ("The One Who Really Loves You," 1962); the Contours ("Do You Love Me," 1962); Marvin Gaye ("Hitch Hike," 1963); Martha and the Vandellas ("Heat Wave," 1963); Diana Ross and the Supremes ("Where Did Our Love Go," 1964); the Four Tops ("Baby I Need Your Loving," 1964); the Temptations ("The Way You Do the Things You Do," 1964); Jr. Walker and the All Stars ("Shotgun," 1965); Gladys Knight and the Pips ("I Heard It Through the Grapevine," 1967); and the Jackson Five ("I Want You Back," 1969).

Berry Gordy wasn't eager to change the way he made pop music just because a bunch of dope-smoking hippies did things differently. But change he did—and when his change of heart came, it was provoked by the overwhelming popularity of one album, *What's Going On,* by Marvin Gaye. Released, against Gordy's better judgment, in

June 1971, the album was a bold musical experiment filled with stream-of-consciousness social commentary. Coming, as it did, from one of the most popular, and reliable, of the teen idols Gordy had so carefully groomed in the previous decade, the album was an unexpected hit—at the time, the best-selling album Motown had ever released. Among those making, and marketing, black music, *What's Going On* went on to become a benchmark, an artistic and commercial triumph frequently, and rightly, compared with the Beatles' *Sgt. Pepper.*

At the time he began work on his Magna Carta for black rock and roll, Gaye was twenty-nine years old, roughly the same age as John Lennon and Paul McCartney. The oldest son of a father ordained a minister in the House of God, a Pentecostal sect, Gaye, like Elvis Presley, grew up on gospel music. He especially admired the great divas of gospel music, magnificently mannered stylists like Mahalia Jackson and Marian Anderson. Despite having a voice of limited range, Gaye learned how to use gospel techniques to summon an astonishing variety of vocal effects. Worrying over the syllables of a song, he could shout hoarsely or glide smoothly into a pure falsetto.

As a teenager, Gaye added jazz and rock and roll to his palette of musical colors, learning how to phrase by studying the recordings of Billie Holiday, and how to put some sweat in his phrasing by listening to Ray Charles. A devotee of doo-wop harmony groups, he defied his father by joining one, the Marquees, while he was still in high school in Washington, D.C. Good enough to cut a record, in 1957, the Marquees weren't lucky enough to have a hit. But two years later, in 1959, Gaye got a second chance when Harvey Fuqua invited him to join his vocal group, the Moonglows, one of the most popular harmony acts of the early rock and roll era. (Alan Freed had given them a start by exchanging airplay for a songwriting credit on their first big hit, "Sincerely," released in 1955.)

Shortly after Gaye joined the Moonglows, they sang the background harmonies on one of Chuck Berry's signature songs, "Back in the U.S.A.," a modest success in 1959. But the Moonglows on their own never regained their old popularity. In 1961, after Fuqua disbanded the group, he and Gaye ended up in Detroit, and went to work for Berry Gordy. "Whereas the girls swooned over Harvey, they died over Marvin," Gordy's first wife, Raynoma, later wrote. "What I loved about him were his many layers and his gentle sensitivity. He always spoke in a low, mellow tone, scarcely above a whisper." He was slim, he was handsome—and in a milieu full of macho men, he was a bashful boy, a young twenty-one.

He joined Gordy's family of musicians, playing piano and drums on sessions, chiming in on background vocals, even writing a song or two. He also married Gordy's sister Anna, an older woman who made sure that her brother fully appreciated Gaye's many musical talents. Recording for the Tamla label and groomed to look supper-club suave, Gaye embarked on a new career as a solo singer, recording such hit songs as "Pride and Joy" (1963), "How Sweet It Is to Be Loved by You" (1964), "Ain't That Peculiar" (1965), and "Your Precious Love" (with Tammi Terrell, 1967).

Although Gaye longed to sing classy ballads with the composure and self-assurance of a Nat "King" Cole, another one of his musical heroes, he was routinely asked in these years to belt out brassy dance tunes. He enjoyed a steady stream of hit recordings. Still, he remained largely unappreciated outside the world of rock and roll, despite his access to an audience vastly larger, and more integrated, than any known by an old-time blues shouter like Wynonie Harris.

Gaye's continuing access to a white teen audience depended on a formula that Berry Gordy had been refining since recording "Lonely Teardrops" with Jackie Wilson in 1958. In return for signing up aspiring but unknown black acts, often from the Detroit area, Gordy received total control. He owned any songs the artists wrote, and he doubled as manager, taking a cut from live appearances. Though his roster of artists was all black, Gordy assiduously cultivated the white teen audience, continuing to book new acts on *American Bandstand*. As Motown's series of hits in the Sixties confirms, Gordy had an ear for what this audience wanted to hear. He liked voices with an intangible sort of adolescent edge, plaintive, keening, guileless. And he liked songs that were aimed at a typical *American Bandstand* fan, set to a simplified beat that almost anyone could dance to: blaring, brusque, visceral, drilled home by the festive sound of clapping hands and banging tambourines. Unrivaled at executing tightly focused rhythm tracks, the Motown band was anchored by a fine jazz-trained drummer, Benny Benjamin, and a peerless bassist, James Jamerson, who for over a decade improvised lines that selectively used harmonic dissonance and unexpected intervals and accents to cut against the grain of the music's overall sound, which was otherwise stereotyped and highly predictable.

As time passed, and Gordy and his Motown staff fine-tuned the musical recipe, the beat got simpler still, the songs grew more and more repetitive, and the sound of the recordings became purposefully strident (following a pattern first established in 1963 by the hit recording of "Heat Wave" by Martha and the Vandellas). At the same time, Gordy closely supervised the image his acts would project on stage. Beautifully choreographed (by Cholly Atkins, a veteran of the swing era), carefully coiffed and costumed, Gordy's acts all had at least the semblance of class. His singers looked sharp. The music was hot. And the beat was blunt. That was the Gordy formula.

Although Marvin Gaye was by no means the flashiest act in Gordy's stable—that honor fell to Diana Ross and the Supremes—he did get consistently good songs. And in 1968, "I Heard It Through the Grapevine" became the first of Gaye's songs to reach out beyond the everyday audience for pop music. Recorded some months earlier, and issued only after Gladys Knight and the Pips had released a tightly coiled and highly successful version of the same song for Gordy's Soul label, Gaye delivered the lyrics as a slow and ominous incantation. The producer, Norman Whitfield, had pitched the song in a key so high that Gaye had to struggle to hit his high notes, giving the lyrics the added piquancy of a singer straining at the limits of his ability.

Gaye's version of "I Heard It Through the Grapevine" became the best-selling record in the history of Motown up to that point, in part because it functioned as a spooky musical capstone to 1968, a tumultuous year, not least for young Americans attuned to the music on the radio. But instead of reveling in his newfound popularity, Gaye was bridling at Gordy's paternalistic regime. He longed to sing the kind of music he really loved, which was old-fashioned ballads. In 1967, he had recorded an unreleased album of standards lushly orchestrated by Bobby Scott (the composer of "A Taste of Honey," a song covered by, among others, the Beatles). In the years that followed, Gaye obsessively returned to Scott's arrangements, taking a master tape of the instrumental tracks and overdubbing ever more ornate and intricate vocal tracks, treating the album, which never appeared during his lifetime, as a private musical talisman, proving, if only to himself, how far he had come in his ability to sell songs of nakedly romantic yearning. Since this was his true ambition, "Grapevine," like the hits that preceded it, felt like a millstone: music that adhered to a style of emotive belting that Gaye had never fully accepted as his own.

In the wake of "Grapevine," Gaye took time off from Motown's musical assembly line. "I dug the hippies," Gaye recalled years later of his mood in these months. "I completely identified. They had the guts to tell the establishment to shove it. They had the imagination to dress differently, think differently, reinvent the world for themselves. I loved that. I also loved their pot."

Rejecting his clean-cut stage image, Gaye discarded his suits and ties and grew a beard. Unwilling any longer to adhere to Gordy's rigid regimen, Gaye refused to go on tour. He refused to cut any more upbeat dance tunes. Instead, he made his first foray into record production, working with the Originals, a new Motown group that specialized in old-fashioned doo-wop harmonies. He composed three gorgeous ballads for the group to sing: "Baby, I'm for Real," "The Bells," and "We Can Make It Baby." Each song was lavishly orchestrated by the arranger David Van dePitte, who surrounded the group's delicate vocal harmonies with swirling violins, a sexy alto saxophone, and a glittering array of tinkling cymbals and bells, creating a dreamlike aura that recalled Gaye's own formative love affair with the harmony singing perfected a decade before by groups like the Moonglows.

In the fall of 1970, Gaye was offered a new song, "What's Going On," composed by two Motown colleagues, Al Cleveland, a staff writer, and Renaldo Benson, a member of the Four Tops who had previously co-written "I Second That Emotion," a hit for another Motown vocal group, Smokey Robinson and the Miracles. A song about a world in chaos, "What's Going On" also evoked, implicitly, the blood still being shed in Vietnam. A prayer for peace, a sermon on social harmony, it had an introspective tone that was unexpected coming from two of Gordy's company songwriters.

At first, Gaye said the song didn't interest him. But Cleveland and Benson kept pestering him to change his mind. Years later, one of Gaye's confidants, Mel Farr, at the time a celebrated pro football player for the Detroit Lions, recalled how, on a visit to the singer's house, Gaye had played "What's Going On" for a group of friends, remarking that it might make a good song for the Originals: "He started fooling at the piano and when we dropped by to see him the next day he was still fooling with it. 'That's not for the Originals, Marvin,' we told him. 'That's for you.' "

Gaye now proceeded to do something all but unprecedented within the Motown system. Late in 1970, while most members of the

Motown staff, including Gordy, Cleveland, and Benson, were in the midst of moving their families, and the company, from Detroit to Los Angeles, Gaye stayed home. Working on his own, without supervision, Gaye began to fool around in the studio. Using the latest studio technology to multitrack his own voice, just as Patti Page had done a generation before, Gaye created an impressionistic pastiche of vocal textures, produced by pitching his voice in various registers and using a variety of timbres, juxtaposing a smooth falsetto, a silky croon, and a raspy groan, gliding from a whisper to a scream, and deploying all these voices in a constantly shifting pattern of changing harmonies. By using the studio to create a kind of musical kaleidoscope, Gaye was able to produce by himself the painful yet enchanting mood of bittersweet longing he had so beautifully conjured up in the love songs he had written and recorded with the Originals.

Functioning as his own producer and free to summon his muse at will, in whatever way he wished—one pictures him at a microphone, eyes closed, enveloped in a cloud of marijuana smoke—Gaye for the first time was able to work as he pleased, at odd hours, toying in the studio with his vocal harmonies, trying out new tracks, adding and subtracting vocal lines and orchestral sounds, mixing in a track of percussively snapping fingers, asking David Van dePitte to create another lavishly romantic string arrangement, and using Mel Farr and his other pals to exchange hip salutations, putting all these pieces together to create the illusion that a singer was singing the song with himself, to himself, commenting on current affairs as if in a trance—and all while a party of old friends swirled around the ghostly troubadour as a small jazz combo played with after-hours ease. (For "What's Going On," as for every song on the album of the same name that was released shortly afterward, the music was anchored by the bass lines improvised, brilliantly, by the peerless Jamerson, who cut loose with perhaps his finest set of recorded performances.)

Since this was Gaye's first new recording in a while, Gordy rushed "What's Going On" into release. But by temperament and conviction, he was unmoved by the stunning originality of Gaye's new music. Still, Gordy *was* moved by the sales that the new music began to rack up. After being released in February 1971, "What's Going On" rose rapidly to number two on the *Billboard* chart of the "Hot 100" singles in America.

Gaye had made his point. And so Gordy allowed him to take the next step. He authorized him to produce, under his own artistic control, a new album, meant to capitalize on the popularity of "What's Going On."

Gaye worked quickly, calling on the talents of Van dePitte again, commissioning new songs from Benson and Cleveland, composing a new song himself, and asking Motown's crack band of studio musicians to go for the sound and feel of "What's Going On" writ large. "I do something and I listen to it and say, 'Wow, this will sound good on this,' " Gaye said of the album's sustained atmosphere of offhand genius: "And I listen to that and say, 'Wait, here I can put behind that, this,' and then I do that, I say, 'Wow, a couple of bells, ding dong, here,' and that's the way you do it. You build. Like an artist paints a picture." By the beginning of May, the album was finished, at least in Gaye's mind.

When Berry Gordy first heard it, he balked. It was one thing to release a single song with stream-of-consciousness lyrics about the state of the nation. But it seemed to Gordy far riskier to release an entire album of such stuff. "He had done nothing for the past year and all of a sudden he wants to do a protest album," Gordy recalled in the memoir he published in 1994. " 'Marvin,' I said, 'don't be ridiculous. That's taking things too far.' "

Gordy eventually relented, though not without pressure from some of his most trusted advisers. Smokey Robinson, the most prolific of Motown's songwriters, warned Gordy that he and the entire Motown staff loved Gaye's album: "We think it's brilliant."

And so it was. Loosely linked by a series of lyrics expressing an almost catatonic mood of doom about the spiritual condition of inner-city America, Gaye's production tied the songs together with music of hypnotic beauty, full of gently pulsating rhythms, sighing strings, sweet saxophone riffs, and lots of tinkling bells. In some of the songs, the singer protested that he and his friends were living in a nightmare world; but Gaye throughout sounded curiously detached, even serene, like a man happily trapped in a charnel house that was not, finally, without compensatory pleasures.

Popular musicians aren't normally capable of expressing feelings of such ambivalence. When *What's Going On* was finally released, in June 1971, Marvin Gaye proved that he could—and so joined a handful of performers, including Dylan and Lennon and McCartney, in expanding the frontiers of rock and roll as a potentially expressive, deeply personal art form.

At the same time, Gaye also laid out, more directly than Dylan, and more lyrically than Lennon or McCartney, the seductions of the cultural moment, and some of its real dangers. He did this most memorably on "Flyin' High (in the Friendly Sky)" perhaps the eeriest of the album's many highlights.

Sung with minimal melodic movement, in a variety of different multitracked voices, "Flyin' High" is, superficially, what Gordy would have called a "protest song." At first glance, it's a cautionary tale, a compassionate vignette of drug addiction, a play on an airline's ad slogan of the day ("Flying high in the friendly sky"). But Gaye isn't outside the landscape of spiritual devastation he surveys: he's singing about himself. This is his version of "Mr. Tambourine Man," his version of "Heroin," his version of "Tomorrow Never Knows," and it's as harrowing and memorable as any of these more frequently celebrated precursors.

Singing in an unnaturally sweet falsetto, Gaye sounds like a drug-addled choirboy. Jamerson's bass prowls around the melody, which floats. The song's protagonist worries about his lusts, but he's helpless to control them; earnestly seeking salvation, he's settling, one more time, for a counterfeit of transcendence.

"And I go to the place where the good feelin' awaits me," Gaye croons sweetly, with angelic yearning. "Self-destruction is in my hand."

It was a lovely piece of music. And as he perhaps intended, it doubled as an epitaph for the halcyon days of intoxicated creativity that would soon enough be drawing to an unhappy close—for Gaye, and also for the larger (counter)culture of rock and roll.

July 3, 1971:

The End

Père Lachaise, the Paris cemetery, has long appealed to romantic sensibilities. Opened in the early years of the nineteenth century, it was a necropolis at the gates of bohemia's capital, the burial site of choice for bourgeois businessmen wealthy enough to lease a plot, and the last stop for a lot of celebrated saints and sinners, lovers and artists, from Eloise and Abelard to Nerval and Proust, Oscar Wilde and Sarah Bernhardt, Gertrude Stein and Edith Piaf (perhaps the most beloved of France's popular singers in the twentieth century). For several years, the most frequently visited site in the cemetery belonged to Allan Kardec, a French spiritualist renowned for his ability to negotiate the boundaries between life and death. Kardec's cult, however, was no match for that which gathered, in the closing decades of the twentieth century, round the grave of a dead American rock star, Jim Morrison of the Doors.

His death was made public on July 5, 1971. Officially, it was said that his heart had failed two days earlier. But friends, and most fans, knew better. A paragon of excess, Morrison in the last years of his short life (he was twenty-seven years old) had committed himself to binges of heavy drinking and drug-taking, fancying himself a *poet maudit* like Rimbaud, high on the nectar of oblivion.

In his prime, performing in 1967 and 1968 as the lead singer of the Doors, he had looked like a Greek god, with a face of angelic sweetness and long tresses of beautiful flowing hair. But he had always acted like a man possessed, prowling the stage in leather pants, high on acid or stoned on pot or smashed on whiskey, trying to live up to his credo: "I am interested in anything about revolt, disorder, chaos—especially activity that seems to have no meaning."

To many fans, Morrison's death seemed perfectly logical, a fine finishing touch to a suicidal work of art. After his death, a cult slowly formed around his memory. For the first time in its history, Père Lachaise began to be mobbed. The cemetery became the fourth most popular place to visit in Paris (after Versailles, the Louvre, and the Eiffel Tower). And the anniversary of Morrison's death became an annual occasion for bacchanalian orgies conducted by amiably besotted young mourners. Faithful to his uncouth code of living, fans desecrated the cemetery with graffiti: ACID RULES; MORRISON THIS WAY; JIM WAS A JUNKIE; THIS IS NOT THE END.

As the years passed, and the pilgrims kept flocking to the grave site, the cult grew ever bigger. A decade after his death, his band was more popular than ever, not least with listeners too young to have seen or heard the Doors in their heyday. In 1980, a biography of Morrison, *No One Here Gets Out Alive,* by Jerry Hopkins and Danny Sugerman, became a best-selling book in the United States. And in 1991, twenty years after his death, Hollywood paid Morrison its highest compliment: Oliver Stone, an Academy Award–winning director, exalted the singer's life, and death, in his film *The Doors*.

"He was Dionysus come to earth, a shaman in a foreign body," a "rock star and poet," a "genius and holy fool"—so says Danny Sugerman in a new preface to the twenty-ninth printing of *No One Here Gets Out Alive*. Unfortunately, a disinterested reader of that book would be hard-pressed to describe Morrison as anything other than a monumental jerk.

When Oliver Stone directed his film *The Doors*, he faced the same problem, posed by the same set of brute facts. Intended as a loving homage, Stone's film offers an inadvertent parody, a portrait of an amateur oracle's excruciatingly dull metamorphosis into a pitiful, drunken slob—not what Nietzsche had in mind when he invoked Dionysus.

It had all begun with a heady vision, a fantasy of making a music of sublime destructiveness, unleashing orgies of "sexual licentiousness," subverting "family life and its venerable traditions," exploring "the most savage natural instincts" in songs that celebrated "that horrible mixture of sensuality and cruelty"—notions of Nietzsche that fascinated Ray Manzarek, a classically trained keyboard player who in 1965 decided to start a rock band.

Looking for help, Manzarek turned to Jim Morrison, a classmate in film school. That summer, during a stroll along Venice Beach (rhapsodically depicted in Stone's film), Morrison, an aspiring poet, sang Manzarek a new song—and the two young men then and there "decided to get a group together and make a million dollars" (as the organist remarked in a 1968 interview). To complete the lineup they recruited John Densmore, a young jazz-oriented drummer, and Robbie Krieger, a guitarist familiar with flamenco as well as the electric blues style made popular by the Rolling Stones. Morrison and Manzarek called their band the Doors—an allusion to a phrase of William Blake's ("There are things that are known and things that are unknown; in between are doors"), and also to *The Doors of Perception,* Aldous Huxley's account of his experiments with mescaline.

Playing first at dives on Sunset Strip, and then at the Whisky-a-Go-Go, Hollywood's premier pop music showcase, the Doors attracted a following large enough to provoke interest from record labels. Signed by a small but trend-setting folk-rock label, Elektra, the Doors released their first album in January 1967. Titled simply *The Doors,* it was a solid debut. The songs ran a gamut from the bawdy blues of Howlin' Wolf ("Backdoor Man") to the Weimar cabaret music of Kurt Weill and Bertolt Brecht ("Alabama Song"), with new songs smartly alluding to the beauties of both dope ("Crystal Ship") and French literature ("The End of the Night," a nod toward the novel by Céline). But what jumped out were the two longest tracks on the album, "Light My Fire," a largely instrumental set of ecstatic variations on a modal riff, and "The End," a creepy little ballad that had evolved, in the course of countless acid-soaked live performances, into a weird, quasi-Oriental epic of lust and morbid longing, with nonsense blues verses punctuated by a shockingly explicit violation of what Freud had regarded as *the* primal taboo: "Father I want to kill you. Mother, I want to . . . Aar-r-r-g-g-g-h-h!"

The album's jacket photo of Morrison could not have been prettier. And in the spring of 1967, as a shortened version of "Light My Fire" began to climb toward the top of the American chart of bestselling singles, reporters flocked around the boyish beauty with Botticelli looks and a shocking song about incest, begging for quotes.

"I think there's a whole region of images and feelings inside us that rarely are given outlet in daily life," Morrison explained of the band and its music. "And when they do come out, they can take perverse forms. It's the dark side. . . . The more civilized we get on the surface, the more the other forces make their plea. We appeal to the same human needs as classical tragedy and early Southern blues. Think of it as a seance in an environment that has become hostile to life: cold, restrictive. People feel they're dying in a bad landscape. People gather together in seance in order to invoke, palliate, and drive away the dead. Through chanting, singing, dancing and music, they try to cure an illness, to bring harmony back into the world."

On one level, Jim Morrison was Ken Kesey's dream come true: a sex symbol who was also a pop apostle of the "other side"—a world to be won through the open use of mind-bending drugs. And in the summer of 1967, while Kesey's original ragtag band of disciples, the Grateful Dead, struggled (without notable success) to reach the larger rock audience, the Doors were making the rounds of American network television.

Invited to appear on *The Ed Sullivan Show,* Morrison was asked to omit a double entendre, an obvious drug reference, in one of the lines in "Light My Fire." He promised that he would—and then broke his promise, leering at the camera, and very clearly enunciating the troublesome word: "higher." In the United States, where it was easy to associate Morrison's conventionally handsome good looks with an all-American pedigree (he was in fact the son of a high-rank-ing U.S. naval officer), the effect was startling: it was as if Ozzie and Harriet's boy-next-door had dropped acid and started snarling ob-scenities.

But it soon enough became clear that Jim Morrison was no Merry Prankster, though not for want of trying. The trouble was with his audience. Far from being converted to a new view of the cosmos, most of them took "Light My Fire," even in 1967, as a cool new ode to sex, drugs, and rock and roll. Even "The End" ruffled few feath-ers: after all, here was a really cute guy behaving in a really gross way—a type tolerated, even beloved, at the fraternity parties com-mon on America's college campuses, where young men traditionally have sowed their wild oats.

As the Doors crisscrossed America, the crowds kept growing. Irri-tated by the prevailing mood of recreational hedonism, Morrison on stage became wilder and wilder. He got in the habit of hurling him-self from the stage. During one famously chaotic concert (in New Haven, Connecticut, in December 1967), he berated the local con-stabulary, who responded with an outburst of old-fashioned vio-lence, beating up the singer after they had arrested him. Mind expansion became a distant memory, as Morrison cut back his intake of pot and acid, and stepped up his drinking. Sometimes he was mes-merizing. Sometimes he simply blacked out.

From the start, of course, rock and roll had entered into a Faust-ian pact with chaotic impulses. For Wynonie Harris, as his loyal fans well understood, "Good Rockin' Tonight" meant fast living and hard drinking. Alan Freed had launched his career with a riot. But during his own descent into intoxicated self-destruction, Jim Morri-son set entirely new standards for disorderly conduct, standards that have remained the envy of every subsequent rock and roll avatar of excess (one thinks of punk bands like the Sex Pistols, and later hard rock bands like Guns n' Roses).

The man who would have been Dionysus became, instead, a figure far closer in spirit to John Belushi's character Bluto, the comic paragon of grossness in the film *Animal House*. "Pecos Bill, Mighty Joe Young and John Henry would be proud to share the volume of outrageous and semi-heroic acts attributed to Morrison," the critic Digby Diehl shrewdly remarked in a piece about the Doors published in 1968: "In addition to prodigious feats of sexuality, he is credited with some bizarre episodes of exhibitionism. At an Ivy League university, Morrison climbed the sixteen-story bell tower with a willing lass; and in a moment of exuberance, swung out on the bell tower shutter, 200 feet above the heads of terrified onlookers—all this stark naked."

When Diehl asked Morrison about his behavior, he explained that his fans demanded it, and that to meet their demands, he now found it "necessary to project more, to exaggerate—almost to the point of grotesqueness."

About appearing grotesque, Morrison had no inhibitions. More and more, he was too drunk to care, and unconcerned, with good reason, about occasionally unpleasant consequences. One night, for example, he drove his car into a tree. Staggering from the vehicle, he summoned an employee to clean up the mess, calm the police, and take him home. Such are the prerogatives of a rock and roll star.

Concerts became an ordeal for the rest of the Doors, who never knew what to expect. But crowds kept coming to the concerts. They were like spectators at an auto race, waiting for a crash.

The crack-up, when it came, was abhorrent, absurd, pathetic. The occasion was a concert staged in an empty airplane hangar in Miami, Florida. It was a steamy night in March 1969, and the promoters had removed every seat in order to sell tickets to the largest possible number of paying customers. With show time nearing, Jim Morrison was nowhere to be seen.

Planning to meet the Doors in Florida, he had spent the previous night in Los Angeles attending *Paradise Now,* an aggressively experimental piece performed by the Living Theater. Inspired by the French playwright Antonin Artaud and his ideas about a "theater of cruelty," and also hoping to negotiate the boundary normally fixed between the artists on stage and the viewers in the audience, the Living Theater in *Paradise Now* aimed to shock: taunting the spectators, denouncing their slavish passivity, their shame at their own animal impulses, the actors feigned fucking, daring the crowd to join them.

When it was all over, Morrison was tired but elated—and primed to emulate the troupe's shock tactics. Preparing to leave for Miami the next morning, he got into a violent row with his longtime girlfriend, Pamela Courson, the only woman up to loving him and hating him with the ferocity that he demanded. Missing his scheduled flight, he took the next available plane and started to drink, tossing back cocktail after cocktail as the jet winged its way toward Florida.

By the time he got to the venue, he was barely coherent and agonizingly late, arriving long after the show had been scheduled to start. The other members of the band were understandably angry. The sold-out audience, crammed together like cattle in a pen, was tired of waiting, and eager for a stiff dose of musical excitement.

The singer, taking a mask from his own ancient gallery of Dionysian disguises, stumbled on stage, his instincts boiling, his thoughts blurred. While the band vamped on a blues riff, the singer, in a half-conscious parody of *Paradise Now,* baited and berated the audience. "You're all a bunch of fuckin' idiots!" he bellowed. "You're all a bunch of slaves!"

The crowd tittered. Slaves just want to have fun.

The master was too drunk to put over a message of psychic metamorphosis and social transformation. After a desultory effort to deliver more or less recognizable versions of some of the songs the crowd had come to hear, Morrison slipped back into a harangue.

"There are no rules!" he shouted, shortly after singing one of his most famous lines, from one of the Doors' most celebrated songs: "We want the world and we want it now!"

A guest walked on stage and handed Morrison a cute baby lamb—a prop meant to provoke a plea for nonviolence and vegetarianism.

"I'd fuck her but she's too young," quipped Morrison. Inured to such outbursts, unlike the intellectuals who had been shocked by the Living Theater the night before in L.A., the good old boys in the crowd whooped and hollered, just like their frat brothers had for "Tutti Frutti" a decade before.

At wit's end, and perhaps as part of a previously planned stunt, Morrison pushed his level of contemptuous exhibitionism up another notch.

As the other members of the band, conceding defeat after clocking in an hour of aimless music-making on stage, started to leave, Morrison resumed his harangue, surrounded now by a number of fans whom he had finally coaxed into joining him on stage.

Somebody poured champagne over Morrison, who stripped off his shirt, now soaking wet. "You didn't come here for music, did you? You came for something more, didn't you? You didn't come to rock 'n' roll, you came for something else, didn't you? You came for something else. WHAT IS IT?"

The crowd roiled and roared.

"You want to see my cock, don't you?"

A member of the Doors' stage crew rushed over to Morrison and grabbed the belt on his pants, pulling up so that he couldn't pull down.

"YEAHHHH!!!" he shouted, waving his wet shirt in front of his crotch. "See it? DID YOU SEE IT?"

The crowd on the floor surged forward. The throng on stage heaved Morrison over the edge. Landing with a thud, he recovered his balance and proceeded to lead several thousand fans in a snake dance.

In an interview shortly before his death, Morrison would call it one of his finest moments. "I think that was the culmination, in a way, of our mass performing career. Subconsciously, I think I was trying to get across in that concert—I was trying to reduce it to an absurdity, and it worked too well."

Years later, the band's drummer, John Densmore, writing in his memoir *Riders on the Storm*, offered a completely different assessment: " 'There's a point beyond which we cannot return. That is the point that must be reached,' Kafka once wrote. Morrison had finally reached it. He had become the cockroach."

Whether one regards the Miami show as a zenith or a nadir, things were never the same—not for Morrison, and not for the Doors.

Four days later, a legal complaint was filed in Miami, charging Morrison with lewd and lascivious behavior, indecent exposure, open profanity, and public drunkenness. Across the country, as newspapers picked up the story, concerts were canceled, invitations to perform withdrawn. The Doors were now a band without a venue.

They struggled to carry on, but Morrison, despite sporadic bursts of energy and interest, had become hopelessly bored by his own fame. Even in a recording studio, he was unable to focus on the music, offering instead uncouth parodies of blues phrasing. Not unaware of what was happening to himself, and still facing the threat of jail for the show in Miami, Morrison flew to Paris in the spring of 1971, apparently hoping that a sojourn in Rimbaud's native land might break his own free fall into oblivion.

The change of scenery didn't work. And so, on July 3, 1971, after a night of hard drinking and (if one can trust the most plausible published accounts) snorting heroin, he finally reached The End "of laughter and soft lies/the end of nights we tried to die."

In 1967, when the world first heard Jim Morrison sing these lines, the sentiments seemed bold and brave, a bracing tonic for a youth culture besotted on a sappy mix of love, peace, and drugged-out bliss.

Four years later, the lines took on a different aura, of self-loathing and involuntary self-revelation. "Our music is like someone not quite at home, not quite relaxed," Morrison once remarked; and so it seemed to be, not least for him.

At the pinnacle of his early fame, Morrison had tried to cast himself willy-nilly as a tragic hero, waging a war on limits. For a moment, in the summer of 1967, that had seemed a war worth waging: a generation, inspired in part by the rock and roll heroes it worshipped, had dreamed of creating new men and new women, undivided, without shame, each one in tune with a unique constellation of animal instincts and creative desires.

But the moment passed. The tragic hero turned himself into a pitiable clown. And the myth of the Doors was reabsorbed by the popular culture it was meant to challenge.

Ten years after Morrison's death, in 1981, *Rolling Stone,* the most prestigious of the American rock periodicals spawned by the abortive cultural revolution of the Sixties, featured a beautiful photo of the rock idol as a Greek god on its cover, with the headline "He's Hot, He's Sexy, He's Dead." "The most important aspect of Morrison Resurrectus," explained the reporter, "is the need today for kids— perhaps all of us—to have an idol who isn't squeaky clean."

Or, as the Doors' Densmore summed up the gist of the piece, and the main maxim of rock and roll ethics in the decades after Morrison's romantic apotheosis: "Permission to party. Well done, Dionysus."

As the end of the millennium drew near, pilgrims continued to flock to Morrison's grave in Père Lachaise. On July 3, 1991, the twentieth anniversary of his death, nearly a thousand fans gathered outside the gates to the cemetery. Fearing a disturbance, the police had closed the grounds for the day. As midnight approached, some of the fans began to hurl beer bottles at the cops. After using a car as a battering ram to break into the park, fans set the car on fire. In the melee that followed, three people were injured, and twenty-one arrested.

The managers of the cemetery shortly afterward announced that, when the term of the Morrison estate's lease on the burial site came up, on July 6, 2001, it would not be renewed. The family would have to move the singer's remains somewhere else.

In France's most famous City of the Dead, at least, the revels would finally be finished. And the cultists, the pilgrims still in search of chaos and freedom, would have to find a new place to worship their holy fool—the most wayward saint yet in the rock and roll pantheon.

6

Stairway

to

Heaven

Ziggy Stardust and the Spiders From Mars

By the end of the Sixties, the Beatles and their disciples had transformed, almost beyond recognition, the world of rock and roll. What once had been dismissed as a form of entertainment suitable mainly for kids was now often credited as a form of culture fit even for discerning adults. In the course of the decade, the music had produced a long string of glamorous celebrities, widely regarded as symbols of some larger social significance, from Mick Jagger to Marvin Gaye and Jim Morrison. These rock stars rivaled any coming from Hollywood—and without having to make demeaning films, like Elvis Presley. At the same time, the keynote acts of the Monterey Pop Festival—Janis Joplin and Jimi Hendrix—had subsequently turned a handsome profit for the companies that sold their recordings, confirming the high commercial value of commodities that could be sold to an avowedly anticommercial subculture. As never before, rock and roll was a potential source of cachet and cold, hard cash, combined.

Still, as the mind-expanding and money-making euphoria of the Sixties started to fade, a new mood, a kind of inchoate malaise, settled over the rock scene. The Beatles had officially dissolved in the spring of 1970, and by the end of the next year, Jimi Hendrix, Janis Joplin, and Jim Morrison had all died of various drug overdoses. In the months that followed, no rock act of remotely similar power and panache had presented itself, sending a small army of industry lookouts into a modest frenzy of worried scouting.

The goal by now was not just to find a hot new band, or even a wild new look, but also—and this was the great lesson learned at the Monterey Pop Festival—to discover a style of music as closely linked to a style of life as the music of the Grateful Dead had been linked to the subculture of San Francisco's psychedelic outlaws. Novelty of any sort, be it sociological or musical, now held out the promise of establishing a new niche in the youth market.

The quest for "The Next Big Thing" was especially ardent in England. Though a relatively small country, England has, ever since the Beatles, played a disproportionately large role in the cultural economy of rock. Since 1963, the looks and sounds fashionable with the island's youth have constantly changed, creating a febrile atmosphere of innovation, and a steady stream of new rock acts, generally more stylish, and startling, than those produced in the United States. At the start of the Seventies, England supported three rival rock weeklies, each one read by obsessive fans and businessmen hoping to exploit their obsessions. With the right sort of publicity from the music press, and support from the country's concentrated network of radio and television outlets, a new British rock act could conceivably redefine the style of teen revolt in a manner of weeks—a feat all but impossible in the United States.

On the night of July 9, 1972, London's media elite assembled in the Royal Festival Hall to see the latest rock and roll prospect. His name was David Bowie, and he'd created a stir in the previous weeks by giving an interview claiming that he was gay; by feigning fellatio with his guitarist on stage; and by wearing lipstick and mascara to go with a puffed ball of hair dyed a shocking shade of red.

As always at such events, the tone was set by a handful of industry heavyweights and media tastemakers. What made the evening unique was the highly visible presence in the audience of the gay press, and a large number of specially invited gay scene-makers. "The crowd isn't noticeably campy," Peter Holmes wrote afterward in London's leading gay paper, the *Gay News*—but the atmosphere, as Holmes evoked it, was nevertheless rich with erotic promise. Aftershave hung heavy in the air, and the compere, when he appeared on stage, announced that he had just had to fight his way through a forest of feather boas.

The lights dimmed, and the hall filled with the steely sound of Beethoven's "Ode to Joy" in a space-age arrangement for electronic synthesizers, the same steely sounds heard on the soundtrack of *A Clockwork Orange* (1971), Stanley Kubrick's lyrical ode to teenage violence in a world run by brainwashing bureaucrats.

Holmes captured the next moment: "A single spot picks out a thin, almost drawn jester. Red hair, white make-up and a skintight, red and green, Persian-carpet-print space suit. All this on top of red lace-up space boots. 'Hello, I'm Ziggy Stardust and these are the Spiders From Mars.' "

Thus spake "Ziggy"—and so began a new era in the packaging of rock and roll celebrities.

Ziggy, as played by Bowie, was a make-believe messiah, a walking publicity ploy, and a cuddly gay pinup, all rolled into one. Bowie had worked up the character in the preceding months, presenting it to the public at large a few weeks earlier, on the album he had called *The Rise and Fall of Ziggy Stardust and the Spiders From Mars*—an album widely hailed by critics in England, not least because of its overt theatrical ambitions and unmistakable aura of high seriousness.

"My performances have got to be theatrical experiences for me as well as for the audience," Bowie had explained to an American journalist the year before, in the course of fielding questions about how he planned to revolutionize the field of rock and roll music. "I think it should be tarted up, made into a prostitute, a parody of itself," declared Bowie. "It should be the clown, the Pierrot medium. The music is the mask the message wears—music is the Pierrot, and I, the performer, am the message."

Inside the Royal Festival Hall, London's smart set beheld the new mask that Bowie's message was now wearing. Ziggy in boots was a parody of Nietzsche's Zarathustra, and an insider's joke, as well, the stage name being an allusion to Iggy Pop (itself the stage name of James Osterberg, a crudely effective American rock and roll daredevil, weaned on the ethos of the Velvet Underground and renowned for slashing and stabbing himself on stage in a bloody display of sick bravado).

Flanked by the Spiders (in fact, a trio of three journeymen rock musicians from Hull), Ziggy and his band roared into "Hang On to Yourself"—a curtain raiser with allegorical bite. A ghostly androgyne, Ziggy offered a pantomime of rock and roll anarchy, projecting a weird aura of icy detachment somehow combined with uninhibited impulsiveness. The band banged out a harshly metallic beat. The singer declaimed the song's lyrics in a broad cockney accent and with demotic exaggeration. The audience was being summoned to a carnival of excess, a ritual of solidarity, an ecstatic loss of personal identity—the sort of thing (not coincidentally) that does sometimes actually happen during rock and roll concerts.

The album that had introduced the Ziggy character had toyed with similar conceits in the controlled context of a studio production. Its most obvious precursor was the Beatles' *Sgt. Pepper's Lonely Hearts Club Band,* though the grammar of the title also recalls another musical, dramatizing another scene of self-destructive permissiveness, *The Rise and Fall of the City of Mahagonny* by Bertolt

Brecht and Kurt Weill (the source of "Alabama Song," which Bowie, like Jim Morrison, liked well enough to record). But Bowie's own *Rise and Fall* was unique: something more than the loosely linked set of songs by the Beatles, and something less than the opera by Brecht and Weill.

The keynote was doom, the subtext chaos. The mood was set by the album's opening track, "Five Years," an evocation of the Last Days. Informed that they only have five years left to live, the residents of Bowie's imaginary metropolis erupt into a desperate orgy, breaking every law, violating every taboo—and leaving a bewildered populace primed for the appearance of a "starman" (whose coming is announced with the sort of sentimental warbling Judy Garland had turned into a trademark cliché in "Over the Rainbow"). When Ziggy, Bowie's salvific hero, first appears, it is as "Lady Stardust" (the song that starts side two of the original album), an omnisexual emblem of animal grace, singing songs of "darkness and disgrace." A "leper messiah," Ziggy falls prey to his own narcissistic delusions (not unlike Jim Morrison)—and with mock piety, offers himself to his fans as a "rock 'n' roll suicide," an admirable icon of redemptive self-destruction, and a mockery of the martyrdom of Jesus Christ.

Bowie was a nearly perfect Pop Proteus: a man of multiple incarnations. He'd arrived in London eight years earlier, performing with a variety of R&B bands under his original surname, David Jones. After attending a storied Bob Dylan concert with the Hawks at the Royal Albert Hall in 1966, all he could talk about was Dylan and the vatic intensity of that performance. Then, in 1967, after changing his stage name to Bowie, he had switched gears again, and reinvented himself as an all-round music man modeled on Anthony Newley, who had been a movie star as a child, a tongue-in-cheek teen rock idol as a young man, and, after 1961, and the opening of his first stage show, *Stop the World—I Want to Get Off,* a successful composer of West End musicals.

Despite all the twists and turns of Bowie's early career, one thing was clear from the start: he was unique among rock artists in his unambivalent embrace of musical theater. As the Sixties went on, he studied mime, learned about Japan's Kabuki theater, cultivated a taste for the French chansons of Jacques Brel, and imbibed Andy Warhol's philosophy of Pop. After scoring an isolated hit in 1969 with "Space Oddity" (a typical wordplay on the title of Stanley Kubrick's film *2001: A Space Odyssey*), Bowie returned to hard rock as his preferred musical idiom. But even when he sang an elemental piece of classic rock and roll like Chuck Berry's "Around and Around" (a 1971 recording of this song, modeled on an earlier version by the Rolling Stones, was originally slated to form part of the *Ziggy Stardust* album), it was with a wink and a nod—as if in knowing parody of rock and roll.

Watching Ziggy in action at the Royal Festival Hall and reporting for *Melody Maker* was Ray Coleman, the jazz buff who had been an early booster of the Beatles. The show was about the making and unmaking of an absurdly overblown, fictive pop star. But Coleman took the parody at face value. (This had happened before in England: Anthony Newley's brief career as a teen idol began after he had starred in a 1959 film satirizing a make-believe teen idol.) "A Star Is Born," read the headline of Coleman's article: and any irony was evidently unintended. "When a shooting star is heading for the peak," Coleman remarked, "there is usually one concert at which it's possible to declare, 'That's it—he made it.' For David Bowie, opportunity knocked loud and clear last Saturday at London's Royal Festival Hall—and he left the stage a true 1972-style pop giant, clutching flowers from a girl who ran up and hugged and kissed him while a throng of fans milled around the stage."

Consecrated by the rock press, Bowie watched sales of his recordings soar in England. Riding a wave of publicity not unlike that heralding the Beatles a decade earlier, he and his handlers set their eyes on the vast American market, their determination to conquer it fortified by a lavish line of credit extended by Bowie's American record label, RCA.

The Ziggy revue landed in America in the fall of 1972. The toast of trend-setters in L.A. and New York City—the sorts of places where influential people actually read British press clips—the show elsewhere was greeted with skepticism and, in many parts of the country, sheer indifference. In the United States, despite massive publicity, Bowie's recordings sold only modestly well—an early indication that the global youth culture created by the Beatles, and ratified at the Monterey Pop Festival, was already beginning to fall apart, fragmenting into different youth subcultures defined by different styles of revolt, and different varieties of rock and roll.

Meanwhile, back in England, where misleading press releases recorded Bowie's overseas progress and helped reinforce the perception that he was a global superstar, popular fascination with Ziggy continued to grow, becoming ecstatic after Bowie's triumphal return to touring in England in the spring of 1973.

One British fan, the writer Harvey Molloy, eleven at the time, later described in the most vivid of terms just what it felt like to be young, excited, and in the presence of Ziggy Stardust in these months. He recalls entering an amphitheater in Manchester that was crammed with kids done up in the regalia of their idol, wearing blue eye shadow, black crushed velvet clothing, and with small star-shaped sequins glued onto their foreheads and cheeks. Molloy, like most of Ziggy's other converts, had committed to memory each song's lyrics, and had, for weeks, looked forward to participating in the liturgy of the event.

"He sings," recalls Molloy of the show's first minutes, "and the world becomes a catalogue of lost objects," doomed to disappear in five years, in the gospel according to Ziggy. "What pleasure comes from imagining the end not only of ourselves but of the entire world! . . . What would the end be like? Would it be final or would some people survive to live without cities, schools, laws and constraints?"

When the Spiders From Mars launch into a prolonged instrumental riff, Molloy feels his mind begin to wander: "I am teleported outside of my mundane life into a vibrant, electric world," simultaneously isolated and fused with everyone else, "neither in the audience nor apart from it, neither separate from my body nor aware of it."

His epiphany is consummated when Ziggy sings the grand finale, "Rock 'n' Roll Suicide," and reaches out to the crowd, as if to heal the sick and raise the dead. "I feel like I'm watching Jesus," recalls Molloy. "He leans over the crowd at the end of the stage, his outstretched hands taunting the front row audience who would give anything to touch him. Sublime, unattainable, out of reach. I know that I will never speak to him; I know that he will never witness the trivial fact of my existence; no Eucharist can allow the congregation to touch the savior."

A figure of serene self-absorption, the ersatz prophet on stage gazes at the undulating, outstretched arms of the crowd as if staring into a mirror. He is alone. So are they. It's just a charade, a make-believe outpouring of divine love.

In the midst of the hoopla, on his way back to England in 1973, David Bowie granted a characteristically disarming interview in which he dissociated himself from his own most famous creation in comments of startling honesty.

"You know," he said to a writer from *Melody Maker,* "the rock revolution did happen. It really did"—society really had been changed, personal revelations really had been provoked by the music of the Beatles and Bob Dylan.

The irony, as Bowie explained, was that often no journalist was there to report what was happening, "so nobody knew when it happened." (Dylan had put it this way: "It was like a flying saucer landed," he remarked in 1985. "That's what the sixties were like. Everybody heard about it, but only a few really saw it.")

Bowie himself had experienced the rock revolution: he was its product. And no matter what his younger fans might feel, Bowie *knew* that the Ziggy revue was, in this sense, unreal: it was mummery, a simulacrum, a theatrical conceit.

"This decadence thing is just a bloody joke," said Bowie to the reporter. "I'm very normal . . . I am me, and I have to carry on with what I started. . . . I never believed a hype could be made of an artist before the artist had got anywhere.

"That's what happened you see. But when I saw our albums were really selling"—as by the time of the interview they were, at least in England—"I knew that one period was over. Well, it wasn't—but at least we'd done something to be hyped about."

Indeed. With David Bowie, hype had become a legitimate, even celebrated aspect of rock and roll as a mode of cultural production. From now on, only someone (like Bowie, like Dylan) who knew better from firsthand experience would be able to separate the genuine from the spurious in what would still be marketed, even in the 1990s, as an ongoing rock "revolution."

But there was one final irony about the David Bowie phenomenon. He had colluded in creating a false impression of himself and the import of his cultural moment. But Ziggy Stardust had real, if transient effects: not least on those young British fans (like Harvey Molloy) who, before Bowie retired Ziggy at a "farewell" concert in July 1973, gave themselves heart and soul to the fake messiah with the flame red hair and the ghostly white face—an all-too-accurate emblem of rock and roll, and what it had become.

1972–1973:

The Harder They Come

By 1972, England wasn't the only place producing prefab icons of rock and roll rebellion. All around the world, wherever films and recordings circulated, rock and roll, and its core values, had taken root locally, generating exotic new variations on familiar themes. Nineteen seventy-two was the year that the film *The Harder They Come* had its world premiere in Kingston, Jamaica. A pioneering venture, produced entirely in a Third World country, the film revolved, in part, around the island's local brand of rock and roll—they called it reggae. Seeking one image to symbolize the film's story line—and also to market the movie to non-Jamaican viewers—the producers made a choice that inadvertently reveals a lot about what rock and roll now stood for, not just in America or England, but around the world.

Featured on posters, and also featured on the cover of the influential soundtrack album, the image is a cartoon. It depicts an impossibly well-dressed outlaw. A pistol-packing fop with a dark black face, he sports a gold chain, shades, a garish yellow leopard-skin patterned shirt, clashing black-and-white zebra-striped trousers, and a wonderfully jaunty yellow beret.

This was Ivan O. Martin, the hero of the film, played by Jimmy Cliff, who was in real life one of the first Jamaican reggae singers to have hits in England and the United States. As he figured in the script of *The Harder They Come,* Ivan O. Martin was a sympathetic figure, a good man undone by a bad society. A country boy with an edge of insolence, Ivan sees his dream of a career in music thwarted by a crooked record producer, and then watches helplessly as his share of the proceeds from a dope deal is siphoned off by equally crooked government officials. In response, Ivan goes on a rampage, murdering more than one man. When a police dragnet descends on the island, it produces front page photos of the previously unknown singer. Thrilled by his newfound infamy and hoping to force the dishonest producer into belatedly promoting his record (the movie's title song), Martin, garishly clothed, arranges a photo call at gunpoint. He wagers that he can turn himself, simultaneously, into a modern-day Robin Hood—and a bona fide pop star.

The ploy works. The outrageous photo stimulates an outpouring of popular demand for the previously ignored recording—and also helps set the seal on the good outlaw's growing legend. Unable to talk disc jockeys and editors out of exploiting the public's fascination with Ivan, the government organizes an island-wide manhunt. The film ends when the army finally corners its prey. Though out of ammo, Martin defiantly confronts his captors in another theatrical pose, emerging from the brush with both pistols cocked, just like in the photograph—an artful gesture that insures he will die a hero, in a hail of meaningless gunfire.

At a time when increasing numbers of critics and publicists were paid by media outlets and record companies to trumpet ephemeral junk, some news still traveled the way it had a quarter century before, in the days of Wynonie Harris: quietly, almost furtively, by word of mouth. So it was that news of *The Harder They Come* began to percolate among rock and roll fans in England and America as 1972 turned into 1973. And as the word spread, Jamaica's unique brand of American rock and roll became a source of growing fascination for fans and musicians alike, creating a new strand of cultural cross-pollination almost as significant as the outlaw blues of Robert Johnson had been a decade before.

An independent Jamaican pop music scene had first emerged in the Fifties, concurrently with the rise of rock and roll in neighboring North America. Since live musicians didn't come cheap, and radios were at first a scarce luxury, most Jamaicans heard the latest pop music at weekly public dances organized by disc jockeys spinning records over mobile "sound systems"—turntables and amplifiers rigged up for outdoor parties. At first, the records were almost entirely imported from the United States. The local record industry was small, and Jamaicans responded with gusto to the jump blues and doo-wop ballads that were the stock-in-trade of early rock and roll. Among the island's most popular stars were Wynonie Harris, Ruth Brown, Fats Domino, and Little Richard. In these years, different sound systems competed by offering the latest import recordings, which were also brought into the country by merchant seamen and migrant workers.

As the Fifties drew to an end, at a time when white teen idols like Ricky Nelson were in the midst of transforming American rock and roll, the Jamaican sound system operators turned to local musicians to supply the continuing demand for sweetly harmonized ballads and swinging dance music. Using American recordings as a guide, the musicians had little difficulty in picking up by ear the new styles, not unlike the teenaged Beatles growing up in Liverpool. At first, the Jamaican players hewed closely to their American models; but as time went by, they began to invert the characteristic rhythmic patterns of boogie-woogie swing, accenting the offbeat, and eventually introducing a new kind of gently lurching syncopation.

By 1970, when Perry Henzell began shooting *The Harder They Come,* Jamaica had developed a thriving local record industry built around successive fads for different local rhythmic styles: first there was ska, starting in 1961, then rocksteady in 1967, and finally, in 1968, came reggae—a term that in the years since has functioned as a generic label for all of the island's modern pop music, making it the Jamaican equivalent of the term "rock."

From the start, the island's music industry had close links with the pop scene in England. A British colony until independence was formally granted in 1962, Jamaica continued to send a great many products—including, at first, its local recordings—back to England for manufacture. Some of the Jamaican records pressed in England stayed there, for sale to immigrants from the West Indies. By the end of the Sixties, the United Kingdom had become the biggest single market for Jamaican music. In 1968, when the British label Trojan released *Uptight,* the first volume in what became a series of budget compilations aimed at immigrants, the album also reached young white Britons, perhaps because the anthology featured several reggae versions of familiar rock and roll songs, including Leiber and Stoller's "Kansas City"; the Beatles song "Ob-La-Di, Ob-La-Da"; and, under the title "Watch This Squad," an eerie rendition of "For What It's Worth," the 1966 hit by the fashionable L.A. band Buffalo Springfield about cops chasing kids in the streets.

Besides songs and listeners, reggae shared with rock and roll a variety of attitudes and techniques. Like American rhythm and blues in the early Fifties, it was an idiom full of sexual innuendo. It gloried in electronic gimmickry, using recording studio techniques to create unnatural timbres and textures: exaggerated echo, muffled vocals, carefully arranged percussion effects, amplified bass lines of visceral forcefulness. And by the end of the Sixties, reggae, like rock, had become a central ingredient in several different types of youth subculture. In Jamaica, it was linked with the unemployed and outcast who inhabited the tin-roof shanties depicted in *The Harder They Come*. In England, by contrast, reggae paradoxically became a tribal music of the skinheads—racist white working-class toughs.

The vitality of the reggae scene struck a chord with Perry Henzell. A white Jamaican of British descent, Henzell had spent the Sixties producing short documentaries, shooting television commercials, and organizing production units for American directors who, impressed by the glamorous setting of the first James Bond film, *Dr. No*, wanted to use Jamaica as a location.

For his first feature film, Henzell and his collaborator, Trevor D. Rhone, devised a script by combining elements of two different mythic figures: the heroic fugitive, and the local rock and roll star. Based loosely on the exploits of a legendary Jamaican criminal named Rhygin, who had undertaken a daring series of robberies and murders in the 1950s, they updated the story by turning the outlaw into an aspiring reggae singer.

As Henzell doubtless knew, the story line wasn't hopelessly far-fetched: just as early rock impresarios like Alan Freed and George Goldner had done business with shady characters like Morris Levy, the prime movers of the reggae world, sound system operators and record producers like Duke Reid and Prince Buster, surrounded themselves with goons and gangsters, sometimes glorified in song as "rude boys."

But as Henzell also knew, there was another, more spiritual strand of the reggae scene that was equally important to his Jamaican audience, and also to a great many musicians. A number of the island's most prominent singers had grown up with gospel music in church. In addition, after independence, Jamaica had witnessed an explosive growth of popular interest in Rastafarianism, a pan-African religion that combined mysticism and political militance with the wearing of long hair knotted in "dreadlocks" and the sacramental smoking of "ganja" (marijuana).

Largely eschewing trained actors for his film, Henzell recruited an ad hoc supporting cast of hoodlums, dope dealers, churchgoers, and Rastafarian holy men, many of whom spoke in a patois so thick that the film used subtitles. Shooting on location in the slums and shantytowns of West Kingston, Henzell exploited the quasi-documentary techniques used so effectively by Richard Lester in *A Hard Day's Night*. Like Lester, too, Henzell built the plot around a sequence of songs, picking his favorite recent reggae hits to supplement a handful of new tunes specially written for the film by Jimmy Cliff.

Like most Jamaican singers of his generation, Cliff had grown up idolizing a variety of American vocalists: Louis Jordan, Fats Domino, Little Richard, and Sam Cooke. Uncommonly polished in stage manner, Cliff had traveled widely in the Sixties, appearing in America and Europe and England and also South America, often performing songs that he had composed in the emotive, neo-gospel soul style then fashionable in America. Cliff's impassioned singing on one of his neo-gospel hymns, "Many Rivers to Cross," is what provoked Henzell's initial interest in him.

With his wiry build and simmering good looks, Cliff was magnificently cast as Ivan. But the real star of the film was the exotic world of reggae and Rastafarianism. Audiences glimpsed various reggae stars in the studio, and also saw vignettes of Rastafarians reverently gathered together to smoke incredibly huge "spliffs" of ganja— scenes from an outlaw subculture as vicariously appealing as the mythic Kansas City celebrated in song by Leiber and Stoller.

Before it was even finished, *The Harder They Come* had become a political football in Jamaica. It was, as *The Hollywood Reporter* remarked, "the first feature from a Third World country"—and a major source of patriotic pride for a great many Jamaicans. At the same time, it was a potential embarrassment, not least for tourism officials, because of its violent content and depiction of rampant corruption.

In a debate recalling that in the early 1950s among Cleveland's black elite over the wholesomeness of Alan Freed's musical fare for upwardly mobile Negroes, the two main Jamaican parties split over the merits of the film. The Conservative Party, in power since independence, made Henzell's life miserable by denying him permits to shoot on location and hiring thugs to terrorize the film crew. But in 1972, when *The Harder They Come* had its premiere shortly after the opposition People's National Party had come to power for the first time, the new prime minister, Michael Manley, was prominently in attendance.

The scene on opening night was chaotic. Inside the Carib Theatre, the largest in the Caribbean, people were jammed two and three to a seat, as the prime minister, politicians, and selected members of Kingston high society were joined by an uninvited mob. As the scenes of slum life flickered across the screen, the crowd roared with gleeful recognition. Outside, another 4,000 people tried in vain to force their way into the theater.

The next day, in order to accommodate popular demand, the film was shown simultaneously in four different cinemas, with couriers shuttling the two available prints from theater to theater. In Jamaica that summer and fall, *The Harder They Come* went on to set a new box office record, outgrossing the island's previous record-holder, *The Sound of Music*—a musical that perfectly symbolizes the goody-goody moralism that, for better or worse, reggae, like rock and roll, mocked, ridiculed, and beat into cultural retreat.

Meanwhile, as plans were laid to open the film in England and America, a soundtrack album, featuring six songs by Cliff, as well as a sampling of six other recently popular reggae tunes, was prepared for global release. The liner notes made a direct appeal to fans steeped in the prevailing ethos of rock and roll, circa 1972: "Shanty Town—Jamaica—where the best grass in the world sells for two dollars an ounce in the street, where shooting a film can be held up when an actor is shot (2 have died since it was completed), where people sing in church until they have an orgasm (thank you Lord)."

When the film finally hit college towns like Boston and Berkeley, some viewers were swept away by "the dazzling, fearsome world Henzell re-creates," in the words of Stephen Davis, a young rock critic who was inspired by the film to visit Jamaica and write several subsequent books about reggae. Not unlike Alan Lomax, who had gone South in search of the men behind the sound of authentic blues, Davis journeyed to Kingston in search of "reggae master musicians as well as the producers, ganja traders, the Rastafarian brethren and elders"—the high priests of the "reggae cosmology," as Davis called it.

Commenting on the range of reactions his movie provoked, Henzell later remarked that "it's two completely different films, really. In North America, Europe and Japan, it's for college-educated people who want to glimpse the other side. In places like Brazil and South Africa, it plays like 'Kung Fu' for illiterate audiences." A quarter century after its first release, the film was still being regularly screened around the world, long after it had fulfilled its function as the *Blackboard Jungle* of Jamaica, introducing a new style of rock and roll to an audience of young people worldwide.

Jimmy Cliff meanwhile proved to be the reggae equivalent of Bill Haley. Lucky to be linked to the right movie at the right time, he was too polished a performer to last long as a credible emblem of what was most authentic about the new musical form. It took several years, but that job finally fell to Bob Marley, someone far better suited to the role. A performer of rare charismatic gifts, with an ambition and reach as a self-taught composer that recall Lennon and McCartney, Marley was originally a member of a vocal trio, the Wailers, which enjoyed great success in Jamaica in the early 1970s, singing a growing number of songs with frankly Rastafarian and political themes. Signed to a global distribution deal by a British-based rock label, Island, the band released an artfully rock-tinged album, *Catch a Fire*, in late 1972, at roughly the same time *The Harder They Come* went into global distribution.

It took several years of touring around the world, and it only occurred after Marley had jettisoned the original Wailers in order to monopolize the spotlight himself, but when his apotheosis finally came, in a legendary series of shows in 1975 at the Lyceum Theatre in London, Marley stood before his racially mixed audience as a latter-day version of Ivan O. Martin: a "visionary Rasta rebel," a figure of defiance and hope. By then, Marley had fully integrated on stage the mystical and militant sides of his outspoken Rastafarianism, projecting an aura of uplifting unruliness—and demonstrating, in a context different from the rock counterculture of the Sixties, the feeling of shared moral energy that a truly committed performer can generate through a hypnotically simple form of music.

So it happened that a singer from a Third World country became one of the decade's quintessential rock and roll stars. As a contemporary critic wrote in England's *New Musical Express,* "The white kids have lost their heroes; Jagger has become a wealthy socialite, Dylan a mellowed, home-loving man, even Lennon has little to say anymore. So along comes this guy with amazing screw top hair, and he's singing about 'Burnin' and Lootin'" and 'brainwash education' and loving your brothers and smoking dope. Their dreams live on."

Just as rock and roll musicians in the Sixties were inspired by the Delta blues, so were musicians in the Seventies and Eighties inspired by the raw style they first discovered on recordings made in Jamaica. As the critics Steve Barrow and Peter Dalton have remarked, "major features of Jamaican dancehall culture—the megawatt sound systems, the exclusive 'one-off' recordings, the foregrounding of drum and bass, and the practice of rapping over rhythm tracks—have been appropriated by rave and dance culture," while other innovations, like the proliferation of different remixes of the same recorded performance, have become a staple feature of mainstream rock and roll, as well as of hip-hop and rap, the two African-American pop music genres most deeply influenced by reggae aesthetics.

In other ways, the global popularity of reggae has had an even deeper long-term impact. The freshness of the island's music inspired veteran American and British rock musicians as different as Paul Simon and David Byrne and Peter Gabriel to cast their net more widely, canvassing other countries for new musical ideas, and opening up to systematic exploitation the last unexplored redoubts of the world's vernacular pop music cultures.

This was a process made paradoxically easy by one simple, overwhelming fact: rock and roll, born in America, reinvented in England, and reinvented again in countries like Jamaica, was, by the end of the Seventies, a truly global phenomenon. It was a cultural form—an ensemble of sounds and styles and patterns of behavior—familiar worldwide, and influential almost everywhere. Looking for something different in Kingston and São Paulo and Capetown, searching for new types of primitive sounds uncorrupted by rotten rules and show biz artifice, the musical explorers, if they dug deep, often enough found a shadow of themselves—rock and roll rebels, in Third World disguise.

August 1, 1973:

American Graffiti

The scene was repeated in theaters across America. The lights dimmed. The film began to roll. A snare drum cracked, with a loud eerie echo. Out of the theater's speakers boomed a voice: "One, two, three o'clock, four o'clock ROCK!"

So began director George Lucas' *American Graffiti*—the first Hollywood blockbuster about rock and roll, and a revealing exercise in nostalgia, suggesting that in the minds of many listeners no longer young, rock's golden age was already over.

Released on August 1, 1973, the film used Bill Haley's old hit and a relentless barrage of equally familiar early rock and roll recordings to turn back the clock and evoke a lost world of youthful innocence. Shot on a shoestring budget, the movie within a year had earned more than $50 million in theater rentals, making it one of the most profitable films in the history of Hollywood.

Lucas was a virtually unknown filmmaker at the time, a twenty-nine-year-old prodigy with only one previous feature to his credit, *THX 1138*, a bleak vision of a future world of robotlike conformity. Born in Modesto, California, in 1944, Lucas had been a big rock and roll fan as a kid. At the age of thirteen, he had gone to see Elvis Presley on his first tour of northern California. A virtual recluse, he would retire to his room every day after school to listen to rock and roll and read comic books. When he was old enough to drive, he added cars to his small list of obsessions. It was only after recovering from a near-fatal car crash in 1962 that Lucas belatedly developed a passion for film, an interest that he pursued at the University of Southern California.

After graduating from USC in 1966, he worked for three years as an administrative assistant to another up-and-coming director, Francis Ford Coppola. Like many Americans of his generation, Lucas was outraged by the endless war in Vietnam, and outlined for Coppola a movie about the war, to be titled *Apocalypse Now*. Earning extra cash as a cameraman, he was at Altamont Speedway in 1969 on the night that a concertgoer was beaten to death while the Rolling Stones played on. Repelled by the brutality of that event, disturbed, too, by the violence enveloping the antiwar movement, Lucas was also stung by the failure at the box office in 1971 of *THX 1138*. He resolved to make a different kind of film—one that would make people feel better about America, and prove his commercial mettle.

"We all know, as every movie in the last ten years has pointed out," Lucas remarked at the time, "how terrible we are, how wrong we were in Vietnam, how we have ruined the world, what schmucks we are and how rotten everything is. It had become depressing to go to the movies. I decided it was time to make a movie where people felt better coming out of the theater than when they went in." The music of Bill Haley would help evoke an era of simpler pleasures: "I wanted to preserve what a certain generation of Americans thought being a teenager was really about—from about 1945 to 1962."

Lucas was scarcely the first person to notice the peculiar power of rock and roll to provoke nostalgia. In the late Fifties, a new term had been coined to classify older recordings with just this power: "oldies but goodies." The phrase had been invented by Art Laboe, a Hollywood disc jockey. After fielding endless requests to play older recordings, he began to air a show entirely dedicated to them. Inspired by the show's success, he issued a compilation album on his own Original Sound label, featuring doo-wop songs like "In the Still of the Nite" by the Five Satins. Entitled *Oldies but Goodies in Hi-Fi,* Laboe's album entered *Billboard* magazine's chart of best-selling albums on September 21, 1959; climbing as high as number twelve, the album remained on the American charts for more than three years. Its popularity demonstrated that, while fads came and went, some rock and roll songs, like "In the Still of the Nite," only a modest hit when first released in 1956, grew more widely popular with age, functioning as modern-day musical madeleines with the mysterious Proustian capacity (as Laboe remarked in the notes to his first album) to "bring back memories of a past love affair or a particular time in one's life."

In his treatment for *American Graffiti,* Lucas bluntly exposed one of the wishes implicit in the popularity of oldies but goodies: "Why can't things stay the way they are?"

Essentially plotless, the film can be summarized simply. Four buddies aged seventeen to twenty-two spend the last night of summer together. The time: August 1962. The place (in the words of Lucas' treatment): "a seemingly adultless, heat-drugged little town." The focus of the action: "a fifties ritual called Cruising. An endless parade of kids bombing around in dagoed, moondisked, flamed, chopped, tuck-and-rolled machines."

The leader of the pack is twenty-two-year-old John Milner, who drives a neon-yellow '32 Ford. The local loser is a pimply geek, nicknamed Toad, who putters into view driving an ignominiously small Vespa motorbike. The other key characters, Steve (who drives a dashing '58 Chevy) and Curt (whose car, a practical Citroën, tells us he's got brains), agonize over whether to leave home for college the next day. By the time dawn breaks, Steve has decided to stay and settle down with his high school sweetheart, while Curt—the film's existential focus—flies off.

The specific characters and course of events scarcely matter, however, as the evening unfolds like a whimsically updated version of *A Midsummer Night's Dream.* Shot almost entirely at night with a cast of unknown young actors and actresses (including several who later became famous, among them Richard Dreyfuss, Ron Howard, and Harrison Ford), the film creates a sustained atmosphere of enchanted goofiness, using neon and mercury vapor streetlights to capture the look that Lucas had specified, "juke-box like: very garish, bright blue and yellow and red." In this version of an old myth, while the young lovers frolic aimlessly, Puck's role falls to a middle-aged disc jockey, Wolfman Jack, the only sympathetic adult on camera, who casts a benign spell over the proceedings.

"I had always been interested in the phenomenon of radio," Lucas later recalled. "I was amused by the fact that people have a relationship with a deejay whom they've never seen but [to] whom they feel very close because they're with him every day. For a lot of kids, he's the only friend they've got." As a young film student at USC in 1965, Lucas had shot a twenty-minute documentary about a Southern California rock radio personality, Bob Hudson. The opening title card said simply, "Radio is a fantasy."

Not the least of Lucas' achievements in *American Graffiti* was his subtle evocation of the dreamworld of rock and roll radio. The pre-text is that everybody, on this last night of summer, is tuned in to hear Wolfman Jack broadcast a night of oldies but goodies. Of course, no group of kids has ever listened in unison to a single radio station from dusk to dawn: it just seemed that way, and it is this semblance that Lucas re-creates with the help of Walter Murch, who mixed the soundtrack.

When Lucas had initially tried to sell *American Graffiti,* a number of studio executives balked. No previous Hollywood project had called for using so many vintage recordings. Each vignette in Lucas' story treatment was calculated to last the length of a rock and roll recording, about two and a half minutes; when Lucas pitched the film, he brought along a cassette of his favorite old recordings as well as the screen treatment. "*American Graffiti* is a musical," the treatment declared: "It has singing and dancing, but it is not a musical in the traditional sense because the characters in the film neither sing nor dance." The idea was to use the old recordings to tie the film's vignettes together—and thus to create a new kind of Hollywood musical, in which the songs in the background formed the film's emotional center. (In some cases, specific songs had formed the basis for the vignettes in the first place.)

Lucas had begun with a list of nearly eighty songs. After filming had started, Universal, the studio that was financing *Graffiti,* protested at the escalating cost (music rights eventually came to al-most $90,000, more than 10 percent of the total budget). The studio wanted Lucas to use only five or six songs, but he refused. Though a few tunes by Elvis Presley were dropped, thirty-nine old recordings were eventually licensed for use—the most ever, till then, in a Holly-wood film.

For the final cut of the film, Lucas and Murch carefully synchro-nized different songs with different scenes, creating an imaginary ra-dio broadcast that established continuity as well as the rhythm of the film. In addition, Murch improvised a new process for mixing the songs, piping them through a variety of speakers in a variety of dif-ferent locations in order to simulate the tinny blare of the outdoor music at the drive-in and the small, pinched tone of a car radio. As the camera and the characters moved through different spaces, the sound changed while the song remained the same. With everyone in the world of *American Graffiti* tuned in to the same wavelength, the familiar old recordings, as they passed by—from "Why Do Fools Fall in Love" by Frankie Lymon to "Ain't It a Shame" by Fats Domino—acquired the weight and inevitability of a cosmic drone: this wasn't the detritus of an infantile pop culture, it was the music of the spheres.

Meanwhile, the audience was invited to look at the recent past as if through the other end of a telescope. Lovingly rendered though the sounds and images on screen were, they seemed to belong to a world so far gone as to be almost beyond recall. "You just can't stay seven-teen forever," one character remarks, though others on screen hotly contest the point. As Lucas explained in an interview shortly after the film was finished, *American Graffiti* is "about teenagers moving forward and making decisions about what they want to do in life. But it's also about the fact that you can't live in the past." To drive that point home, Lucas insisted on ending the film with title cards describing the fate of the four principal characters (two survive, but two die: Milner in a car crash, Toad in Vietnam).

Despite the somber tone of these final cards, *American Graffiti* left a contradictory impression, rooted at least in part in Lucas' own am-bivalence about whether he meant to bid the past farewell or to give it a new lease on life.

"I know what I liked as a kid," Lucas later explained to a biogra-pher, "and I still like it."

In shooting *American Graffiti*, Lucas got to stage, and viewers got to see, a painstaking reproduction of a certain moment in cultural time. Lucas had assumed that the core audience for his film would be kids between the ages of sixteen and twenty—but he was mistaken. Intelligently handled, a dream of eternal youth conveyed by sounds as much as images could be marketed to a public that turned out to be surprisingly large, at least in the United States.

For months after it was first released, *American Graffiti* drew crowds across America, turning the film into one of the most successful movies released till then. It was not the first time that a movie rooted in the culture of rock and roll had become a major hit: that distinction belongs to *Easy Rider,* Hollywood's 1969 homage to the worldview of Ken Kesey. But *American Graffiti* was a much bigger hit—and its long-term consequences were deeper, and more varied.

A generation of younger filmmakers, raised, like Lucas, on television and comic books and rock and roll, turned for inspiration toward the past, reinventing—to take only the case of Lucas himself—the Flash Gordon movie serials from the Thirties (in *Star Wars* and its sequels), and the Uncle Scrooge comic books from the late Forties and early Fifties (in one keynote sequence in the first of the *Indiana Jones* films). Thanks to directors like Lucas, rock and roll faced serious new competition from Hollywood for the money and enthusiasm of teenagers.

At the same time, the traditional Hollywood musical virtually disappeared after *American Graffiti.* Instead of a singer bursting into song on camera—a naturalistic convention still honored by the Beatles in their films—movie music was now emphatically prerecorded. It was left to the visual artistry of the filmmaker to link a set of familiar sounds to a tableau that underlined, and amplified, one possible imaginative response to the music. Once a sound floating free over the airwaves, inviting listeners to indulge in private reveries, rock and roll increasingly entered into an alliance with tightly scripted images—in films, on commercials, and (in the Eighties and after) in the short films and promotional videos that record companies produced and distributed to the new music video networks on cable and satellite television.

Buoyed by the box office clout of *American Graffiti,* studios in these years became adept at churning out big-budget pictures that combined a coming-of-age story line with a suitably high-octane rock and roll soundtrack. If music helped sell a film, the film just as often returned the favor. The soundtrack album of *American Graffiti* became the most popular compilation of vintage Fifties rock and roll since Art Laboe's original *Oldies but Goodies* album in 1959, selling more than one million copies. In the years that followed, similar collections proliferated, from *Saturday Night Fever* in 1977 to *The Big Chill* in 1983, and from *Dirty Dancing* in 1987 to *Wayne's World* in 1992.

This was not an unmixed blessing. To anyone raised on the old songs on these soundtracks, from Marvin Gaye's "I Heard it Through the Grapevine" on *The Big Chill* to the Ronettes' "Be My Baby" on *Dirty Dancing,* it sometimes seemed that a handful of recordings had achieved a new, and terrible, sort of immortality: and that these musical traces of youthful inspiration, products of whimsy preserved on tape, were fated to be repeated over and over again, in film after film, in ad after ad, aimed at the young, and at those who wished they still were, until nobody, young or old, could any longer experience the core feelings—of wonder and surprise—that rock and roll had really excited, once upon a time.

October 1975:

Rock and Roll Future

It had begun with a rare surge of spontaneous enthusiasm for a new performer, shared among a handful of club-goers on the East Coast. By the spring of 1974, the euphoria had spread to a small but influential group of rock critics, wired into the infrastructure of media outlets that had sprung up, after the Summer of Love, to report on happenings in America's hip youth culture. And finally, one and a half years later, in the fall of 1975, the cause of the commotion became a focus of national attention.

In the eyes of some, it was very glad news: a savior had appeared. His name was Bruce Springsteen. And he was going to be America's greatest pop music hero since Elvis Presley, never mind the Beatles.

Almost every aspect of the Springsteen phenomenon was remarkable. The unrestrained enthusiasm of a small coterie of admirers became the basis for a calculated outpouring of exaggerated praise that, in its intelligence and sustained intensity, made the coverage of Ziggy Stardust seem amateurish by comparison. The performer himself, aware of the mounting hubbub, had spent endless hours in the studio, trying to craft a transcendent musical masterpiece. Executives at the performer's record label, Columbia, invested tens of thousands of dollars in a marketing campaign of unprecedented sophistication. Critics chimed in with rave reviews. And by the fall of 1975, with his album in stores and the star on his first national tour, Springsteen was being widely hailed as a rock and roll Messiah: not a pretend one, like Ziggy Stardust, but a real one—a figure blessed with the miraculous ability to lift up people's spirits (and drive their blues away).

That was when the mass media took over. By the end of October, *Time* and *Newsweek,* magazines read by millions of Americans, had both run major pieces—in the same week!—examining the Springsteen phenomenon.

Never before in the history of rock and roll had a single performer been featured simultaneously on the cover of America's two major news magazines. Never before had concerted public proclamations about the significance of a rock and roll performer played such a central role in creating the impression that he was, in fact, significant. Never before had there been such obvious reason to wonder whether the proclamations were actually true.

Springsteen, twenty-six, had been playing in rock bands since the Sixties. Signed to Columbia in 1972 by John Hammond, he had quickly recorded two albums, *Greetings from Asbury Park, N.J.,* released in January 1973, and *The Wild, the Innocent and the E Street Shuffle,* released nine months later. Neither album sold many copies. Critics in the United States, writing in newly influential pop music publications like *Rolling Stone* (the mass-circulation biweekly founded in 1967), nevertheless expressed guarded admiration for both discs, especially the second, a roller-coaster ride through a variety of riffs more or less familiar to anyone steeped in the rock and roll of the Sixties, but elaborated in long, breathless songs about an urban frontier peopled with romantic tramps and outlaws, each one with his or her own mock-heroic stage name: Rosalita, Big Balls Billy, Kitty, Weak-kneed Willie.

In the winter of 1974, Springsteen barnstormed up and down the East Coast. What on record had seemed overwrought on stage became overwhelming. The reason had only partly to do with the quality of the music. Springsteen was a rudimentary guitarist, and his baritone was a raspy instrument. His band, too, though tightly rehearsed, was little more than a glorified bar band, which was not surprising, since Springsteen had recruited its five members (bassist, drummer, organist, pianist, and saxophonist) from bands playing in various New Jersey bars. But if the music was sometimes rough-hewn, and if the band (especially compared to British rivals) was so casually outfitted as to make almost no visual impression at all, Springsteen himself projected a strong aura of blue-collar authenticity, and the band's gritty performances were rarely less than exhausting. Fiercely committed to putting on a memorable show, he and the band made a practice of playing marathon sets that routinely lasted over two hours, until he, or his audience, or both, seemed on the verge of collapse. That was what, finally, provoked wonderment and joy: the sheer do-or-die *spirit* with which Springsteen played his music, night after night, week after week.

"Rock and roll came to my house where there seemed to be no way out," he said to one reporter in these years, explaining his own sense of having been "saved" by rock and roll. "And it came into my house—snuck in, ya know, and opened up a whole world of possibilities. Rock and roll. The Beatles opened doors. Ideally, if any stuff I do could ever do that for somebody, that's the best. Can't do anything better than that. Rock and roll motivates. It's the big, gigantic motivator, at least it was for me. There's a whole lot of things involved, but that's what I think you gotta remain true to. That idea, that *feeling*. That's the real spirit of the music"—and it was that spirit that came across in his performances in these months.

In April 1974, prompted by the buzz on the streets, two young writers—Dave Marsh, then the music editor of a Boston alternative weekly, *The Real Paper,* and Jon Landau, a columnist for *The Real Paper,* and also, as music editor of *Rolling Stone,* perhaps the most influential rock critic in America—went to check out a Springsteen show in a Boston-area bar. "Both of us had seen a lot of music performed in a lot of bars," Marsh later wrote, "but never with an effect like that." In the first of his two books on Springsteen, *Born to Run*—a surprise best-seller in the United States—Marsh described his reaction in frankly religious terms. "The advent of Bruce Springsteen," he wrote, "seemed nothing short of a miracle to me."

And so it seemed as well to Jon Landau: "On a night when I needed to feel young," he wrote a month later, "he made me feel like I was hearing music for the first time."

Landau was one of several writers who had risen to prominence in the Sixties by analyzing the significance of rock and roll. Unlike most of his peers, he knew how to play an instrument, the guitar, and (at the invitation of Jerry Wexler at Atlantic Records, who doubtless saw in Landau a younger version of himself) had gotten involved in producing records, working among others with the MC5, a quintet of self-avowed rock and roll revolutionaries. Appreciating though he did the broader cultural ramifications of the music, Landau was far more interested in how essentially unschooled performers could flourish as showmen expert in the enigmatic art of thrilling large audiences with feats of musical magic. College-educated and bookish, he was fascinated by musicians who were neither. Otis Redding, for example, he praised for being "openly and honestly concerned with pleasing crowds," and also for being "truly a 'folk' artist," unwilling to modulate his music according to passing trends. In an essay published in 1968, he expressed his distaste for the Dionysian posturing of the Doors, and wondered out loud why "it wasn't good enough just to sing about cars, balling, dances, school and summertime blues."

It's small wonder, then, that Bruce Springsteen struck a chord with Landau. He did after all just sing about cars, balling, dances, school, and summertime blues. The world that Springsteen evoked was not, finally, all that different from the one depicted in *American Graffiti*. Even better, Springsteen seemed like the real thing—he was a paragon of populist musical virtues, evidently as untainted and pure in his own way as Robert Johnson or Otis Redding, despite growing up within earshot of Alan Freed's radio show.

"He has far more depth than most artists," Landau explained to *Newsweek* in 1975, "because he really has roots in a place—coastal Jersey, where no record company scouts ever visit." (It was true that John Hammond had not had to leave Midtown Manhattan in order to discover Springsteen—but that was because the singer had come to him.)

In May 1974, after seeing Springsteen live for the second time, Landau—knowing that his words carried uncommon weight within the American music business—wrote an impassioned essay, declaring "I saw rock and roll future and its name is Bruce Springsteen."

Though written for a local Boston weekly, Landau's sentiments were soon enough blazoned in advertisements, paid for by Springsteen's record company. Landau's imprimatur had three immediate effects. The first was to set Springsteen himself a daunting, and perhaps impossible task—to fulfill Landau's prophecy. The second was to force every self-respecting rock critic in America to sit up and take notice. Last but not least, Landau's emphatic words of praise convinced Springsteen's record label to embark on an intensive, and expensive, new effort to market his first two albums.

These were months in which it was clear, certainly to Jon Landau and his peers in the critical community, that the explosive growth of rock and roll had produced paradoxical consequences. More people than ever before were listening to the music—on radio, on television, on film, and not least on recordings, which were selling in larger quantities than ever. But the more pervasive rock and roll became, the less it seemed to matter.

The key problem was simple. As the appetite of younger listeners for rock music had continued to grow, the companies and media outlets competing to satisfy their appetite had begun to specialize, offering different kinds of rock to different target audiences, splitting apart a market that had been unified as recently as 1967, when the Beatles released *Sgt. Pepper.* In the mid-Sixties, radio stations around the world, when they played rock and roll, had generally played more or less the same handful of songs, insuring that the music, when it became popular, reached a large and diverse cohort of listeners. A decade later, the situation was entirely different. In America, rock was easy to hear—indeed, it had all but driven most other forms of music off the radio—but stations rarely played the same songs. Some, sticking with Top 40, played only current hits. Others specialized in oldies but goodies, sometimes concentrating on music from the Fifties, sometimes on music from the Sixties. Some played only "urban" or primarily black artists, while still other stations played only "progressive" artists like David Bowie and Led Zeppelin, acts that sold large numbers of long-playing albums without having a number one single on the Top 40. (By the Nineties, the rise of alternative rock would leave the market even more fragmented.)

In this situation, no one could any longer reasonably expect one radio station to air all the rock music that was worth hearing, just as no one of sound mind would actually wish to hear all the rock and roll records that were now being released. A rock act of real cultural consequence in one country—David Bowie in England, for example—might well become moderately popular in another country, but without having any cultural consequence there at all (such was Bowie's fate in America).

For anyone weaned, like Jon Landau, on the sentiments of shared self-discovery unleashed first by Elvis Presley and then by the Beatles, the new regime was hopelessly frustrating. Motivating his personal quest for "The Next Big Thing" was an inchoate but powerful yearning—for a new rock hero as real and mythic (and as popular) as Elvis and the Beatles. It was precisely this need that Bruce Springsteen seemed to meet. Even better, he seemed to meet it instinctively, spontaneously, without coaching or self-conscious theatricality (unlike Bowie), and also without (as the press duly noted) the use of illegal drugs. He seemed, in short, a throwback to rock's golden age of innocence.

Once Columbia had renewed its publicity campaign for Springsteen in earnest, over the summer of 1974, the singer was in a strange sort of box. Asked to deliver the "future" of rock and roll, he was also now widely expected to function as if he were a " 'folk' artist" (to use Landau's rubric), by using inspiration and intuition to create a fresh new music as ostensibly uncontrived and primordial as that widely believed to have been produced by the first heroes of rock and roll.

Trying to rise to the challenge, Springsteen wrote a new song, "Born to Run," which would become the title track of his next album. Composed like an old-fashioned teen anthem from the early Sixties, Springsteen and his band spent weeks working up an elaborate arrangement in the studio, using multiple overdubs to create a cavernous, majestic, quasi-orchestral sound without actually using an orchestra (though Springsteen had played with that idea, too, cutting an early, rejected version of the song with strings).

Given an advance tape of "Born to Run" by Springsteen, Landau shared it with writers he trusted to be helpful. But as the pressure mounted to produce nothing less than a masterpiece, and his own self-confidence began to falter, Springsteen anxiously reached out for someone who could offer him expert musical advice, the kind of advice that George Martin had given the Beatles. (Up till then, Springsteen had produced his own music in conjunction with his manager, a burly ex-Marine of limited musical talents named Mike Appel.)

The person that Springsteen turned to was Jon Landau—who, having foreseen the future, was now asked to help make his prediction come true.

As 1974 turned into 1975, Springsteen and his band, working with Landau, concentrated on the task at hand. Exploiting the singer's natural aura of artless honesty, Landau implicitly cast his leading man as a new kind of star-spangled superhero, doing with a rock star what filmmaker John Ford had done with John Wayne: taking a minor artist and turning him into a major symbol, a larger-than-life personification of America, Land of the Free.

By the start of summer 1975, the songs for the next album were written, and the recording was largely finished. Executives at Columbia loved what they heard, and decided to invest still more money in promoting Springsteen. "You don't go right to the public to sell a new performer," remarked Bruce Lundvall, the man in charge of Columbia's marketing efforts, speaking to a reporter from *Business Week:* "You sell him to your own company first, then to the trade, then to the record buyers."

At the end of August, on the eve of the album's release, Springsteen and his band were booked into the Bottom Line, a 400-seat nightclub in Greenwich Village that functioned at the time as an industry showcase for new talent. Columbia filled the house night after night with record label staffers, and also made certain that elite tastemakers were on hand to witness the event. Springsteen's appearances also drew long lines of ordinary fans, frantic to obtain one of the artificially scarce tickets, reinforcing the impression that history—real history—was being made. (The atmosphere was not unlike that generated three years earlier when David Bowie had debuted Ziggy Stardust in London at the Royal Festival Hall.)

Since one of the Bottom Line shows was recorded for broadcast, and subsequently circulated widely as an unauthorized album, it is possible to verify some of what was happening musically, and take some measure of the bizarre disproportion between the mood of frenzied excitement communicated by the press coverage and the modest but real charm of the performance at issue.

As Dave Marsh described one show, accurately enough, "the songs invariably build from a whisper to a scream"—subtlety was not one of Springsteen's gifts. Drawing material from all three of his albums, the singer turned several of his songs into epic sagas. One of them, "Kitty's Back," routinely lasted more than eighteen minutes. The music, as it survives on the broadcast recording, is notable for its nervous, unrelenting drive—and also for its unblushing exploitation of crude musical devices, such as the wildly rushing tempo used to climax the song "Rosalita."

These devices were amplified on stage by a host of stunts that dated back to the era of vaudeville and blackface. At the end of one show, described by John Rockwell, a *New York Times* rock critic assigned to profile Springsteen for *Rolling Stone*, Springsteen feigned fainting into the arms of his most important stage foil, Clarence Clemons. A pawn in what had become a quintessential rock and roll mise-en-scène, Clemons was Springsteen's designated "Superspade" (to borrow the charged term used by Robert Christgau in his critique of the Monterey Pop Festival). A modestly talented saxophonist, Clemons had one priceless asset: he was a big, burly black man who was quite willing to clown around for white folk, just like Louis Jordan or Louis Armstrong.

"I don't think I can go on, Clarence," Springsteen croaked at this point in the show. "It's cholesterol on my heart. My doctor told me if I sing this song once more, he wouldn't be responsible. But I gotta do it, Clarence, I gotta." With that, Springsteen hurled himself into the last chorus of "Twist and Shout"—the very same ersatz gospel song that the Beatles had used a decade earlier to bring down the house.

It was a gesture of breathtaking bravado, and, in the view of Rockwell, it epitomized Springsteen's genius: "It was pure corn, of course, but a perfect instance of the way Springsteen can launch into a bit of theatricalized melodrama, couch it in affectionate parody, and wind up heightening his own overwhelmingly personal rock & roll impact." (The reader was left to wonder what, precisely, distinguished a "rock & roll impact" from any other sort.)

The furor over *Born to Run* was an eye-opening experience. For the first time, the key players—music critics, record executives, publicists, disc jockeys, editors in the mainstream media—gained an appreciation for the marvelous circularity of the process of rock star-making as it had evolved: if it was declared loudly enough that a musician had wider cultural significance, it was feasible to manufacture, however briefly, at least a simulacrum of wider cultural significance, insofar as this could be measured by the attention paid to a performer by the mass media. "Is it all publicity?" asked Bruce Lundvall at the time. "Some of it is, sure. But Springsteen has to be good enough to sell records over the long haul."

As the passage of time would show, Bruce Springsteen was in fact good enough "to sell records over the long haul." Indeed, in 1984, his seventh album, *Born in the U.S.A.*, became the object of an even more intensive marketing blitz that, before it was finished, completely overshadowed what Columbia had done with *Born to Run,* and turned it into one of the top-selling records of all time, with over fifteen million copies sold worldwide.

Yet Springsteen's triumph was in some ways Pyrrhic, since it had some perverse and presumably unintended consequences. Like David Bowie as Ziggy Stardust, Bruce Springsteen as "Bruce Springsteen, American Superhero" was widely perceived as a quasi-religious, larger-than-life medium of spiritual uplift. Both Bowie and Springsteen nurtured this impression by shrewdly manipulating the whole range of mass media that had grown up around rock and roll since the Beatles. But by shrewdly manipulating the media, both artists— Bowie did this deliberately—turned the public image of themselves, and their music, into fetishized commodities, prefab tokens of a rapturous transcendence, producing a variety of goods that could be purchased and (for the truly idolatrous) reverently collected. With the successful mass-marketing in the United States of Bruce Springsteen, American Superhero (the very image of redemptive innocence), following on the heels of the successful mass-marketing in England of Ziggy Stardust (the very image of redemptive self-destruction), the age of innocence in rock was well and truly over—probably forever.

In 1997, music historian Fred Goodman justly summed up the larger meaning of the Springsteen phenomenon. "His ultimate embrace of music as business made it impossible to separate the acts of faith from the acts of fortune or to tell which one was pursued in the service of the other. As a business strategy it was superb. . . . But as an action, its meaning was completely different from that of the protest movement, to which it owed so much of its persona."

Fiercely committed though his stage performances showed him to be, Bruce Springsteen in 1975 didn't challenge the supremacy of crass commercialism in the music business. He unwittingly consummated it—and so revealed, just as Jon Landau had promised that he would, "rock and roll future."

December 2, 1976:

"Anarchy in the U.K."

They had worked long and hard to make themselves notorious. But even a band as audacious as the Sex Pistols and a manager as mischievous as Malcolm McLaren were unprepared for the uproar they provoked in one minute and forty seconds of airtime on a live London television show.

Their appearance had been an afterthought. On December 2, 1976, EMI, the British record label that had just released the first recording by the Sex Pistols, learned that another of the label's bands, Queen, would not be available to do a scheduled live interview later that afternoon on the *Today* program. *Today* was a talk show aired over Thames TV in London weekdays at teatime. EMI hoped that a last-minute appearance by the Sex Pistols might help to boost interest in the band's new single, "Anarchy in the U.K.," released the previous Friday. For McLaren and the Sex Pistols, the show was an opportunity—but also a risk. The Sex Pistols had already achieved a certain measure of infamy for their vehement, sometimes violent live shows. Now they were being invited to charm, or somehow to outrage charmingly, a daytime television audience.

On the face of it, the odds of success were low. For much of the previous year, the Sex Pistols had been at the center of a gathering storm of controversy, more or less orchestrated by their manager McLaren, then thirty years old. An elfin figure with merry eyes and a shock of red hair, McLaren had gotten into rock and roll through the rag trade. In collaboration with Vivienne Westwood, his wife as well as a seamstress and designer, McLaren had opened a shop in 1971 called Let It Rock. Located on World's End, off the King's Road, the shop doubled as a retail outlet and a hangout for rock musicians, both aspiring and established. Four years later, bored with the idea of Let It Rock and fired with enthusiasm for bands like the New York Dolls and the Ramones from New York City's burgeoning post–Velvet Underground rock scene, McLaren and Westwood changed the shop's name to Sex, redesigned the interior, and added clothes with a fetishistic flair: rubber shirts, chain link necklaces, studded leather dog collars. Capitalizing on the evident appeal of the new look to a new breed of rock musician, McLaren lit on the idea of forming a band that would help publicize the store.

Thus was born the Sex Pistols. By 1976, as McLaren's band started to make its mark, McLaren and Westwood changed the look and name of their shop again, and Sex gave way to Seditionaries. While McLaren turned his attention to managing the band, Westwood produced a new look that visually elaborated the message of the new band's music. There was, for example, the "anarchy" shirt, produced in conjunction with the Sex Pistols' new song, "Anarchy in the U.K." Dyed with stripes, it was stenciled with slogans ("Only Anarchists Are Pretty"), stitched with a crazy quilt of politically contradictory patches (a portrait of Karl Marx, a Nazi swastika), and completed with an armband inscribed with a word that perfectly summed up the overall look of the shirt and sound of the Sex Pistols: CHAOS.

The band itself had formed around a nucleus of two longtime friends, Paul Cook, eighteen, a drummer and fan of rude-boy reggae, and Steve Jones, nineteen, an electric guitarist and accomplished thief who had stolen the public address system used by David Bowie at Ziggy Stardust's "farewell concert." Drawn to Sex after reading an article about the shop in a music magazine, Cook and Jones met McLaren, Westwood, and, through them, another aspiring young rock musician, Glen Matlock, eighteen, a bassist who proved to have a knack for composing catchy riffs. Sometime in the summer of 1975, this trio began to rehearse as a unit, and McLaren decided to complete the band by finding a suitable singer. Informed that John Lydon, another of the shop's customers, might be a possibility, McLaren asked him if he could sing. "Only out of tune," Lydon quipped—and according to legend, that clinched the deal.

Though he was the last to join, Lydon quickly became the band's focus of attention. He wore torn T-shirts held together by safety pins, a uniform of distress that set off handsomely a face of contorted expressiveness. "He looks like a disgraced Angel Gabriel," journalist Caroline Coon wrote, exaggerating only slightly, in an early profile of the band: "Meningitis in childhood accounts for his slight stoop. He has ice-blue eyes, parchment white skin and a head of ginger/blond/yellow hair. It's all spikey and damp like the well-kissed fur of a child's teddy bear. But he can be as cold and as closed as a fist of steel."

When EMI signed the Sex Pistols in the fall of 1976, it seemed to be a coup. Critics for Britain's weekly pop papers had already been bowled over by the band's brutally simple style of hard rock—they called it "punk," borrowing the term from rock writers in America. The music was abrasive, the look repulsive, the concerts wild—a "Warhol monster mash," as one observer described the scene. Still, a good many critics agreed that the Sex Pistols stood at "the vanguard of a new youth culture," as Caroline Coon trilled.

And what a culture it was. At punk shows, the kids didn't exactly dance, they "pogoed"—leaping stiffly up and down, as if on a pogo stick. Because Lydon tended to expectorate when he sang, the audience had gotten in the habit of spitting back—a ritual called "gobbing." And then there was the fighting. Wherever they went, the Pistols took with them a threat of violence. One of John Lydon's pals was John Simon Ritchie, better known under his stage name, Sid Vicious. A quintessential punk long before he became a bona fide member of a punk band, Ritchie got ready for a Sex Pistols show by fortifying himself with a prodigious quantity of amphetamine sulphate and liquor, often supplemented with heroin. Mild-mannered when sober, he was a monster when high. At one Sex Pistols show, he chain-whipped a writer suspected of harboring reservations about the band. At another, he expressed his irritation with a warmup group by hurling a glass that hit a pillar and shattered, wounding one bystander in the eye, and landing Ritchie in jail.

When McLaren and the Sex Pistols arrived at the Thames TV studios on the afternoon of December 2, they were parked in a waiting room and plied with drinks—not a bright idea. Although they had been quizzed in the past by music writers and television reporters, this was to be the band's first—and last—live television interview.

Just how much the producers of the *Today* show knew about the Sex Pistols is unclear. Fortunately, Thames TV had aired a documentary on the punk scene just a few days before. So the *Today* show's presenter, Bill Grundy, began by introducing a clip from the film. "Chains round the neck," Grundy quipped breathlessly, scarcely concealing his contempt. "And that's just it, fellas, yeah, innit? Eh? I mean, it is, just that, fellas. Yeah? They are punk rockers. The new craze they tell me. They are heroes, not the nice clean Rolling Stones"—an utterly bizarre comment, indicative of the host's addled state. "You see, they are as drunk as I am. . . . They are a group called the Sex Pistols. And I'm surrounded by *all* of them. . . . Just let us see the Sex Pistols in action. Come on, chicks."

Shot, in part, at a Sex Pistols concert filmed in November, the clip gave viewers a glimpse of the deranged atmosphere created by the band. By the fall of 1976, Lydon had reinvented himself, performing under the stage name of Johnny Rotten. Wild hair framed a bug-eyed look of mad concentration. His hunched back gave him a grotesque profile. Wearing a filthy white shirt festooned with "I Survived the Texas Chain-Saw Massacre" stickers, he sang pitched forward, howling at the microphone, twitching spasmodically. Those listening as he sang looked stylishly damaged, boys and girls wearing Gothic eye shadow, speed freaks in torn T-shirts, chains round their necks, hair gelled and dyed and carefully molded into strange shapes.

Once the clip was over, Grundy turned to face his visitors. Slouched into their seats and looking soused and sullen, the four Sex Pistols were joined on camera by four of their most telegenic fans, each one a work of art, not least Siouxsie Sioux (born Susan Janet Dallion), already an aspiring singer in her own right: with her zigzag eye shadow and platinum-blond thatch of spiky hair (though without the naked breasts and swastika armband that had already made her a London club legend), Siouxsie was a perfect example of punk style—edgy, inscrutable, a paragon of bored perversity.

Addressing the band, Grundy popped an obvious question: "Are you serious?"

"Oh yeah," answered Glen Matlock with mock earnestness.

"You are serious?"

"Mmmmm."

Bemused and evidently uncertain how to proceed, Grundy began again: "Beethoven, Mozart, Bach and Brahms have all died . . ."

"They're all heroes of ours," sneered Lydon.

"Suppose they turn other people on?" parried Grundy.

Lydon, muttering, was barely audible: "Well that's just their tough shit."

Grundy: "It's what?"

Lydon: "Nothing. A rude word. Next question!"

A rude word: now there was something to run with. Grundy asked Lydon to speak up. What had he said? Lydon complied. "Shit."

Grundy next challenged Steve Jones to "say something outrageous."

Jones: "You dirty bastard."

Grundy: "Go on, again."

Jones: "You dirty fucker!"

Grundy: "*What* a clever boy!"

Jones: "You fucking rotter!"

Grundy: "Well that's it for tonight . . ."

As a moment of history in the making, this pathetic telecast scarcely stands comparison with the great rock and roll events of the Fifties and Sixties, when first Elvis Presley and then the Beatles electrified vast audiences of viewers in America and England. By comparison, virtually no one had seen the Sex Pistols on the *Today* show.

It didn't matter. An elemental modern taboo had been violated. Profanities had been indiscriminately televised. Even worse, they had been uttered at an hour—teatime—when innocent children might well be listening.

The next day, the British tabloids all ran banner headlines about the incident: "THE FILTH AND THE FURY!" "WHO ARE THESE PUNKS?" "THE FOUL MOUTHED YOBS" "ROCK GROUP START A 4-LETTER TV STORM" "THE PUNKS—ROTTEN AND PROUD OF IT!"

Before this onslaught of mainstream publicity, the recording of "Anarchy in the U.K." had seemed likely to turn the Sex Pistols into rock stars of a fairly conventional sort. The song used one of Matlock's simple riffs to accompany a jarringly half-rhymed call to arms, written by John Lydon: "I am an antichrist/I am an anarchist." Sung with malicious glee, and clearly enunciated in the kind of theatrical cockney that David Bowie had introduced into British rock, the blasphemy of the lyric was hard to ignore, even in the finished recording, which partially buried Lydon's vocal beneath layer upon layer of buzzing electric guitars and thrashing drums. Still, the record was actually rather elegant, as hard rock went, since it had been immaculately produced by Chris Thomas, a classically trained musician who had broken into the business by working with George Martin and the Beatles (and who would go on to work closely with one of the most musically gifted of the post-punk British bands, the Pretenders). As a critic remarked in one early review, for the British music weekly *Sounds*, "Anarchy in the U.K." had "so many of the traditional ingredients of high-energy rock that it makes nonsense of all those hysterical letter-writers who see the Pistols as a threat to Music As We Know It. Conversely, it also makes nonsense of any claims that the Pistols are revolutionaries."

This was before the band's appearance on the *Today* show. Punk till then had been a movement known only to a handful of London's trendiest young sophisticates. After the TV show, life began to imitate art. However conservatively structured it was as a piece of music, the song was still called "Anarchy in the U.K." Now, thanks to the uproar over the band's impromptu profanities, there really *was* a hint of anarchy in the U.K., not least among those still young enough to care about rock and roll.

That December, for example, an aspiring songwriter and singer named Declan McManus was working as a computer operator, punching cards in a big glass box in downtown London for the Elizabeth Arden cosmetics company. He had been a youthful Beatles fan, and listened to a lot of different kinds of pop and rhythm and blues. Punk scarcely interested him, as either a form of music or a style of dress—until the *Today* show. "I was still working when the Sex Pistols went on television and said 'fuck,' " McManus recalled years later, "you know, and it was really outrageous. And I had to go to work that [next] day, and sit with everybody . . . middle-aged guys reading the newspaper, the steam coming out of their ears. It was really funny."

Since he got the joke, McManus became, in effect, a punk, like it or not. And when the uproar over the Grundy show produced, as one of its by-products, a scramble among British record companies to sign edgy new talent, McManus got his break; under the stage name of Elvis Costello, and promoted as part of his record label's roster of punk acts, he went on to record some of that era's smartest rock and roll.

The Sex Pistols were meanwhile in a peculiar bind. After several days of hesitation, EMI, feeling pressure from the public and from some members of its board, ordered the record division to jettison the Sex Pistols, and to stop manufacturing and distributing "Anarchy in the U.K." Trapped like "flies in the amber of their own notoriety" (in the critic Jon Savage's bitter phrase), the band was banned from performing at most British venues. And when it did appear, mayhem and violence routinely resulted, as fans eagerly rose to the challenge of behaving as idiotically as the band had on the *Today* show.

The maelstrom left McLaren crazily exhilarated. His own vision of the band and what it could become had been marked by two different experiences: the French student revolt of May '68 and the kinky decadence of the downtown New York rock scene. Apart from these overriding influences, McLaren subscribed to a simple set of imperatives: "Be childish. Be irresponsible. Be everything this society hates." As backward-looking in his way as either George Lucas or Bruce Springsteen, McLaren longed to recapture the purity of the primal rock and roll event, the moment when "Rock Around the Clock" incited British youth to run riot. One of his heroes was Larry Parnes, the pioneering British rock impresario who had given his pretty boys stage names like Billy Fury. McLaren had taken the same basic idea, and turned it upside down, promoting an ugly squatter with a stage name to match his demeanor: Johnny Rotten.

"We wanted to create a situation where kids would be less interested in buying records than in speaking for themselves," McLaren declared. And as the critic Greil Marcus has put it, one result of "Anarchy in the U.K.," produced in the few days it was for sale, and reinforced by its censorship, was the unplanned irruption of "a sort of giant answer record," a set of songs composed in response, "in dozens of languages, all over the world. It was a potlatch of yesses and noes that sounded" (at least to Marcus) "like a conversation in which everything was at stake—a potlatch that, for a time, sounded like a conversation in which everyone was taking part," where, as Marcus puts it, everyone was "destroying all limits on everyday speech, and turning it into public speech." In the months following the release of "Anarchy in the U.K.," a handful of new bands and novice musicians, inspired by its riotous spirit, produced a striking series of fresh-sounding rock and roll recordings, from the Adverts' "One Chord Wonders" to the Gang of Four's "Return the Gift."

But the unfettered creative exuberance of such acts was the exception, not the rule. This was the heyday of so-called new wave, as the British industry labeled any new music more or less inspired by the Sex Pistols. In London, the hot venue was the Roxy, in Neal Street, Covent Garden. Steeling themselves for a night of gobbing and pogoing and shattering glass, talent scouts from the major labels crowded into the club, poised to sign up any band with the right sound and attitude. As *Music Week,* one of the British trade magazines, put it, punk and new wave "might be THE NEXT BIG THING so long awaited." The bands came cheap—many of them consisted of utter amateurs, after all—and the recipe for success (as Jon Savage later summed it up) was blessedly simple:

"1!—A fussy drummer and 2!—a bassist playing repeated single notes . . . 3!—a guitarist who turned up his amp to eleven and tried to keep up and 4!—a singer who barked angry lyrics (about media,

TV, fascists and the like) in such a garbled fashion that only slogans were decipherable."

In the winter of 1977, meanwhile, the Sex Pistols, whose influence was ubiquitous, were missing in action. Their record couldn't be bought, and no British music hall was willing to book them. But McLaren, instead of devising a strategy to regain control of events, kept hatching new schemes to increase the level of chaos. "Once he wanted me to go to Madame Tussauds and set fire to the Beatles," Vivienne Westwood has recalled. Though she refused, the gesture is a telling symptom of McLaren's brand of anarchy: the target, after all, was not British society as such. It was waxen effigies of a rock and roll sacred cow.

In February 1977, McLaren capitalized on the discontents that were roiling his temporarily unemployed band to engineer the exit of bass player Glen Matlock, the group's most proficient musician and best-looking member. To replace him, McLaren hired John Simon Ritchie, aka Sid Vicious, who was perfectly ugly and also musically incompetent.

"I don't understand why people think it's so difficult to learn to play guitar," Vicious remarked to Caroline Coon. "I found it incredibly easy. You just pick a chord, go twang, and you've got music." With his spiky hair, leering attitude, and the needle tracks he flaunted on his bare arms, he at least had the right *look*.

Most of what followed was pure farce. There was, for example, the photogenic and very formal signing of the new band with Vicious to a new label, A&M, on March 10: the ceremony was staged in front of Buckingham Palace. From there the group was whisked by limousine to a press conference at the Regent Palace Hotel. Thrilled to discover an open bar, amply stocked with libations for thirsty reporters, Vicious, who was a big baby of the purest impulsiveness, attacked the drink with unrestrained glee, swilling vodka by the bottle.

When the lads stumbled blindly into their limousine for the next stop on their journey to the top of the pops, they proceeded to the London headquarters of A&M. Here the aim was to schmooze with the staff and foster enthusiasm for the band among the company's publicists. En route, alas, a brawl erupted between Vicious and drummer Paul Cook. By the time the limo arrived, Cook had a bloody nose and Vicious had a bloody foot and no shoes (during the melee, they had been tossed out the window). Steve Jones was so drunk he staggered by mistake into the women's bathroom, creating instant panic among the female staff. Sid Vicious lurched into another room and, as McLaren later recalled, began to bark at a secretary: "My foot's bleeding, can you find a fucking plaster for me, you bitch!" Feeling ill, he dashed to a toilet. Before the visit was over, he had fallen out a window.

The Sex Pistols' contract with A&M was terminated the next day. Once again, they were pariahs. Once again, the publicity was priceless. And once again, McLaren was exhilarated, perhaps because he assumed, rightly as events would show, that sooner or later a new record label would rise to the challenge of exploiting this fantastic new band of rock and roll outlaws.

Three months later, McLaren and the band signed their third contract in less than a year, this time with Virgin, at the time a relatively small, independent label run by Richard Branson, a swashbuckling young entrepreneur already on his way to becoming the most prominent British tycoon of his generation. In June, six months after the Grundy show, Virgin finally released the second single by the Sex Pistols, "God Save the Queen." Keeping the lads under wraps, a task made easy by the fact that they were still banned from most British venues, Branson had the satisfaction of seeing his gamble pay off handsomely. Another exquisitely produced piece of musical chaos, outfitted with another finely crafted set of incendiary lyrics, "God Save the Queen" was released to coincide with the Queen's Silver Jubilee, a nationwide celebration of Elizabeth II and her twenty-five years on the throne. Within days of release, "God Save the Queen" shot to the top of the British charts of best-selling records. An album (including both "Anarchy in the U.K." and "God Save the Queen") was belatedly released in November 1977. It, too, quickly became a number one album in England.

An American tour began a few weeks later, though the land of Bruce Springsteen showed even less interest in Johnny Rotten than it had in Ziggy Stardust. The first show was on January 3, 1978. Twelve days later, after a bizarre trek to a few improbably all-American outposts, such as Tulsa, Oklahoma, the tour was over, and so were the Sex Pistols. On stage in San Francisco, Lydon uttered his famous last lines as Johnny Rotten: "Ever have the feeling you've been cheated?"

By then, the Sex Pistols had in fact quite successfully realized a large number of Malcolm McLaren's basic ideas. The band had brought back to life the tumult and sense of shocked surprise that rock and roll had first provoked in the Fifties, and it had done so in a roar of raw noise with a threat of real violence. Even better, all this had happened in a way that was perversely puerile, just as McLaren had enjoined: "Be childish. Be irresponsible. Be everything this society hates."

But by behaving in this way, the Sex Pistols also helped to destroy the unified youth culture that had for so long fascinated McLaren. Once upon a time, rock impresarios as different as McLaren and Jon Landau, inspired by the examples of Elvis Presley and the Beatles, had hoped that rock and roll could inform a powerful collective force for social change, differ though they might about what change was desirable. But where the Beatles had urged a generation to "Come Together" in song, the Sex Pistols instead generated endless conflict: they polarized and repelled, inadvertently accelerating the forces of fragmentation that had already begun to overtake the established global youth culture as a whole, and rock and roll in particular.

Although the Sex Pistols succeeded, briefly, as the Beatles had before them in 1963, in galvanizing a genuine outburst of expressive freedom among a certain number of aspiring British musicians, what McLaren proudly came to call "The Great Rock 'n' Roll Swindle" was anything but liberating in its longer-term effects. Because McLaren insisted on demystifying the role that he and Westwood had played in the process of producing and promoting the Sex Pistols as a carefully designed package, selling images of teen revolt, he also reinforced the cynicism that was already a salient feature of the rock music business.

And there was, after all, a lot to be cynical about, at least if one was honest about the virtues of punk from a business point of view. If it was unruliness and noise that the kids wanted, the record companies were happy to oblige them, so long as the bands adhered to a minimal level of punctuality and professional courtesy. The trick was to snap up bands so new they could hardly play; make sure the musicians had a look that was stylishly repulsive; and never forget the paradoxical formulas that Andrew Loog Oldham had perfected ten years earlier with the Rolling Stones: in the kingdom of cutting-edge rock and roll, bad is good, ugly is beautiful.

Throughout the Eighties and Nineties, as the rock business became more nimble at exploiting rough sounds and raw styles, the same basic formulas were applied to a variety of different rock bands playing in a variety of genres, from gangsta rap to grunge. A familiar scenario went like this: First came an outpouring of enthusiasm, as media mavens got excited about hearing kids push the limits of their all but nonexistent musical abilities. (The enthusiasm was more intense if the band first recorded for a small, independent record label.) Then came a solemn projection of the broader social implications, as a music usefully associated with yet another colorful tribe of rebellious young people was presented to the marketplace with subversive flags flying. (The press had a crucial role to play here, since rock journalists ever since the Sixties have wanted to see themselves as custodians of subversive social significance—this is about the only thing that keeps the job interesting.) Last but not least came the commercial apotheosis and simultaneous critical backlash, provoked when some specific band, perhaps one with uncommonly talented or especially good-looking young musicians, actually succeeded in the mass market—thus "selling out," and betraying the subversive flags that had been flying.

The cycle of changing styles was of course sometimes unpleasant, not least for the musicians. But if all went well, the record companies could count on making a certain amount of money. And the cycle could then begin again, as talent scouts fanned out in search of "The Next Big Thing."

One knowledgeable critic, the late Robert Palmer, entitled one of his books *Rock & Roll: An Unruly History*. The subtitle is misleading. After the experience of punk rock, the general patterns of the music's commercial exploitation were perfectly predictable. For anyone who had grown up on rock and roll, McLaren's original vision—of childish revolt and cultural chaos—was as familiar as the leering punks who crowded the screen in the opening shot of *Blackboard Jungle*.

What was "unruly," in short, was *not* rock and roll as a cultural form, but rather the central fantasy it was exploiting—in 1955; in 1976; and ever since.

My Way

The news broke in the afternoon of August 16, 1977. Elvis Aron Presley, universally recognized as the King of Rock and Roll, was dead at the age of forty-two. To a lot of people, it seemed impossible. Presley had been the idol of a still youthful generation. Like a hero of Greek mythology, he belonged to a world apart. It was perhaps a delusion spawned by the mass media, but his fame seemed immortal—and his death therefore unimaginable.

Details at first were sketchy. After being found unconscious at his Graceland mansion in Memphis, Presley had been taken by ambulance to Baptist Memorial Hospital. He was declared dead at 3:30 P.M., after efforts to revive him failed. Later that evening, a local medical examiner met with reporters and announced that Presley had died of "cardiac arrhythmia"—in other words, his heart had stopped beating. There was no evidence of any other disease, he said. And, he added, contradicting a rumor that had started to spread, Elvis Presley did not die of drug abuse.

That night, two of America's national television networks broadcast special reports. On ABC, the show's host, Geraldo Rivera, expressed relief that Elvis at least "had not followed in the melancholy rock 'n' roll tradition of Janis Joplin, Jim Morrison, Jimi Hendrix." On NBC, by contrast, David Brinkley, the moderator, explicitly broached the possibility that Elvis had in fact died of drug abuse, no matter what the examiner in Memphis was saying.

One of Brinkley's guests that evening was Steve Dunleavy. A pugnacious tabloid journalist, Dunleavy had just published a lurid little book entitled *Elvis: What Happened?*, written in collaboration with three disgruntled former Presley employees, Red West, Sonny West, and Dave Hebler. Seizing the chance to publicize their book, Dunleavy retailed for Brinkley some of the book's revelations about "the dark side of the brightest star in the world": for example, Presley's fondness for fooling around with women half his age; his streak of paranoia that sometimes issued in outbursts of reckless gunplay; and his uncontrollable appetite for a vast array of different prescription drugs—uppers, downers, powerful painkilling narcotics.

But perhaps the most mind-boggling thing in Dunleavy's best-selling exposé, the first of many devoted to Presley and his private life, was the evidence it offered, not of Presley's lust for girls, guns, and pills, but rather of his apparently earnest belief in his own supernatural powers. "While the rest of the world recognizes that Elvis Aron Presley is something more than an ordinary human being, the one person who believes that most passionately is Presley himself," wrote Dunleavy, summarizing some of the gossip he had been fed. "He is addicted to the study of the Bible"—a strange thing to label an addiction! He was also "addicted," Dunleavy asserted, to "mystical religion, numerology, psychic phenomena, and the belief in life after death. He believes that he has the strength of will to move clouds in the air, and he is also convinced that there are beings on other planets. He firmly believes he is a prophet who was destined to lead, designated by God for a special role in life."

A great many of Presley's fans, certainly, regarded him with a reverence more befitting a prophet than a mere entertainer. By dusk on the night of August 16, a large and growing crowd of fans had formed outside Graceland to share their prayers and pay their final respects. Meanwhile, reporters with cameras and klieg lights roamed the scene and police struggled to maintain order.

Among a great many Americans of a certain age, a strange and confusing set of sentiments had been stirred up. "So that was his end," the writer Nick Tosches has recalled: "I was nonplussed. I had not known Elvis Presley as a man. I had never even met him. I started then to realize that, on some level of faint illogic, I had never truly thought of him as a creature of flesh and blood but rather as an absurd effulgence of hoi polloi mythology, an all-American demigod who dwelt, enthroned between Superman and the Lone Ranger, in the blue heaven of the popular imagination."

As dawn broke, mourners continued to pour into Memphis. Overwhelmed by the sight of the throng gathering outside Graceland, Presley's father, Vernon, announced that the casket would be opened for a public viewing that afternoon. By then, some 80,000 people were waiting to file past.

Elsewhere, mourners bought records and sent flowers, hundreds of thousands of flowers, producing the busiest day in its history for the floral company FTD, and forcing flower shops in Memphis to fly in five extra tons of flowers to fill the orders going to Graceland—tangible evidence of the extent and startling intensity of popular sentiment.

All through that evening, long after the sun had set, people continued to snake their way up the hill to the room in the mansion where Presley's body was on display. The writer Roy Blount, Jr., had flown to Memphis earlier that day to see for himself what was happening. "Elvis in his coffin was fat, glowering, and surrounded by similar-looking but vertical heavies who pushed us viewers along," Blount recalls: "He didn't look cool. Neither did the thousands of people who gathered at the gates of Graceland. People fainted left and right, from the heat, the crowding, and the historical moment. And because if you fainted, you got carried into the grounds."

As reporters scrambled to cover the story, new details about Presley's death began to emerge. Unable to sleep, he had gone to the bathroom, taking with him a book, *The Search for the Face of Jesus,* about the Shroud of Turin. (Later, more authoritative sources would report that the book he took into the bathroom was really entitled *Sex and Psychic Energy.*) It was in the bathroom, while studying his book and "straining at stool," that Presley's heart had given out.

This was the official version. Meanwhile, rumors were flying. According to one, Presley had not died a natural death at all. He had been killed. With a fine sense of poetic irony, as if to honor Presley's own fascination with the martial arts, the assailant, it was said, had felled the King with a lethal karate chop.

According to another set of rumors, Presley in fact was not dead after all. He had simply staged a death scene.

In the goriest version of this rumor, Presley had murdered a look-alike in order to make his escape. In another, even more improbable version, Presley had convinced an admirer, also a look-alike, to commit suicide so that the real Elvis could disappear into a life of happy anonymity.

Last but not least, there was the rumor that Presley's purported death was a hoax, staged with the complicity of the Memphis police and medical authorities. The corpse was really a wax dummy. This was the most benign version of the rumor, and its persistence formed the basis for the reports that cropped up a decade later that Elvis was in fact alive and well and living in Kalamazoo, Michigan, of all places, where a series of witnesses in the late Eighties spotted him performing a number of reassuringly mundane chores, for example, standing in a grocery store checkout line, waiting to purchase a fuse.

On August 18, 1977, the day of Presley's funeral, the governor of Tennessee ordered flags flown at half mast. The cortege consisted of a white hearse followed by a color-coordinated fleet of white limousines and white luxury cars. Leaving Graceland, the cortege made its way across Memphis to the Forest Hill cemetery. There the singer was laid to rest in a mausoleum near the grave of his mother. After the formal ceremony was finished, tens of thousands of bystanders, frenzied in grief, poured into the site to get closer to the fallen idol—and, if possible, to snatch some memento or relic. By nightfall, Presley's grave had been stripped clean of every last flower.

Over the next several weeks, more than one million people, by one estimate, visited the Presley grave site in Forest Hill cemetery. The site was impossible to secure. And after an attempt was made to rob the grave in October, Vernon Presley arranged to have the remains of mother and son moved to the Meditation Garden in back of Graceland.

This was the first of a series of increasingly sophisticated efforts by the Presley estate to contain and control the wild outpouring of spontaneous sentiment. After Vernon Presley's death in 1979, Graceland was incorporated as a tourist attraction. By the 1990s, the house and garden were attracting roughly 700,000 visitors annually, making it the most visited historic home in America, apart from the White House.

Shortly after Presley's death, Tom Parker, his longtime manager, is supposed to have said that "It don't mean a damn thing. It's just like when he was away in the Army." Even credited to Parker, the quote is almost too crass to be credible; but the prediction turned out to be true. Elvis in death has generated as much passion, and profit, as he ever did during his life.

Presley's posthumous career began in earnest that fall, with a grotesquely fascinating television special, aired in October. The show documented two of his last live performances, one in Omaha, Nebraska, the other in Rapid City, South Dakota, on June 21, 1977—the kind of midsize heartland cities where Presley, to his dying day, was still the King.

His final years were of course a far cry from his heyday in the mid-Fifties, and an even bigger change from his years of hibernation in Hollywood, when Parker had hidden his boy from public view and put him to work doing a series of dreary star turns in light comic films. But in 1969, shortly after appearing on an American television network for the first time since his show with Frank Sinatra in 1960, Presley had made a ballyhooed return to public performing. Buoyed by the adulation of the audiences, he came to depend on the income the concerts produced, turning himself into a one-man musical circus that traveled to over 130 cities, doing more than 1,000 shows from 1969 to 1977. Venturing ever farther afield, from New York and Las Vegas to Omaha and Rapid City, Presley performed in smaller and smaller venues in smaller and smaller cities where he was still virtually guaranteed to sell out the local coliseum, if only because the fans there had never before had a chance to see him, or any other living legend, live, in the flesh, on stage, for one night of carnival bliss. An appearance by Elvis Presley was, for the fans in a town like Rapid City, a truly extraordinary event, something to anticipate, experience, and remember.

The idea of using such a concert as the pretext for a network television special had been sold by Parker to CBS earlier in the year. But when executives at CBS initially previewed the footage from Omaha and Rapid City, they balked at airing it. Monstrously overweight, Presley had been stuffed like a sausage into one of his custom-tailored jumpsuits, powder blue, lavishly embroidered, clasped tight with a gigantic studded belt that doubled as a girdle.

Sweating profusely, often singing with his eyes shut, as if to blank out reality, Presley looked dazed and confused, like a necromantic Doughboy: chin doubled, belly bloated, his face the color of flour, ashen white. David Bowie may have enacted a rock 'n' roll suicide at the end of his Ziggy Stardust revue—but this was Bowie's conceit brought vividly, brutally to life.

In the two concerts captured on film for posterity, Presley gave desultory renditions of classic rock hits like "Hound Dog." But when the spirit moved him—when the lyrics to some appropriately bathetic ballad like "Unchained Melody" suddenly seemed to grab his interest—his voice came flooding forth, astonishingly intact, still a controllable instrument, as if the singer, by straining every fiber, could momentarily convey in song a raw passion that was, and remains, even years later, truly awful in its concentrated beauty.

The highlight of Presley's last television special was an especially painful and pathos-filled version of "My Way." When it was released as a posthumous single, the recording of this live performance became Presley's last major international hit, turning a treacly ballad into a paradoxical monument to rock and roll as a form of transcendental self-immolation.

"My Way" had first been recorded a decade earlier, by another mythic singer, Frank Sinatra. Based on the music to a French song, "Comme d'Habitude" ("As Usual"), the new English lyrics had been written, with Sinatra in mind, by Paul Anka—one of the most successful of the early rock and roll teen idols inspired by Presley and featured on *American Bandstand.* Sinatra himself regarded "My Way" as a piece of fluff for kids—he first recorded it at a time when he was still trying to pitch some of his recorded music at the teen market. But by 1971, when Presley first took a stab at singing the song in a studio (a recording that remained unreleased until 1995), Sinatra had turned "My Way" into the climax of his concerts. As writer Will Friedwald once put it, hearing Sinatra sing "My Way" at the end of a show became like "standing in front of Macy's on Thanksgiving morning, watching the Frank Sinatra balloon float by. Nothing gets in the way of this choreographed exhibition of burgeoning ego."

Given the totemic association of the song with Sinatra, it took a certain nerve (mixed with arrogance) for Presley to integrate "My Way" into his live shows, featuring it on the most popular of his later albums in the United States, *Aloha From Hawaii via Satellite,* a live recording made in January 1973. Obviously drawn by the mythic largeness that the song had acquired, Presley at first could scarcely match the bombastic majesty of Sinatra's rendition. But in his last performances, after Presley had become all too visibly unwell, the song took on an altogether darker hue, quite different from anything evoked by Sinatra, or even by Presley himself four years earlier.

Anka's lyrics were meant to convey magisterial self-command. But as Presley sang the familiar words on June 21, 1977, in the live version that became a posthumous hit single, the lyrics conveyed a mood of stately disintegration, evoking the morbid pride of a man taking solace from the certainty that he is, as if in a dream, slowly, and not without pleasure, killing himself.

Even though the song's melody presents few real challenges, Presley had to work, and work hard, to hit his notes. On camera, he sweats and wobbles as he sings, like a punch-drunk boxer on the ropes. When the public first saw and heard this performance, Presley had been dead for almost two months. The nature of his fate, visible in his face, balanced the bathos of Anka's lyrics. The song's opening lines were delivered with grim aplomb: "Now the end is near, and I face the final curtain." Elvis was singing his own epitaph—as surely he must have known.

It was this last, memorably morbid version of "My Way" that inspired Malcolm McLaren and the Sex Pistols (with Sid Vicious singing) to film, record, and rush into release a version of their own. The film shows Vicious in a concert setting, wearing formal attire. He starts by singing the song straight, roars into a punk parody, and finishes by pulling out a pistol and randomly shooting into the crowd (as if to emulate André Breton's "simplest surrealist act").

If Elvis was a zombie, Vicious had the look of a serial killer. Adding yet another set of morbid associations to the song's innocuous English lyrics, Vicious shortly afterward stabbed his girlfriend to death, and a year later killed himself with an overdose of narcotics.

Years after, the critic Greil Marcus argued that "Elvis's tawdry death sanctioned that of Sid Vicious, and when Vicious went out with 'My Way' . . . his death sanctioned Elvis's." While it is hard to see how a song can retroactively sanction a death, there is a point to this remark. Through the ever more tangled web of associations conjured up by his life and his music, dead Elvis loomed larger than ever, still a sovereign symbol of rock and roll. He remained the music's single greatest figure, an apotheosis of a way of life that Malcolm McLaren once described as "the one adult mode that inhabitants of the adolescent mode can imagine living in—because it is not really an adult state but is rather the ultimate adolescent fantasy of adulthood," a state in which Herculean feats of self-indulgence could be undertaken with a childish disregard for the consequences.

As time passed, more and more sordid details began to emerge about the true wages of Presley's immense fame. In the fall of 1979, the ABC television network broadcast a widely watched special report on Presley's death. Two years later, Albert Goldman published a scurrilous, best-selling biography.

What emerged was the picture of an infantilized sovereign, living a life of indescribable freedom and incredible luxury, innocent of lofty ambitions, drunk on his own crazy fountain of youth, heedless of conventional limits, able to satisfy virtually any passing impulse on whim, even able, if he chose, to blot out the everyday aches and pains of ordinary existence. Presley, it turned out, was a drug addict of epic proportions. In the seven and a half months leading up to his death in August of 1977, records showed that one Memphis doctor, George C. Nichopoulos, had prescribed him 1,790 amphetamines, 4,996 sedatives, and 2,019 narcotics. A blood sample drawn at the autopsy after Presley's death indicated that the singer had consumed a banquet of pills that beggared belief. Analysis revealed toxic levels of Quaalude and near-toxic levels of Codeine, Valium, and Placidyl, not to mention traces of Valmid, Pentobarbital, Butabarbital, and Phenobarbital—a lethal cocktail of sedatives and narcotics.

So Elvis was a soul mate of Sid Vicious, after all: the legendary momma's boy had died a junkie.

Yet at exactly the same time, the dead singer was undergoing an altogether different, superficially unrelated metamorphosis, emerging—amazingly enough—as some kind of saint in the minds of countless enthusiasts. For every story about Elvis as a drug-addled slob, there were dozens more that seemed to demonstrate his undying love for his mother, his kindness to strangers, his acts of unstinting charity.

Moved no doubt by their memories of the "good" Elvis, five people gathered outside Graceland on the evening of August 15, 1978, to mark the first anniversary of Elvis's last, dark night of the soul. According to the lore that has grown up since, each one solemnly lit a candle and placed it on top of the stone wall that borders the front of Graceland. Throughout the night, the five kept vigil. So began what today is called Elvis Week—a ritualized outpouring of reverent affection for the fallen idol.

Every August, tens of thousands of pilgrims converge on Memphis, to tour Presley's mansion, to visit the Meditation Garden, to gawk at Elvis imitators, to visit museums and galleries, to attend a memorial service, to buy trinkets and souvenirs. But the most dramatic moment always comes at sundown on August 15. The simple vigil of 1978 has been turned into an annual procession up the hill to the grave site, where mourners bearing candles briefly commune with the dead man's living spirit.

While they wait their turn, the pilgrims can read the latest messages and prayers inscribed in Magic Marker and paint on the outer stone wall of Graceland:

ELVIS LIVES IN US
ELVIS, YOU ARE MY BRIDGE OVER TROUBLED WATERS
I DID DRUGS WITH ELVIS
THERE IS ONLY ONE KING AND WE KNOW WHO HE IS
ELVIS IS LOVE
ELVIS DIDN'T DESERVE TO BE WHITE
ELVIS, IT TOOK 20 YEARS TO GET HERE. NEXT STOP, HEAVEN.

The graffiti (which is periodically scrubbed clean so that new visitors can join the conversation) suggests that something more than a hobby is at issue. For many participants, Elvis Week has obviously become a quasi-religious occasion. The Meditation Garden is an American Lourdes, a place where miracles sometimes happen. Every year on August 15, the sick and the lame hobble up the hill, full of hope. As every one of the faithful well knows, on the first anniversary of Presley's death, a fan aimed his camera skyward and photographed a cumulus cloud forming a familiar profile, right down to the famous pompadour. Elvis is watching over them.

Addressing co-religionists in a letter printed in an Elvis fan club publication, an enthusiast from Belgium put it this way: "Dear friends, our LOVE and RESPECT for Elvis are unlimited . . . and we are in touch in full appreciation of our personal battle to do the best for Elvis. . . . Let's continue to work hard for him, because his LIGHT on our world today is the guarantee to give HOPE and PEACE for the next generations. . . . *We believe in Elvis just like we believe in GOD* . . . and I'm sure that we are on the right way."

Presley might have thought so, too. On more than one occasion, he expressed his own hunch that he was someone blessed with divine powers. "I don't mean to sound sacrilegious," George Klein, a Memphis disc jockey, longtime Presley crony, and media factotum remarked ten years after his death, "but he was Jesus-like. One time, when we were on the road, Elvis stopped the car. 'See that cloud,' he said. 'I'm going to move that cloud.' And the cloud moved. Maybe the wind blew it, I don't know. Elvis just looked at us and smiled."

The cult of Elvis poses perhaps the ultimate riddle of rock and roll. How could such a simple and sometimes nihilistic type of music strike such a deep and essentially religious chord among so many listeners?

Perhaps the answer lies outside rock and roll as a cultural form. Perhaps the cult of Elvis, like the cult of Jim Morrison, is best understood as the latest chapter in a much older story: the emergence of music in the modernizing West as a substitute for religion. In an elegant essay, the historian H.G. Koenigsberger has surveyed "the rise of music to a quasi-religious status and cult, as a psychological compensation for the decline of all forms of traditional religion." Feared by the medieval church and also by puritan reformers for its potentially wayward effects on the soul, music gradually came to be seen in the West as the most divine of art forms, and a fitting medium for the worship of God. Once the Promethean rebels of the early nine-teenth century had severed music from its liturgical moorings, a path was cleared for the deification of music and the musician. "Here the gods are at work," said Goethe of Beethoven, expressing sentiments obviously shared by more than one Elvis Presley fan. "Just as Chris-tianity arose in the international civilization of the Roman Empire," Wagner declared two generations later, "so music emerges out of the chaos of modern civilization. Both proclaim: 'Our kingdom is not of this world.' "

In 1957, at a time when Elvis Presley was still a young man and superficially on top of "this world," he expressed a telling ambiva-lence about the immensity of his worldly fame and the enormity of the carnal passions he had so visibly provoked, perhaps because he had not entirely purged himself of the old puritan distrust of music and its potential for exciting errant raptures. After Easter services that year, Presley approached the pastor at his church. According to someone who overheard their conversation, "He said, 'Pastor, I am the most miserable young man you have ever seen. I have got more money than I can ever spend. I have thousands of fans out there, and I have a lot of people who call themselves my friends, but I am miser-able. I am not doing a lot of things that you have taught me, and I am doing some things that you taught me not to do.' "

He struck a similar tone of anxious bewilderment in comments to a reporter he made at roughly the same time. "I never expected to be anyone important," the twenty-two-year-old rock star said. "Maybe I'm not now, but whatever I am, whatever I will become will be what God has chosen for me.

"Some people I know can't figure out how Elvis Presley happened. I don't blame them for wondering that. Sometimes I wonder myself."

It is something like this sense of wonder at the marvelous creative abilities of a simple country boy, tinged with awe at the reckless power of that boy's imagination and appetites running wild, that Elvis Aron Presley evidently managed to convey to millions of people round the world. And it was a similar sort of wonder, at the essen-tially mysterious power of a song with a big beat, even the simplest of songs, to uplift and transfigure the soul, that surely helped fuel the rise to global prominence of rock and roll, from Elvis to the Beatles and beyond.

If the desires and yearnings nourished by that cultural form were as often as not puerile and self-destructive, just like those that Presley, at the end of his life, indulged without inhibition or limit, a transcendental aura still surrounds him, as it surrounds every other avatar of excess consecrated by the rock culture industry, from Jim Morrison and Sid Vicious and Kurt Cobain to rappers like Tupac Shakur and the Notorious B.I.G., both gunned down in the 1990s.

In the world turned upside down by Elvis Presley, it was as if the sinners had become saints, ignorance had become bliss, and the freedom of a child at play was the very image of true happiness. Even better, the feeling of bliss conveyed by the music, like the image of freedom the idol embodied, could be bought and sold and shared. For the faithful—the young and the forever young at heart—attendance at concerts and the collecting of recordings functioned as sacraments, the key elements in a novel kind of consumer religion.

To an outsider, the kind of cults that have formed around Elvis Presley and the Beatles and Bob Dylan and Jim Morrison and Ziggy Stardust and Bruce Springsteen may well seem absurd. But such was the regime founded by the King of Rock and Roll—the once and future Messiah of a new cultural form.

"No Future"

Nearly a quarter century after Elvis Presley's death, rock and roll is as lucrative as ever: a prominent, apparently permanent feature of global culture. Without going anywhere near a living musician, one can hear the strains of various rock songs, not just on TV and in films and on the radio, but in grocery stores, in elevators, on one's telephone line while waiting to get advice on fixing one's computer. A music that once provoked the wrath of censors has become the Muzak of the Millennium.

Of course, while shopping for lettuce one is likely to hear the Beatles, and not Tupac Shakur; Whitney Houston, and not Nirvana. Some styles of rock and roll remain, by design, offensive—calculated to irritate and annoy. Gangsta rap couldn't fulfill one of its functions if its collage of beats and violent imagery failed to outrage. And the young, who enjoy provoking outrage, remain the core of the music business's market: a 1991 survey of the global record industry revealed that people under the age of twenty-five accounted for well over half of total revenues.

Since Presley died, the world of rock and roll has become ever more fragmented, especially in the United States, where radio stations compete by delivering narrowly defined audiences to their advertisers. Genres are largely defined by the key radio formats: Top 40 (current hits no matter what style—an endangered format), urban contemporary (current dance music and romantic ballads, primarily performed by black musicians), alternative rock (music aimed largely at college students, primarily performed by white musicians, often inspired by the Velvet Underground and the Sex Pistols), hard rock (party music, aimed largely at young men, including heavy metal and grunge, invariably performed by white musicians, often inspired by the Rolling Stones), classic rock (mainly music from the Seventies and Eighties inspired by the Stones, the Beatles, and Dylan), and oldies (from the Fifties or Sixties). In addition, there are more esoteric subgenres, rarely heard on radio though often heard in clubs, for example, trip-hop and techno, synthetic cocktails of sound with a carefully calibrated number of electronically generated beats per minute.

As never before, retailers know in detail what kinds of rock actually sell, and to whom. In May 1991, *Billboard* introduced new charts based on information supplied by SoundScan, a research firm that accurately monitors sales by gathering the information from electronic cash registers that read the bar codes on albums. The new charts were revealing. The most aggressively puerile kinds of hard rock and rap sold far more than the old charts had indicated; and so did classic rock and roll recordings first issued in the Sixties and Seventies. (The charts also revealed the commercial clout of country-western, the only popular alternative to rock and roll in the Nineties, if one can really call it an alternative: the decade's most popular country artist, Garth Brooks, routinely performed classic rock songs by artists like Billy Joel and Little Feat in an energetic stage act that recalled Bruce Springsteen.)

It is unlikely that the fragmentation of the audience for pop music generally, or rock and roll specifically, will be reversed any time soon. As they always have, fans and connoisseurs reject much of what they hear. Many hard rock fans despise rap, and vice versa. Many alternative rock fans despise dance music, and vice versa. Given how deeply divided the current pop scene is, it seems highly unlikely that any future rock and roll star, however popular, will have the kind of broad cultural and social impact that Elvis had in the Fifties, or the Beatles had in the Sixties.

Michael Jackson's fate in the Eighties is symptomatic. In the two years after its release in 1982, his album *Thriller* sold some twenty-five million copies, more than any previous album in history, a record that still stands. Jackson became world-famous; but as Greil Marcus has remarked, his music asked "not to be judged by the subjective quality of the response it provoked, but to be measured by the number of objective commercial exchanges it elicited." Jackson was able to gratify his personal dream of winning renown in the *Guin-*

ness Book of World Records. He was rich enough to become the owner of much of the Lennon-McCartney songbook, charming (or cunning) enough to wed Elvis Presley's only child, Lisa Marie. But he lacked her dad's aura of yearning spirituality—and he couldn't buy the cultural significance of the Beatles, since it wasn't for sale. One need only contrast the reception of *Thriller* to the "subjective quality of the response" to the Beatles' *Sgt. Pepper*. There is no comparison.

In 1987, three years after the international carnival of consumption and media coverage ignited by Michael Jackson (which I witnessed firsthand, and contributed to, writing not one, but two pieces about Jackson for *Newsweek*), I was in Memphis, Tennessee. Once again, I was on assignment for *Newsweek*, this time to write about a dead white male. Gathering material for a planned cover story on the cult that had grown up around Elvis Presley in the decade after his death, I had spent several days wandering around the city, being debriefed by officials at Graceland, and interviewing Sam Phillips, among others.

One evening, I walked to a bluff overlooking the Mississippi, to watch the sunset. Since I'd grown up in the Midwest, and had spent time watching the muddy river before, I knew better than to expect a romantic panorama: but during my visit, my imagination had been fired by the idea of the blues coming up the river from New Orleans, so a romantic panorama, at least in my mind's eye, is what I was pondering.

As I pictured the musicians who had gone upriver from New Orleans to Memphis, St. Louis, and Chicago, the image of Louis Armstrong, grinning, trumpet in hand, came to mind. Armstrong, I mused, had made musical history with the Hot Five and Hot Seven in 1927, recording songs like "Potato Head Blues" and "Struttin' With Some Barbecue." Thirty years later, in 1957, Elvis Presley was making his own kind of musical history, with four consecutive number one hits: "Too Much," "All Shook Up," "(Let Me Be Your) Teddy Bear," and "Jailhouse Rock." And thirty years after that, the pop music act of the hour was an Irish "new wave" rock band, U2, at the pinnacle of its fame with songs like "With or Without You" and "I Still Haven't Found What I'm Looking For," and I was in Memphis to write about a mythic American hero.

I thought about all the musical history that had unfolded in the thirty years after 1927: an era in which jazz and the Broadway musical achieved a definitive form, and also the golden age of gospel singing, the golden age of Western swing, the golden age of Delta blues: an era associated with names like Sidney Bechet, Dock Boggs, Bing Crosby, Paul Whiteman, George Gershwin, Blind Willie Johnson, Jimmie Rodgers, Cole Porter, Fats Waller, the Boswell Sisters, Duke Ellington, Fred Astaire, Mildred Bailey, Benny Goodman, Bob Wills, Robert Johnson, Billie Holiday, Count Basie, the Soul Stirrers, Lester Young, Charlie Parker, Big Joe Turner, Rodgers and Hammerstein, Frank Sinatra, Ella Fitzgerald, Peggy Lee, Thelonious Monk, Hank Williams, Wynonie Harris, Fats Domino, Chuck Berry, Little Richard . . .

I then thought about what had happened to American popular music in the post-Elvis era, the era chronicled for a good part of this book.

Eschewing the balmy "moon-June" lyrics typical of an earlier era, rock and roll had introduced a refreshing realism about sexuality into popular music; it had reinforced the rhythmic complexities first made widely popular through the earlier vogues for ragtime, jazz, swing, and boogie-woogie; however imperfectly, it had irrevocably consummated the musical marriage between black and white in America, helping to bring the music of African-American performers to an audience vastly wider than anything even Louis Armstrong could have imagined. In the course of accomplishing all this, rock and roll had produced some music of stirring beauty.

But it had also produced artifacts of stunning ugliness. Punk rock had been a quintessence. Since then, most popular rock and roll acts have been musically crude or gleefully obscene or just plain silly, and sometimes (as witness highly touted albums by Marilyn Manson and the Wu-Tang Clan in the last half of the 1990s) all three at once—as if to mark the triumph of the psychopathic adolescent that Norman Mailer had warned would become the "central expression of human nature before the twentieth century is over."

For years, I had celebrated rock in print as a vibrant, triumphant hybrid of everything interesting about America's older vernacular musical traditions. But as I watched the sun set and thought about Louis Armstrong and what had come after, I was assailed with a doubt. What if rock and roll, as it had evolved from Presley to U2, had destroyed the very musical sources of its own original vitality? The music popular in America between 1927 and 1957 represented a real flowering of diverse forms. Rock and roll as represented by the Sex Pistols—or even by U2—was narrow and coarse by comparison.

I walked back to my car. Shortly after picking it up a few days before at the Memphis airport, I had discovered the radio station I would listen to for the rest of my stay. It played nothing but black church music, twenty-four hours a day. I turned on the radio and listened. Gospel music had survived. But for how much longer?

By 1987, my own writing about rock for *Newsweek* had developed into a pattern: short notices of esoteric bands that struck my fancy, and longer features about celebrities, like Michael Jackson, that had struck the public's fancy. The short notices had no real meaning in the context of *Newsweek,* since the bands I fancied rarely appealed to the typical *Newsweek* reader. (I can still recall the consternation produced when I informed my editors that I wished to devote space to covering a British band called the Jesus and Mary Chain.) Meanwhile, the longer features had become an ordeal, for reasons that the British writer John Mortimer has nicely illustrated. Describing his own "quest" to secure an interview with Mick Jagger, "the middle-aged Puck," Mortimer recounted how, after an almost interminable series of delays, he was finally summoned from his hotel room with the news that Mr. Jagger was "ready to receive me in audience. I got off the bed feeling rather as Sir Galahad might have done when he was told there was someone at the front door who had come to deliver the Holy Grail, and would he please come down and sign for it."

Disenchanted by my epiphany in Memphis, and unwilling to spend the rest of my life begging for quotes from cosseted celebrities, I resolved to stop writing about rock and roll on a regular basis (though it took me several years to make good my resolution).

Of course, the history of rock and roll did not stop when I stopped writing about it, any more than it stopped after Elvis Presley died. New styles continue to come and go, some smooth, some rough, some pure, some wildly hybrid (like the London-based bhangra groups currently fusing Punjabi folk music with American Sixties funk). Since retiring from my beat, I have been happy to tune in to the rock scene casually, free of any obligation to celebrate it or dissect it, or even take it very seriously. I get a kick out of seeing my own kids get excited by new records by bands like Rage Against the Machine. And I get a kick myself out of a few newer bands. Current rock songs still color my world, and inflect the texture of my daily life.

Yes, there are other kinds of music I care for more. No, I would not wish to be stranded on a desert island with nothing but rock and roll records.

But the fact remains that the style of syncopated dance music that Elvis Presley made globally popular (and that Louis Armstrong had helped to invent thirty years before) really is the closest thing we have to a musical lingua franca as the twentieth century ends.

Whatever its expressive limitations—and they are manifold—rock and roll speaks to millions. Out of the chaos of our time has come a prerecorded music bearing the promise of redemption through Dionysian revelry. "Tutti Frutti" and "Hound Dog" and "Lonely Teardrops" and "She Loves You" and "What's Going On" and "Born to Run" and "Anarchy in the U.K." (and, yes, "With or Without You," too) have probably touched more lives more deeply than any opera by Wagner or any symphony by Beethoven.

And because people around the world want to hear this sound, and share in the fantasies it still excites, rock and roll is here to stay—for better; for worse; and for a long time to come.

Notes and Discographies

A work of synthesis is only as good as its sources, discussed chapter by chapter in detail below. All quoted material comes from these sources; and though I have tried to do without an extensive scholarly apparatus, I trust that I have given enough information that other researchers will be able, if they wish, to retrace my steps.

The accompanying discographies make no pretense at comprehensiveness. I have included pertinent data on original recordings, and also information about the reissues, bootlegs, unauthorized cassettes, etc., used in preparing the text, supplemented by occasional comments about other anthologies and reissues available at the time of writing.

A few reference works, used extensively throughout, should be listed at the outset. Above all, I had constantly to hand Joel Whitburn's invaluable series of works compiling data from *Billboard* magazine; each one of these books contains a listing, in alphabetical order, of every artist who had a recording listed on the pertinent *Billboard* chart. Of the Whitburn volumes, the most impressive, as a piece of informed speculation about the country's pop music marketplace going back to the last century, is *Joel Whitburn's Pop Memories, 1890–1954* (Menomonee Falls, Wisconsin, 1986)—since *Billboard* only began publication of song charts in 1913, lists of popular recordings from earlier decades are pieced together from other sources. In addition, no one seriously interested in American pop should be without *Joel Whitburn's Top Pop Singles* (which starts in 1955), *Joel Whitburn's Top R&B Singles* (which goes back to 1942), *Joel Whitburn's Top Country Singles* (starting in 1944), and *Joel Whitburn's Top Pop Albums* (from 1955 on); all of these volumes are periodically updated. Whitburn's books are my source for information about *Billboard* chart positions.

There is a similar series of volumes for the British pop charts, edited by Jo and Tim Rice, Paul Gambaccini, and Mike Read: *The Guinness Book of British Hit Singles,* which starts in 1952, and *The Guinness Book of British Hit Albums,* which starts in 1958. Again, these books are regularly revised (I used editions published in 1983 and 1984, respectively). All chart information about British recordings comes from these two works.

The best one-volume encyclopedia for pop is Phil Hardy and Dave Laing, eds., *The Da Capo Companion to 20th-Century Popular Music* (New York, 1995). Also useful is Donald Clarke, ed., *The Penguin Encyclopedia of Popular Music* (London, 1989). I referred as well to Barry Kernfeld, ed., *The New Grove Dictionary of Jazz* (London, 1988).

Although there are several good previous general histories of rock and roll, some of them noted below, in principle and in practice I treated none as factually reliable.

1 Life Could Be a Dream

December 28, 1947: "Good Rockin' Tonight"

There are several sources on the life and character of Wynonie Harris. Preston Love's quoted memories of Harris are recorded in his liner notes to an excellent reissue, Wynonie Harris, *Oh Babe!* (Route 66 Kix-20, Swedish LP, 1981). Roy Brown's recollections appear in a John Broven interview with Brown, "Good Rockin' Tonight," *Blues Unlimited,* No. 123, January–February 1977, p. 6. Brown's own quote ("I'm the highest-paid blues singer in the business") appeared in an autobiographical essay, printed in 1954 in *Tan* magazine, and reprinted in its entirety (with vintage photos) as the liner notes to Wynonie Harris, *Playful Baby* (Route 66 Kix-30, Swedish LP, 1986). See also the notes by Per Notini and Bengt Weine to the first in the Route 66 series of reissues, Wynonie Harris, *Mr. Blues Is Coming to Town* (Route 66 Kix-3, Swedish LP, 1977). The Albert Murray quote comes from *Stomping the Blues* (New York, 1976), p. 17 (though Murray never mentions Wynonie Harris, one indication of the curious jazz purism of his analysis, as witness, too, his treatment, later, of Louis Jordan and Ray Charles). For the debate over the first rock record, see Jim Dawson and Steve Propes, *What Was the First Rock 'n Roll Record?* (Boston, 1992), pp. 29–33—an entertaining and in-formative book. Joe Turner is quoted in a helpful (as always) essay by Whitney Balliett, in *American Singers* (New York, 1988), pp. 42–49. The Henry Glover quote is from John Broven, *Walking to New Orleans* (Sussex, England, 1974), p. 23. The quotes from Syd Nathan about his career, and about signing Wynonie Harris, come from a talk to his sales staff recorded in 1951, and reissued as a track on the fourth, "bonus" CD of *The King R&B Box Set* (King KB-SCD-7002, US CD, 1995). The description of Nathan as like "Porky Pig" appears in Dorothy Wade and Justine Picardie, *Music Man* (New York, 1990), p. 59. Other sources: Ross Russell, *Jazz Style in Kansas City and the Southwest* (Berkeley, 1971), pp. 16–17; Frank Buchmann-Moller, *You Just Fight for Your Life: The Story of Lester Young* (New York, 1990), p. 42; Dan Morgenstern, liner notes to *The Original Boogie Woogie Piano Giants* (Columbia KC 32708, US LP, 1974); Russell Sanjek, *American Popular Music and Its Business*, Volume III (New York, 1988), pp. 215–50.

Discography: Wynonie Harris, "Good Rockin' Tonight" (King 4210, #1, race, May 1948). Lucky Millinder, "Who Threw the Whiskey in the Well?" (Decca 18674, #1, race; #7, pop, June 1945). Wynonie Harris and Joe Turner, "Battle of the Blues," Parts I and II (Aladdin 3184, 1947). Wynonie Harris, "Bloodshot Eyes" (King 4461, #6, rhythm and blues, August 1951). Early Harris material is compiled on Wynonie Harris, *Here Comes the Blues: Roots of Rock 'n' Roll, Volume 4* (President PLCD 559, UK CD, 1997). The most convenient anthology of Harris' King material is *Bloodshot Eyes: The Best of Wynonie Harris* (Rhino R2 71544, US CD, 1994). The best King R&B anthology is the box set mentioned above. There are now three good samplers of vintage jump blues, documenting "The Birth of Rock 'n' Roll": *Juke Box Jive* (Charly CPCD 8270-2, UK CD, 1997), *Bootin' the Boogie* (Charly CPCD 8300-2, UK CD, 1997), and *Good Rockin' Tonight* (Charly CPCD 8362-2, UK CD, 1998). A nice compilation of boogie-woogie from the height of the fad is *Boogie Woogie*, three volumes (Jasmine JASMCD 2538-40, UK CD, 1993). For Kansas City jump, the essential starting point is Count Basie, *The Complete Decca Recordings* (Decca GRD-3-611, US CD, 1992); also revealing: Andy Kirk and His 12 Clouds of Joy, *March 1936* (Mainstream MRL 399, US LP, n.d.). My knowledge of Big Joe Turner comes from several different LPs and CDs from differ-ent eras, which I will not list here, with two exceptions: the estimably annotated *I Don't Dig It* (Jukebox Lil, JB-618, Swedish LP, 1985); and the estimably programmed *Joe Turner's Blues* (Topaz TPZ 1070, UK CD, 1997), which collects the best of the early (1938–1946) recordings with a variety of great pianists (including Pete Johnson, Willie "The Lion" Smith, Art Tatum, and Albert Ammons). The most comprehensive reissue is the three-CD *Big, Bad and Blue: The Big Joe Turner Anthology* (Rhino 71550, US CD, 1995), which is lumbered with a lot of mediocre stuff produced during his Atlantic years—an illustration of just how much "dumbing down" rock and roll has often entailed. There are lots of Louis Jordan reissues, but the real eye-opener (and full of *great* music) is the eight-CD boxed set *Louis Jordan: Let the Good Times Roll: The Complete Decca Recordings, 1938–1954* (Bear Family BCD 15557, German CD, 1992).

October 29, 1949: Red Hot and Blue

The opening passage describes an aircheck of *Red Hot and Blue,* a fifteen-minute segment broadcast on WHBQ, Memphis, December 3, 1951. (For help in obtaining this and other vintage airchecks mentioned below, I thank JillEllyn Riley, who in 1989, when I got my copies, was an assistant curator at the Museum of Broadcasting in New York City.) WHBQ's program director is quoted in Louis Cantor, *Wheelin' on Beale* (New York, 1992), p. 165: Cantor's book, as the subtitle says, is primarily about "How WDIA-Memphis Became the Nation's First All-Black Radio Station and Created the Sound That Changed America"; but it is also a rich source about Memphis in the Fifties. Other sources on Phillips: Stanley Booth, *Rythm Oil* (New York, 1992), pp. 48–49; Colin Escott with Martin Hawkins, *Good Rockin' Tonight* (New York, 1991), pp. 5, 19–20. For radio in this era, see Arnold Shaw, *The Rockin' 50s* (New York, 1974), pp. 61–66; John A. Jackson, *Big Beat Heat* (New York, 1990), pp. 40–42; and—most revealing of all—Zenas Sears, memoirs reprinted in the liner notes to Billy Wright, *The Prince of the Blues* (Route 66 Kix-13, Swedish LP, 1980). For an overview of Delta blues (a topic intensively researched and debated by scholars), see Robert Palmer, *Deep Blues* (New York, 1981).

Discography: For a good introductory survey of the different blues genres, listen to the four-CD set *The Blues: A Smithsonian Collection of Classic Blues Singers* (Smithsonian RD 101, US CD, 1993); the music Phillips would have played is on disc four.

April 1950: Fender Guitars

The standard source on Leo Fender and his electric instruments is now Richard R. Smith, *Fender: The Sound Heard 'Round the World* (Fullerton, CA, 1996), the only work based on research in the company archives. The Fender quote is from Tom Wheeler, "Leo Fender: One of a Kind," *Guitar Player,* May 1978, p. 32ff. See also Leo Fender, "Pro's Reply," *Guitar Player,* September 1971, pp. 9, 38; Charles Shaar Murray, *Crosstown Traffic* (New York, 1990), pp. 210–13; Jon Pareles, "The Right Instrument at the Right Time," *The New York Times,* April 7, 1991, p. H27; Michael Lydon, *Boogie Lightning* (New York, 1974), pp. 145–58; and Tony Bacon, *The Ultimate Guitar Book* (New York, 1991). On the microphone and popular singing technique, see Henry Pleasants, *The Great American Popular Singers* (New York, 1984), pp. 25–26. A useful introduction to the technology of rock music-making is Chris Lent, ed., *Rockschool 1 & 2* (New York, 1987): Volume 1 is on string instruments, Volume 2 on keyboards and electronics.

Discography: John Lee Hooker, "Boogie Chillen" (Modern 627, #1, race, 1949). Arthur Smith and his Crackerjacks, "Guitar Boogie" (MGM 10293, #8, folk; #25, pop, 1948). Les Paul, "Hip-Billy Boogie" (Capitol 15070, flip side of "What Is This Thing Called Love?," #11, pop, 1948).

Winter 1950-1951: "The Tennessee Waltz"

Jerry Wexler recalls his role in the changing nomenclature of American pop, and also in the career of Patti Page, in Jerry Wexler and David Ritz, *Rhythm and the Blues* (New York, 1993), pp. 59–66. For Pee Wee King, and the first version of "Tennessee Waltz," see Irwin Stambler and Grelun Laulon, *The Encyclopedia of Folk, Country and Western Music* (New York, 1983), pp. 376–78. For Patti Page's version, see the interview with her in Joe Smith, *Off the Record* (New York, 1988), pp. 51–53; and Joseph P. Laredo, liner notes to *The Patti Page Collection* (Mercury 314 510 433 2, US CD, 1991).

Discography: Pee Wee King and His Golden West Cowboys, "The Tennessee Waltz" (RCA 2680, #3, folk, 1948). Erskine Hawkins, "The Tennessee Waltz" (Coral 60313, #6, rhythm and blues, 1950) (thanks to James Isaacs and Stereo Jack for locating and taping for me a copy of this now rare 78). Patti Page, "The Tennessee Waltz" (Mercury 5534, #1, pop, 1950). Les Paul and Mary Ford, "The Tennessee Waltz" (Capitol 1316, #6, pop, 1950).

Winter 1950–1951: "Teardrops From My Eyes"

The classic profile of Ahmet Ertegun is by George W.S. Trow, origi-
nally in *The New Yorker*, reprinted in *Within the Context of No
Context* (Boston, 1982), pp. 101–230—his off-the-cuff quip about
Ruth Brown and Doris Day is on p. 179. "Urbanized, watered-down
versions of real blues" etc. comes from Arnold Shaw, *Honkers and
Shouters* (New York, 1978), see esp. p. 373, though Shaw's whole
chapter (pp. 370–415) on Atlantic is useful. See also Charlie Gillett,
*Making Tracks: Atlantic Records and the Growth of a Multi-Billion-
Dollar Industry* (New York, 1974); Dorothy Wade and Justine Pi-
cardie, *Music Man: Ahmet Ertegun, Atlantic Records and the
Triumph of Rock 'n' Roll* (New York, 1990); Peter Grendysa, liner
notes to *Atlantic Rhythm and Blues, 1947–1974* (Atlantic 7 81293-
1-F, US LP, 1985); Jerry Wexler, interview in Ted Fox, *In the Groove*
(New York, 1986), pp. 123–55; and Jerry Wexler and David Ritz,
Rhythm and the Blues (New York, 1993): the description of Ertegun's accent is on p. 76. Norman Mailer's 1957 essay "The White
Negro" is reprinted in *Advertisements for Myself* (New York, 1959),
pp. 337–58, and also in *The Time of Our Time* (New York, 1998).

Discography: Stick McGhee and His Buddies, "Drinking Wine,
Spo-Dee-O-Dee, Drinking Wine" (Atlantic 873, #2, race, 1949).
Ruth Brown, "Teardrops From My Eyes" (Atlantic 919, #1, rhythm
and blues, 1950). A nice overview of Brown's work on Atlantic is the
two-CD set *Ruth Brown: Miss Rhythm: Greatest Hits and More* (Atlantic 7 82061-2, US CD, 1989). Atlantic has been especially adept
at preserving its past achievements in comprehensive reissues. The
most recent is the eight-CD *Atlantic Rhythm and Blues, 1947–1974*
(Atlantic 82305, US CD, 1991).

1951: Top 40

My description of life on the Great Plains is drawn from personal experience: my formative years were spent in Lincoln, Nebraska, where
my parents lived for a decade, starting in 1953, and where I grew up
listening to Omaha's Top 40 radio stations, as well as several other
influential early Top 40 stations, including KOMA in Oklahoma
City and WLS in Chicago. My primary source for the information
about Storz is Herman Land, "The Storz Bombshell," *Television
Magazine*, special issue on Radio, May 1957, pp. 85–92. Also essential was Joe Nick Patoski, "Rock 'n' Roll's Wizard of Oz," *Texas
Monthly*, February 1980, p. 101ff, a sharp profile of Gordon McLen-

don, who developed Top 40 concurrently with Storz. Also useful is the inside look at a Top 40 station in the mid-Sixties by Renata Adler, "The New Sound," *The New Yorker,* February 20, 1965, pp. 63–121. See also Ken Barnes, "Top 40 Radio," in Simon Frith, ed., *Facing the Music* (New York, 1988), pp. 8–50; and Arnold Shaw, *The Rockin' 50s* (New York, 1974), pp. 67–72. On the instinctive appeal of repetition, and also on the complex ornamentation and improvisation that repetitive musical forms facilitate, consult Peter Van Der Merwe, *Origins of the Popular Style: The Antecedents of Twentieth-Century Popular Music* (Oxford, 1989), a remarkable musicological account of blues strands in modern popular music, written by a South African scholar; see esp. pp. 107–9.

March 21, 1952: The Moondog Coronation Ball

All contemporary quotes are drawn from John A. Jackson, *Big Beat Heat: Alan Freed and the Early Years of Rock & Roll* (New York, 1991), that rarity among such books: a carefully researched, truly informed historical account. For a look back at the riot, with quotes from audience members, see Tom Junod, "Oh, What a Night!," *Life,* December 1, 1992, pp. 32–37. Alan Freed, *Moondog House,* airchecks recorded on March 22, 1952, and March 31, 1952.

Discography: In addition to airchecks from the Museum of Broadcasting, I consulted the excerpts from the Freed shows appearing on *Dedication,* Volumes 1, 2, and 3 (Silhouette S.M. 10006, 10007, 10008, US LP, 1982).

August 1952: "Kansas City"

Minstrelsy has become an academic minefield, with advocates of the idiom's "subversive" potential (such as Eric Lott) locked in combat with proponents of "whiteness" studies (for example, David R. Roediger), who regard any defense of minstrelsy as just a new-fangled version of old-fashioned (white) racism. For an approach more deeply rooted in a knowledge of the music industry, see Allen Lowe, *American Pop: From Minstrel to Mojo: On Record, 1893–1956* (Redwood, NY, 1997). See also the fine, persuasive study by Roger D. Abrahams, *Singing the Master: The Emergence of African American Culture in the Plantation South* (New York, 1992), and, for a survey of the larger subject, Eileen Southern, *The Music of Black Americans* (New York, 1983), and Peter van der Merwe, *Origins of the Popular Style* (Cambridge, 1989). On Leiber and Stoller, the primary source is Robert Palmer, *Baby That Was Rock & Roll* (New York, 1978); other quotes come from the superb interview in Ted Fox, *In the Groove* (New York, 1986), pp. 156–86 (see pp. 163–64 for remarks on "K.C. Lovin' "), and also a shorter conversation in Joe Smith, *Off the Record* (New York, 1988), pp. 120–24. The detail about the left-wing commune comes from an interview conducted by Michael Roloff with Leiber and Stoller and recounted by Greil Marcus in *Dead Elvis* (New York, 1991), pp. 100–101, 105. For a classical composer's informed appreciation of the *music* written by Leiber and Stoller, see William Bolcom's liner notes to his 1978 Nonesuch recording, with his wife, mezzo-soprano Joan Morris, of *The Other Songs of Leiber and Stoller*.

Discography: Charles Brown, "Hard Times" (Alladin 3116, #7, rhythm and blues, March 1952). Little Willie Littlefield, "K.C. Lovin' " (Federal 12110, recorded August 1952). Wilbert Harrison, "Kansas City" (Fury 1023, #1, rhythm & blues; #1, pop, April 1959). Willie Mae "Big Mama" Thornton, "Hound Dog" (Peacock 1612, #1, rhythm and blues, March 1953). For Little Willie Littlefield more generally, I referred to a reissue, *K.C. Lovin'* (K.C. 101, UK LP, 1977), which contains fourteen tracks. And for the minstrel roots of modern pop music, consult the astonishing early discs of the indispensable nine-CD set *American Pop: An Audio History,* the companion to Allen Lowe's book, mentioned above (West Hill Audio Archives WH-1017, Canadian CD, 1998).

Summer 1953: Elvis Hears Voices

The primary source for all future work on Elvis Presley is now the painstakingly researched biography by Peter Guralnick, *Last Train to Memphis: The Rise of Elvis Presley* (Boston, 1994); before him there was Jerry Hopkins, whose *Elvis: A Biography* (New York, 1971) contains some material from people who were dead by the time Guralnick wrote. See also Guralnick's liner notes to *Elvis, The King of Rock 'n' Roll: The Complete 50's Masters* (RCA, 1992). My own approach has been formed in dialogue throughout the years with Greil Marcus; his essay on Presley in *Mystery Train* (New York, 1975) remains a model of intelligent writing about rock and roll. I have also drawn on impressions I formed during interviews I conducted in the spring of 1987 with Sam Phillips and Marion Keisker for a *Newsweek* cover story on Presley published in the issue dated August 3, 1987, pp. 48–55. It is, in part, on the basis of these interviews that

I have decided to ignore the claim of Sam Phillips to have been at the Sun studio the day Elvis first recorded; I regard his insistence on this point as petty jealousy, since Marion Keisker never pretended that she had "discovered" Elvis—it was Sam Phillips, after all (as she always pointed out), who reacted to the music on the tape. The most reliable source for the history of Sam Phillips and Sun Records is Colin Escott with Martin Hawkins, *Good Rockin' Tonight: Sun Records and the Birth of Rock 'n' Roll* (New York, 1991), but see, too, the liner notes by Hank Davis to the six volumes (each containing 4 CDs) of *From the Vaults: The Complete Sun Singles* (Bear Family BCD 15801, 15802, etc., German CD, 1994–1998); Davis is the source for the story of how Phillips turned a joke by Junior Parker into a hit—see his essay for Volume 1, p. 18. The best profiles of Sam Phillips are by Peter Guralnick, in *Lost Highway* (Boston, 1979), and by David Halberstam, in *The Fifties* (New York 1993), pp. 456–79—Halberstam is useful on the era more generally.

Discography: Elvis Presley, "My Happiness" and "That's When Your Heartaches Begin," private acetate recordings, 1953; first publicly issued in the five-CD *Elvis, The King of Rock 'n' Roll: The Complete 50's Masters* (RCA 07863/66050-2, US CD, 1992). Presley's earliest vocal efforts are worth comparing with his later gospel work, especially the four sides he cut in 1957, now all collected on the two-CD *Elvis Presley: Amazing Grace* (RCA 07863, US CD, 1994). For the Ink Spots, a good recent anthology is *Swing High, Swing Low* (Living Era AJA 5082, UK CD, 1991). For the black gospel music Presley would have heard in Memphis, listen to *Bless My Bones: Memphis Gospel Radio in the Fifties* (Rounder 2063, US LP, 1988). The deeper, African-American sources of quartet singing are plumbed in a fine two-LP compilation, with brilliant notes by Doug Seroff, *Birmingham Quartet Anthology: Jefferson County, Alabama (1926–1953)* (Clanka Lanka 144, 001/002, Swedish LP, 1980).

March 15, 1954: "Sh-Boom"

My primary source for "Sh-Boom" and its importance was Arnold Shaw, *The Rockin' Fifties* (New York, 1974), pp. 73–33—Shaw was personally involved in brokering the publishing rights to "Sh-Boom." See also the discussion by Jim Dawson and Steve Propes, *What Was the First Rock 'n Roll Record?* (Boston, 1992), pp. 137–41, which quotes the *Cashbox* editorial on "cat" music by Ertegun and Wexler.

For doo-wop—and also for factual details about the Chords—my primary source was Philip Groia, *They All Sang on the Corner* (Port Jefferson, NY, 1983)—a book written with great affection and careful attention to factual details. Greil Marcus has some beautiful pages on the topic, too, in *Lipstick Traces* (Cambridge, MA, 1989), see pp. 258–61. See, too, the pioneering essay by Barret Hansen, "Doo-Wop" in Jim Miller, ed., *The Rolling Stone Illustrated History of Rock & Roll* (New York, 1976); Martin Gottlieb, "The Durability of Doo-Wop," *The New York Times*, January 17, 1993, pp. 1H, 25H; and Martin Gottlieb, "On the White Side of Crossover Dreams," *The New York Times*, February 14, 1993, p. 6E.

Discography: The Chords, "Sh-Boom" (Cat 104, #2, rhythm and blues, #5, pop, July 1954). The Crew-cuts, "Sh-Boom" (Mercury 70404, #1, pop, July 1954). For the music of the Chords, I referred to *The Best of the Chords* (Cat 1000, US LP—a bootleg from the early Eighties, I would guess), which collects fourteen mostly dreary tracks. For the Crew-cuts, I used *Rock and Roll Bash* (Bear Family 0 4794/1399, German LP, 1986), an anthology of sixteen equally dreary tracks. For doo-wop more generally, there are two superb four-CD anthologies: *The Doo Wop Box* (Rhino R2 71463, US CD, 1993) and *The Doo Wop Box II* (Rhino R2 72507, US CD, 1996)—both sets include excellent notes by experts on the genre.

July 30, 1954: Elvis Discovers His Body

The primary source is the relevant chapter in Peter Guralnick, *Last Train to Memphis* (Boston, 1994), pp. 89–125 (for Elvis telling his girlfriend June Junesco how he felt when he sang, see p. 319). See also Jerry Hopkins, *Elvis: A Biography* (New York, 1971), pp. 71–72, for Dewey Phillips' recollection of the event (once considered credible by Guralnick himself, in his liner notes to *Elvis Presley—The Sun Sessions* CD [RCA 6414-2-R, US CD, 1987]). See, too, Albert Goldman, *Elvis* (New York, 1981), p. 120; Elaine Dundy, *Elvis and Gladys* (New York, 1985), pp. 179–80. Colin Escott with Martin Hawkins, *Good Rockin' Tonight: Sun Records and the Birth of Rock 'n' Roll* (New York, 1991), p. 65.

Discography: "That's All Right" b/w "Blue Moon of Kentucky" (Sun 209, recorded July 1954). "Good Rockin' Tonight" (Sun 210, recorded September 1954). The indispensable anthology for Presley in the Fifties is the five-CD *Elvis, The King of Rock 'n' Roll: The Complete 50's Masters* (RCA 07863/66050-2, US CD, 1992). Also of great interest are Presley's radio performances on *The Louisiana Hayride*, starting with renditions of "That's All Right" and "Blue Moon of Kentucky" on October 16, 1954: in all, fifteen *Hayride* air shots recorded between 1954 and 1956 survive in varying states of sonic decay, and they are all collected on Elvis Presley, *The Louisiana Hayride* (IMC Licensing SA, Bobby and Ray Williams Partnership, US CD, 1997).

November 24, 1954: Copyrighting "Rock and Roll"
The source for facts, and quotes, in this chapter is John A. Jackson, *Big Beat Heat* (New York, 1991), pp. 72–87; and Fredric Dannen, *Hit Men* (New York, 1990), pp. 41–43.

Spring 1955: Blackboard Jungle
For an example of real scholarship in the field of cultural studies, one cannot do better than Thomas Doherty, *Teenagers and Teenpics: The Juvenilization of American Movies in the 1950s* (Boston, 1988), esp. pp. 105–39. For *Blackboard Jungle,* I also found useful Andrew Dowdy, *Movies Are Better Than Ever* (New York, 1973), pp. 142–46; Mark Thomas McGee and R.J. Robertson, *The J.D. Films* (Jefferson, NC, 1982), pp. 25–30; and Peter Biskind, *Seeing Is Believing* (New York, 1983), pp. 197–217. Details about the recording of "Rock Around the Clock" come from Jim Dawson and Steve Propes, *What Was the First Rock 'n Roll Record?* (Boston, 1992), pp. 142–49, and the interview with Milt Gabler in Ted Fox, *In the Groove* (New York, 1986), pp. 91–92. The standard biography of Bill Haley is by John Swenson, *Bill Haley: The Daddy of Rock and Roll* (New York, 1982); see also Colin Escott, liner notes to *Bill Haley and His Comets: The Decca Years and More* (Bear Family BCD 15506, German CD, 1990). On juvenile delinquency as a source of popular moral concern in these years, see, besides the Doherty book cited above, Michael Barson and Steven Heller, *Teenage Confidential: An Illustrated History of the American Teen* (San Francisco, 1998), pp. 32–51. Information on Alan Freed and the making of *Rock Around the Clock* comes from John A. Jackson, *Big Beat Heat* (New York, 1991), pp. 94–95, 120–24. The reaction in England is described in Ian Whitcomb, *After the Ball* (New York, 1972), pp. 225–28; John Lennon's reaction is recorded in Philip Norman, *Shout!* (New York, 1981), p. 32.

Discography: Bill Haley and the Saddlemen, "Rock the Joint" (Essex 303, 1952). Bill Haley and His Comets, "Crazy Man Crazy" (Essex 321, #12, pop, 1953). Bill Haley and His Comets, "(We're Gonna) Rock Around the Clock" (Decca 29124, #23, pop, 1954; #1, pop; #3, rhythm and blues, 1955). Bill Haley and His Comets, "Shake, Rattle, and Roll" (Decca 29204, #7, pop, 1954). The full sonic impact of the original master of "Rock Around the Clock" is most evident on the version of the song that appears on the five-CD *Bill Haley and His Comets: The Decca Years and More* (Bear Family BCD 15506, German CD, 1990); too bad most of the rest of this interminable reissue consists of musical garbage. One wonders if Haley's fate at the hands of critics might be kinder if more of them listened to his most interesting legacy, the pre-Decca recordings: while writing I referred to the compilation Bill Haley and His Comets, *Rock the Joint!* (Roller Coaster ROLL 2009, UK LP, 1985), twenty-two fascinating pieces of musical Americana.

2 Rock and Roll Music

March 15, 1955: "Ain't It a Shame"

For Fats Domino and the New Orleans R&B scene more generally, the primary source remains the pioneering study by John Broven, *Walking to New Orleans* (Sussex, England, 1974). For Fats Domino, see also Jeff Hannusch and Adam Block, liner notes to the four-CD set Fats Domino, *They Call Me the Fat Man* (EMI E2-96784, US CD 1991); and Peter Guralnick, "Fats Domino," in Jim Miller, ed., *The Rolling Stone Illustrated History of Rock & Roll* (New York, 1980), pp. 45–47. For more on Dave Bartholomew, see Dawn Eden, liner notes to Dave Bartholomew, *The Genius of Dave Bartholomew* (EMI 0777-7-80184-21, US CD 1992). The information on Randy Wood comes mainly from Arnold Shaw, *The Rockin' 50s* (New York, 1974), pp. 126–29. See also the interview with Pat Boone in Joe Smith, *Off the Record* (New York, 1988), pp. 109–11 (the source of the quote about singing a duet with Domino). See also the (anonymous) liner notes to *Pat Boone* (Dot 3012, US LP, 1956).

Discography: Fats Domino, "Ain't It a Shame" (Imperial 5348, #1, rhythm and blues; #10, pop, 1955). Pat Boone, "Ain't That a Shame" (Dot 15377, #1, pop, 1955). A fine overview is the four-CD set Fats Domino, *They Call Me the Fat Man* (EMI E2-96784, US CD 1991). For the early work, I also referred to the original Imperial albums, too numerous to mention, and also these reissues: *The Fats Domino Story,* Volumes 1 and 2 (United Artists UAS 30067, 30068, UK LP, 1977); and Fats Domino, *Boogie Woogie Baby* (Ace CHD 140, UK LP, 1985). For Pat Boone, I listened to *Pat Boone* (Dot 3012, US LP, 1956)—the first rock and roll album I was able to convince my parents to buy for me. For a revealing look at how Randy Wood worked the rock and roll side of the pop fence in these critical months, see *Dot Records "Cover to Cover"* (Ace CDCHD 609, UK CD, 1995), an anthology of thirty mind-boggling Dot covers of early R&B songs (many of them pop hits) by Boone, Gale Storm, the Fontane Sisters, and Tab Hunter, among others.

May 21, 1955: "Maybellene"

My primary source for the quotes and stories in this chapter is Chuck Berry, *The Autobiography* (New York, 1987), which I consider largely credible, not least in its emphasis on how deliberately (and cynically, in the end) Berry pitched his music to white teenagers. See also Patrick William Salvo, interview with Chuck Berry, 1972, reprinted in Peter Herbst, ed., *The Rolling Stone Interviews, 1967–1980* (New York, 1981), pp. 224–34; Jim Dawson and Steve Propes, *What Was the First Rock 'n Roll Record?* (Boston, 1992), pp. 181–85; John A. Jackson, *Big Beat Heat* (New York, 1991), pp. 98–102, 104–07; Arnold Shaw, *Honkers and Shouters: The Golden Years of Rhythm and Blues* (New York, 1978), pp. 289–93.

Discography: Bob Wills and His Texas Playboys, "Ida Red" (Vocalion 05079, 1938). Bob Wills and His Texas Playboys, "Ida Red Likes the Boogie" (MGM 10570, #10, country and western, 1950). Chuck Berry, "Maybellene," #1, rhythm and blues; #5, pop, 1955). For Bob Wills, I referred (among other albums) to *Bob Wills Country and Western Classics,* a fine three-LP set with extensive notes by Rich Kienzle (Time-Life Records TLCW-07, US LP, 1982). The original "Ida Red" appears on the two-LP set *Bob Wills and His Texas Playboys: The Golden Era* (Columbia C2 40149, US LP, 1987). A good overview of Berry's career is the three-CD set *Chuck Berry: The Chess Box* (Chess CHD3-80,001, US CD, 1988). Presley does "Maybellene" on Elvis Presley, *The Louisiana Hayride* (IMC Licensing SA, Bobby & Ray Williams Partnership, US CD, 1997).

September 14, 1955: "Tutti Frutti"

The primary source of information on Little Richard and the "Tutti

Frutti" sessions is Charles White, *The Life and Times of Little Richard* (New York, 1984); this invaluable book is an authorized oral history that collates retrospective accounts by (for example) Art Rupe and Bumps Blackwell, as well as extensive reminiscences of Richard himself. Also crucial: the notes by Rob Finnis, Rick Coleman, and Ray Topping for *Little Richard: The Specialty Sessions* (Ace ABOXCD 1, UK CD, 1989); the observation about "Tutti Frutti" only going over in whites-only clubs comes from Richard's friend Henry Nash, quoted in the large book included with this superb set, p. 21. See also Jonas Bernholm, liner notes to Billy Wright, *Prince of the Blues* (Route 66 Kix-13, Swedish LP, 1980) and Jim Dawson and Steve Propes, *What Was the First Rock 'n Roll Record?* (New York, 1992), pp. 185–89. For how Richard appeared in the eyes of a peer, see James Brown with Bruce Tucker, *The Godfather of Soul* (New York, 1990), pp. 85–86.

Discography: Little Richard, "Tutti Frutti" (Specialty 561, #2, rhythm and blues; #17, pop, 1955–1956). For the career of Little Richard more generally, I referred to the six-CD set *Little Richard: The Specialty Sessions* (Ace ABOXCD 1, UK CD, 1989), which contains every surviving scrap of tape from the years 1955 through 1957—a historian's dream, a listener's nightmare (there are plenty of more digestible anthologies to pick from). Interesting early stuff is collected on *Little Richard: "Shut Up!" A Collection of Rare Tracks, 1951–1964* (Rhino R1 70236, US LP, 1988)—this includes the young Jimi Hendrix doing "Hound Dog" with Richard in '64! More early stuff, along with some rare Billy Wright material, is on Little Richard/Billy Wright and the Tempo Toppers, *Hey Baby, Don't You Want a Man Like Me?* (Ace CHA 193, UK LP, 1986).

November 1955: "Why Do Fools Fall in Love"

The source of the Lymon quotes in this chapter is Art Peters, "Comeback of a Child Star," *Ebony*, Volume 22, Number 3, January, 1967, p. 42. Most of the information is drawn from Philip Groia, *They All Sang on the Corner* (New York, 1983), pp. 119–24, and also the booklet by Philip Groia, Bob Hyde, and Marcia Vance, for the five-LP set, *Frankie Lymon/The Teenagers: For Collectors Only* (Murray Hill 000148, US LP, 1986); see also Ted Fox, *Showtime at the Apollo* (New York, 1983), pp. 201–2. For George Goldner, see Jerry Wexler and David Ritz, *Rhythm and the Blues* (New York, 1993), pp. 139, 163–64; Dorothy Wade and Justine Picardie, *Music Man* (New York,

1990), pp. 57, 82, 87–88, 95–96, 108–16, 119–21; Fredric Dannen, *Hit Men* (New York, 1990), pp. 40–41; and Ted Fox, *In the Groove* (New York, 1986), interview with Jerry Leiber and Mike Stoller, pp. 182–83. The Arlene Smith quote is from Charlotte Greig, *Will You Still Love Me Tomorrow?* (London, 1989), interview with Arlene Smith, pp. 11–20; see also Mike Redmond and Steve West, liner notes to the three-LP set *Arlene Smith and the Chantels: For Collectors Only* (Murray Hill 000385, US LP, 1987). For Ronnie's swoon at Lymon's voice, see Ronnie Spector with Vince Waldron, *Be My Baby* (New York, 1990), pp. 13–16. For Richard Barrett, see liner notes to *The Best of the Valentines* (Murray Hill 000202, US LP, 1986).

Discography: Frankie Lymon and the Teenagers, "Why Do Fools Fall in Love" (Gee 1002, #1, rhythm and blues; #6, pop, 1956). In writing this chapter, I referred to the five-LP set *Frankie Lymon/The Teenagers: For Collectors Only* (Murray Hill 000148, US LP, 1986). There are also a variety of more selective anthologies available on CD.

December 19, 1955: "Blue Suede Shoes"

The primary source for this chapter was Colin Escott with Martin Hawkins, *Good Rockin' Tonight: Sun Records and the Birth of Rock 'n' Roll* (New York, 1991), pp. 125–43; supplemented by Colin Escott with Martin Hawkins, book for *The Carl Perkins Box* (Charly Sun Box 101, UK LP, 1982). Shortly before he died, Perkins himself co-wrote with David McGee *Go, Cat, Go: The Life and Times of Carl Perkins* (New York, 1996); see esp. pp. 128–91. Also useful (as always): the chapter in Jim Dawson and Steve Propes, *What Was the First Rock 'n Roll Record?* (Boston, 1992), pp. 190–93. An early and still noteworthy profile of Perkins appears in Michael Lydon, *Rock Folk* (New York, 1971), pp. 25–45. Material about Presley and Sun in 1955 comes from Escott and Hawkins, *Good Rockin' Tonight*, pp. 67–84, and also from Peter Guralnick, *Last Train to Memphis* (Boston, 1994). The description of the honky-tonk by Rich Kienzle appears in his liner notes to *Columbia Country Classics, Volume 2: Honky Tonk Heroes* (Columbia 46030, US CD, 1990).

Discography: Carl Perkins, "Blue Suede Shoes" (Sun 234, #1, country and western; #2, rhythm and blues; #2, pop, 1956). The definitive look at the first decade (1954–1964) of Perkins' ill-fated career is the five-CD set *The Classic Carl Perkins* (Bear Family BCD 15494, German CD, 1990), which contains 134 songs recorded for three different labels, and chronicles a honky tonk singer's unsuccessful (and unhappy) quest to comprehend the teen poetics of the Fifties and write another song with the commercial clout of "Blue Suede Shoes." An early sign of trouble: recording "Pink Pedal Pushers" for Columbia in 1958.

3 All Shook Up

June 5, 1956: Elvis From the Waist Down

For Milton Berle and the early years of American television, see David Halberstam, *The Fifties,* pp. 185–87. The June 5, 1956, performance of "Hound Dog" is most readily available on Andrew Solt, *Elvis: The Great Performances, Volume 1: Center Stage* (Buena Vista Home Video, 1990). The July 1 version, with Steve Allen, is available on *Elvis '56,* a video documentary first aired on Cinemax in 1987. For backstage details and the reaction, see Peter Guralnick, *Last Train to Memphis: The Rise of Elvis Presley* (Boston, 1994), pp. 283–86; and Jerry Hopkins, *Elvis: A Biography* (New York, 1972), pp. 125–26. For the Oakland concert, see Ralph J. Gleason, "Dawn of True Sexual Hysteria," *Rolling Stone,* February 1, 1969, p. 20. For Jack Gould, see the obituary in *The New York Times,* May 25, 1993, p. B6. Ann Fulchino quoted in Leonard Bennett, "Who the Hell Is Elvis Presley?," *Cabaret,* August 1956, p. 22. Jerry Leiber quoted in Peter Cronin, Scott Isler, and Mark Rowland, "Elvis Presley: An Oral Biography," *Musician,* October 1992, p. 67. The comment on sexual mores in the Fifties comes from Anne Stevenson, writing about Sylvia Plath in her book *Bitter Fame* (New York, 1989). Some of the information about the Bellboys I've drawn from the original liner notes to Freddie Bell and the Bell Boys, *Rock and Roll . . . All Flavors* (Wing MG 20289, US LP, 1957). Also useful: Jim Dawson and Steve Propes, *What Was the First Rock 'n Roll Record?* (Boston, 1992), pp. 114–18.

Discography: Willie Mae "Big Mama" Thornton, "Hound Dog" (Peacock 1612, #1, rhythm and blues, 1953). Elvis Presley, "Hound Dog" b/w "Don't Be Cruel" (RCA 6604, #1, country and western; #1, rhythm and blues; #1, pop, 1956). It is interesting to note that "Hound Dog" was the big R&B hit of this two-sided classic recording, while "Don't Be Cruel" was the bigger C&W hit (never mind that it was composed by a black songwriter, Otis Blackwell).

March 25, 1957: Ricky Nelson Impresses His Girlfriend

There are two biographies of Rick Nelson, the better by Joel Selvin, *Ricky Nelson: Idol for a Generation* (Chicago, 1990), which includes the details about the teen's Hollywood "hipster" phase, smoking pot, etc.: see p. 113. But I consulted as well Philip Bashe, *Teenage Idol: The Complete Biography of Rick Nelson* (New York, 1992). Also useful are Steve Kolanjian's liner notes to *Ricky Nelson,* Volume 1 (EMI CDP-7-92771-2, US CD, 1990). Vintage clips of Ricky on TV are included in *A Tribute to Ricky Nelson* (Rhino Home Video, 1989). In 1995, Front Row Entertainment released four videos with eight episodes of the TV show—of special interest is "Rick's Big Night" from 1957, which features the freshly minted teen idol singing Carl Perkins' "Boppin' the Blues" (as well as "Honeycomb"). *The Ozzie and Harriet Show* is analyzed by John R. Holmes in "The Wizardry of Ozzie: Breaking Character in Early Television," *Journal of Popular Culture,* Volume 23, Number 2, Fall 1989, pp. 93–102. Other quotes come from "Ozzie and Harriet . . . They Never Leave Home," *Look,* October 24, 1950, p. 83; and Jack Gould, "Radio and Television," *The New York Times,* October 4, 1952. In their reference book *The Complete Directory to Prime Time Network TV Shows* (New York, 1979), Tim Brooks and Earle Marsh include a handy list of songs turned into pop hits by television exposure, on p. 817. See also David Halberstam, *The Fifties* (New York, 1993), pp. 474–79 (on Rick Nelson); and Peter Guralnick, *Last Train to Memphis: The Rise of Elvis Presley* (New York, 1994), p. 338 (on Presley's TV ratings).

Discography: Ricky Nelson, "A Teenager's Romance" b/w "I'm Walking" (Verve 10047, #2 b/w #4, pop, 1957). *Ricky* (Imperial 9048, #1, pop albums, 1957). The hits from 1957 through 1971 are collected on three different compilations: *The Best of Ricky Nelson,* Volume 1 (EMI CDP-7-92771-2, US CD, 1990); *The Best of Rick Nelson,* Volume 2 (EMI CDP-7-95219-2, US CD, 1991); *The Best of Rick Nelson 1963–1975* (Decca/MCA MCAD-10098, US CD, 1990). James Burton's most torrid rockabilly licks appear on the third and fourth albums by Nelson, *Ricky Sings Again* and *Songs by Ricky;* both appear on one CD that, though not impossible to find, looks like it is probably unauthorized: *Ricky Nelson Volume 2* (TNT 9061/9082, US CD, 1991).

August 5, 1957: American Bandstand

For the teenage marketplace, see Dwight MacDonald's classic profile of Eugene Gilbert, "A Caste, a Culture, a Market," *The New Yorker,* November 22, 1958, pp. 57–94; November 29, 1958, pp. 57–107; and also Thomas Doherty's chapter on "The Teenage Marketplace" in *Teenagers and Teenpics* (Boston, 1988), pp. 42–70. A good contemporary industry view of Dick Clark and the *Bandstand* phenomenon is offered in Bob Rolontz, "The Philadelphia Story," in two parts, *Billboard,* March 10 and March 17, 1958. Other primary sources used in this chapter: Dick Clark, "R 'n' R: The Basic Form of Pop Music," ABC television feature, Summer 1958; Gael Greene, "Dick Clark," in six parts, *New York Post,* September 22–28, 1958; Leslie Lieber, "Why Everybody Likes Dick Clark," *This Week,* November 16, 1958. The authorized autobiography, Dick Clark and Richard Robinson, *Rock, Roll and Remember* (New York, 1976), though filled with inadvertently revealing information, should now be used only in conjunction with John A. Jackson, *American Bandstand: Dick Clark and the Making of a Rock 'n' Roll Empire* (New York, 1998). Two other book packages authorized by Clark: Michael Shore with Dick Clark, *The History of American Bandstand* (New York, 1985); and, with great photos, Dick Clark with Fred Bronson, *Dick Clark's American Bandstand* (New York, 1997). Gerald Early, one of our sharpest writers on the color line in American pop, has sharp comments to make on the *Bandstand* aesthetic and Berry Gordy, in "One Nation Under a Groove," *The New Republic,* July 15 and 22, 1991, pp. 30–41. For the passage by Eldridge Cleaver, see *Soul on Ice* (New York, 1968), pp. 197–98. For the Castles, Handy, and the fox-trot, see Tim Gracyk, liner notes to *James Reese Europe's 369th U.S. Infantry "Hell Fighters" Band* (Memphis Archives MA7020, US CD, 1996)—Europe became the first important black bandleader of this century when the Castles hired him as their music director and accompanist.

Discography: If someone were creating a time capsule with only three discs to represent the Dick Clark era in the history of rock and roll, I would choose: *Teenage Crush* (Ace CDCHD 640, UK CD, 1997), twenty-eight ballads compiled by John Broven, Trevor Churchill, and Rob Finnis, who have picked songs that make up a "soundtrack to teen angst," Fifties-style; and the first two volumes of *The Golden Age of American Rock 'n' Roll* (Ace CDCHD 289 and 445, UK CD, 1991 and 1993), each containing thirty tracks, again lovingly compiled by Trevor Churchill, Rob Finnis, and John Broven: with these sets you get a feel for the kitsch glory and feckless fun of the period's best rock and roll, without having to endure long stretches of unamusing treacle.

October 21, 1957: Jailhouse Rock

Information on the making of *Jailhouse Rock* comes from Peter Guralnick, *Last Train to Memphis: The Rise of Elvis Presley* (Boston, 1994), pp. 404–420. On rock films and "juvenilization," see Thomas Doherty, *Teenagers and Teenpics* (Boston, 1988), pp. 71–104; and, for the *Variety* article of March 5, 1958, "Film Future: GI Baby Boom," pp. 230–31.

   Discography: Jailhouse Rock (RCA EPA-4114, 1957): the soundtrack was originally released on an extended-play 45 that spawned three hit songs: "(You're So Square) Baby I Don't Care," released only on the EP (#14, rhythm and blues, 1958) and—released as a separate single—"Jailhouse Rock" b/w "Treat Me Nice" (RCA 7035, #1 b/w #11, country and western; #1 b/w #7, rhythm and blues; #1 b/w #18, pop, 1957). Presley's topping of all three *Billboard* charts suggests his continuing across-the-board popularity in 1957 with black and white listeners, and this is a fact worth stressing: the Beatles never came close to this kind of transracial appeal in America. A variety of alternate takes of the film music are available on the latest reissue of *Jailhouse Rock* (RCA 07863/67453-2, US CD, 1997); what the alternates show is that Presley was a very methodical craftsman in the studio, laboring over every small detail of his music.

October 15, 1958: "Lonely Teardrops"

For Berry Gordy, the historian now has to contend with *To Be Loved* (New York, 1994), a "memoir" full of ellipses, but nevertheless of interest; the quote about rock and pop appears on p. 99. Far more revealing is the bitter memoir by Gordy's first wife, which is full of juicy details about the early years, details that I, for one, find credible: see Raynoma Gordy Singleton, *Berry, Me, and Motown: The Untold Story* (Chicago, 1990), especially Chapter 2, which contains a description of Gordy's triumphant production of "Lonely Teardrops" that is far more gripping than anything in Gordy's own book. For Motown more generally, the standard history remains Nelson George, *Where Did Our Love Go?* (New York, 1985). Jerry

Leiber's comments about Motown are recorded in Ted Fox, *In the Groove* (New York, 1986), p. 181. For a reliable précis of what is currently known about Billy Ward, see Peter A. Grendysa's liner notes, informative as always, for *Sixty Minute Men: The Best of Billy Ward and the Dominoes* (Rhino R2-71509, US CD, 1993). For a pioneering appreciation of Jackie Wilson's artistry, see Joe McEwen, "Jackie Wilson," in Jim Miller, ed., *The Rolling Stone Illustrated History of Rock & Roll,* second edition (New York, 1980), pp. 117–19; and see, too, Billy Vera and Robert Pruter, liner notes for the three-CD set *Mr. Excitement!* (Rhino R2/R4 70775, US CD, 1992); and Bill Millar, liner notes to *Reet Petite* (Ace CH125, UK LP, 1984).

Discography: The Dominoes, "Rags to Riches" (King 1280, #2, rhythm and blues, 1953). Billy Ward and the Dominoes, "St. Therese of the Roses" (Decca 29933, #13, pop, 1956). Jackie Wilson, "Reet Petite" (Brunswick 55024, #62, pop, 1957). Jackie Wilson, "To Be Loved" (Brunswick 55052, #7, rhythm and blues; #22, pop, 1958). Jackie Wilson, "Lonely Teardrops" (Brunswick 55105, #1, rhythm and blues; #7, pop, 1958). For the Dominoes, the handiest current anthology is *Sixty Minute Men: The Best of Billy Ward and the Dominoes* (Rhino R2-71509, US CD, 1993). For Jackie Wilson, the set to have is *Mr. Excitement!* (Rhino R2/R4 70775, US CD, 1992), which (among its other virtues) includes "St. Therese of the Roses"— a pop and *not* an R&B hit, notice—and *two* versions of "Danny Boy" (this is the only anthology that does not whitewash, so to speak, Wilson's genuine love of saccharine pop). Presley's imitation of Wilson—he refers to Billy Ward and the Dominoes by name—appears on Elvis Presley, *The Million Dollar Quartet* (RCA 2023-2-R, US CD, 1989), an off-the-cuff jam session that occurred one afternoon when Presley dropped by the Sun studio to say hello, and discovered that Carl Perkins was in the midst of a session.

November 22, 1959: Payola

The quiz show scandals, and their link with McCarthyism, are discussed in David Halberstam, *The Fifties* (New York, 1993), pp. 643–66. Primary source material used for the Alan Freed part of the story includes stories in *The New York Times,* November 22, 1959, p. 1; November 24, 1959, p. 31; November 26, 1959, p. 51; December 1, 1959, p. 34; April 26, 1960; and May 20, 1960. For Freed at the last broadcast of his WNEW TV show, see *Time,* vol. 74, December 7, 1959, p. 47; and *Life,* December 7, 1959, pp. 30–31. For AS-CAP's animus against rock and roll, see Russell Sanjek and David Sanjek, *American Popular Music Business in the 20th Century* (New York, 1991), pp. 155–95. The Dick Clark quotes are drawn from the official record: U.S. House of Representatives, *Responsibilities of Broadcasting Licensees and Station Personnel: Hearings Before a Subcommittee of the Committee on Interstate and Foreign Commerce,* 86th Congress, 2nd Session on Payola and Other Deceptive Practices in the Broadcasting Field (Washington, D.C., 1960), pp. 1167–1368.

May 12, 1960: Elvis Comes Home

The details about the taping of the Sinatra special come from Herb Zuker, "A Quiet Day at Miami Beach," *TV Guide,* May 7–13, 1960, p. 15; Alan Levy, "Elvis Comes Marching Home," *TV Guide,* May 7–13, 1960, pp. 10–13; "Teen Idols on TV," *Life,* May 16, 1960, pp. 103–4; and Murray Schumach, "Money No Object for Sinatra Show," *The New York Times,* May 13, 1960, p. 63 (the source of the Sammy Cahn quotes). See also Kitty Kelly, *His Way: The Unauthorized Biography of Frank Sinatra* (New York, 1987), pp. 277–78. And also Peter Guralnick's liner notes to *Elvis: From Nashville to Memphis, the Essential 60's Masters I* (RCA 07863-66160-2, US CD, 1993). Parts of the show itself can be seen in *This Is Elvis,* directed by Andrew Solt and Malcolm Leo, with forty-five additional minutes of footage in the home video format (Warner Home Video, 1981); and in Solt's *Elvis, The Great Performances, Volume Two: The Man and the Music* (Buena Vista Home Video, 1990).

Discography: Presley's session of April 3–4, 1960, in its entirety, as it was recorded, can be heard on the first disc of the five-CD set *Elvis: From Nashville to Memphis, the Essential 60's Masters I* (RCA 07863-66160-2, US CD, 1993). Most of the session was quickly released as a large part of one album, with three tracks held back for release later in the year as singles: *Elvis Is Back* (RCA LSP 2231, #2, pop albums, 1960); "It's Now or Never" (RCA 47-7777, #1, pop; #7, rhythm and blues, 1960); "Are You Lonesome To-night?" b/w "I Gotta Know" (RCA 47-7810, #1 b/w #20, pop; #3, rhythm and blues; #22, country and western, 1960). Frank Sinatra, *Nice 'n' Easy* (Capitol 1417, #1, pop albums, 1960).

4 Glad All Over

November 9, 1961: Brian Epstein Enters the Cavern

For the canonic account, see Brian Epstein, *A Cellarful of Noise* (London, 1964), pp. 46–47 (for November 9, 1961, in the Cavern); as should be clear from my chapter, I find it impossible to credit some details in Epstein's memoir, which is the chief source for the story that he had never laid eyes on the Beatles before his lunchtime visit to the Cavern. Cf. Peter Brown and Steven Gaines, *The Love You Make: An Insider's Story of the Beatles* (New York, 1983), pp. 55–83, on Brian Epstein—the best available retrospective account; it is Brown who is quoted describing the young Brian Epstein. For the Liverpool veteran who recalls seeing Epstein at a Beatles show in the summer of 1961, see Chris Salewicz, *McCartney: The Definitive Biography* (New York, 1986), p. 110; on p. 117, Salewicz also quotes Sam Leach, the promoter of Operation Big Beat, on the beginning of Beatlemania. For the Epstein employee who recalls seeing his boss gazing at the Beatles photo, see Ian Whitcomb, *Rock Odyssey* (New York, 1983), p. 98; Whitcomb also has the best brief analysis of the early Merseybeat style, on pp. 95–96. For a good print of the photograph in question, see Allan Kozinn, *The Beatles* (London, 1995), pp. 28–29. For the early Beatles, see Philip Norman, *Shout! The Beatles in Their Generation* (New York, 1981). Lennon's *Mersey Beat* biography of the Beatles is reprinted in Ray Coleman, *Lennon* (New York, 1984), pp. 149–50. The circumstances under which Lennon first met McCartney are recounted by Jim O'Donnell in an "hour by hour account of how the Beatles began," published in 1994, and bearing a title of typically pseudo-religious portent: *The Day John Met Paul.* For the most authoritative reconstruction of the Beatles' live repertoire in these years, and also for details about the concerts they played, see Mark Lewisohn, *The Complete Beatles Chronicles* (New York, 1992). On British art schools and their influence on rock, see Simon Frith and Howard Horne, *Art Into Pop* (London, 1987), pp. 80–86. Susan Sontag's famous 1964 analysis of camp sensibility, "Notes on 'Camp,' " appears in her first collection of essays, *Against Interpretation* (New York, 1968). The career of Larry Parnes is briefly retailed in Johnny Rogan, *Starmakers and Svengalis: The History of British Pop Management* (London, 1988).

Discography: The Beatles' early version of "Be-Bop-A-Lula" has been released several times in several different forms; in writing this chapter, I referred to *The Beatles Live! at the Star Club in Hamburg, Germany; 1962* (Bellaphon BLS5560, German LP, 1977). Very early amateur recordings of "That'll Be the Day" and "In Spite of All the Danger" from 1958, and "Hallelujah, I Love Her So," "You'll Be Mine," and "Cayenne" from 1960, appear on *The Beatles Anthology 1* (Apple CDP 7243 8 34445 2 6, US CD, 1995).

1961-1962: Robert Johnson: King of the Delta Blues Singers

For Robert Johnson, I drew on Peter Guralnick, *Searching for Robert Johnson* (New York, 1989); Stephen C. LaVere, biography and notes in booklet for *Robert Johnson: The Complete Recordings* (Columbia C2K 46222, US CD, 1990); Charles Shaar Murray's discussion in *Crosstown Traffic: Jimi Hendrix and the Rock 'n' Roll Revolution* (New York, 1989), pp. 106–20; Greil Marcus, *Mystery Train* (New York, 1975), pp. 21–40 (it is Marcus who calls Johnson "a sort of invisible pop star"); Frank Driggs, liner notes to *Robert Johnson: King of the Delta Blues Singers* (Columbia CL 1654, US LP, 1961); and Rudi Blesh, *Shining Trumpets: A History of Jazz* (New York, 1946). For John Hammond, Alan Lomax, and the original quest to find Johnson, see Alan Lomax, *The Land Where the Blues Began* (New York, 1993), pp. 12–15; John Hammond with Irving Townsend, *John Hammond on Record* (New York, 1977); and John Cowley, notes to *Walking Blues* (Flyright FLY 541, UK LP, 1978). The *Life* headline about Leadbelly is quoted in Lawrence Cohn, liner notes to *Leadbelly: King of the 12-String Guitar* (Columbia CK 46776, US CD, 1991). On the folk music craze, by far the best account, and a brilliant analysis, appears in Robert Cantwell, *When We Were Good: The Folk Revival* (Cambridge, MA, 1996); see also "Public Eyes Folksy Melodies as Remedy for War Tensions," *Billboard*, January 6, 1951 (for the popularity of "Tennessee Waltz" and "Goodnight Irene" showing the appeal of "a bright, homey, simple, folksy melody sort of tune"). On Johnson's influence in the Sixties, see Peter Guralnick, "Eric Clapton at the Passion Threshold," *Musician*, February 1990, p. 46 ("This was an image that I was very, very keen to hang on to"); Keith Richards, "Well, This Is It," in booklet for *Robert Johnson: The Complete Recordings* (Columbia C2K 46222, US CD, 1990). For Johnson's influence on later hard rock, and on the meaning of freedom as "a lack of social ties" in heavy metal, see Robert Walser, *Running With the Devil: Power, Gender, and Madness in Heavy Metal Music* (Hanover, NH, 1993), pp. 8, 52.

    Discography: Robert Johnson: King of the Delta Blues Singers (Columbia CL 1654, US LP, 1961). Johnson finally made the *Billboard* charts—and earned a gold record!—with the CD reissue, *Robert Johnson: The Complete Recordings* (Columbia C2K 46222, #80, pop albums, 1990).

September 4, 1962: "How Do You Do It?"

The only reliable chronology, packed with details about the Decca and Parlophone auditions, is Mark Lewisohn, *The Complete Beatles Chronicles* (New York, 1992); Lewisohn's book also reproduces Epstein's letter of December 8, 1961, on p. 54; Epstein's typed playlist for the June 6, 1962, audition, on p. 70; and the early British press clip on the Beatles, describing their resurrection of "original style rock 'n' roll music," on p. 61. All the Paul McCartney quotes come from the Paul McCartney interview in Mark Lewisohn, *The Beatles Recording Sessions* (New York, 1988), p. 7. The critic quoted as calling "Ask Me Why" a pastiche is Ian MacDonald, whose *Revolution in the Head: The Beatles' Records and the Sixties* (New York, 1994) is consistently the shrewdest track-by-track commentary on the music. George Martin's version of history is recorded in *All You Need Is Ears* (New York, 1979), by George Martin with Jeremy Hornsby; see esp. pp. 120–32—all Martin quotes come from this autobiography. A caveat: I have ignored Martin's chronology of events wherever it does not jibe with the documents that Lewisohn has subsequently located. For more on the Coasters, see Bill Millar, *The Coasters* (London, 1974); and also the interview with Leiber and Stoller in the booklet for *The Coasters: 50 Coastin' Classics* (Rhino R2 71090, US CD, 1992).

    Discography: The Beatles, "Love Me Do" (Parlophone R 4949, #17, UK pop, 1962; Tollie 9008, #1, US pop, 1964). The Beatles, "Please Please Me" (Parlophone R 4983, #2, UK pop, 1963; Vee-Jay 581, #3, US pop, 1964). Versions by the Beatles of "Hello Little Girl," "Like Dreamers Do," and other early songs can now be heard on *The Beatles Anthology 1* (Apple CDP 7243 8 34445 2 6, US CD, 1995), which also includes the Coasters songs from the Decca audition, the band's September 4 recording of "How Do You Do It?," and the first up-tempo version of "Please Please Me" recorded on September 11, 1962; a version of "I'll Be on My Way" appears on *The Beatles Live at the BBC* (Apple CDP 7243 8 31796 2 6, US CD,

1994). The canonic early Beatles songs were issued on *Please Please Me* (Parlophone PMC 1202, UK LP, 1963) and *With the Beatles* (Parlophone PMC 1206, UK LP, 1963). In addition, many of Lennon and McCartney's earliest songs were recorded (and made popular) in these months by other Liverpool artists, many of them managed by Brian Epstein: the best collection of this material, *The Songs Lennon and McCartney Gave Away* (EMI NUT 18, UK LP, 1979), includes versions of "Love of the Loved," "Hello Little Girl" and "I'll Be on My Way" by Cilla Black, the Fourmost, Billy J. Kramer and the Dakotas, etc.

April 28, 1963: Andrew Loog Oldham Enters the Crawdaddy Club

The definitive source for the early years of the Rolling Stones is Bill Wyman with Ray Coleman, *Stone Alone: The Story of a Rock and Roll Band* (New York, 1990), which carries the story through the death of Brian Jones in 1968; since Wyman kept a diary as well as a scrapbook of contemporary press clippings, his account is far more reliable than most rock memoirs. The standard biography, still useful, is Philip Norman, *Symphony for the Devil: The Rolling Stones Story* (New York, 1984). I also found useful Barry Miles, *The Rolling Stones: A Visual Documentary* (London, 1984), a comprehensive chronology of tour dates and recording sessions. Also invaluable: David Dalton, *The Rolling Stones: The First Twenty Years* (New York, 1981), a compendium of contemporary press reports and interviews. To be used with more caution are Stanley Booth, *Keith: Standing in the Shadows* (New York, 1995), an uncharacteristically careless account, and Christopher Andersen, *Jagger Unauthorized* (New York, 1993), a gossipy biography that asserts (on the basis of what evidence is, as always, unclear) that Jagger and Oldham slept together in their Hampstead flat. For Oldham himself, see his essay, ". . . A Way of Life," in the booklet for *The Rolling Stones Singles Collection: The London Years* (Abkco 1218-2, US CD, 1989), pp. 66–67; and see, too, the chapter in Johnny Rogan, *Starmakers and Svengalis* (London, 1988), pp. 235–48. Compare George Melly, *Revolt Into Style* (London, 1970), pp. 90–95 (it is Melly who recalls Oldham looking at Jagger "as Sylvester looks at Tweetie Pie"); Melly also has interesting things to say (on pp. 163–66) about Mary Quant and the influence of fashion on British pop.

Discography: The Rolling Stones, "Come On" b/w "I Want to Be

Loved" (Decca F 11675, #21, UK pop, 1963). Muddy Waters, "I Want to Be Loved" (Chess 1596, US, 1955). For the early Stones, the best overview is the three-CD set *The Rolling Stones Singles Collection: The London Years* (Abkco 1218-2, US CD, 1989). Perhaps the most revealing single glimpse of the band live in its earliest R&B days was recorded at the Camden Theatre in London in March, a set of four songs: "Route 66," "Cops and Robbers," "You Better Move On," and "Mona." By the time this was recorded, Jagger sounds less labored and more insouciant in his minstrelsy manner. The complete, unedited Camden set in true stereo appears most recently on a bootleg CD, the Rolling Stones, *Raw Power* (Blue Moon BMCD41), that also has lots of other interesting early stuff.

November 11, 1963: BEATLEMANIA!

The Wagner quote is from the 1872 introduction to "Art and Revolution," in Richard Wagner, *The Art Work of the Future,* trans. W.A. Ellis (Lincoln, NE, 1993), p. 24. Unless otherwise indicated below, all of the quotes in this chapter—from Lennon, McCartney, from various fans, from Ed Sullivan, from the British press, and from the American press—appear in Michael Braun, *"Love Me Do!"—The Beatles' Progress* (London, 1995); originally published in 1964, Braun's book is both the first and best account of Beatlemania. Lennon's later disavowal of the mania surrounding the Beatles is expressed most famously in his 1971 interview with Jann Wenner, reprinted in *The Rolling Stone Interviews, 1967–1980* (New York, 1981), pp. 128–55. Ray Coleman's recollections of first interviewing Lennon in 1963 appear in his biography, *Lennon* (New York, 1984), p. 196. Maureen Cleave is quoted in Philip Norman, *Shout! The Beatles in Their Generation* (New York, 1981), p. 175. For Dezo Hoffmann's first impressions, see Pearce Marchbank, ed., *With the Beatles: The Historic Photographs of Dezo Hoffmann* (London, 1982), p. 10—also a crucial collection of early Beatles iconography. The famous *Times* of London piece of December 27, 1963, is reprinted in Elizabeth Thomson and David Gutman, eds., *The Lennon Companion* (London, 1987), pp. 27–29. Lennon's confession of ignorance about Aeolian cadences came in a 1980 interview in *Playboy* magazine. For the Epstein quote, see *The New Yorker,* "The Talk of the Town," December 28, 1963, p. 23. Dick Clark's story about "She Loves You" appears in Dick Clark and Richard Robinson, *Rock, Roll and Remember* (New York, 1978), p. 326.

The exchange at the British embassy, as well as the quips about crummy musicianship, appear in "George, Paul, Ringo, and John," *Newsweek,* February 24, 1964, pp. 54–57—a slightly different version of the embassy caper also appears in Braun's book. A useful anthology of Beatle quips at press conferences can be found in Barry Miles, ed., *Beatles in Their Own Words* (London, 1978), pp. 47–69. The circus atmosphere of the Beatles' first visit to America is on full view in a video documentary created out of the footage shot by Albert and David Maysles, *The Beatles: The First U.S. Visit* (MPI Home Video, 1990)—an amazing document, and obviously one inspiration for *A Hard Day's Night.* Also visually arresting for this period are the relevant volumes in the eight-cassette video version of *The Beatles Anthology* (Apple Home Video, 1996). For the dustup between George Melly and John Lennon, see Melly, *Revolt Into Style* (London, 1970), p. 77. On the making of *A Hard Day's Night,* see Andrew Yule, *Richard Lester and the Beatles* (New York, 1994), pp. 1–20. The quote from Richard Lester comes from an interview appended to the 1995 video "special edition" of *A Hard Day's Night.* For what the Beatles ad-libbed in the film, see the Voyager CD-ROM of *A Hard Day's Night* (Irvington, NY, 1993), which includes the original script, along with a transcript of the improvised dialogue. As always, dates and statistics have been taken, whenever possible, from Mark Lewisohn, *The Complete Beatles Chronology* (New York, 1992).

Discography: In an effort to delineate the progress of the Beatles, and indicate, however crudely, the time lag between their fame in the U.K. and the explosion of public fascination in the U.S., I have listed every major charting single and album in this period in the U.K. and U.S. in the chronological order of its appearance on the charts. "From Me to You" (Parlophone R 4983, #1, UK pop, April 1963). *Please Please Me* (Parlophone PMC 1202, #1, UK pop albums, April 1963). "She Loves You" (Parlophone R 5055, #1, UK pop, August 1963). *With the Beatles* (Parlophone PMC 1206, #1, UK pop albums, November 1963). "I Want to Hold Your Hand" (Parlophone R 5084, #1, UK pop, December 1963). "I Want to Hold Your Hand" (Capitol 5112, #1, US pop, January 1964). "She Loves You" (Swan 4152, #1, US pop, January 1964). "Please Please Me" b/w "From Me to You" (Vee-Jay 581, #3 b/w #41, US pop, February 1964). *Meet the Beatles!* (Capitol 2047, #1, US pop albums, February 1964). *Introducing the Beatles* (Vee-Jay 1062, #2, US pop albums,

February 1964). "Twist and Shout" (Tollie 9001, #2, US pop, March 1964). "Can't Buy Me Love" (Parlophone R 5114, #1, UK pop; Capitol 5150, #1, US pop, both in March 1964). "Do You Want to Know a Secret" (Vee-Jay 587, #2, US pop, March 1964). "Love Me Do" b/w "P.S. I Love You" (Tollie 9008, #1 b/w #10, US pop, April 1964). *The Beatles' Second Album* (Capitol 2080, #1, US pop albums, April 1964). "A Hard Day's Night" (Parlophone R 5160, #1, UK pop; Capitol 5222, #1, US pop; both in July 1964). *A Hard Day's Night* (Parlophone PMC 1230, #1, UK pop albums, July 1964). *A Hard Day's Night* (United Artists 6366, #1, US pop albums, July 1964). *Something New* (Capitol 2108, #2, US pop albums, August 1964). The most important supplement to these studio recordings is the BBC sessions. A good but small selection has been officially issued on a two-CD set, *The Beatles Live at the BBC* (Apple 7243 8 31796 2 6, US CD, 1994). Any serious historian of the moment, however, will need to dig into the world of bootlegs: for this chapter, I referred to *The Beatles: The Complete BBC Sessions* (Great Dane, 9236/9, Italian CD, 1993); this set, nine CDs in all, is lovingly produced, with an elaborate booklet indicating any missing known broadcasts (of which there are several from the early days). Listening, in order, to these shows is a real ear-opener. Despite the frequent repetition of their own current hits, the series demonstrates the band's offhand mastery of what we today think of as the canonic songs of early rock and roll. It is the Beatles, in these broadcasts even more than in their studio recordings, who effectively created this canon—just as Frank Sinatra (following in the footsteps of Lee Wiley, among others) did something similar for the classic prerock American pop songbook in his Capitol albums from the Fifties.

July 25, 1965: Dylan Goes Electric

For Dylan's much-cited quote on his reaction to the Beatles in February 1964, see Anthony Scaduto, *Bob Dylan* (New York, 1971), pp. 203–4. Dylan's 1958 taped comments are transcribed from *Highway 61 Revisited,* a 1993 television documentary directed by James Marsh (and shared with me by Greil Marcus, who had a taped copy); recounting the story behind Dylan's song, this is one of the best rock documentaries I have ever seen. Dylan's notes for *Another Side of Bob Dylan* are quoted from Bob Dylan, *Lyrics* (New York, 1985), pp. 154, 152 (not all of these notes were used on the jacket). Unless otherwise indicated, all other Dylan quotes come from Robert

Shelton, *No Direction Home: The Life and Music of Bob Dylan* (New York, 1986). Both Scaduto and Shelton have now been supplemented by Clinton Heylin, *Bob Dylan: Behind the Shades* (New York, 1991)—see p. 104 for an account of Dylan being mobbed in London in 1964. See also Clinton Heylin, *Bob Dylan: The Recording Sessions* (New York, 1995), an invaluable annotated guide to *all* of Dylan's studio recordings, including those that are still officially unreleased. Ray Coleman's account of interviewing Dylan in 1964 appears in his biography *Lennon* (New York, 1984), p. 246. For Dylan and the Butterfield band at Newport in 1965, see especially Joe Boyd interviewed by Jonathan Morley, "Newport '65," in John Bauldie, ed., *Wanted Man: In Search of Bob Dylan* (New York, 1990), pp. 57–66. Footage of Dylan's 1965 Newport show appears in "Plugging In," the fourth cassette in *The History of Rock 'n' Roll* (Time-Life Home Video, 1995). For parts of this chapter, I have drawn freely from a previous essay of mine on Dylan, most widely available in Elizabeth Thomson and David Gutman, *The Dylan Companion* (London, 1990), pp. 18–32.

Discography: Following the format used in the Beatlemania section, here is a list of albums and singles in chronological order, through *Highway 61 Revisited*, as they charted in the U.S. and U.K.: *The Freewheelin' Bob Dylan* (Columbia 8786, #22, US pop albums, September 1963). *The Times They Are A-Changin'* (Columbia 8905, #20, US pop albums, March 1964). *The Freewheelin' Bob Dylan* (CBS BPG 62193, #1, UK pop albums, May 1964). *The Times They Are A-Changin'* (CBS BPG 62251, #4, UK pop albums, July 1964). *Bob Dylan* (CBS BPG 62193, #13, UK pop albums, July 1964). *Another Side of Bob Dylan* (Columbia 8993, #43, US pop albums, September 1964). *Another Side of Bob Dylan* (CBS BPG 62515, #8, UK pop albums, November 1964). "The Times They Are A-Changin' " (CBS 201751, #9, UK pop, March 1965). "Subterranean Homesick Blues" (Columbia 43242, #39, US pop; CBS 201753, #9, UK pop, both in April 1965). *Bringing It All Back Home* (Columbia 9128, #6, US pop albums; CBS BPG 62515, #1, UK pop albums, both in May 1965). "Maggie's Farm" (CBS 201781, #22, UK pop, June 1965). "Like a Rolling Stone" (Columbia 43346, #2, US pop, July 1965; CBS 201811, #4, UK pop, August 1965). *Highway 61 Revisited* (Columbia 9189, #3, US pop albums; CBS BPG 62572, #3, UK pop albums, both in October 1965.) I am not a fan of the available Dylan anthologies, especially the five-LP set *Biograph* (Columbia

C5X 38830, US LP, 1985), which mixes the good, the bad, and the ugly in cheerful disregard for chronological development. Without going into hopeless detail, especially about bootlegs, I found four recordings essential for tracking Dylan's metamorphosis from a folk hero into a rock and roll star: *Halloween Mask* (Red Line WPOCM 0888 F 004-2, Italian CD, 1988), a two-CD set, recorded live at Carnegie Hall, October 31, 1964—all acoustic, but you can tell which way the wind is blowing; *Now Ain't the Time for Your Tears* (Swingin' Pig TSP-CD-057, Luxembourg CD, c. 1994), recorded live at the Free Trade Hall in Manchester, U.K., May 7, 1965, again all acoustic, but with the British audience reacting as if to a pop star (which he was by then in the U.K.); *Thin Wild Mercury Music* (Spank SP-105), a collection of studio alternates and outtakes, mainly with electric accompaniment, recorded between January 15, 1965, and January 21, 1966; and—the astonishing apotheosis, at long last officially issued—*Bob Dylan Live 1966: The "Royal Albert Hall" Concert* (Columbia C2K 65759, US CD, 1998)—a two-CD set of Dylan (in fact recorded live in Manchester on May 17), one CD acoustic, one CD with the Hawks, all in stereo: this was the kind of concert that transfixed aspiring British musicians like David Bowie (for whom, see the relevant chapter in this book).

October–November 1965: Rubber Soul

John Lennon's comment about Bob Dylan's cap is recorded in Michael Braun, *"Love Me Do!"—The Beatles' Progress* (London, 1964), p. 83. The meeting between Dylan and the Beatles in New York in August of 1964 is recounted in a variety of places: a particularly detailed version appears in Peter Brown and Steven Gaines, *The Love You Make: An Insider's Story of the Beatles* (New York, 1983), pp. 155–58. Paul McCartney recalled the evening in an interview printed in *Mojo*, November 1993, the source for the "meaning of life" revelation. The most cogent analysis of the relevant songs, by a musically literate writer who also appreciates the larger context of rock music that inspired the band, is *Revolution in the Head: The Beatles' Records and the Sixties* by Ian MacDonald (New York, 1994). An interesting academic essay on *Rubber Soul* by ethnomusicologist Terence J. O'Grady is reprinted in Elizabeth Thomson and David Gutman, *The Lennon Companion* (London, 1987), pp. 69–71. McCartney has recorded his debt to James Jamerson in Dr. Licks, *Standing in the Shadows of Motown: The Life and Music of*

Legendary Bassist James Jamerson (Wynnewood, PA, 1989), p. 102. Lennon's comments about the frustrations for the Beatles in concert, and also about the composition of "In My Life," appear in Ray Coleman, *Lennon* (New York, 1984), p. 299. George Martin's comment about *Rubber Soul* appears in Mark Lewisohn, *The Beatles: Recording Sessions* (New York, 1988), p. 69. The McCartney quotes about the importance of pot, and about Dylan's reaction to the Beatles' music in May 1966, is from an interview about Dylan's influence on the Beatles by Paul Du Noyer, in John Bauldie, ed., *Wanted Man: In Search of Bob Dylan* (New York, 1990), p. 72. The impact of *Rubber Soul* on the Bay Area's proto-hippies is recounted in Charles Perry, *The Haight-Ashbury: A History* (New York, 1984), pp. 37–38.

Discography: The Beatles, *Help!* (Parlophone PMC 1255, #1, UK pop albums; Capitol 2386, #1, US pop albums, both in August 1965). The Beatles, *Rubber Soul* (Parlophone PMC 1267, #1, UK pop albums; Capitol 2442, #1, US pop albums, both in December 1965). Outtakes and alternate versions appear on *The Beatles Anthology 2* (Apple CDP 7243 8 34448 2 3, US CD, 1996).

5 Break on Through

December 4, 1965: The Acid Test

The primary source remains one of the great pieces of Sixties reportage, Tom Wolfe, *The Electric Kool-Aid Acid Test* (New York, 1968), esp. Chapter 18, "Cosmo's Tasmanian Deviltry," pp. 203–21 —among other things, Wolfe's account is a tour de force of subtle moral commentary. Other sources include Sandy Troy, *One More Saturday Night* (New York, 1991), pp. 1–10 (pretty good illustrations); Sandy Troy, *Captain Trips: A Biography of Jerry Garcia* (New York, 1994), esp pp. 70–72. For oral history, the book to read is Robert Greenfield, *Dark Star: An Oral Biography of Jerry Garcia* (New York, 1996), pp. 3–86: this is the most atmospheric, and authoritative, of the Garcia books. One of the Rock Scully quotes comes from *Dark Star,* pp. 76–77; another comes from Rock Scully with David Dalton, *Living With the Dead: Twenty Years on the Bus with Garcia and the Grateful Dead* (New York, 1996), p. 10. I admire Robert Stone's heartfelt elegy, "End of the Beginning," in *Garcia* (New York, 1995), pp. 32–34. On the history of LSD and its impact on the Sixties, see Jay Stevens, *Storming Heaven: LSD and the American Dream* (New York, 1987), an intelligent and spirited general account, obviously written by someone who knows what he is talking about. For Kesey and the Rolling Stones, see the accounts given in both *Symphony for the Devil* (New York, 1984) by Philip Norman (on p. 165) and *Stone Alone* (New York, 1990) by Bill Wyman with Ray Coleman (on p. 358); David Dalton, in *The Rolling Stones,* has Jones and Richards dropping the acid the night before, at the Acid Test in San Jose, but this seems highly unlikely, since none of the interviews with participants that I've seen mention any of the Stones being there.

Discography: Though a few early recordings of the Dead exist, I haven't heard them. Still worth a listen is the first official studio album, *The Grateful Dead* (Warner 1689, #73, US pop albums, 1967). The only recording that I think captures the band as I heard it in its psychedelic heyday is *Two From the Vault* (Grateful Dead Records, GTDCD40162, US CD, 1992), a recording of shows held on August 23 and 24, 1968, at the Shrine Auditorium in Los Angeles; if you buy only one Dead CD, this is the one. This is not the place for a complete discography of the Bay Area acid rock scene: Joel Selvin has an excellent one in his book *The Summer of Love* (New York, 1994). Still, worth hearing just to recapture the crazy musical mood of the moment: *The Amazing Charlatans* (Big Beat CDWIKD 138, UK CD, 1996), an anthology of the scene's founding band; and the three-CD set *Jefferson Airplane Loves You* (RCA 07863 61110-2, US CD, 1992), which apart from the expected hits has some powerfully freewheeling, previously unreleased live material, recorded at the Fillmore in May 1967.

February 8–13, 1966: Andy Warhol, Up-Tight

I have relied extensively on information in Andy Warhol and Pat Hackett, *POPism: The Warhol 60s* (New York, 1980), a terrific, sometimes creepy memoir, and the source of various Warhol quotes: see pp. 69 ("everything went young"), 33 (on amphetamine), 113 ("Art just wasn't fun"), 56 ("too gifted"), 63 ("the big social thrust"), 7 ("hand gesture"), 134 ("the Pop idea"), 63 (on amphetamine keeping life amusing), 157 ("looked just like a stage set"), 50 ("the meaning goes away"). David Bourdon, *Warhol* (New York, 1989), is a lavishly illustrated overview, written from a sympathetic, yet skeptical, point of view. Photos are collected in Stephen Shore and Lynne Tillman, *The Velvet Years: Warhol's Factory, 1965–67*

(New York, 1995), which is also the source of my quotes from Sterling Morrison—see p. 89. For the Velvet Underground, the best source remains Victor Bockris and Gerard Malanga, *Up-Tight: The Velvet Underground Story* (New York, 1983), a labor of love, preferable in its heavily illustrated first edition; some more details appear in Victor Bockris, *Transformer: The Lou Reed Story* (New York, 1994). For Nico, see Richard Williams, liner notes to Nico's album *The Marble Index* (Elektra 74029-2, US CD reissue, 1991); and James Young, *Nico: The End* (Woodstock, New York, 1993)—a stunning chronicle of the road life of the aging rock star, and a truly harrowing look into the music's heart of darkness. For La Monte Young, see the liner notes to *Second Dream of the High-Tension Line Stepdown Transformer, from the Four Dreams of China* (Gramavision R2-79467, US CD, 1991) and also the liner notes to *The Well-Tuned Piano 81X25* (Gramavision 18-8701-1, US LP, 1987); the entry on Young by Norman Lebrecht in his *Companion to 20th Century Music* (New York, 1992) is characteristically incisive and witty. For gossip, see Legs McNeil and Gillian McCain, *Please Kill Me: The Uncensored Oral History of Punk* (New York, 1996), pp. 3–24: my quote from Cale appears on p. 9.

Discography: The Velvet Underground and Nico (Verve 5008, #171, US pop albums, 1967). The 1965 home demo tapes have been reissued as disc one of the five-CD set *The Velvet Underground: Peel Slowly and See* (Polydor 31452 7887-2, US CD, 1996), an exemplary chronicle of the band's career. For Nico, the key albums from this period are *Chelsea Girl* (1967; reissued on Polydor 835 209-2, US CD), and her first two albums with Cale, *The Marble Index* (Elektra 74029, US LP, 1968; reissued with additional material on Elektra 74029-2, US CD, 1991), and *Desertshore* (Reprise 6424, US LP, 1970, reissued on Reprise 6424-2, US CD, 1993).

June 1, 1967: Sgt. Pepper's Lonely Hearts Club Band

For the Beatles in their acid phase, see above all the fine essay by Barry Miles, chopped up as part of James Henke and Parke Puterbaugh, eds., *I Want to Take You Higher: The Psychedelic Era, 1965–1969* (San Francisco, 1997): Miles, a proprietor of Indica, saw it all as it happened—his is a trustworthy and sympathetic account. Oddly enough, his quasi-authorized biography of Paul McCartney, *Many Years From Now* (New York, 1997) is not nearly as lively, though it does have a lot of useful information on this period. Compare the typically careless, but not unperceptive, account in Albert Goldman, *The Lives of John Lennon* (New York, 1988), pp. 195–99. And see, too, Peter Brown and Steven Gaines, *The Love You Make: An Insider's Story of the Beatles* (New York, 1983), which is mean-spirited, but often has the ring of truth. For the making of *Sgt. Pepper* from the producer's point of view, see George Martin with William Pearson, *With a Little Help From My Friends: The Making of Sgt. Pepper* (New York, 1994). For an analysis of the music, I turned repeatedly to Ian MacDonald, *Revolution in the Head: The Beatles' Records and the Sixties* (New York, 1994). For Peter Blake as a figure in postwar British art, see Robert Hewison, *Too Much: Art and Society in the Sixties, 1960–1975* (London, 1986); for Blake and the Beatles, see Martin's book on *Sgt. Pepper,* Chapter 14; Gold-man's Lennon biography, pp. 259–61 (a very funny and caustic ac-count, based on an interview with Blake); and also Simon Frith, *Art Into Pop* (London, 1987); Blake also contributes some comments to the booklet accompanying the CD reissue of *Sgt. Pepper.* For the re-ception of *Sgt. Pepper,* I rely on my own memories of the summer of 1967, which I started in L.A. and ended in Athens, Greece; but cf. Langdon Winner's much-quoted contemporary observation: "At the time *Sgt. Pepper* was released I happened to be driving across coun-try on Interstate 80. In each city where I stopped for gas or food— Laramie, Ogallala, Moline, South Bend—the melodies wafted in from some far-off transistor radio or portable hi-fi. It was the most amazing thing I've ever heard." This is no exaggeration: it's a state-ment of plain fact.

Discography: The Beatles, *Revolver* (Parlophone PMC 7009, #1, UK pop albums; Capitol 2576, #1, US pop albums, 1966). The Bea-tles, "Strawberry Fields Forever" b/w "Penny Lane" (Parlophone R 5570; #2, UK pop; Capitol 5810, #1 b/w #8, US pop, both in Febru-ary 1967). The Beatles, *Sgt. Pepper's Lonely Hearts Club Band* (Par-lophone PCS 7027, #1, UK pop albums; Capitol 2653, #1, US pop albums, both in June 1967). For outtakes etc. get *The Beatles An-thology 2* (Apple CDP 7243 8 34448 2 3, US CD, 1996)—these are most interesting in the case of "Strawberry Fields." To hear what McCartney wanted his electronic loops to sound like, it is worth lis-tening to his favorite piece of electronic music in these years, Karl-heinz Stockhausen's *Gesang der Junglinge,* completed in 1956 and available currently in Volume 3 of the Stockhausen Gesamtausgabe, *Elektronische Musik* (Stockhausen-Verlag 3, German CD, 1991).

June 16–18, 1967: Monterey Pop

A good place to start is Stephen K. Peeples, liner notes to the 1992 *Monterey Pop* CD reissue, and also the various remarks by performers at the festival recorded in that set's lavish book; in conjunction with the crystal-clear live recordings that were cleared for reissue (a quarter century later, the Grateful Dead still would have nothing to do with Lou Adler, so their set is omitted), the reissue offers a comprehensive sonic overview (Rhino R70596, US CD, 1992—a 1997 reissue omits the large book). In addition, there are now three documentaries that have been pulled from D.A. Pennebaker's footage: the original (and still unsurpassed) rock festival documentary, *Monterey Pop* (which reveals Woodstock, the festival and the film, as the bloated mud-bath they both were); *Jimi Hendrix at Monterey,* an hour-long tape built around Hendrix's still shocking performance; and *Shake: Otis Redding Plays Monterey,* which is the most entertainingly professional stretch of music-making the festival has bequeathed to posterity. The best behind-the-scenes account is Joel Selvin, photos by Jim Marshall, *Monterey Pop* (San Francisco, 1994). Cf. Joel Selvin, *Summer of Love* (New York, 1994), who offers incisive portraits of Chet Helms and Janis Joplin. Chet Helms' quote about "irresponsible dollars" appears in Joan Didion's piece in the *Saturday Evening Post,* reprinted as the title essay in her book *Slouching Towards Bethlehem* (New York, 1968). Robert Christgau's *Esquire* essay on Monterey was reprinted in his book *Any Old Way You Choose It* (New York, 1972). The remarks about Hendrix by Jerry Wexler appear in Jerry Wexler and David Ritz, *Rhythm and the Blues* (New York, 1993), pp. 197–98. The thumbnail biography of Jimi Hendrix is based on that offered by Charles Schaar Murray in his peerless study *Crosstown Traffic: Jimi Hendrix and the Rock 'n' Roll Revolution* (New York, 1989).

Discography: The Monterey International Pop Festival (Rhino R70596, US CD, 1992): this four-CD set has lots more music than the movie, and includes all of Janis Joplin's hair-raising first run-through of her set with Big Brother and the Holding Company. Jimi Hendrix's first album was out by the time of Monterey, and it still sounds stunning, especially the 1997 CD version remastered by Hendrix's original engineer, Eddie Kramer: *Are You Experienced?* (MCA 11602, US CD, 1997). For the pop version of the hippie utopia, it is hard to beat listening to the Mamas and the Papas in their prime: *Greatest Hits* (MCA 11740, US CD, 1998) is a good place to start. I also recommend the aptly titled *Psychedelic Pop* (BMG 75517 49507 2, US CD, 1996), which, besides obvious Top 40 hits like "White Rabbit" and "Eight Miles High" and "Incense and Peppermints," has a really esoteric item featuring Jimi Hendrix playing, with a UK group called Eire Apparent, "The Clown." Wow.

June 7, 1968: "Sympathy for the Devil"

For the Stones' part of the story, I relied on Philip Norman, *Symphony for the Devil* (New York, 1984), supplemented by Bill Wyman with Ray Coleman, *Stone Alone* (New York, 1990). For Godard, I referred to Richard Roud, *Godard* (London, 1970); Tom Milne, ed., *Godard on Godard* (New York, 1968); Vincent Canby, "What Godard Hath Wrought," *The New York Times*, March 29, 1970; and Andrew Sarris, "Films in Focus," *The Village Voice*, April 30, 1970. For the wider youth rebellion of the Sixties, I am drawing implicitly from my own experience, and also from the detailed account of the political, and specifically American, side of the story, in a previous book, *"Democracy Is in the Streets": From Port Huron to the Siege of Chicago* (New York, 1987). For Altamont as myth and fact, see Greil Marcus, "Myth and Misquotation," in his book *The Dustbin of History* (Cambridge, MA, 1995), pp. 36–46. Marcus also includes a variant account of what happened from another eyewitness, Stanley Booth, a writer responsible for the most intelligent and beautiful paean to the satanic majesty of the Stones on the Altamont tour, *Dance With the Devil: The Rolling Stones and Their Times* (New York, 1984), which opens with an atmospheric epigraph from Norman Mailer: "We want the heats of the orgy and not its murder, the warmth of pleasure without the grip of pain, and so the future threatens a nightmare, and we continue to waste ourselves."

Discography: The Rolling Stones, "Jumpin' Jack Flash" (Decca F 12782, #1, UK pop, May 1968; London 910, #3, US pop, July 1968). The Rolling Stones, *Beggar's Banquet* (Decca SKL 4955, #3, UK pop albums; London 539, #5, US pop albums; both in December 1968).

1970–1971: What's Going On

For the life of Marvin Gaye, the primary source is David Ritz, *Divided Soul: The Life of Marvin Gaye* (New York, 1985), and also Ritz's many subsequent liner notes for various compilations of Gaye's work. See especially Ritz's notes for the 1994 CD reissue, in

Motown's "Marvin Gaye Edition," of *What's Going On*. For Motown more generally, I largely relied on Nelson George, *Where Did Our Love Go?: The Rise and Fall of the Motown Sound* (New York, 1985); my account of the making of the album *What's Going On* follows the one given (on pp. 175–79) by George, who interviewed several of the songwriters and session musicians (Ritz, by contrast, seems to have interviewed only Gaye about the album). See also Berry Gordy, *To Be Loved: The Music, the Magic, the Memories of Motown* (New York, 1994), and Raynoma Gordy Singleton, *Berry, Me, and Motown: The Untold Story* (Chicago, 1990). Last but not least, there is a great deal of invaluable material to be found in Dr. Licks, *Standing in the Shadows of Motown: The Life and Music of Legendary Bassist James Jamerson* (Wynnewood, PA, 1989).

Discography: Gladys Knight and the Pips, "I Heard It Through the Grapevine" (Soul 35039, #1, rhythm and blues; #2, pop, 1967). Marvin Gaye, "I Heard It Through the Grapevine" (Tamla 54176, #1, rhythm and blues; #1, pop). The Originals, "Baby, I'm for Real" (Soul 35066, #1, rhythm and blues; #14, pop, 1969). The Originals, "The Bells" (Soul 35069, #4, rhythm and blues; #12, pop, 1970). The Originals, "We Can Make It Baby" (Soul 35074, #20, rhythm and blues; #74, pop, 1970). Marvin Gaye, "What's Going On" (Tamla 54201, #1, rhythm and blues; #2, pop, 1971). Marvin Gaye, *What's Going On* (Tamla 310, #6, pop albums, 1971). For an anthology of the Moonglows that includes Gaye's few sessions with the fabled doo-wop group, try *Blue Velvet: The Ultimate Collection* (MCA Chess CHD2-9345, US CD, 1993). Gaye's ballad sessions with Bobby Scott exist in several forms: they were first made available on the four-CD set, *The Marvin Gaye Collection* (Motown MOTD4-6311, US CD, 1990). The same songs were then issued again, with completely different vocal tracks (and several additional alternate versions), on *Vulnerable* (Motown 314530786-2, US CD, 1997). Both of these reissues could have been done with more class and thoroughness. Better is Berry Gordy's official monument to his own genius, *Hitsville USA: The Motown Singles Collection, 1959–1971* (Motown 37746363122, US CD, 1992), 104 songs on four CDs.

July 3, 1971: The End

In writing about Jim Morrison and the Doors, I have used John Densmore, *Riders on the Storm* (New York, 1990), to confirm stories that also appear in Jerry Hopkins and Danny Sugerman, *No One Here Gets Out Alive* (updated mass market edition: New York, 1995), a book that seems generally trustworthy. See, too, the methodically compiled chronology by Greg Shaw, *The Doors on the Road* (New York, 1997), which includes day-by-day information, including (among other interesting tidbits) a verbatim transcript of what Morrison was caught saying on tape at the infamous Miami show (the most controversial of his comments, alas—about the crowd's desire to see his cock—were uttered after the chaos in the crowd forced the audience member to shut off the tape recorder). There is an active market in quasi-authorized Doors tapes, so I have been able to hear the tape, such as it exists, of the Dinner Key show in Miami on March 1, 1969 (Volume 15 of *The Doors: Live Shows* series). See Joan Didion, *The White Album* (New York, 1979), pp. 21–25, for revised excerpts from a piece first published in 1968 in *Esquire*; and see, too, *The Doors: The Complete Lyrics* (New York, 1991). Bob Seymore, *The End: The Death of Jim Morrison* (New York, 1990), is generally worthless, but revealing, since it is the work of a man obsessed. I also referred to Jan E. Morrison, "Miami," electronically published in August 1997 on the Internet (at www.doors.com); and Frank Lisciandro, *Morrison: A Feast of Friends* (New York, 1991), a persuasive portrait of an enigma from the point of view of countless associates and friends, whose comments are offered in the form of a collective oral history. Quotes, in order, are from: Jim Morrison, promotional (auto)biography for Elektra Records, distributed as a press release with review copies of the first Doors album in 1967, p. 1; Danny Sugerman, "Foreword" to the 1995 edition of Hopkins and Sugerman, *No One Here Gets Out Alive*, p. xvii; Friedrich Nietzsche, *The Birth of Tragedy*, trans. Walter Kaufmann (New York, 1967), #2, p. 39; the Ray Manzarek quotes, and several subsequent Jim Morrison quotes (including "I think there's a whole region"), all come from the first major journalistic essay about the Doors: Digby Diehl, "Jim Morrison and the Demonic Psyche," *Eye*, April 1968; Morrison's quote on Miami as a culmination appears in Ben Fong-Torres, "Jim Morrison's Got the Blues," *Rolling Stone*, March 4, 1971; John Densmore's remarks on Miami, and on Morrison's long-term impact, both appear in *Riders on the Storm*, pp. 212, 272.

Discography: There are only one and a half Doors albums that belong in a basic rock and roll record collection: *The Doors* (Elektra

74007, #2, pop albums, 1967); and half of *Strange Days* (Elektra 74014, #3, pop albums, 1967). From there, it's all downhill. But listeners can judge for themselves. Storied as a live act, they were often quite mediocre live, as witness the selection of material that has belatedly been released officially in *The Doors Box Set* (Elektra 62123-2, US CD, 1997), four CDs of hits, plus several hours of the Doors live: too much.

6 Stairway to Heaven

July 9, 1972: Ziggy Stardust and the Spiders From Mars

There are several credible biographies of Bowie. For the early years, the best in my judgment is *David Bowie: Living on the Brink* (New York, 1997), by George Tremlett, a British journalist for *New Musical Express,* among other papers, who interviewed Bowie a number of times in the 1960s, before he became famous. For the Ziggy period, the richest source is Henry Edwards and Tony Zanetta, *Stardust: The David Bowie Story* (New York, 1986). Zanetta was one of the few people close to Bowie from 1972 through 1974. Additional information—including the claim that Bowie saw Dylan at the Royal Albert Hall—comes from Jerry Hopkins, *Bowie* (New York, 1974), which seems generally reliable, though plodding. For the show on July 8, see Peter Holmes, "Gay Rock," *Gay News,* July 1972; and Ray Coleman, "A Star Is Born," *Melody Maker,* July 15, 1972. For Bowie's ambitions: John Mendelsohn, "David Bowie? Pantomime Rock?," *Rolling Stone,* April 1, 1971 ("music is the Pierrot"). The *Melody Maker* interview—Michael Watts, "Oh You Pretty Thing," January 22, 1972—has been reprinted along with the pieces by Holmes and Coleman in Elizabeth Thomson and David Gutman, eds., *The Bowie Companion* (London, 1995). For Angie's version of her makeover of Bowie, see Angie Bowie, *Free Spirit* (London, 1981), pp. 80–81. Harvey Molloy's memoir, "Ziggy '72: A Catalogue of Lost Objects," first came to my attention when it was posted on the unofficial "The Ziggy Stardust Companion" Web site maintained by Mike Harvey at http://ourworld.compuserve.com/homepages/mbh/start.htm.contents; a revised draft was kindly supplied by Mr. Molloy himself, who in 1998 made his living as an architect in New Zealand.

Discography: Listed in chronological order are the relevant recordings that charted in the U.K. and U.S., through *Aladdin Sane,* the last album done before Bowie retired the Ziggy character: David Bowie,

"Space Oddity" (Philips BF 1801, #5, UK pop, September 1969). "Changes" (RCA 0605, #66, US pop, April 1972). *Hunky Dory* (RCA 4623, #93, US pop albums, April 1972). "Starman" (RCA 2199, #10, UK pop, June 1972; RCA 0719, #65, US pop, July 1972). *The Rise and Fall of Ziggy Stardust and the Spiders From Mars* (RCA 8287, #5, UK pop albums, July 1972; RCA 4702, #75, US pop albums, June 1972). "John, I'm Only Dancing" (RCA 2263, #12, UK pop, September 1972). *Hunky Dory* (RCA 8244, #3, UK pop albums, September 1972). *Space Oddity* (RCA 4813, #17, UK pop albums; RCA 4813, #16, US pop albums, both in November 1972). *The Man Who Sold the World* (RCA 4816, #26, UK pop albums; RCA 4816, #105, US pop albums, both in November 1972). "The Jean Genie" (RCA 2302, #2 UK pop, December 1972; RCA 0838, #71, US pop, November 1972). "Space Oddity" (RCA 0876, #15, US pop, January 1973). "Drive-In Saturday" (RCA 2352, #3, UK pop, April 1973). *Aladdin Sane* (RCA Victor RS 1001, #1, UK pop albums; RCA 4852, #17, US pop albums, both in May 1973). *David Bowie Sound + Vision* (Ryko RCD 90120/21/22, US CD, 1989) offers a good overview of his career, though it skimps on *Ziggy* material in favor of rarities (including Bowie's fey version of "Around and Around"). The crucial live disc to hear is *David Bowie Santa Monica '72* (Mainman Golden Years GY002, UK CD, 1994), from tapes of a concert that was broadcast. If you want to hear Anthony Newley's otherwise unbelievable incarnation as a rock idol—and the best evidence of his extraordinary influence on Bowie's singing style—try *Anthony Newley's Greatest Hits* (Deram 820 694-2, UK CD, 1990).

1972–1973: The Harder They Come

Of books on reggae, a good place to start, in my view, is Steve Barrow and Peter Dalton, *Reggae: The Rough Guide* (London, 1997). Also worthwhile is Lloyd Bradley, *Reggae on CD: The Essential Guide* (London, 1996); and a useful anthology edited by Chris Potash, *Reggae, Rasta, Revolution: Jamaican Music From Ska to Dub* (New York, 1997). Some details about Jimmy Cliff come from a Warner Bros. press kit dated September 1978 and prepared to publicize the release of Cliff's album *Give Thanx*. The passage about *The Harder They Come* from *The Hollywood Reporter* appears in Volume 223, Number 44, Wednesday, November 15, 1972. The premiere is described by Henzell in the four pages of "background information" distributed with the American press kit for *The Harder*

They Come soundtrack album (Mango SMAS-7400, 1972), and also in a short item on the film published in the column "Scenes" in *The Village Voice,* January 11, 1973. The Stephen Davis quotes come from the pioneering book he produced with photographer Peter Simon, *Reggae Bloodlines: In Search of the Music and Culture of Jamaica* (London, 1977), pp. 3–4. For Marley as "a visionary Rasta rebel," and also the *New Musical Express* passage, see Stephen Davis, *Bob Marley* (New York, 1985), pp. 150, 169.

Discography: Jimmy Cliff, *The Harder They Come* (Mango SMAS-7400, US LP, 1972). The first two volumes of the *Tighten Up* series have been reissued as *Tighten Up Vols. 1 & 2* (Trojan CDTRL 306, UK CD, 1992). Bob Marley's myth-making concert in London is available on *Bob Marley and the Wailers Live!* (Tuff Gong 422-846 203-2, US CD reissue of the 1975 album). The best introduction to reggae is *Tougher Than Tough: The Story of Reggae* (Mango 162-539 935-2/518 399-2, US and UK CD, 1993), a four-CD set with extensive notes.

August 1, 1973: American Graffiti

The various quotes from George Lucas' original screen treatment come from Dale Pollock, *Skywalking: The Life and Films of George Lucas* (Hollywood, 1990), which is also the source of most biographical information. The long quote about Vietnam and "what schmucks we are" appears in Peter Biskind, *Easy Riders, Raging Bulls* (New York, 1998), a juicy insider's account, in the words of the subtitle, of "how the sex-drugs-and-rock-'n'-roll generation saved Hollywood": see p. 235 ("saved," one hopes, is used with some irony). Other quotes from Lucas come from Larry Sturhahn, "The Filming of *American Graffiti*: An Interview With Director George Lucas," *Filmmakers' Newsletter,* Volume 7, Number 5, March 1974.

Discography: Oldies but Goodies (Original Sound 5001, #12, US pop albums, 1959). *American Graffiti* (MCA 8001, #7, US pop albums, 1973).

October 1975: Rock and Roll Future

"Rock and roll came to my house": interview with Robert Duncan, *Creem,* quoted in Dave Marsh, *Born to Run* (New York, 1979), p. 74. "Both of us had seen": Dave Marsh, *Glory Days: Bruce Springsteen in the 1980s* (New York, 1987), p. xiv. "On a night when I needed to feel young": Jon Landau, *The Real Paper,* May 22, 1974, quoted in

Marsh, *Born to Run,* p. 103. Landau's comments on rock and art, and rock as a folk music, come from his book of collected essays, *It's Too Late to Stop Now* (San Francisco, 1972), pp. 155, 132. "He has far more depth": Jon Landau, quoted in Maureen Orth, "Making of a Rock Star," *Newsweek,* October 27, 1975, p. 60. For the Bottom Line showcase dates, see Dave Marsh, "A Rock 'Star Is Born' Performance Review," *Rolling Stone,* September 25, 1975; and John Rockwell, "New Dylan From New Jersey? It Might as Well Be Springsteen," *Rolling Stone,* October 9, 1975. "His ultimate embrace of music as business": Fred Goodman, *The Mansion on the Hill: Dylan, Young, Geffen, Springsteen, and the Head-on Collision of Rock and Commerce* (New York, 1997), p. 351; Goodman's book is one of the most detailed, and well-informed, accounts to date of how the business of rock and roll has been conducted since the 1960s, though it is not always fair to Springsteen and Landau and also adheres to an unrealistic standard of moral purity in the music business. I should add that in 1974 and 1975, I worked on the staff of *The Real Paper,* where I was friendly with both Dave Marsh and Jon Landau; in addition, I should make clear my personal indebtedness to Landau, who, along with Greil Marcus, was instrumental in my being hired, in 1975, as the original editor of *The Rolling Stone Illustrated History of Rock & Roll.* I wrote nothing in these months myself about Springsteen only because Landau and Marsh had already provided ample coverage. In recounting the sense of yearning for a rock Messiah, I do not mean to pretend that I did not labor under similar illusions: most of us did who were writing about rock in those days.

Discography: Springsteen's commercial breakthrough came in the summer and fall of 1975, when each of his first three albums at last made the *Billboard* charts, as indicated: *Greetings From Asbury Park, N.J.* (Columbia 31903, #60, US pop albums, July 1975). *The Wild, the Innocent and the E Street Shuffle* (Columbia 32432, #59, US pop albums, July 1975). *Born to Run* (Columbia 33795, #3, US pop albums, September 1975). Key live shows from this period, available on bootlegs: *Bruce Springsteen: The Greatest Performance, Westbury, NY, Westbury Music Fair, February 23, 1975* (Parrot, US CD, n.d.); *Bruce Springsteen/Live* (Coral NR 909-2, Brazilian LP, n.d.)—this is the version, on vinyl, of the Bottom Line show of August 15, 1975, that I referred to; and *Ain't Nobody Here From Billboard Tonight* (Moonlight ML 9619/20, Czech CD, 1996), from a show broadcast from the Roxy Theatre in L.A. on October 17, 1975.

December 2, 1976: "Anarchy in the U.K."

The basic source is Jon Savage, *England's Dreaming: Anarchy, Sex Pistols, Punk Rock and Beyond* (London, 1991)—exhaustive, savvy, thoroughly researched, it is one of the very best historical books on rock ever published: on Bill Grundy and the *Today* show, and its aftermath, see esp. pp. 257–75; McLaren's credo ("Be childish," etc.) was composed for an experimental film produced in 1970—see p. 44; for the quote from *Music Week* ("THE NEXT BIG THING"), see p. 279; Savage's sarcastic recipe for punk success ("A fussy drummer," etc.) is on p. 301; for "flies in the amber of notoriety," see p. 273. For an essentially sanguine assessment of punk rock and its larger historical importance, see Greil Marcus, *Lipstick Traces: A Secret History of the 20th Century* (Cambridge, MA, 1989); his comments on the response to "Anarchy in the U.K." appear on p. 437. "The vanguard of a new youth culture": *Melody Maker* critic Caroline Coon, writing in her oddly titled book *1988: The New Wave Punk Rock Explosion* (London, 1977), p. 5—this was one of the first books about the phenomenon; the Vicious quote ("go twang") is on p. 60. "Warhol monster mash": Peter York, "Post-Punk Mortem," originally published in *Harpers & Queen,* July 1977, reprinted in York, *Style Wars* (London, 1980), p. 134. "So many of the traditional ingredients": Alan Lewis, star single review of "Anarchy in the U.K.," *Sounds,* November 27, 1976. "Once he wanted me to go to Madame Tussauds": Vivienne Westwood, quoted in Shane Watson, "My Brilliant Career," *UK Elle,* November 1995, p. 58. For Chris Thomas and his contribution to the overall sound of the Pistols on record, see the chapter on Thomas in John Tobler and Stuart Grundy, *The Record Producers* (London, 1982), pp. 227–44. The Elvis Costello quote comes from an interview conducted for Andrew Solt and Jeffrey Peisch, producers, *The History of Rock 'n' Roll* (Time-Life Home Video, 1995), Episode 9, "Punk." The best anthology of vintage photos and press clips is Ray Stevenson, editor, *Sex Pistols File* (London, 1978). For the view from the lead singer's standpoint, see John Lydon with Keith and Kent Zimmerman, *Rotten* (New York, 1995). For a knowing, and subtle, sociological analysis, see Dick Hebdige's now classic *Subculture: The Meaning of Style* (London, 1979), esp. pp. 90–99, on the dynamics of "incorporation." And last but not least, for an insider's demystifying account of how the post-punk alternative rock game is played, see Steve Albini, "The Problem With Music," in Thomas Frank and Matt Weiland, eds., *Commodify Your Dissent* (New York, 1997), pp. 164–76 (Albini has produced Nirvana, among other indie bands).

Discography: Sex Pistols, "Anarchy in the U.K." (EMI 2566, #38, UK pop, December 1976). Sex Pistols, "God Save the Queen" (Virgin VS 181, #2, UK pop, June 1977). Sex Pistols, "Pretty Vacant" (Virgin VS 184, #6, UK pop, July 1977). Sex Pistols, "Holidays in the Sun" (Virgin VS 191, #8, UK pop, October 1977). Sex Pistols, *Never Mind the Bollocks Here's the Sex Pistols* (Virgin V 2086, #1, UK pop albums, November 1977; #106, US pop albums, December 1977). There's a confusing gray market of Pistols demos and live shows. Worth hearing is the original, unproduced version of the album, widely bootlegged in England as *Spunk;* also worth hearing is a live show recorded on September 24, 1976, at the 76 Club in Burton on Trent. Both items are on a two-CD set, *Pretty Vacant* (Receiver RRDCD 004, UK CD, 1991). For a sense of the scene's early atmosphere, listen to *The Roxy London WC2 (Jan–Apr 77)* (Harvest SHSP 4069, #24, UK pop albums, 1977). For those in search of more tips, Jon Savage's book, cited above, includes a discerning and thorough discography.

August 16, 1977: My Way

For the first reports on Presley's death, and the mood on Memphis on the day Elvis died, as well as carefully documented details about the autopsy and how the truth about Presley's death was ferreted out, see Charles C. Thompson II and James P. Cole, *The Death of Elvis: What Really Happened* (New York, 1991): the two men played a pivotal role in reporting the Presley drug abuse story for ABC-TV's *20/20* news program in 1979; for the rumors that were swirling in Memphis immediately after the autopsy, see p. 54. I have also drawn from the Associated Press story, carried across the country, which was modified as August 17 went on, using as my source the morning and evening editions of the *Austin American-Statesman* (I was living in Texas at the time, and this was the local paper); the afternoon edition of the AP story carried the interview with Sonny West conducted by columnist Bob Greene for the *Chicago Sun-Times.* Also a good gauge of reaction at the time are the newsweekly articles, by Jay Cocks for *Time* and Maureen Orth for *Newsweek,* both reprinted in Kevin Quain, ed., *The Elvis Reader* (New York, 1992), pp. 57–67. "He is addicted to the study of the Bible": Red West, Sonny West, Dave Hebler, as told to Steve Dunleavy, *Elvis:*

What Happened? (New York, 1977), p. 157. "I was nonplussed": Nick Tosches, "Elvis in Death," in Quain, ed., *The Elvis Reader,* p. 273. "He didn't look cool": Roy Blount, Jr., "Elvis!," from *Esquire,* December 1983, reprinted in Quain, ed., *The Elvis Reader,* p. 75. For Elvis in Kalamazoo, see Pete Cooke, "I've Seen Elvis and He's Alive and Well!," originally published in *Weekly World News,* June 28, 1988, reprinted in Quain, ed., *The Elvis Reader,* pp. 82–83; 1988 is the year that such stories began to proliferate: see, e.g., the front page of the *National Examiner* for October 4, 1988, reprinted in Greil Marcus, *Dead Elvis* (New York, 1991), p. 24. Presley's 1977 version of "Unchained Melody" can be heard (and seen) only in *Elvis: The Great Performances: Center Stage* (Buena Vista Home Video, 1990). "The Frank Sinatra balloon": Will Friedwald, *Sinatra! The Song Is You* (New York, 1995); he offers useful details about the origins of "My Way" and its evolution in Frank Sinatra's repertoire on pp. 445–47. "Elvis's tawdry death sanctioned that of Sid Vicious": Marcus, *Dead Elvis,* p. 83. "The ultimate adolescent fantasy": Malcolm McLaren, quoted in Jon Savage, *England's Dreaming: Anarchy, Sex Pistols, Punk Rock and Beyond* (London, 1991), p. 14. The most thoughtful account of the Elvis cult is John Strausbaugh, *E: Reflections on the Birth of the Elvis Faith* (New York, 1995); he quotes some of the graffiti on the stone wall outside Graceland on p. 43. Other examples of graffiti, as well as George Klein describing Elvis as "Jesus-like," come from the *Newsweek* cover story I wrote—see Jim Miller, "Forever Elvis," *Newsweek,* August 3, 1987, pp. 51, 48; while working on this cover story, I spent time with a variety of Elvis faithful, ordinary fans, and executives at Graceland, an experience that implicitly informs what I have written here. The essay by H.G. Koenigsberger, "Music and Religion in Modern European History," appears in J.H. Elliot and H.G. Koenigsberger, eds., *The Diversity of History: Essays in Honour of Sir Herbert Butterfield* (Ithaca, NY, 1970), pp. 37–78. And compare Simon Reynolds, *Blissed Out: The Raptures of Rock* (London, 1990), a collection of smart essays by a British rock critic who is more deeply influenced by the rhetoric of Christian mysticism than he may realize, since he has absorbed the rhetoric through the writing of a declared atheist, the French theorist Georges Bataille.

Discography: Frank Sinatra, "My Way" (Reprise 0817, #27, US pop; Reprise 20817, #5, UK pop, both in April 1969—it stayed on the British charts for an incredible forty-two weeks, a British record).

Elvis Presley, "My Way" (RCA PB-11165, #22, US pop; RCA PB-1165, #9, UK pop, both in December 1977). Sex Pistols, "My Way" (Virgin VS 220, #7, UK pop, July 1978). Paul Anka's own version of the song can be heard in a handy compilation of his greatest hits, *30th Anniversary Collection* (Rhino R2 71489, US CD, 1989). The official overview of Presley's last decade is *Walk a Mile in My Shoes: The Essential 70's Masters* (RCA 66670-2/07883, US CD, 1995). But for anyone truly curious about Elvis and the final days, accept no substitute and listen to *Elvis In Concert* (RCA APL 2-2587, US LP, 1977); from shows taped in June 1977 comes a surreal tragicomedy that will make you laugh, cry, etc.—a weirdly fitting relic of the Elvis cult, a shocking document of a slow-motion suicide, and also, intermittently, a moving glimpse of rock and roll spirituality at its most besotted.

EPILOGUE

For a comprehensive overview of the global recording industry as the Nineties began, see Anthony Gottlieb, "Almost Grown: A Survey of the Music Business," *The Economist*, December 21, 1991. For Marcus on Michael Jackson, see Greil Marcus, *Lipstick Traces* (Cambridge, MA, 1989), p. 109. And for Mortimer on Mick Jagger, see John Mortimer, *In Character* (London, 1983), p. 150.

Acknowledgments

I relied on several friends to read over the manuscript before it was finished, to flag errors and to comment on the manuscript's intelligibility and literary merit. For reading early versions, I thank Samantha Dunn, Stephen Farber, Hillary Frey, Jonathan Veitch, Marc Woodworth, and Alexander Woolfson. One of my students at the New School, Joshua Karant, read the manuscript with special care, as did David Sanjek, archive director of Broadcast Music Incorporated, whom I asked to point out any factual errors he noticed. One of my oldest friends in Boston, James Isaacs, did the same, and also offered editorial suggestions. Another old friend, Peter Guralnick, was at crucial points a friendly critic as well as a source of historical information. Last but not least, my copy editor, Fred Chase, also caught and corrected several factual mistakes.

The book was finished during a sabbatical from the Graduate Faculty of the New School for Social Research, and with the help of a fellowship from the Guggenheim Foundation.

Last but not least, I must thank Greil Marcus. Without the example of his own work, not to mention his unflagging critical intelligence over the course of our friendship, I may not have learned so well, or so young, a crucial lesson: that, in the words of Montaigne, *"La plus grande chose du monde, c'est de savoir être a soi"*—be true to yourself.

James Miller is professor of political science and director of liberal studies at the Graduate Faculty of the New School for Social Research. A Guggenheim Fellow and twice a winner of the ASCAP–Deems Taylor Award for excellence in writing about music, he has covered the rock scene for national publications since 1967, when one of his early record reviews appeared in the third issue of *Rolling Stone* magazine. Since then, his reviews, profiles, and essays on music have appeared in *New Times, The New Republic, The New York Times,* and *Newsweek,* where he was a book reviewer and pop music critic between 1981 and 1990. The original editor of *The Rolling Stone Illustrated History of Rock & Roll* (which first appeared in 1976), he also contributed an essay on his favorite rock album, *Presenting the Fabulous Ronettes* (1964), to an anthology edited by Greil Marcus, *Stranded: Rock and Roll for a Desert Island* (1979). He is the author of four previous books: *The Passion of Michel Foucault* (1993), an interpretive essay on the life of the French philosopher, a National Book Critics Circle Finalist for General Nonfiction; *"Democracy Is in the Streets": From Port Huron to the Siege of Chicago* (1987), an account of the American student movement of the 1960s, also a National Book Critics Circle Finalist for General Nonfiction; *Rousseau: Dreamer of Democracy* (1984), a study of the origins of modern democracy; and *History and Human Existence—From Marx to Merleau-Ponty* (1979), an analysis of Marx and the French existentialists. A native of Chicago educated at Pomona College and Brandeis University, where he received a Ph.D. in the History of Ideas, he lives with his wife and three sons in West Roxbury, Massachusetts.